International and Interregional Migration

Theory and Evidence

World Scientific Studies in International Economics
(ISSN: 1793-3641)

World Scientific Studies in International Economics includes works dealing with the theory, empirical analysis, and evaluation of international economic policies and institutions, with topics covering international macroeconomics and finance, international trade theory and policy, as well as international legal and political economy. Monographs and edited volumes will comprise the core of the publications.

Vol. 66 *International and Interregional Migration: Theory and Evidence*
edited by Francisco L. Rivera-Batiz (Columbia University, USA)

Vol. 65 *International Trade Theory and Competitive Models: Features, Values, and Criticisms*
by Ronald W. Jones (University of Rochester, USA)

Vol. 64 *Information Spillovers and Market Integration in International Finance: Empirical Analyses*
by Suk-Joong Kim (University of Sydney, Australia)

Vol. 63 *Dimensions of Trade Policy*
by Martin Richardson (Australian National University, Australia)

Vol. 62 *International Trade and Labor Markets: Welfare, Inequality and Unemployment*
by Udo Kreickemeier (TU Dresden, Germany)

Vol. 61 *Achieving Financial Stability: Challenges to Prudential Regulation*
edited by Douglas D. Evanoff (Federal Reserve Bank of Chicago, USA),
George G. Kaufman (formerly Loyola University Chicago, USA),
Agnese Leonello (European Central Bank, Germany) &
Simone Manganelli (European Central Bank, Germany)

Vol. 60 *International Macroeconomic Interdependence*
by Paul R. Bergin (UC Davis)

Vol. 59 *Contributions to the Economics of International Labor Standards*
edited by Arnab K. Basu (Cornell) & Nancy H. Chau (Cornell)

Vol. 58 *International Economic Integration and Domestic Performance*
edited by Mary E. Lovely (Syracuse University, USA)

Vol. 57 *Trade Policies for Development and Transition*
by David G. Tarr (The World Bank, USA)

The complete list of the published volumes in the series can be found at
http://www.worldscientific.com/series/wssie

66 World Scientific Studies in International Economics

International and Interregional Migration

Theory and Evidence

Francisco L. Rivera-Batiz
Columbia University, USA

World Scientific
NEW JERSEY • LONDON • SINGAPORE • BEIJING • SHANGHAI • HONG KONG • TAIPEI • CHENNAI • TOKYO

Published by

World Scientific Publishing Co. Pte. Ltd.

5 Toh Tuck Link, Singapore 596224

USA office: 27 Warren Street, Suite 401-402, Hackensack, NJ 07601

UK office: 57 Shelton Street, Covent Garden, London WC2H 9HE

Library of Congress Cataloging-in-Publication Data

Names: Rivera-Batiz, Francisco L., author.

Title: International and interregional migration : theory and evidence / Francisco L. Rivera-Batiz.

Description: Hackensack, N.J. : World Scientific, 2018. | Series: World scientific studies in international economics | Includes bibliographical references.

Identifiers: LCCN 2017051778 | ISBN 9789813208704 (hardcover)

Subjects: LCSH: Emigration and immigration--Economic aspects. | Migrant labor--Economic aspects. | Emigration and immigration--Government policy. | Illegal aliens--Government policy. | Brain drain.

Classification: LCC JV6217 .R58 2018 | DDC 304.8--dc23

LC record available at https://lccn.loc.gov/2017051778

British Library Cataloguing-in-Publication Data

A catalogue record for this book is available from the British Library.

For any available supplementary material, please visit
http://www.worldscientific.com/worldscibooks/10.1142/10413#t=suppl

Desk Editor: Jiang Yulin

Typeset by Stallion Press
Email: enquiries@stallionpress.com

Printed in Singapore

To my dear wife, Sandra

Contents

About the Author

Francisco L. Rivera-Batiz is a professor emeritus of economics and education at Columbia University where he remains teaching at the School of International and Public Affairs. At Columbia, he has had appointments in the Economics Department, the School of International and Public Affairs and at Teachers College (Columbia's Graduate School of Education), and has been the Director of the Program in Economic Policy Management, the Latino Studies Program, and the Institute for Urban and Minority Education. Rivera-Batiz has also held teaching or research appointments at the University of Chicago, Harvard University, Indiana University at Bloomington, the University of Massachusetts at Amherst, the University of Pennsylvania, Rutgers University in New Brunswick, and the University of Wisconsin at Madison.

Rivera-Batiz has written and published extensively on topics relating to labor migration, international economics, regional science, growth, and the economics of education. His articles have been published in leading academic journals such as *The American Economic Review*, *International Economic Review*, *Journal of Development Economics*, *The Quarterly Journal of Economics*, *The Journal of Population Economics*, and *Regional Science and Urban Economics.* His books include *The Political Economy of the East Asian Crisis and Its Aftermath: Tigers in Distress*, co-edited with A. Lukauskas (Edward Elgar, 2001), *International Finance and Open Economy Macroeconomics*, co-authored with L. Rivera-Batiz (Prentice Hall, 1993), and *U.S. Immigration Policy Reform in the 1980s: A Preliminary Assessment*, co-edited with S. Sechzer and I. Gang (Praeger, 1991). He is currently Editor-in-Chief of the *World Scientific Encyclopedia of International Economics and Global Trade.*

Born in Puerto Rico, Rivera-Batiz obtained his Bachelor's degree from Cornell University in 1975 and a Ph.D. in Economics from the Massachusetts Institute of Technology in 1979.

Acknowledgments

First of all, I wish to acknowledge the enormous intellectual debts I have accumulated over the years in relation to my work on international and interregional migration. My special gratitude goes to Jagdish N. Bhagwati, co-author of one of the papers included in this volume, and to Michael J. Piore, for their support throughout the last 40 years, as teachers, dissertation advisors, mentors and friends. The research presented in this volume stands in the shoulders of these two giants in the field of international migration.

Some of the papers in this collection have had the benefit of collaborations with several colleagues. I wish to particularly thank Ira N. Gang, with whom I have had a long and productive research partnership and friendship. I also wish to thank Na Feng and Myeong-Su Yu not only for their kind permission to publish our papers but also for their invaluable intellectual contributions to this work. I am also very grateful to Melisa Morales for her efficient research assistance, without which this project would not have been completed.

I would finally like to express my appreciation to the original publishers of the following articles for their permission to reprint them.

Chapter 1. Trade Theory, Distribution of Income and Immigration was originally published in *The American Economic Review*, Vol. 73, No. 2 (May 1983), pp. 183–187.

Chapter 2. The Effects of Immigration in a Distorted Two-Sector Economy was originally published in *Economic Inquiry*, Vol. 19, No. 4 (October 1981), pp. 626–639.

Chapter 3. The Short-Run Economic Effects of Immigration: Some General Equilibrium Simulations was originally published in William G. Vogt and Marvin H. Mickle, eds., *Modeling and Simulation, Vol. 17*, North Carolina: Instrument Society of America, 1986, pp. 215–222.

Chapter 4. The Labor Market Effects of Immigration in the United States and Europe: Substitution vs. Complementarity (co-authored with Ira N. Gang) was published in *Journal of Population Economics*, Vol. 7, No. 2 (June 1994), pp. 157–175.

Chapter 5. International Migration, Non-Traded Goods and Economic Welfare in the Source Country was originally published in *Journal of Development Economics*, Vol. 11, No. 1 (August 1982), pp. 81–90.

Chapter 6. International Migration, Remittances and Economic Welfare in the Source Country was originally published in *Journal of Economic Studies*, Vol. 13, No. 3 (October 1986), pp. 3–19.

Chapter 7. International Migration, Non-Traded Goods and Economic Welfare in a Two-Class Economy: A Reply was originally published in *Journal of Development Economics*, Vol. 16, No. 3 (December 1984), pp. 325–330.

Chapter 8. The Impact of International Migration on Real Wages: Another Look was originally published in *Journal of Development Economics*, Vol. 31, No. 1 (July 1989), pp. 185–192.

Chapter 9. The Service Sector, Monopolistic Competition and the Impact of Emigration was originally published in *Economics Letters*, Vol. 12, No. 3 (June 1983), pp. 327–332.

Chapter 10. International Migration, the Brain Drain and Economic Development was originally published in Amitava Krishna Dutt and

Jaime Ros, eds., *International Handbook of Development Economics*, Cheltenham: Edward Elgar, 2008, pp. 119–136.

Chapter 11. English Language Proficiency and the Economic Progress of Immigrants was originally published in *Economics Letters*, Vol. 34, No. 2 (November 1990), pp. 295–300.

Chapter 12. How Do Migrants from Latin America and the Caribbean Fare in the U.S. Labor Market? was originally published in *The World Economy*, Vol. 30, No. 9 (September 2007), pp. 1399–1429.

Chapter 13. Undocumented Workers in the Labor Market: An Analysis of the Earnings of Legal and Illegal Mexican Immigrants in the U.S. was originally published in *Journal of Population Economics*, Vol. 12, No. 1 (February 1999), pp. 91–116.

Chapter 14. Illegal Immigrants in the U.S. Economy: A Comparative Analysis of Mexican and Non-Mexican Undocumented Workers was originally published in Slobodan Djajic, ed., *International Migration: Trends, Policy and Economic Impact*, London: Routledge, 2001, pp. 180–203.

Chapter 15. Can Border Industries Be a Substitute for Immigration? was originally published in *The American Economic Review*, Vol. 76, No. 2, (May 1986), pp. 263–268.

Chapter 16. A Kinder, Gentler Immigration Policy: Forget Comprehensive Reform — Let the States Compete (co-authored with Jagdish N. Bhagwati) was originally published in *Foreign Affairs*, Vol. 92, No. 6 (November/December 2013), pp. 9–15.

Chapter 17. Economic Strain, Education and Attitudes towards Foreigners in the European Union (co-authored with Ira N. Gang and Myeong-Su Yun) was originally published in *Review of International Economics*, Vol. 21, No. 2 (May 2013), pp. 177–190.

Chapter 18. Education and Attitudes towards Internal Migrants in China (co-authored with Na Feng) was originally published in Na

Feng, ed., *Essays on Education, Political Movements and Income Growth in China*, Ann Arbor, Michigan: Proquest Publishing LLC, 2016, pp. 122–187.

Chapter 19. Modeling Urban Agglomeration: Producer Services, Linkage Externalities and Specialization Economies was originally published in William G. Vogt and Marvin H. Mickle, eds., *Modeling and Simulation, Vol. 19*, North Carolina: Instrument Society of America, 1988, pp. 113–119.

List of Tables

List of Figures

Introduction

Global migration flows have grown sharply over the last few decades. Just as international trade in goods and services has expanded by historical proportions, so has the movement of people. It was estimated that in 1960 there was a stock of about 75 million people residing in countries other than their country of birth; by 2015, this figure had grown to 244 million. In the developing world, the emigration rates of the highly-skilled have climbed over time and generally exceed those of less-skilled workers; in a number of countries as much as one-third or more of the college-educated have moved out of their countries of birth, including Afghanistan, Cambodia, Haiti, Jamaica, Liberia, Sierra Leone, and others.

Interregional migration flows have also increased. Rural to urban migration has led to sprawling cities, particularly in developing nations. In 1960, 34 percent of the world population resided in urban areas, by 2015 over 54 percent was located in cities. In China alone, official estimates were that in 2015 there were over 277 million rural to urban migrants.

This book contains a selection of articles examining the causes and consequences of international and interregional migration flows. How do immigrants benefit or hurt the recipient countries? And what benefits or costs do they have for the sending nations? These are some of the questions that these articles seek to answer.

Part 1: The Economic Consequences of Immigration

The chapters in this part of the volume seek to determine the various effects of immigration on the recipient economies. The simplest theoretical framework within which the impact of immigration can be analyzed is one that focuses on the aggregate labor market effects of immigration. In this partial equilibrium approach, often adopted by labor economists, an influx of immigrants raises the recipient country's or region's supply of labor, generating a surplus of workers that depresses wages and pushes down the employment opportunities of natives.

Chapter 1 shows that the answers provided by a simple labor market model can be as well simple-minded and misleading. The analysis in this chapter shows how international trade economists think about the impact of immigration, leading them to the conclusion that immigration may in fact have very little if any effect on wages or the employment opportunities of those already in the recipient country. What explains this lack of impact? As the chapter shows, the explanation is that immigrants tend to generate their own demand for labor through general equilibrium effects involving the reallocation of production in the recipient economy or region. As the migrants place downward pressure on wages, this makes employment in labor-intensive sectors, such as agriculture or services, more profitable. As a result, employers have an incentive to increase their output of labor-intensive products (agricultural and service sector production, for instance, rises), which shifts upwards the overall demand for labor. The increased demand for labor then lifts up wages and the employment opportunities of domestic workers as well, offsetting the initial impact of the migrants. In international economics, this paradoxical result, where an influx of labor leads to no change in wages, is called the Rybczynski effect, in the name of the economist who first postulated it. It suggests that economies have the ability to absorb labor supply increases without resulting in negative consequences for the existing workers.

The conclusion that immigration may not affect the economic welfare of non-migrants is obtained under a set of conditions that are enumerated in Chapter 1. It assumes, for example, that there is perfect inter-sectoral and interregional mobility of capital across the economy, so that when lower wages stimulate increased demand for labor in sectors where migrants have moved in, capital will be able to easily move to those sectors, thus generating the employment opportunities noted before. But in most economies capital does not move so handily across regions and sectors in the short-run, and so wages may be depressed by immigrants within this time horizon. In addition, the discussion assumes that labor markets are competitive and do not suffer from distortions that generate unemployment. Furthermore, only goods that are traded in labor markets are considered, but in most economies a significant share of production occurs in nontraded goods sectors. The following chapters examine the consequences of immigration when these assumptions are relaxed.

Chapter 2 develops a theoretical two-sector model of an economy, where one sector is characterized by rigid wages and suffers from unemployment and a second, traditional sector with labor markets that are competitive and flexible wages. In this framework, immigration increases the unemployment of non-migrants, turns income distribution against labor and in favor of the non-labor input in the traditional sector, and has an ambiguous, but possibly negative, effect on the total income of the non-immigrants. This last result contrasts with the result discussed in Chapter 1 (derived under the assumption of no domestic distortions), that immigration may not affect negatively the income of the non-migrants at all. The reason behind the possible negative effects of immigration on the income of natives is that the migrants, by decreasing wages in the traditional sector, induce a movement of domestic workers out of that sector and into the modern sector. But the modern sector has only a fixed number of jobs available (given the fixed administered wage). Those additional domestic workers, then, either become unemployed, or cause other workers to become unemployed. This reduces national income.

Do the results of this theoretical approach apply to the case of immigrants to the United States? How significant are the potentially negative effects of immigration suggested in this chapter? The following chapter provides some answers.

Chapter 3 examines the effects of immigration in a model where the production structure of the economy or region under consideration is decomposed into three sectors: agriculture, manufacturing and services. Although services and agriculture are assumed to function under competitive labor markets, the manufacturing sector is considered to be operating under rigid wages and unemployment. As in the previous chapter, immigration in this context reduces wages in the competitive labor markets of the economy. Since wages in manufacturing are assumed to be sheltered from the effects of immigration, the drop in the wages offered in competitive labor markets will widen the wage differential between manufacturing and the rest of the economy. This induces some workers to quit their jobs in agriculture and services in order to search for employment in manufacturing. But since the employment level in the latter is unresponsive to immigration, the outcome is increased unemployment.

To provide some understanding of the relative magnitude of the effects involved in thc analysis presented in this chapter, a simulation of the effects of an inflow of immigrants of 10 percent (as a proportion of the native-born labor force), was carried out under various assumptions regarding the values of the various parameters in the model. Several conclusions stand out.

Firstly, the numerical values of the real-wage elasticities of demand for labor in each sector of the economy or region appear to be critical in determining the magnitude of the effects of immigration. The elasticities specify by how much employment changes in response to the drop in wage rates in competitive labor markets generated by immigration. This influences, in turn, the impact on output, prices of services, unemployment, and so forth.

A second conclusion evident from the simulations is the importance of the effects of immigration on the nontradable goods and services sector. Nontradable goods and services are highly labor-intensive and show a relatively large labor demand elasticity, compared to other sectors in the economy. They are therefore more strongly affected by the labor inflow. Given the significance of nontradable goods and services sectors in most economies — composing over 60 percent of gross national product (GNP) in most industrial countries — an infrequently recognized positive effect of immigration lies on the increased rates of return that the labor inflow makes possible to employers in this sector and the reduced prices of these goods and services made available to consumers.

Following much of the existing literature in the field, the chapters just discussed assume that immigrants and existing workers in the labor market have identical characteristics and are therefore perfect substitutes in production. Chapter 4 recognizes that the labor market consequences of immigrants from various countries or ethnicities on native-born workers vary according to their respective skills and characteristics. In this case, the impact of immigration on the earnings of native-born workers is closely linked to whether these groups are substitutes or complements.

Chapter 4 presents estimates of the complementarity and substitution relationship between immigrant and native labor in the United States and the European Community. The paper relies on a theoretical model that focuses on the various inputs that individuals may supply to the production process, which includes primarily unskilled labor, education and on-the-job experience. As a result, workers get rewarded for the amounts of unskilled labor, education and experience that they provide to their employers, receiving implicit rates of return on each of these inputs. The wage received by a person is an overall composite of the rewards that he/she receives for his/her unskilled labor, education and experience. How do immigrants affect the income of native-born workers? Given the amounts of unskilled labor, education and experience that a person is endowed with, a disturbance in the rates of return to these three inputs will result in a change in wages. In this framework, an inflow of immigrants affects residents by altering the returns to unskilled labor, education and experience (immigration augments the supplies of these inputs in local labor markets). By how much the rates of return are affected depends not only on the magnitude of the labor inflow and the relative endowments of education, experience and unskilled labor that the immigrants have, but also on the degree of complementarity or substitutability among the inputs. If, for instance, education and unskilled labor are complements, then an inflow of highly schooled immigrants raises the return to unskilled labor; if the two inputs are substitutes, however, the return to unskilled labor declines. The empirical analysis in Chapter 4, based on the estimation of a translog production function, indicates that, in both the United States and Europe, education is complementary with unskilled labor and experienced labor in production.

The impact of immigration is highly complex in this framework. Immigrants with various endowments of unskilled labor, education and experience have different effects on the rates of return to these inputs in local labor markets. Given these changes in rates of return, the effects of these disturbances on the wages of natives vary according to the endowments of unskilled labor, education and experience of the different groups of residents. Chapter 4 presents estimates of the impact of a wide array of immigrant groups on a variety of resident groups. As can be expected, domestic groups with human capital endowments that diverge from those of the immigrants experience wage increases as a result of immigration (because they are complements). Domestic groups with human capital endowments similar to the immigrant population experience wage reductions (since the groups are substitutes). But although there is great diversity in the sign of the estimated impact of different immigrant groups on resident's wages, Chapter 4 shows that the absolute magnitude of the effects tends to be small, a result that is shared by a survey of the existing research by the National Academy of Sciences in 2016.

Part 2. The Impact of International Emigration: The Effects of the Brain Drain

This part of the volume shifts the analysis to the source countries, discussing how emigration may impact the wages, employment, production, and economic welfare of those left behind.

At the theory level, the analysis of the consequences of emigration in the source countries can go along lines similar to those followed by the discussion in Part 1 on immigration. Instead of an increase in the labor force, emigration causes the opposite: a reduction in the domestic labor supply. As implied from that analysis, a simple-minded, partial equilibrium labor market approach suggests that the direct impact of a reduced labor force in the source country would be to generate labor shortages and raise wages. However, as was also presented in Chapter 1, the conclusion of international trade theory is that inter-sectoral changes can allow the economy to adjust to changes in the labor force and ameliorate or eliminate the impact of emigration. For instance, as workers emigrate and wages go up, sectors that are capital-intensive will have an incentive to expand, which reduces aggregate labor demand and puts downward pressures on wages. So, as discussed before, output composition effects may diminish or even eliminate the effects of emigration on wages and income distribution, at least in the long-run when capital is able to move across sectors.

Using a different perspective, looking at the issue from the consumption side, if the country is a small open economy, the trade-theoretic literature concludes again that emigration would not affect the economic welfare of the non-migrants. This is because the presence or the absence of the migrant group in the population implies the same terms of trade, and hence the same trade opportunities, for the non-migrants. The same array of products is available for consumption in world markets at the same world market prices. Of course, emigration for a large country can turn the terms of trade against it and cause a loss of economic welfare for the source country.

Chapter 5 re-examines the welfare effects of emigration on the source country by introducing a dichotomy between traded and non-traded goods and services. In this framework, emigration always worsens the economic welfare of the non-migrants, even if there are fixed terms of trade facing the economy and even if capital is perfectly mobile across sectors; changes in the price of nontraded goods and services give rise to the deterioration in economic welfare. Looking at it from the consumption side, the emigration tends to eliminate any internal exchange of traded for nontraded goods and services existing between migrants and non-migrants. As a result, this disruption of internal trade in (internationally) nontraded goods and services in the source country results in a loss of economic welfare for those left behind. The loss is reflected in the higher prices of nontraded goods that the remaining population may face.

The results in Chapter 5 apply particularly to the emigration of skilled workers, the so-called brain drain. These workers are often employed in local service sectors that are not traded internationally. Their emigration can therefore result in acute shortages in the supply of essential services, from school teachers and professors to doctors and nurses. Note that, as the previous literature indicated, the emigration of workers employed in sectors that produce exports and imports is not subject to these effects because local consumers can import these products from abroad when the laborers leave the country. But when the workers are employed in service sectors that produce internationally-nontraded goods, the impact of emigration is more significant and potentially disastrous because domestic consumers can only obtain those services locally. If doctors and nurses emigrate, the supply of health services can collapse, resulting in higher prices and acute shortages. In this case, as Chapter 5 emphasizes, the brain drain can have a sharply negative effect on the economic welfare of those left behind.

Any negative consequences of emigration must be weighed against the potential benefits of the remittances that the migrants send back home. In 2016, the World Bank estimated that developing countries received US$429 billion in remittances from their migrants abroad, exceeding the net private debt and portfolio equity capital flowing into the region that year. For some countries, remittances constitute a major source of income. In the Kyrgyz Republic, remittances accounted for 35 percent of its gross domestic product (GDP) in 2016, in Nepal and Liberia the corresponding figure was 30 percent, in Haiti it was 28 percent, in Tonga it was 27 percent, and so on for other labor-exporting countries

Remittances clearly constitute an improvement in the standard of living for family members who are recipients of such income. Some questions are often raised as to the extent to which the remittances simply raise current consumption instead of stimulating investment and future economic growth. But a significant portion of what is considered consumption spending out of remittances consists of household investments in housing, automobiles and durable goods, whose long-term wealth-raising capacities are substantial. Furthermore, the use of remittances for community investment projects is not insignificant and also acts to stimulate local development. Finally, the increased consumption spending does act to generate local economic activity and exerts a positive, multiplier impact on the rest of the economy.

Chapter 6 extends the theoretical framework developed in Chapter 5 to examine the impact of remittances on source countries. The analysis separates the population in the home (sending) country into two groups: a group that contains the families of the migrants — who receive the remittances — and the rest of the source country population or non-migrants. These are the conclusions: First, emigration tends to raise nontraded goods prices (a result already noted) and remittances reinforce this impact. Secondly, emigration turns income distribution in favor of labor and against capital, and remittances (whether intended for consumption or investment purposes) again strengthen this pattern. Finally, although remittances provide a net gain to the migrant families that are recipients of the funds, their impact on real income is diminished by the nontraded goods' price increase they ignite. The net balance of the impact of remittances on non-migrant welfare is positive, as they generate internal trade (within the economy) between the now wealthier migrant families on the one hand and non-migrants on the other. The mechanism through which non-migrants benefit is the increase in the relative price of nontraded goods, which redistributes real income from the migrant families (which become net consumers of nontraded goods) to non-migrants (net sellers of nontraded goods).

Chapter 7 is a reply to an article published in the *Journal of Development Economics* in 1984 by Henry Thompson. In his paper, Thompson extends the framework presented in Chapter 5 to analyze the effects of emigration on the real income of source-country capital and labor. The two factors of production are considered to be separate groups, each consuming different fractions of traded and nontraded goods. Thompson then argues that emigration may actually reduce real wages in the source country, in spite of the fact that nominal wage rates do rise. The increase in the prices of nontraded goods caused by emigration may, according to Thompson, offset the higher nominal wages.

The purpose of Chapter 7 is to develop a more general approach to the problem of examining the impact of emigration in a situation where there are two distinct segments of the population, with separate demand functions and disparate factor endowments. For these purposes, a model of emigration is developed for an economy in which two classes of individuals exist, with each class having separate utility functions (and therefore demand functions) as well as different endowments of capital and labor: One class is rich in capital (owns relatively more capital than labor) and one is labor-rich (owns relatively more labor than capital). This is a more realistic setting, as most emigrants often withdraw some of their wealth from the source country. In addition, if one thinks of capital as including human capital, the emigration of skilled workers implies a joint flight of labor and human capital from the economy. The brain drain can thus be visualized as consisting of the emigration of labor and human capital bundled together.

Emigration in the framework developed in Chapter 7 can be of capital-rich or labor-rich individuals. If labor-rich persons emigrate (and they take both their capital and labor with them), then the economy's labor endowment will decline proportionally more than its capital endowment. This causes a decline in the output of the labor-intensive nontraded goods, an excess demand for these commodities and a consequent rise in their prices. If emigration of capital-rich individuals occurs, however, the results are exactly the opposite. The impact of emigration on the real income of the non-emigrants must then be subdivided into its impact on the two classes remaining in the home economy. In his comment, Thompson considers a special case of the one developed in Chapter 7, in which emigrants only take labor with them. More generally, however, emigration will consist of individuals owning both capital and labor. In this situation, if the emigrants form part of a class endowed with a relatively large fraction of capital — which they take with them — then the prices of the labor-intensive nontraded goods would decline. As a result, the real income of the non-emigrants forming part of the capital-rich class would unambiguously improve, while the impact on the real income of the non-emigrants who have higher labor endowments, is ambiguous and can actually decline if the fraction of nontraded goods they consume is small enough.

Chapter 8 is a comment on a paper published in the *Journal of Development Economics* in 1984 by Muhammad G. Quibria. In his paper, Quibria reexamines Thompson's analysis of the impact of emigration on real wages concluding that in the framework adopted in that article "there is no ambiguity in the link between emigration and real wages", and that "the result appears quite robust to different production-side specifications". Chapter 8 confirms that Quibria is correct in his conclusion that, under the assumptions utilized in Thompson's paper, real wages always rise with emigration. But the chapter also shows that there is still an ambiguity on the effects of emigration on real income within the two-class model developed in Chapter 7. Furthermore, the chapter also argues that the connection between emigration and real wages is closely dependent on the production-side specifications of the model utilized. If those specifications are altered to incorporate, for instance, increasing returns, emigration can reduce real wages.

Chapter 8 develops a model of emigration in the presence of increasing returns, where the nontraded goods sector is characterized by a market structure of monopolistic competition where firms face a declining average cost curve. In this case, emigration would push upwards nominal wages, raising unit labor costs and, thus, the prices of nontraded goods. In addition, the shrinking domestic consumption of nontraded goods caused by emigration leads some nontraded goods producers to exit the market, which results in greater monopoly power for those firms that remain. These firms raise their price markups and the prices of nontraded goods end up increasing proportionally more than nominal wages. By reducing the number of domestic producers and their scale of operations, emigration can lower labor productivity and, thus, depress real wages.

Chapter 9 follows on the analysis presented in Chapter 8 by showing that there is a further negative consequence of emigration: the reduced market size in the nontraded goods and services sector causes a drop of product variety which reduces economic welfare. Many nontraded goods and services are best characterized as being slightly-differentiated commodities, produced under conditions of monopolistic competition and increasing returns to scale. One reason is because nontraded goods depend on local (home market) demand and cannot rely on international trade to attain some eventual minimum average cost. In addition, many services involve a close interaction between producer and consumer (as in the case of health services, education, etc.) and they are thus more subject to the product differentiations arising from such interaction. This chapter shows that, in a framework where nontraded goods and services are produced under conditions of monopolistic competition and product differentiation, emigration will have a negative effect on the economic welfare of those left behind by reducing the diversity of nontraded goods and services available. In a sense, emigration imposes a negative externality on the non-migrants by reducing the extent of the market and, thus, the variety of nontraded goods and services

Chapter 10 surveys the literature on the economics of international migration, with a focus on the emigration of professional and technical workers referred to as the brain drain. The chapter discuses first the recent trends in global migration flows, delineating the efforts of some international organizations — such as the Organisation for Economic Co-operation and Development (OECD) and the United Nations — to gather cross-country data on migration and seek to provide more uniform, comparable statistics. The chapter then proceeds to examine the determinants of international labor flows, looking at the balance of expected costs and benefits that lead to individual migration decisions, the labor market returns of migration, the issue of migrant selectivity, the role of families in migratory behavior, and the impact of networks and chain migration. The chapter also examines the political economy of immigration policy, describing how interest groups and attitudes towards migrants may influence immigration policy. The survey concludes with a discussion of the literature on the economic consequences of migration for developing countries. This includes a description of the distributional as well as the welfare impact of the migration flows.

Part 3. How Do Migrants Fare?

A large body of research has now accumulated studying the immigrants' economic outcomes. In the United States, the evidence suggests that the labor market performance of immigrants relative to natives has generally deteriorated since the 1960s. But there are differences among immigrant groups in how well they do in the United States, depending on their skills.

The vast majority of immigrants to the U.S. come from countries whose native language is that other than English. As a result, the nature of their participation in the U.S labor market is closely mediated by English language proficiency. Although there are employment opportunities — in services, agriculture and in ethnic enclaves — that do not require extensive use of English for their performance, one expects lack of English language proficiency to block successful entry into mainstream U.S. labor markets, impeding upward labor mobility and constraining earnings

Chapter 11 examines the role of English language proficiency in determining the wages of immigrants. The chapter utilizes for the first time a data set that provides test-based measurements of individual English language proficiency: the 1985 National Assessment of Educational Progress (NAEP) Young Adult Literacy Assessment survey. This nationally representative household survey of persons aged 21 to 25 years old provides scores on a reading proficiency test administered to each individual sampled in addition to the usual background information. Through the use of these test-based, English reading proficiency measurements, instead of the self-assessed measures used in the previous literature, this chapter sketches a more reliable picture of the role played by language on wages.

The research presented in Chapter 11 estimates human capital wage equations for male and female immigrants and second-generation individuals (persons whose mother and/or father are foreign-born) using English reading proficiency scores as one of a set of explanatory variables. The chapter shows that lack of English reading proficiency is a significant factor constraining the wage opportunities of immigrants and may explain a substantial fraction of the relatively lower wages received by non-English speaking immigrants in the U.S.

Migration from Latin America and the Caribbean (LAC) constitutes over 50 percent of the foreign-born population residing in the United States. In 2015, there were about 22 million persons born in LAC residing in the U.S., out of a total foreign-born population of 43 million. Chapter 12 examines how these migrants fare in U.S. labor markets. It is concluded that, on average, LAC immigrants have substantially lower earnings than those from other parts of the world. Furthermore, their economic outcomes have sharply deteriorated relative to other immigrants in recent decades. In 1980, Latin American and Caribbean migrants on average earned 76.1 percent of the weekly wages received by other immigrants. By 2005, the corresponding percentage was 54.7 percent, a drop of over 20 percentage points.

Why have the labor market outcomes of LAC migrants deteriorated relative to other migrants? The empirical work presented in chapter 12 shows that the most significant factor explaining both the lower relative wages of LAC migrants and the deterioration of those wages relative to other migrants is the comparatively low — and declining — educational attainment of these migrants relative to other immigrants and natives in the US. In 1980, for example, the percentage of migrants from LAC with less than a 12th-grade (high school) education was equal to 58.3 percent, which was almost twice the corresponding figure for natives in the US and 1.4 times higher than for immigrants from other regions. By 2005, the percentage of Latin America and Caribbean immigrants with less than a 12th-grade schooling was 43.3 percent, which was about four times the equivalent percentage for natives and 3.5 times the proportion for other immigrants. This relative skill deterioration among LAC migrants accounts for 45 percent of the relative wage loss of these migrants between 1980 and 2005 for men and 50 percent of the loss for women.

Compounding the declining relative skills of LAC migrants are changes in US labor markets since the early 1980s that have made rates of return to education skyrocket while the wages of workers with relatively lower skills have worsened. The research presented in this chapter also shows that rates of return to education among LAC migrants are lower than those of other migrants and have not increased in line with those of other immigrant groups. As the previous chapter emphasizes, English-language proficiency is another important force explaining the declining wages of LAC migrants relative to other migrants. Indeed, immigrants from LAC countries tend to have substantially lower English-language proficiency. In addition, rates of return to English-language skills increased sharply between 1980 and 2005.

Part 4. Undocumented Workers and Immigration Policy

A growing proportion of global migration flows consists of persons who have illegally crossed country borders or over-extended their entry visas and are therefore residing in those countries without any legal visa or immigration documents. Estimates suggest that, although a variety of nations have significant undocumented immigrant populations, the U.S. has by far the highest number, estimated to be about 11 million in 2017.

Chapter 13 examines the labor market outcomes of undocumented Mexican immigrants in the United States. It explores one of the key issues surrounding undocumented workers, which is the extent to which they are exploited, or discriminated against, in host country labor markets by being paid wages that are substantially below those paid to legal workers with identical characteristics.

Chapter 13 utilizes information on Mexican undocumented immigrants collected by a unique data set: the 1989–1992 Legalized Population Survey (LPS), a national sample of 6,193 illegal immigrants who were residing in the United States in 1987/1988 when they sought legal permanent residence through the Immigration Reform and Control Act of 1986 (IRCA). IRCA constituted the major illegal immigration reform legislation of the 1980s in the United States, introducing sanctions for employers knowingly hiring undocumented workers, increasing border enforcement, and introducing an amnesty program through which illegal immigrants could obtain permanent resident status. The sample of undocumented immigrants examined in this study was interviewed in 1989 and then in 1992, as they applied for legal status. In this chapter, the labor market outcomes of the Mexican undocumented workers in the sample were compared to those of a group of legal Mexican immigrants sampled by the U.S. Bureau of Census during the corresponding years.

The findings in Chapter 13 confirm that Mexican undocumented workers receive substantially lower earnings relative to legal immigrants. It shows that, on an hourly basis, male Mexican legal immigrants in the United States in 1987/1988 earned 41.8% more than undocumented workers while female legal immigrants earned 40.8% more. At the same time, the chapter also shows that undocumented immigrants have lower average educational attainment than legal immigrants, lower English language proficiency, and a smaller number of years of residence in the United States. Could these differences in characteristics explain the legal–illegal wage gaps? The results presented in Chapter 13 indicate that differences in the measured human capital, occupational, and demographic characteristics of legal and illegal immigrants *do not* explain most of the observed wage gap between the two groups, whether for males or females. Indeed, differences in measured characteristics explain only 48.7% of the observed log-wage gap between legal and illegal male immigrants, and 43% of the observed log-wage gap for women. This strongly suggests the presence of systematic discrimination against undocumented workers.

It is still possible, though, that the legal–illegal gap in wages is related to the presence of differences in *unmeasured* characteristics of legal and illegal workers, such as employment instability. In order to provide an answer to the question of whether illegal status itself, and not unmeasured individual characteristics, is the culprit behind the lower wages of undocumented workers when compared to other immigrants, Chapter 13 carried out an analysis of the longitudinal data available for undocumented workers before and after legalization. Since unmeasured characteristics are likely to remain constant for any particular individual before and after legalization, this analysis is not subject to the criticism leveled against the cross-sectional analysis. The longitudinal analysis shows that undocumented immigrants did catch-up substantially with the legal immigrants once they were legalized and it offers even stronger evidence that undocumented immigrants sustain significant and systematic wage discrimination when compared to other migrants.

Chapter 14 provides an analysis of the labor market performance of the overall undocumented immigrant population in the United States — Mexican and non-Mexican — through the use of the LPS survey mentioned earlier. It finds substantial differences in the characteristics of the Mexican and non-Mexican undocumented migrant samples. In fact, the analysis presented in Chapter 14 shows that the popular perception of undocumented immigrants as unskilled workers with low levels of schooling is incorrect since it only characterizes Mexican immigrants. Among non-Mexican undocumented workers, the paper shows that the mean years of schooling for persons aged 25 years of age or older was 10.4 years in 1987/1988, which was about the same as the average years of schooling of the overall immigrant population counted in the 1990 U.S. Census of Population. By contrast, Mexican undocumented immigrants were found to have an average of 6.3 years of schooling. Chapter 14 also presents the results of empirical human capital earnings equations, showing that the average rate of return to education among Mexican undocumented male workers is substantially lower than for the non-Mexican illegal immigrants. Finally, the chapter concludes that despite the substantially higher earnings that non-Mexican undocumented immigrants display compared to Mexican undocumented workers, both groups earn substantially less than the overall immigrant population.

The continuous flow of undocumented workers from Mexico to the United States has given rise to a wide range of proposals aimed at containing the migratory tide. One of them is Mexican border industrialization, the incarnation of the view that immigration should be controlled at the border, through the creation of an economic fence absorbing the potential migrants. Border industrialization received a strong boost in the mid-1960's with the establishment of the Mexican Border Industrialization Program (BIP). The BIP combined trade, fiscal, and other incentives to encourage the formation of assembly plants (maquiladoras) in Mexico, particularly in the border region. Though the BIP was only part of a wider border industrialization process, it has been particularly connected to U.S. immigration policy. Indeed, the BIP was established in the aftermath of the bracero program (that ended in 1965) and its main purpose was to absorb the former braceros into the Mexican labor force so as to prevent their illegal migration to the United States. The growth of assembly plants in Mexico's border region has now grown to over 3,000, offering employment to about one million workers.

Chapter 15 questions the view that assembly plants and border industrialization in Mexico reduce undocumented migration to the U.S. First, surveys of assembly plants in Mexico show that, under usual circumstances, they offer wage rates in the range of 5 to 30 percent above the corresponding official minimum wages, but these do not represent a significant reduction of U.S.–Mexico real wage differentials. By moving to the United States, undocumented migrants could obtain as much as an 800–1300 percent increase above the Mexican minimum wages, depending on occupation, region of employment, etc.

Assembly plants have provided the border region with high rates of employment growth at wages above the Mexican average for a number of decades now while undocumented migration to the U.S. has expanded. This is inconsistent with the view that Mexican border industrialization is capable of reducing illegal immigration. Indeed, as Chapter 15 suggests, the impact of the maquiladoras on migration to the United States is dependent on whether these firms are able to raise employment by more than they increase the labor supply in the border area through induced migration from southern regions. The chapter presents an intertemporal model of labor migration where expectations of future labor market conditions affect current labor migration decisions. It builds on the fact that although information about employment opportunities in destination areas is usually available — through networks of friends, relatives, etc. — it is impossible to know in advance exactly how many jobs will develop or how many applicants will seek employment. This is particularly so when the distances involved are large, as they are in the case of international and interregional migration. In addition, since migration will usually be undertaken for an extended period of time (depending on the temporariness of the migration), there is an intertemporal aspect involved: expectations must be formed not only about current but also about future employment prospects. Expectations formation, then, is central to determining the impact of job creation in the border on induced interregional migration flows in Mexico and, as a consequence, unemployment and/or underemployment along the border region

The results of the model developed in Chapter 15 suggest that Mexican border job creation, when expected to be sustained over time, and if a feasible alternative for migrant workers, is likely to generate an excess supply of migrants from other regions in Mexico, that could potentially raise the level of unemployment and underemployment along the border. These unemployed or underemployed migrants can then create a pool of workers from whom undocumented migration to the U.S. can be more easily fueled.

Chapter 16 presents a new proposal to reconsider efforts to reform undocumented migrant policy in the United States. Comprehensive immigration reform appears difficult to achieve at the present time, given the polarization of views on both legal and undocumented immigrants between Democrats and Republicans, and even among Republicans. Even if reforms were to be approved, it is likely that the measures adopted will be punitive in nature, including greater emphasis on employer sanctions and heightened border security, both of which have been tried now for many decades without much impact on the flow of undocumented workers to the U.S. What such measures would do, however, is to further increase the risk to the lives of the undocumented migrants as they try to cross the border over more dangerous terrain.

Given these realities, Chapter 16 argues that the United States should stop attempting to eliminate illegal immigration and focus instead on policies that treat the undocumented with humanity. Doing so would mean adopting a variety of measures to diminish the public's hostility to undocumented immigrants. Principal among them would be a shift from a top-down approach to a bottom-up one: letting states compete for illegal immigrants. States with laws that are unfriendly to illegal immigrants would lose them and their badly needed labor to states that are more welcoming. The result would be a competition that would do far more to improve the treatment of undocumented immigrants than anything coming from Washington. Of course, states cannot intrude on the parts of immigration enforcement over which the federal government has exclusive authority, such as border control and civil rights. But there are a number of steps states can take to make life easier for illegal immigrants, such as issuing them driver's licenses and making accessible to them everything from health care to university scholarships.

This process has already happened. Undocumented immigrants are voting with their feet, leaving or bypassing states that treat them harshly and flocking to those with more benign policies. For instance, from 1990 to 2010, when tough border enforcement policies (which naturally focused on the Border States) were in vogue, Arizona, California, New Mexico, and Texas saw their collective share of illegal immigrants decline by 17 percent. In California alone, the percentage of all illegal immigrants residing there fell from 43 percent to 23 percent. Similarly, the economists Sarah Bohn, Magnus Lofstrom, and Steven Raphael have calculated that Arizona's 2007 Legal Arizona Workers Act, which banned businesses from hiring illegal immigrants, led to a notable decline in the proportion of the state's foreign-born Hispanic population. The resulting blow to economic activity in anti-immigrant states has often been drastic; employers in agriculture and construction, for example, regularly complain about the absence of workers. As a result, one may anticipate a race to the top, where not only do pro-immigrant states benefit economically by welcoming the migrants but also anti-immigrant states face increasing economic pressures to change their policies. As this dynamic plays out, and as states compete for illegal immigrants, the migrants will face less harassment and be able to better integrate into their communities.

Part 5: Attitudes towards International and Interregional Migrants

The attitudes adopted by natives towards migrants represent a critical force in the migration process. Political movements may reflect the perceptions — or misperceptions — that natives have towards immigrants and can exert a powerful influence on immigration policies. In addition, how natives react to migrants can have a significant influence on how the migrants adjust to their destinations. But what determines attitudes towards migrants? The chapters in this part of the volume examine the forces that influence how people form their perceptions of migrants.

Chapter 17 considers the attitudes towards foreigners in countries that form part of the European Union (EU). The analysis in this chapter uses data on attitudes obtained from Eurobarometer Surveys, which sample the public opinion of a geographically distributed population of households across Europe. In addition to information on household economic and demographic behavior, the 1988, 2003, and 2008 Eurobarometer surveys contained questions on attitudes towards immigrants and foreigners. The research in Chapter 17 measures attitudes towards foreigners on the basis of the responses of the residents of EU countries to two questions. In 1988, they were asked: "Is the presence of (non-European Community) foreigners good or bad for the future of our country?" In 2003 and 2008, survey participants were asked: "Do immigrants contribute a lot to your country?"

Chapter 17 postulates that there are two sets of factors influencing attitudes towards foreigners. One set of factors is economic. It is hypothesized that in countries facing economic strain, with stagnant or collapsing income and/or employment opportunities, immigrants will be partly blamed for the economic stress thus generating the resentment of the native-born population. Whether immigration does actually lower wages or reduce employment opportunities is a matter of debate and earlier chapters in this volume have discussed the diverse theory and evidence on these issues. But whether immigrants do in effect take jobs away from natives or reduce their wages may not be directly relevant to the formation of attitudes, which are based on *perceptions* about how immigrants affect the economy, perceptions that are not necessarily based on reality.

The second set of factors influencing attitudes towards immigrants is ethnic or racial prejudice. In the U.S., historically, there is substantial evidence that racial prejudice was a major factor behind restrictionist movements that reduced immigration flows from particular countries or regions, such as China and Mexico. Racial prejudice and xenophobia have also been found in many of the anti-immigrant activities observed in the last few years in European and other countries.

Chapter 17 finds a sharp increase in anti-foreigner attitudes in Europe between 1988 and 2003 and a decline between 2003 and 2008. In 1988, 31.4 percent of the sample felt that foreigners did not contribute a lot to the future of their country, but by 2003 as much as 50.9 percent felt that immigrants did not contribute to their countries, although by 2008 this had dropped to 45 percent. The chapter then examines the relative significance of a set of variables influencing the attitudes of EU citizens towards foreigners by estimating probit equations of the likelihood that people in the sample had negative attitudes towards foreigners. It is found that people who directly compete (or have competed) in the labor market with immigrants do have stronger negative attitudes towards foreigners, *ceteris paribus*. This includes the unemployed but also employed workers who may perceive that their wages are negatively affected by immigrants.

Educational attainment is found to be a strong antidote to anti-foreigner sentiments. Both rising educational attainment and increasing effectiveness of education in reducing anti-foreigner sentiments lay behind the turnaround in negative attitudes towards immigrants from 2003 to 2008. At the same time, the decomposition analysis carried out in this chapter suggests there may be a long-term, rising trend in racial bias and xenophobia sustaining anti-foreigner sentiment in Europe. While this trend is more than compensated by the effects of education between 2003 and 2008, in the earlier period, from 1988 to 2003, it was strong enough to give rise to increasingly negative attitudes towards foreigners.

The data available for the research presented in Chapter 17 end in 2008 and it was preceded by a period of declining unemployment and economic boom. This situation, however, has sharply turned around since that time. Europe currently faces an extended recession, rising unemployment and an uncertain economic future. Insofar as Chapter 17 finds that economic strain is associated with negative attitudes towards immigrants, the current economic situation is likely to reverse the reductions in anti-foreigner sentiments that developed between 2003 and 2008.

There is very little research on attitudes towards interregional migrants, when compared with the voluminous literature on international migrants. Chapter 18 is one of the exceptions. It presents the results of an analysis of the determinants of attitudes towards internal migrants in China. The number of internal migrants in China accelerated after the early 1980s. Before that time, the so-called hukou household registration system restricted severely rural to urban movements. Imposed in the 1950s, the hukou system requires that every person register their permanent residence and type of work with local government authorities. In order to migrate, the person either requests an official change of hukou location — which was originally very difficult but has progressively become easier since the 1980s — or migrates without such change of residence, either by using temporary migration permits or other means (giving rise to so-called non-hukou migrants). The official estimates based on the 2010 Census are that the number of non-hukou migrants in China (often referred as the country's floating population or *liu dong ren kou*) was about 221 million, up from about an estimated 40 million in 1990.

Chapter 18 uses survey data from the 2005 wave of the Chinese General Social Survey (CGSS), which includes a series of detailed questions asking respondents to identify their opinions towards migrants. The CGSS is an annual survey that includes a random cross-sectional sample of the population in China each year and interviews a set of individuals 18 years of age or older, asking them a core set of detailed background questions on their socioeconomic status as well as that of the households where they reside. These are five questions relating to attitudes towards migrants in the 2005 CGSS: (1) Are you willing to work with them? (2) Can you tolerate them living in your neighborhood? (3) Can you tolerate them living next to you? (4) Are you willing to invite them as guests in your home? (5) Do you consent that your sons, daughters and other relatives court them? The sample of people included in the analysis reported in this chapter consists of urban residents in China.

Chapter 18 carries out a statistical analysis where the dependent variable used in the estimation for each question is a categorical variable equal to one if the answer for the attitude question is yes or zero if the answer is no. The set of explanatory variables include some of the same determinants of attitudes towards immigrants discussed in relation to Chapter 17, such as educational attainment, age, family income, labor market status, and a set of other variables that potentially influence attitudes towards migrants. The chapter estimates probit equations of the likelihood that the respondents in the sample had positive attitudes towards migrants

The research presented in Chapter 18 indicates that educational attainment does not dampen negative attitudes towards migrants in China. This is different from the results obtained by international research on attitudes toward immigrants, such as those presented in Chapter 17, in which education has been found to have a negative influence on anti-migrant sentiments. What explains this difference? One hypothesis is that urban residents in China may be fearful that the massive flow of non-hukou migrants will deteriorate their quality of life due to congestion, increased crime, etc. These perceptions may not be based on reality, but fueled by prejudice among urbanites. In addition, the school system in urban areas in China may not be contributing towards reducing anti-migrant attitudes as it does in many countries. The hukou system has acted effectively to make migrants a separate group in society, segregating migrant children from the children of urban residents, and generating a population with limited legal rights, stimulating the perception that they are inferior to urban residents. More specifically, the suzhi (素质 — personal quality) discourse which was gradually adopted by the school system, presumably to make the population "better-behaved", "more refined", or "higher-quality", has used migrants as a negative stereotype, portraying them as uncultured, ignorant and unrefined people whose behavioral characteristics should be avoided.

The analysis presented in Chapter 18 has a number of policy implications. There is clearly a need for a plan to incorporate migrant-sensitive curricula and teacher training into schools and colleges in China. In addition, the hukou system that has governed migration policy for decades needs to be reformed in order to end the institutional marginalization of migrants in urban areas. Since social benefits, including public education and health benefits, are attached to the person's hukou, the system has excluded migrants from having the same rights as urban residents. Experiments to modify the hukou system have emerged in some areas, such as Guangdong. And in 2014, China's State Council announced a set of hukou policy reforms intended to allow migrants greater access to public services in cities, such as in education, health care and social security. But the reform is gradual and favors towns and small cities while in larger cities (above 3 to 5 million in population), changes in registration will remain difficult for migrants. A deeper reform needs to be implemented.

Part 6: Interregional Migration and Geography

Interregional migration is often undertaken by rural migrants seeking the improved standard of living offered in urban areas. From the consumption side, one of the most popular incentives for migration is the gain in utility that consumers can obtain in urban areas. These can originate in the greater supply of local public goods or the access to a greater variety of local goods and services in the larger market areas created by urbanization. At the same time, the strongest incentives for migration are the higher wages and increased employment opportunities available in cities. The latter have been a central topic in urban and regional economic theory for centuries, going back to the early work of Adam Smith associating city size with increased trade and economic growth.

Chapter 19 forms part of a new literature that emerged in the late 1980s and early 1990s seeking to explain the geographical distribution of economic activity using frameworks that adopt models of increasing returns to scale, imperfect competition and product diversity. This new geography literature includes the work of Masahisa Fujita, Paul Krugman, Enrico Moretti, Konrad Stahl, and J. Vernon Henderson, among others. This chapter, which is based on a previous paper published in *Regional Science and Urban Economics* in 1988, is part of this budding literature and represents research that was simultaneously and independently being applied in other areas of economics, such as the endogenous technological change models developed by Paul Romer.

Chapter 19 develops a theoretical model focusing on how the agglomeration of producers in urban areas generates external economies of scale due to increased specialization that raise productivity and allow greater wages. More specifically, the model examines the role played by business services in generating external economies of scale in urban industrial production. The increased productivity that the presence of these business services allow induces industrial firms to agglomerate in urban areas.

The model in Chapter 19 conceptualizes the business services sector as supplying an array of specialized, differentiated intermediate inputs within a market structure of Chamberlinian monopolistic competition. As migration into cities occurs, two forces enter into play. On the one hand, the conventional effect of an increase in the labor force is to reduce the city's wage rate due to diminishing returns. However, an increase in the size of the urban population augments the size of the industrial sector and it shifts upwards the demand for producer services. The latter leads to an expansion in the variety of such services. With a wider diversity of service firms available, the industrial sector can obtain more specialized services and its productivity is therefore enhanced. This productivity increase is then embodied into higher wage rates. The net impact of increased population on the equilibrium wage rate in the city is related to the relative importance of the "diminishing returns" and the "increased productivity or linkage externality" effects just discussed.

Part 1

The Economic Consequences of Immigration

Chapter 1

Trade Theory, Distribution of Income and Immigration*

1.1 Introduction

The mass migration of unskilled labor from poor to rich countries has become a subject of intense concern in the rich countries. This can be noticed from the growing public outcry on the topic, and from the vocal debates on immigration policy thriving among policymakers. This paper examines the impact of mass immigration utilizing the analytical framework of so-called trade theory. As such, its emphasis is on general equilibrium effects and on the constraints imposed by the openness of the economy on such effects. The analysis will center on the distributional impact of immigration. This is a matter which has generated much controversy, as some groups in the economy (such as labor) have opposed immigration on the basis they are hurt by immigrants, while others (such as producers facing intense import competition from developing countries) have lobbied for increased immigration on the basis they may not subsist without them.

*This chapter was originally published in *The American Economic Review*, Vol. 73, No. 2 (May 1983), pp. 183–187.

This paper was written while I was a Post-Doctoral Fellow at the University of Chicago. The helpful comments of Luis Rivera-Batiz are gratefully acknowledged. The research embodied in this paper was supported in part by a grant from the National Research Council of the National Academy of Sciences.

1.2 Output Composition Effects and Immigration

In spite of the popular belief that immigration turns income distribution against labor and in favor of capital, standard trade theory offers the strong presumption that immigration may actually have no significant effects on income distribution at all. Consider the standard trade model of a small economy producing two traded goods, X and Y, under conditions of perfect competition and constant returns to scale. There are fixed endowments, $\bar{K}_n$ and $\bar{L}_n$, of nationally owned capital and labor, which are perfectly mobile among sectors in the economy and operate in perfectly competitive factor markets. These define the national transformation curve AZ, shown in Figure 1.1. With an international price ratio given by $\bar{P}\bar{P}$ (whose slope is $-P_X/P_Y$, with P_X and P_Y being the prices of X and Y in international markets), the production point of the economy would be at E. The "income distribution locus" for labor is given by WM. This curve shows the share of output that national labor would receive (earn) at different points on the national transformation curve. For instance, given production point E, we can draw the ray OE from the origin to that point. The WM locus is constructed so that the intersection of the ray OE with WM (at point C) gives

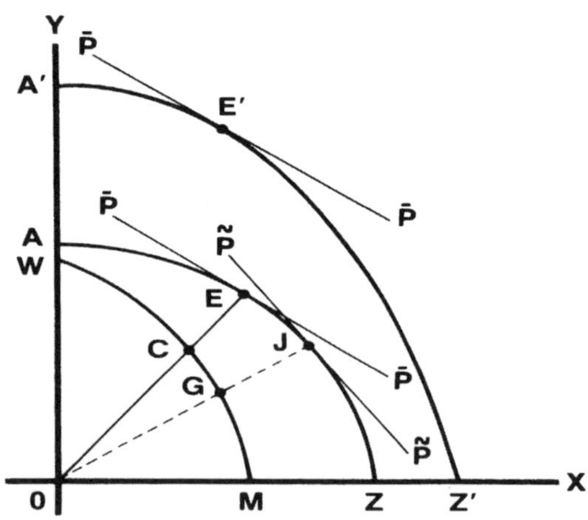

Figure 1.1. Output Composition Effects and the Distributional Impact of Immigration.

us the relative claim of labor on national output. The length of the segment *OC* represents labor's claim on output, while *CE* represents capital's claim; *OC/CE* then represents the factor share of labor relative to capital. Similarly, other points along *WM* represent labor's factor share associated with other production points along the *AZ* curve. The shape of *WM* is determined by the behavior of factor shares as output is varied along *AZ*. The factor earnings of capital relative to those of labor are given by $\theta = r\bar{K}_n/w\bar{L}_n$, where r and w are the factor prices of capital and labor. Since national factor endowments are fixed, θ will change only in response to changes in relative factor prices. As drawn, labor's share relative to capital's decreases as production of X increases. The explanation lies on the assumption that sector X is relatively capital intensive. As output of X increases, this sector's demand for labor will not increase by as much as sector Y releases its own labor. Excess labor supply results and the wage-rental ratio decreases.

What is the impact of immigration in this framework? An increase in the aggregate labor endowment would shift the economy's transformation curve upwards, as illustrated by the move from AZ to $A'Z'$. Aggregate production would then move to E', where $\bar{P}\bar{P}$ is tangent to $A'Z'$. Note, however, that the equilibrium of the national residents, lying along the national transformation curve AZ, remains unchanged at point E.[1] As a consequence, the income distribution curve *WM* is unaffected, leaving labor's earnings share unchanged at OC/OE and capital's at CE/OE. This result may be puzzling. One's tendency is to think that the additional labor should reduce wage rates since, with diminishing returns, more intensive use of labor reduces its marginal product. What must be understood, however, is that the additional labor force can be absorbed without any sector having to use labor more intensively. This occurs because of output composition effects. The additional labor does put downward pressures on the wage-rental ratio. But this increases the relative profitability of the labor-intensive Y sector. As a result, the output of commodity Y increases while the output of X decreases (at the aggregate level). Sector Y, though, demands relatively more labor than sector X. This means sector Y can absorb all the immigrant labor without either sector having to use more labor-intensive techniques. The overall increased demand for labor in the economy eliminates any tendencies for wage rates to decline.

These results can be extended without much difficulty to include more industries and factors, so long as the number of (internationally) traded goods, n, equals the number of factors, r. With more than two sectors, however, the output composition effects keeping factor prices constant can be quite complicated. The general conclusion is that some industries (at least one) will grow while others (at least one) will contract (See Jones and Scheinkman, 1977). Cases where $r \neq n$ are considered below.

The result that immigration does not affect income distribution is dependent on a number of crucial assumptions. The next sections examine these assumptions, starting with the fixed terms of trade one.

1.3 Changes in Relative Prices and Immigration

Immigration has been observed to have important effects on the price competitiveness of the industries it helps expand in the economy. By increasing the supply of domestic labor-intensive importables (and if this increase is perceptible in world markets), immigrants will reduce their relative price, inducing an improvement in the economy's terms of trade (Peter B. Kenen, 1971). Let us suppose, then, that an increase in P_X/P_Y occurs simultaneously with the immigration. Figure 1 shows this shift by means of the switch from $\bar{P}\bar{P}$ to $\tilde{P}\tilde{P}$. The national production point then moves from E to J. As a consequence, factoral income distribution is now affected: point G along WM represents a decrease in the wage-rental ratio and a corresponding increase in the share of capital relative to labor. The reduction in w/r arises from the decreased demand for labor relative to capital as the economy's production of good X increases and that of Y decreases. The effect on the size distribution of income depends on two considerations. First, the more labor an individual owns relative to capital, the more likely she or he will be hurt by the immigration. Second, the larger the person's propensity to consume exportables, the more likely his or her real income will be reduced by the immigration-cum-relative price disturbance. The net balance of these two effects on individuals depends on their factor endowments and tastes. If the economy is composed of a group of rich capitalists who consume mostly commodity Y, and a group of poor workers who consume mostly X, then the size distribution of income will clearly worsen. Note finally that if immigration is accompanied by a *decrease* in the relative price of X in terms of Y, then the distributional impact will be to benefit labor and hurt capital!

Relative prices can be affected even if the economy faces fixed terms of trade. This occurs because of the presence of (internationally) nontraded goods, such as services, whose prices are determined by local demand and supply. Actually, the impact of immigration on the nontraded goods sector may be of immense importance, due both to the size of the sector in most developed countries (composing as much as 56 percent of GNP in the United States), and because of its significance in employing immigrants (more than one-third of all legal immigrants entering the United States in 1977, for example, declared occupations associated with nontraded goods sectors).

Assuming fixed terms of trade, we can aggregate exportables and importables into a composite traded good which can be represented by X. If Yrepresents nontraded goods, Figure 1.1 can still be used as a tool of analysis. Suppose point E is the pre-migration equilibrium and that, with nontraded goods prices unchanged, immigration moves aggregate production to point E'. This would reduce the economy's output of traded goods (X) and increase that of nontraded goods. The additional supply of nontraded goods would then induce a reduction in their price, which is shown by the switch from $\bar{P}\bar{P}$ to $\tilde{P}\tilde{P}$. The final production point for the nationals would be at point J. As a consequence, income distribution is affected by the same considerations noted earlier in this section. Functional income distribution, for instance, would turn against labor and in favor of capital. In addition, those individuals who consume relatively more nontraded goods would tend to benefit (see my 1982b article for details; these results must be qualified when there are more than two industries and factors, see my 1982a paper).

1.4 Sector-Specific Factors and Income Distribution

It was shown above that output composition shifts can prevent immigration from affecting income distribution. The operational importance of this effect, however, depends on how easily inputs can be shifted among sectors in the economy. Within short periods of time, it may be reasonable to expect capital to be relatively immobile. If capital is considered sector specific, then, in effect, there will be three inputs in the economy: X industry capital, Y industry capital, and labor, and three factor prices to analyze: the rental rates in each sector, and the wage rate. In this context, immigration will tend to decrease the wage rate and increase rental rates in each sector. This is because the sector-specific capital generates diminishing returns at the economy-wide level (see Mussa, 1974). The additional workers decrease the marginal productivity of labor, and increase that of capital in each sector. Consequently, the distribution of earnings will turn against labor and in favor of capital. The size distribution of income will also be affected, with those individuals owning more capital relative to labor gaining, not only from the discussed shift in factor prices, but also because capital owners receive a (scarcity) rent on the use of the immigrant labor.

When sector-specificities characterize only the short run, capital will move over time into production of the labor-intensive commodity. Wages will then increase and rental rates decrease back towards their original levels. Long-run equilibrium will involve no distributional effects; only over the adjustment process will income distribution change (see my 1982c article, and Sapir, 1983).

Up to this point, I have considered labor to be perfectly homogeneous and freely mobile. This contrasts with many applied studies on immigration, which tend to view the labor market in the recipient countries as being segmented into quite distinct sectors, each characterized by a quite distinct type of labor (see Piore, 1979). Accordingly, let us suppose that sector X uses only skilled labor while sector Y uses only unskilled labor. If mass immigration of unskilled workers occurs, the wage rates of both skilled and unskilled labor decrease and the rental rate on capital increases. As in the case of sector-specific capital, the economy is subject to aggregate diminishing returns, implying the additional unskilled workers must reduce their wage rate and increase capital's rental rate. The wages of skilled workers, on the other hand, decrease because the initial impact of the immigrants is to increase the rental rate in sector Y, inducing capital to leave sector X. With less capital to work with, skilled workers will face lower marginal products, and thus lower wages. So, even if nationals are predominantly employed in industries where there are few immigrants, they will still not necessarily be insulated from the effects of immigration.

In contrast to the many restrictions governments impose on immigration, international capital mobility seems to be relatively more free from controls. If capital is freely mobile among countries, what difference does this make in terms of the present discussion? As it has been shown, unskilled labor immigration increases the rental rate on capital. This would then induce an inflow of foreign capital into the economy, which would partially reverse the losses of labor relative to capital.

1.5 Immigration in the Presence of Distortions

Most economies are plagued by economic distortions, originating from both private and public manipulation of the marketplace. Examining the distributional impact of immigration under these conditions is thus imperative. I consider first immigration in the presence of a tariff, assumed to be placed on the (labor-intensive) importables. In terms of Figure 1.1, the tariff-inclusive price is now represented by means of $\bar{P}\bar{P}$. Consequently, the economy's initial production point is E. Immigration would then move the economy's equilibrium to E', but leave national production at point E. Factoral income distribution would remain unchanged. The size distribution, however, will tend to worsen. Immigration increases the economy's output of importables, and thus tends to reduce imports. This reduces the tariff revenues collected by national customs authorities. As a result, the nonimmigrants, to whom it can be assumed the revenues are distributed, will face a reduction of their real income. Given that domestic output of importables is still produced at the artificially high price imposed by the tariff, the loss in the real income of nationals must be collected by someone else. It is actually received by the immigrants, who are paid at a marginal product whose value is inflated by the tariff — inclusive price, and is thus higher than its worth at international prices (see Bhagwati, 1982). Given the loss of tariff revenues, and if the allocation of these is made on the basis of income, then those individuals at the lower tail of the income distribution, who benefit relatively more from the revenues, will lose relative to high-income groups.

The presence of factor market distortions brings into focus the analysis of unemployment. A useful scheme to describe some aspects of labor markets in developed countries is to decompose the economy into a unionized sector that sets artificially high wages and generates unemployment, and a competitive sector with flexible wages and full employment. Labor market equilibrium is assumed to occur when the expected wage in the protected sector (equal to the union wage weighted by the probability of employment) is equal to the wage in the competitive sector. Immigration of labor into the competitive sector lowers its wage rate, inducing nationals to migrate to the unionized sector until the increase in unemployment in that sector lowers the expected wage rate enough to maintain parity with the competitive wage. As a result, nonunion workers will lose relative to union workers. This loss occurs in the form of lower wage rates in the competitive sector and higher unemployment rates in the unionized sector (see my 1981 article).

1.6 Conclusions

Some crucial aspects regarding the distributional impact of unskilled labor immigration have been examined in this paper. The weight of the analysis is that immigration does tend to turn the functional distribution of income against labor and in favor of non-labor factors. This result, however, is not exactly obvious, and depends on the importance of output composition effects, international capital movements, and changes in relative prices, among other things.

Notes:

[1]Curve AZ is a hypothetical one in the post-migration situation since what is observed is the aggregate curve, $A'Z'$. It is still, however, a useful tool of analysis given that it allows us to compare the pre- and post-immigration situations of the national population (see Jagdish Bhagwati and R. Brecher, 1981).

References

Bhagwati, Jagdish N., *Import Competition and Response*, Chicago: University of Chicago Press, 1982.

——, and Brecher, R., "Foreign Ownership and the Theory of Trade and Welfare," *Journal of Political Economy*, June 1981, 89, 497–511.

Jones, R. W. and Scheinkman, J., "The Relevance of the Two-Sector Production Model in Trade Theory," *Journal of Political Economy*, October 1977, 85, 909–935.

Kenen, P. B., "Migration, the Terms of Trade and Economic Welfare in the Source Country," in J. N. Bhagwati *et al.*, eds., *Trade, Balance of Payments and Growth, Amsterdam*: North-Holland, 1971, 238–260.

Mussa, M., "Tariffs and the Distribution of Income," *Journal of Political Economy*, December 1974, 82, 1191–1203.

Piore, M., *Birds of Passage: Migrant Labor and Industrial Societies*, Cambridge: Cambridge University Press, 1979.

Rivera-Batiz, F., "The Effects of Immigration in a Distorted Two-Sector Economy," *Economic Inquiry*, October 1981, 19, 626–639.

——, (1982a), "Nontraded Goods and the Pure Theory of International Trade with Equal Numbers of Goods and Factors," *International Economic Review*, June 1982, 23, 401–409.

——, (1982b), "International Migration, Nontraded Goods and Economic Welfare in the Source Country," *Journal of Development Economics*, September 1982, 11, 81–90.

——, (1982c), "On the Distributional and Welfare Impact of Immigration: Costs and Benefits," mimeo, University of Chicago, October 1982.

——, "The Economics of the 'To and Fro' Migrant: Some Welfare-Theoretic Considerations," *Scandinavian Journal of Economics*, 1983, 85(3), 403–413.

Sapir, A., "Foreign Competition, Immigration and Structural Adjustment," *Journal of International Economics*, 14 (1983), 381–394.

Chapter 2

The Effects of Immigration in a Distorted Two-Sector Economy*

2.1 Introduction

Most of the literature on the theory of international migration has examined the effects of immigration by analyzing the effects, on the nonimmigrants in a distortion-free economy, which arise from an exogenous inflow of foreign labor.[1] This approach may be criticized on two grounds.[2] Firstly, since the migrant inflow is treated as exogenous, the analysis cannot explain why immigration occurs at all. Secondly, given that the models assume that the economy is free of domestic distortions, they cannot examine the impact of immigration on such a crucial variable as unemployment.

In this paper, we try to avoid the shortcomings of the traditional literature by developing a two-sector model in which immigration is

---

*This chapter was originally published in *Economic Inquiry*, Vol. 19, No. 4 (October 1981), pp. 626–639.

This paper draws on the second chapter of my Ph.D. thesis. For their guidance and encouragement, I am deeply indebted to Jagdish N. Bhagwati and Michael J. Piore, members of my dissertation committee. I also wish to acknowledge the helpful comments of Henry S. Farber, third member of the committee, Lance Taylor, and the members of seminars at Indiana University, the University of Massachusetts, and the Massachusetts Institute of Technology. I have to especially thank Arthur De Vany and the referees for their valuable comments and suggestions, which substantially improved this paper. Financial assistance was provided by a dissertation grant from the Ford Foundation.

endogenous, and in which a sector-specific administered wage generates unemployment. Our recipient economy is divided into two sectors: a modern sector which is categorized by the production of an exportable good, a high administered wage and unemployment, and a traditional sector specializing in the production of an import-competing good, with full employment, flexible wages, and especially characterized by using foreign, or migrant, labor, plus domestic labor, in production.

In Section 2.2 we state our basic two-sector model; in Section 2.3 we derive how immigration responds to the exogenous variables in the system; in Section 2.4 we analyze the impact of immigration on unemployment, national income, factoral income distribution, etc., and in Section 2.5 we restate our conclusions, assess the assumptions we have made to derive them, and discuss the main implications of the analysis.

2.2 The Model

The economy consists of two sectors: a modern sector and a traditional sector. The short-run production function for the output of the modern sector, X_1, is:

$$X_1 = F_1(N_1), \quad F_1' > 0, \quad F_1'' < 0, \tag{1}$$

where N_1 is the labor employed in the sector, F_1' is the derivative of F_1, with respect to N_1, and F_1'' is the second derivative. Diminishing returns are a result of the fixed non-labor input in production in the short-run.[3] The output of this sector is considered to be an exportable so that the total consumption of modern-sector goods, C_1, is:

$$C_1 = X_1 - E, \tag{2}$$

where E represents net exports of sector 1, and where consumption is a function of real income, Y, and the price ratio $P \equiv P_2/P_1$, where P_1 is the price of export goods and P_2, is the price of imports, so that:

$$C_1 = C_1(\bar{P}, Y), \quad C_{11} > 0, \quad C_{12} > 0, \tag{3}$$

with C_{11} equal to the partial derivative of the function C_1 with respect to $\bar{P}$, where $\bar{P}$ is equal to the international price ratio (assuming that the country is "small"), and with C_{12} equal to the partial with respect to Y.

Note that Y is equal to (from the budget constraint):

$$Y = C_1 + \bar{P}C_{12}, \tag{4}$$

where we utilize the price of the modern sector good, P_1, as numeraire, and where C_1, is the domestic consumption of commodity 2.

The modern sector is especially characterized by an administered wage. This wage is assumed to be set by a trade union whose goal is to maximize the total wage bill in the modern sector, regardless whether all wage earners are employed.[4] It is easy to show that, if the wage bill is maximized, the union must set the wage rate in the modern sector at the point where the elasticity of demand for labor in the modern sector is equal to 1; that is, where

$$\eta_D \equiv -\frac{\bar{w}_1}{N_1}\frac{dN_1}{d\bar{w}_1}, \tag{5}$$

where η_D is the (wage) elasticity of demand for labor, $\bar{w}_1$ is the administered wage and N_1 is employment in the modern sector. The administered wage is taken to be exogenous by firms in the modern sector[5] so that, from the usual first-order condition for profit maximization:

$$F_1' = \bar{w}_1, \tag{6}$$

where we have made use of the assumption that modern-sector goods are the numeraire. We also assume that $\bar{w}_1$ is set above the market-clearing wage so that unemployment is generated. In this case, the total labor supply to the modern sector, L_1 is equal to:

$$L_1 = N_1 + U_1, \tag{7}$$

where U_1 is the number of unemployed workers in that sector. Note, finally, that the administered wage is rigid and is completely determined by technology.

The traditional sector produces an importable good, X_2, through a production function:

$$X_2 = F_2(N_2 + L_M), \quad F_2' > 0, \quad F_2'' < 0, \tag{8}$$

where N_2 is employment of domestic labor in the sector, L_M is employment of foreign labor, and F_2' and F_2'' are first- and second-order derivatives of F_2. We assume as before that there is a fixed, non-labor, input which generates diminishing returns. Employers in the traditional sector use domestic and foreign labor. Foreign labor, unavailable locally, must be imported from abroad. Depending upon the preferences of the foreign population, an offer curve of foreign (or migrant) labor to the traditional sector exists with:[6]

$$w_m = g(L_m, \bar{Y}), \quad g_1 > 0, \quad g_2 > 0, \tag{9}$$

where w_m is the wage paid to the foreign (migrant) laborers, L_m, and Y is the average income of the worker in the less-developed country from which he comes, which we assume, for simplicity, to be fixed exogenously at a level equal to $\bar{Y}$. The partial derivative of g with respect to L_m, g_1, is positive because, as the wage offered increases, more migrants are available whose reservation wage is less than the wage paid. Also, $g_2 > 0$ because, as the average income abroad increases, the opportunity cost of migrating increases and, thus, the migrants' reservation wage increases.

Assuming that there are no government restrictions on immigration (we will examine these later on), then the traditional-sector firms can import foreign labor freely, and net profits in that sector (net of the costs of the non-labor input), Π, are given by:

$$\Pi = \bar{P}F_2(N_2 + L_m) - w_2 N_2 - L_m g(L_m, \bar{Y}),$$

where w_2 is the competitive wage rate in sector 2. Profits are maximized with respect to N_2 and L_m, given $\bar{P}$ and $\bar{Y}$; The first-order conditions for a maximum[7] are:

$$\bar{P}F_2' = w_2 \tag{10}$$

and

$$\bar{P}F_2' = w_M. \tag{11}$$

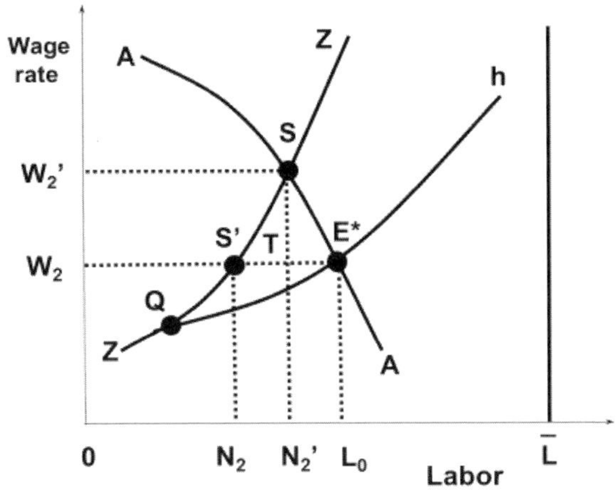

Figure 2.1. The Effects of Immigration in the Traditional Sector.

The equilibrium condition in (10) is just the usual equality of the wage rate with the marginal value product of labor, and (11) states that the services of migrant labor are imported[8] up to the point where their wage rate, w_M, equals their marginal value product, $\overline{PF_2'}$.

The equilibrium conditions in (10) and (11) are portrayed in Figure 2.1, where we show the labor market equilibrium of sector 2. The marginal product curve, $\bar{P}F_2'$, is represented by AA, the domestic labor supply curve to the sector is ZZ, and the total labor supply curve to the sector (the domestic supply curve augmented by the foreign labor supply) is ZQh. Equilibrium would then occur at point E^*, with an equilibrium wage, for both domestic and foreign labor, of w_2; employment of domestic labor equal to ON_2; and employment of migrants equal to $L_0 - N_2$.

We assume there is a fixed total labor supply (of non-migrants) in the economy, $\bar{L}$, so that:[9]

$$\bar{L} = N_2 + L_1. \tag{12}$$

What determines the intersectoral allocation of this fixed labor supply? One possibility is that labor moves along sectors so as to equalize wage rates. More realistically, however, is the assumption that workers recognize the presence of unemployment in the modern sector and compare the going wage in the traditional sector with the *expected wage* in the modern sector, which is defined as the administered wage weighted by the probability of employment in the modern sector, ϵ. We define ϵ, in turn, to be equal to the ratio of job vacancies to the supply of workers available to fill those vacancies:

$$\epsilon \equiv \frac{\theta N_1}{L_1 - (1-\theta)N_1}, \tag{13}$$

where θ is the fraction of the employed which turn-over in each time period.

What (13) says is that the θN_1, slots available are randomly allocated among those workers who do not retain their slots.[10] The inter-sectoral labor market equilibrium condition is, then:

$$w_2 = \epsilon \bar{w}_1. \tag{14}$$

Total consumption of traditional-sector goods, C_2, is:

$$C_2 = X_2 + M, \tag{15}$$

where M is equal to the net imports of traditional-sector goods, and C_2 is determined from (4) above. The balance of payments equilibrium condition is

$$E = g(L_M, \bar{Y})L_M + \bar{P}M, \tag{16}$$

which reflects the fact that migrant workers are assumed to be foreign residents so that their income is considered to be a payment for the import of services.

2.3 The Determinants of Immigration

Our model is now complete. Substituting (1) and (8) into (2) and (15) respectively, we obtain 11 equations: (2), (3), (4), (6), (7), (10), (11), (12), (14), (15), and (16) in 11 variables: C_1, C_2, N_2, N_1, L_1, U_1, L_M, Y, E, M, and w_2, with parameters given by:$\bar{P}$, $\bar{Y}$, $\bar{L}$ and θ. This system can be solved to determine the effects of exogenous parameters on L_M by totally differentiating each of the above-mentioned equations and combining them until only dL_M, appears as an endogenous variable. The reduced form result is the following:

$$dL_M = \frac{\gamma}{1-\gamma}d\bar{L} - \frac{\gamma N_1(\bar{w}_1 - w_2)}{(1-\gamma)w_2}d\theta - \frac{\gamma F_2'}{(1-\gamma)\bar{P}F_2''}d\bar{P}$$
$$- \frac{g_1}{(1-\gamma)g_1}d\bar{Y} \tag{17}$$

where

$$\gamma \equiv \frac{\bar{P}F_2''w_2}{g_1[w_2 - \bar{P}F_2''(U_1 + \theta N_1)]} < 0.$$

The first observation which can be discerned from (17) is that an increase in the non-immigrant labor force reduces the amount of immigration $(\partial L_M/\partial \bar{L}) < 0$. The reason for this is that the increase in the domestic labor supply decreases the wage rate in the traditional sector and, thus, the profitability of importing cheap foreign labor decreases relative to the hiring of domestic residents. A second exogenous variable affecting immigration is the turnover rate in the modern sector of the recipient economy. As the turnover rate increases, the profitability of finding employment in the modern sector increases so that domestic labor moves, or migrates, internally out of the traditional sector and into the modern sector. The scarcity of labor in the traditional sector then increases the wage rate there, which, finally, triggers an increase in the import of foreign labor (from (17), $\partial L_M/\partial\theta > 0$).

A third factor affecting immigration is the price ratio, $\bar{P}$. An increase in the price of traditional-sector goods relative to modern-sector goods, that is, an increase in $\bar{P}$, leads to a shift of the demand for labor in the traditional sector upwards, which increases the wage rate in that sector and, thus, increases immigration $(\partial L_M/\partial \bar{P} > 0)$. A fourth variable affecting the number of immigrants in the recipient economy is the level of foreign income, $\bar{Y}$. An increase in $\bar{Y}$ shifts the offer curve of foreign labor upwards, which makes its hiring more expensive. The quantity demanded of foreigners declines, and immigration decreases $(\partial L_M/\partial \bar{P} < 0)$.

2.4 The Effects of Immigration

Our strategy in this section is to examine how the different endogenous variables in the recipient economy change if we assume that immigrant workers are not allowed to enter the recipient economy. Our purpose is to compare the immigration and the no-immigration situation.

Let us consider the labor market effects of, non-infinitesimal[11] immigration first. If no foreign labor were allowed into the economy, the labor market equilibrium in the traditional sector would occur at point S, as shown in Figure 2.1. It is clear, then, by comparing point S with point E^*, that immigration decreases the employment of domestic labor (from ON_2' to ON_2) as well as the equilibrium wage rate in that sector (from w_2' to w_2). The native workers released from the traditional sector then move to the modern sector so as to equalize the expected wage in the latter with the, now lower, wage in the former. But as long as the modern sector's administered wage is fixed, employment in that sector will also remain unchanged. This implies that immigration, by inducing a movement of native labor out of the traditional and into the modern sector, increases the unemployment rate of domestic labor.

In the goods market, immigration reduces the production of imported goods by non-immigrants, even though their production of exported goods stays fixed. This effect arises because immigration reduces the employment of non-immigrants in the traditional sector, causing their production to decline; since employment is fixed in the modern sector, there is no change in the production of modern-sector goods. Note that even though production of traditional-sector goods by non-immigrants declines, production by the immigrants more than offsets this decline.

What is the distributive impact of immigration? As seen above, the additional supply of labor implied by the immigrants leads to a reduction in the wage rate in sector 2, as well as to a reduction in the expected income in sector 1 (compared to a situation without immigration). Since there is a rigid wage in sector 1, employment is fixed and, thus, the returns to the sector-specific non-labor input in that sector are invariant with respect to the immigrants. The returns to the sector-specific input in sector 2, however, increase since the additional labor increases the marginal product of that input. So, immigration leads to a redistribution of income from labor to the non-labor input in sector 2. In terms of Figure 2.1, the total returns to labor in sector 2 decline from an amount represented by the area of the rectangle $OW'_2SN'_2$, under no immigration, to an amount represented by the area of the rectangle $OW_2S'N_2$, under immigration. The returns to the non-labor input in that sector, on the other hand, increase by an amount equal to the area $W'_2SE^*W_2$.

The final aspect of immigration which we want to analyze is its impact on the overall income of the non-immigrants. Assuming that the only change is in the presence of foreign workers, (2), (4), and (15) can be differentiated to obtain:

$$dY = dX_1 - dE + \bar{P}dM. \tag{18}$$

But, from (16):

$$dE = W_M dL_M + \bar{P}dM, \tag{19}$$

and $dX_1 = 0$ since, by differentiating (8) and substituting into (18) we get:

$$dY = \bar{P}F'_2(L_2)dL_2 - W_M dL_M, \tag{20}$$

where L_2 represents total employment in the traditional sector. But if one compares a situation of no immigration with one of free immigration, then $dY = Y_r - Y_1$ is equal to domestic income under no immigration, and Y_1 is equal to domestic income if foreign labor is freely allowed into the economy. Referring to Figure 2.1, then, we also know that $dL_2 = N'_2 - L_0$ and $dL_M = N_2 - L_0$. If we then approximate the marginal product of labor curve in the traditional sector by means of a Taylor series around L_0, we obtain:

$$dY \cong \left[\bar{P}F'_2(L_0) + \frac{\bar{P}}{2}F''_2(L_0)(N'_2 - L_0) - W_M(N_2 - L_0)\right], \tag{21}$$

where we have neglected the higher-order terms in the Taylor-series approximation. Simplifying equation (21), and noting that $W_M = \bar{P}F_2'(L_0)$, we finally obtain:

$$dY \cong \bar{P}F_2'(L_0)(N_2' - N_2) + \frac{\bar{P}}{2}F_2''(L_0)(N_2' - L_0)^2. \qquad (22)$$

That is, the impact of immigration on the total income of the native population is ambiguous. The first term in (22) represents the loss in income resulting from the increase in unemployment brought about by immigration and described in detail above. Note that, in the absence of the administered-wage distortion in the modern sector, this term would disappear. This is easily verified by noting that, without distortions, $dX_1 \neq 0$ and, thus, differentiating (1) and substituting into equation (18) one would obtain:

$$dY \cong \bar{P}F_2'(L_0)(N_2' - N_2) + F_1'(N_1)(N_1' - N_1) + R, \qquad (23)$$

where N_1' represents employment in the modern sector under restrictionism, N_1 employment under free immigration, and R represents second order terms. But since, in the absence of distortions, wage rates must equalize across sectors in the economy, then $\bar{P}F_2' = F_1'$, and since there is fixed labor supply of native workers: $N_2' - N_2 = N_1' - N_1$. By substituting these into (22), one would obtain that $dY \cong R$, where R is negative (as can be verified from equation (21)). That is, in the absence of distortions, immigration can only increase the income of the non-immigrants.[12] The main intuitive reason behind the decrease in national income represented by the first term in (22) is, then, that immigration, through its effects on the domestic intersectoral labor mobility, causes an increment in the importance of the administered wage distortion.[13]

Going back to equation (22), we can see that immigration may still increase the income of the non-immigrants even if the administered-wage distortion in the modern sector exists. This will occur if the second term in (22) dominates the first term. The economic meaning behind this second term, in (22), can be easily visualized from Figure 2.1. Allowing immigration into the economy leads to an increase in the total employment of labor in the traditional sector by an amount equal to $L_0 - N_2'$. This additional labor increases the rent obtained by the non-labor input by an amount represented in Figure 2.1 by the area of STE*. This rent represents a net gain in income for the non-immigrants. Only if this gain is large enough to offset the income losses due to increased unemployment,[14] as represented by the first term in equation (22), will immigration increase the total income of the non-immigrants. This depends, of course, on such factors as the elasticity of the marginal product of labor curve in the traditional sector, the optimal amount of immigration, etc.

2.5 Conclusions

In this paper we have developed a two-sector model of an economy which faces unemployment and in which immigration is endogenous, responding positively to rises in the wage rate offered in the traditional sector of the economy. Our main conclusions are that immigration, within this framework, increases the unemployment of domestic residents, turns income distribution against labor and in favor of the non-labor input in the traditional sector, and has an ambiguous, but possibly negative, effect on the total income of the non-immigrants. This last result contrasts with the traditional result, derived under the assumption of no domestic distortions, that immigration cannot affect negatively the income of the domestic residents at all. The reason behind the possible negative effects of immigration on the income of the non-immigrants is that immigration, by decreasing wages in the traditional sector, induces a movement of domestic workers out of that sector and into the modern sector. But the modern sector has only a fixed number of jobs available (given the fixed administered wage). Those additional domestic workers, then, either become unemployed, or cause other workers to become unemployed. This increases the waste in the economy and, thus, reduces domestic income.

Note also that our results contradict the views of some authorities, who argue that the relaxation of the U.S. immigration laws with respect to Mexicans, for example, does not decrease domestic welfare on the basis of the fact that the introduction of migrant workers does not lead to increases in domestic unemployment in the areas or sectors in which they compete with domestic workers. As one expert puts it:

"Does illegal migration 'create unemployment' among the U.S. domestic work force? If illegal immigration from Mexico were decreasing job opportunities for significant numbers of American workers — either directly or indirectly — it follows that unemployment rates should be higher in those parts of the country having large concentrations of Mexican illegals, and lower in areas with few illegals. Of course, this is not the case: some of the lowest unemployment rates in the U.S. are found in the 'Sunbelt' areas having the largest concentration of illegal Mexican migrants."[15]

According to our framework, the fact that unemployment rates in high immigration areas are very low does not affect the conclusion that unemployment is affected positively by immigration, because the import of foreign workers induces an internal migration of native workers out of the high-immigration, mostly agricultural, areas and into the modern, mostly industrial areas, leading to congestion and unemployment in the latter, not in the former. It is a matter of future research to examine further the empirical importance of these movements.[16]

Many argue that the importation of foreign labor into the U.S. arises because of the decline of the domestic labor supplies available to employers in the traditional sector. This has been one of the most systematic reasons given by recruiters of foreign labor in some sectors of U.S. agriculture. Even at the present time, with the immense flow of both legal and illegal foreign workers into the U.S., the use of such workers is still rationalized as being the result of a labor shortage. Actually, this movement of U.S. labor out of the traditional to the modern sector has been quite stable over time. As Sjaastad has estimated: "since 1950, an average of about 4 percent of the total farm population left agriculture each year. That such a high pace of evacuation can continue for an extended period of time is remarkable in itself, and cannot conceivably continue indefinitely if for no other reason than complete exhaustion of farm labor."[17] This evidence on the decline of the supply of domestic labor to the traditional sector, however, has been questioned by many who argue that foreign labor substitutes for domestic labor, when it is imported, and that traditional-sector employers could indeed find domestic labor only if they were not more interested in employing the cheaper foreign labor. These differing points of view have led to many controversies as to the effects migrant labor has on the employment of domestic workers. For example, when the *Bracero* program ended in 1965, a controversy rose between the then Secretary of Labor, W. Willard Wirtz (and other pro-labor groups), and agricultural employers. "The growers argued that without *Braceros*, they would be unable to harvest their crops, that domestic workers were both unwilling and unable to do the back-breaking work of harvesting. Wirtz replied that domestic workers would be available if the workers were paid a decent wage."[18] Even though it has been a source of great controversy, it seems to us that these two seemingly conflicting hypotheses can be integrated, in terms of our framework. Suppose that, as the evidence tends to point out, there is a decline in the labor supply of the traditional sector due, perhaps to an increase in the time horizon[19] of the domestic agricultural population or to an increase in the turnover rate in the modern sector. This implies that, at the original wage rate, the employers in the traditional sector would face a shortage of (domestic) labor. Assuming that the import of foreign labor is not allowed, there would be a rise in the wage rate as well as a (net) decline in the employment in the sector. If immigration were allowed, the consequent increase in the (total) supply of labor would lead to a decrease in both the wage rate and the employment of domestic workers. In this case, then, the two views on immigration mentioned above are correct: employers do face a (domestic) labor shortage, because of the (leftward) shift of the labor supply curve; pro-labor groups, on the other hand, are also right, in the sense that employers could indeed find domestic labor, if only they were to let the wage rate increase, through a movement along the new labor supply curve. The real question is not, then, that the shortage be eliminated (without the import of foreign labor), but how much the wage rate has to increase in order to induce domestic workers to supply labor to the traditional sector. The answer to this question, of course, depends on the (wage) elasticity of labor supply. The evidence, though not entirely conclusive, tends to suggest that the supply of labor to the traditional sector in the U.S. is highly elastic and mobile, responding quite rapidly to changes in the relative wage rate.[20] It means that restricting the import of foreign labor will probably increase substantially the employment of domestic labor in the traditional sector *vis-a-vis* the situation without restrictions. But, given the high elasticity, there would be much less improvement in the wage rate.[21]

Our analysis is developed under a substantial number of assumptions, which include the two-sector model description of the recipient economy, the presence of diminishing returns in both sectors, etc. It is clear that our results would change significantly if these assumptions were relaxed. Immigration, in the presence of increasing returns in the recipient economy, for example, will tend to increase, rather than decrease, domestic income, so long as population growth is the binding constraint in the economy. It is our belief, however, that the model's assumptions do not strain the analysis too much. A crucial building block in the model is the assumption that immigration occurs only in the traditional sector of the economy. We agree that this is a simplifying assumption, but it may very well serve as a crude approximation to the actual behavior of unskilled immigration in some developed economies. With respect to the U.S., it seems that Mexicans (which are the majority of immigrants) do tend to be employed, an increasingly so, in the import-competing sectors we described above as traditional.[22]

Finally, we would like to mention possible extensions to our analysis, and suggestions for further research. Given the endogeneity of immigration in our model, the logical extension is to examine the effects of government restrictions on immigration, and of optimal immigration quotas, given any domestic distortions or possible externalities. It would also be possible to consider how immigration policies can help attain any noneconomic objectives of the decision-makers in the economy. Our model could also be expanded into a two-country model, in which case the general equilibrium impact of international migration on both the recipient and the source country could be examined. Using this framework it would then be possible to relax our assumption that only international labor migration occurs, by allowing capital to flow between the two countries too. In this context capital outflows may very well substitute for labor migration or vice versa.

Notes:

[1]See, for example, Kenen (1971), Bhagwati and Rodriguez (1976), Mishan and Needleman (1966, 1968). Some of this literature is concerned with the economic effects of emigration, but the analysis is exactly analogous under immigration.

[2]There is a further problem which is not examined in this paper. This is that the immigrants are not considered to be part of the domestic population in the recipient economy and, thus, their income, consumption, etc., is considered to be foreign, rather than domestic. This is accurate only so long as the immigrants do not intend to become residents of the recipient country (as in the case of '*braceros*' and 'guest workers'), or in a short-run framework in which the immigrants are not yet domestic residents. Note, however, that the question of how new residents would affect the income, consumption, etc. of the existing residents is still a relevant question, especially in view of its policy implications.

[3]One of our main interests is how immigration affects the mobility of domestic labor within the economy, among sectors. In order to concentrate our attention on labor mobility, we are assuming that mobility in the non-labor input does not occur. This is correct only if that input is sector-specific, and/or if the concern is only with the short-run.

[4]There are many other alternative goals that may enter into the utility or preference function of a trade union, but the wage bill maximand is perhaps the most simple and typical. See Dunlop (1966, Chapter 3).

[5]In a more complex treatment one would have to assume that both unions and firms bargain over, and can influence, the administered wage. See Calvo (1978) for some models of this type.

[6]Actually, in the long-run, and in a more complete treatment, the immigrants' offer curve, g, will also depend on the recruitment activities of the employers. These involve the provision of employment information and work contracts to the foreign workers, and the financing of their transport costs, temporary housing expenses, etc. For a detailed analysis of recruitment, see Rivera-Batiz (1979).

[7]Second-order conditions can be easily shown to be satisfied so long as $g_{11} > 0$, that is, so long as the offer curve of foreign labor is upward-sloping.

[8]We assume that sector 2 behaves as a perfect competitor in importing labor, rather than as a monopsonist. In the latter case, equation (11) would have to equalize the marginal value product of foreign labor with its marginal cost. We also implicitly assume that the fixed, non-labor input is held by the sector, so that its rate of return must equal its marginal value product.

[9]Note that (12) assumes that workers must, beforehand, decide to supply labor to either the modern or the traditional sector, but not to both. Given the presence

of unemployment in the modern sector, this implies that unemployed workers in that sector will not take a job in the traditional sector. The main reason for this assumption is that employment in the traditional sector would obstruct to some extent the search process of the worker in the modern sector. This assumption is certainly restrictive but it simplifies the analysis, and it is the one which has been utilized in most studies on the theory of job search anyway.

[10]An alternative is to assume that all jobs are allocated randomly in each time period, that is, that $\theta = 1$. This hiring-hall system, though widely utilized in the literature, does not seem to be consistent with our assumption that there be a trade union strong enough to set wages in the modern sector. Our main results, in any case, are quite robust with respect to different assumptions about the probability of employment in the modern sector. For more details, see Stiglitz (1974, appendix).

[11]This distinction between finite and infinitesimal migration has been made by Tobin (1974) and Bhagwati and Rodriguez (1978, p. 89–92). An infinitesimal amount of immigration would have no effects on the marginal product of labor in sector 2 and, thus, it would have no effect at all on the domestic economy.

[12]This conclusion is also obtained by Bhagwati and Rodriguez. See also Kenen (1971, pp. 246–47), Reder (1963, p. 223), and Berry and Soligo (1969, pp. 779–784).

[13]Actually, this result runs along the same lines as those of the studies on growth under the presence of distortions. See Bhagwati, (1971, pp. 69–70).

[14]Note that an increase in unemployment does not represent a complete loss in welfare for the non-immigrants, since the unemployed would probably increase their consumption of leisure. Given our description of the labor market in the modern sector, however, the direct loss obtained by being involuntarily unemployed, (that is, by being unable to obtain a job by just reducing the reservation wage below the going wage rate) would more than offset any positive leisure gain.

[15]Cornelius (1978, pp. 57–58). The same view is shared by Reubens (1978, pp. 118–19).

[16]As is discussed below, Wise (1974) and Smith and Newman (1977) have some evidence supporting our view.

[17]Sjaastad (1961, p. 27). See also Reubens (1978, p. 118).

[18]Wise (1974, p. 547).

[19]Note that our intersectoral mobility condition, (14), is a static one. A more sophisticated version would assume that the worker, in evaluating to which sector to supply labor, would consider both the present and the future average wage expected to be prevalent in the modern sector. The worker would then supply labor to that sector which gives him a higher discounted present income, over his time horizon. If wages in the traditional sector are assumed to remain more or less constant over the working life of the individual, while wages in the modern sector increase, because of on-the-job training, etc., then changes in such parameters as ‘time preference’ and ‘time horizon’ will affect the allocation of labor between sectors. If the time horizon of the individual increases, the modern sector will become relatively more attractive, compared

to the traditional one, because of its rising wages. Labor would then move to the modern sector until the present values of income in both sectors were equalized. For a more detailed examination, see Rivera-Batiz (1979, Essay 2).

[20]See Wise (1974), also Sjaastad (1961), and Smith and Newman (1977).

[21]Evidence on the impact of the termination of the Bracero program in California suggests that the end of the program may have led to an increase in domestic agricultural employment of as much as 262%. Agricultural wages were also found to increase, but only by 67%. See Wise (1974, p. 555).

[22]See Cornelius (1978. p. 54).

References

Berry, R. and Soligo, R., "Some Welfare Aspects of International Migration," *Journal of Political Economy*, Sept./Oct. 1969, 77, 778–794.

Bhagwati, Jagdish N., "The Generalized Theory of Distortions and Welfare," in *Trade, Balance of Payments and Growth*, ed., J. N. Bhagwati *et al.*, North Holland, Amsterdam, 1971, 69–90.

——— and Rodriguez, Carlos, "Welfare-Theoretical Analyses of the Brain Drain," in *The Brain Drain and Taxation*, ed., J. N. Bhagwati, North Holland Amsterdam, 1976, 85–111.

Calvo, Guillermo A., "Urban Unemployment and Wage Determination in LDCS: Trade Unions in the Harris-Todaro Model," *International Economic Review*, 19, February 1978, 65–81.

Cornelius, Wayne A., "Mexican Migration to the United States: Causes, Consequences and U.S. Responses," *Migration and Development Study Group Discussion Paper*, No. C/78-9, MIT, July 1978.

Dunlop, John T., *Wage Determination under Trade Unions*, Kelley, New York, 1966.

Harris, John R. and Todaro, Michael P., "Migration, Unemployment and Development: A Two-Sector Analysis," *American Economic Review*, 60, March 1970, 126–142.

Kenen, Peter B., "Migration, the Terms of Trade, and Economic Welfare in the Source Country," in *Trade, Balance Payments and Growth*, ed., J. N. Bhagwati, et al., North Holland, Amsterdam, 1971, 238–260.

Mishan, E. J. and Needleman, L., "Immigration, Excess Aggregate Demand and the Balance of Payments," *Economica*, 33, May 1966, 129–147.

———, "Immigration: Some Long Term Consequences," *Economia Internazionale*, 21, May 1968, 281–300.

Piore, Michael, "Notes for a Theory of Labor Market Stratification," in *Labor Market Segmentation*, eds., R. Edwards, M. Reich, and D. Gordon, Heath and Co., Massachusetts, 1975, 125–150.

———, *Birds of Passage: Migrant Labor and Industrial Societies*, Cambridge University Press, Cambridge, 1979.

Reder, Melvin W., "The Economic Consequences of Increased Immigration," *Review of Economics and Statistics*, 14, August 1963, 221–230.

Reubens, Edwin El, "Aliens, Jobs and Immigration Policy," *The Public Interest*, Spring, 1978, No. 51,

Rivera-Batiz, Francisco, "Three Essays on the Theory of Labor Migration," unpublished Ph.D. thesis, Massachusetts Institute of Technology, June 1979.

Sjaastad, Larry, "Occupation Structure and Migration Patterns," in *Labor Mobility and Population in Agriculture*, ed., Iowa State University Center for Agriculture and Economic Adjustment, Iowa State University Press, Iowa, 1961.

Smith, Barton and Newman, Robert, "Depressed Wages Along the U.S.–Mexico Border: An Empirical Analysis," *Economic Inquiry*, 15, January 1977, 52–66.

Stiglitz, Joseph, "Wage Determination and Unemployment in LDCs," *Quarterly Journal of Economics*, 88, May 1974, 194–227.

Tobin, James, "Notes on the Economic Theory of Expulsion and Expropriation," in *The Brain Drain and Taxation*, ed., J. N. Bhagwati, Amsterdam, 1976, 279–290.

Wise, Donald E., "The Effects of the Bracero on Agricultural Production in California," *Economic Inquiry*, 12, December 1974, 547–558.

Chapter 3

The Short-Run Economic Effects of Immigration: Some General Equilibrium Simulations*

3.1 Introduction

Estimates indicate at least one million and perhaps as many as one million and a half immigrants move into the United States as a net inflow each year. Of these, approximately 500,000 a year are admitted legally under permanent resident status and 100,000 under temporary worker programs. The rest are accounted for by illegal immigration. The magnitude of this flow has set afire controversy over its possible impact on the recipient regions in the United States. It is the purpose of this paper to provide some exploratory numerical figures on the matter.

Traditionally, the literature on the effects of immigration has been of a partial equilibrium nature and ignored the constraints that openness of the economy imposes on the behavior of key domestic variables such as prices [see Reder (1963), Wachter (1979), Johnson (1980), Chiswick (1982) and De Leew (1985)]. In recent years, however, general-equilibrium modeling and open economy considerations have started to emerge in the analysis of immigration [see the survey

*This chapter was originally published in William G. Vogt and Marvin H. Mickle, eds., *Modeling and Simulation, Vol. 17*, North Carolina: Instrument Society of America, 1986, pp. 215–222.

by Rivera-Batiz (1983)] and Greenwood and McDowell (1985) as well as the papers by Rivera-Batiz (1981) and Baldwin-Grossman (1984). This work, though, appears to be highly fragmented, with different authors using quite particular frameworks and ignoring the considerations stressed by other writers (some, for example, ignore unemployment; others ignore the service sector, et cetera). The present paper provides an integrated approach to the impact of immigration. The next section states the theoretical model and provides a guide to the solution of the set of production, demand and consistency equations describing the recipient region. The third section shows — using comparative statics — how the general equilibrium solution is disturbed by an inflow of foreign unskilled labor. In Section 3.4 these changes are then simulated using available data for actual parameters relevant for the case of United States immigration.

3.2 The Theoretical Model

The production structure of the economy or region under consideration is decomposed into three sectors: agriculture, manufacturing and services. Since most services cannot be profitably traded outside the local markets where they are sold [see Kravis, Heston and Summers (1983)], they are referred to as nontradables, whereas agriculture and manufacturing are mostly tradables, that is, they face stringent interregional and international competition. The output of each commodity, X_j (the subscripts j = 1, 2 and N index agriculture, manufacturing and services, respectively), is produced through the use of labor, X_j, and a composite of nonlabor inputs, K_j. Given our emphasis on the short-run and the fact that different sectors use different non-labor inputs (land in agriculture, capital in manufacturing and services), it will be assumed that non-labor inputs cannot be shifted among sectors. Labor, on the other hand, will be assumed to be perfectly-mobile, an assumption reflecting evidence showing that the wage elasticity of labor supply to any given sector in the U.S. economy appears to the high, especially with regard to those occupations in which immigrants are predominantly employed [see Wise (1974), and Smith and Newman (1977)]. The general–equilibrium model utilized is therefore of the two-goods, three-factors type, as described by Jones (1971).

Instead of assuming perfectly-competitive labor markets, we assume that the economy or region under analysis is characterized by segmented labor markets [see Mincer (1976), Piore (1975) and Harris and Todaro (1969)]. We consider manufacturing to be subject to a rigid wage, $\bar{w}$, set a level higher than the available in the rest of the labor market, which is competitive and clears at a wage rate equal to w. The distortionary, rigid wage element in manufacturing can be associated with minimum wage laws or unionization but, whatever is the case, it implies that unemployment will be a natural, market outcome. The explanation is that, given a certain rate of labor turnover among employees in manufacturing, some workers will take their chances and wait and/or search for employment in entry-level positions bearing the relatively higher wage rate in that sector. Since the job search process is generally obstructs full-time employment — especially when it involves some geographic mobility — one can expect that the search for employment in manufacturing will generate some job quits in other sectors. Unemployment is the outcome. The labor market equilibrium condition in this case is then given by:

$$w = \bar{w}\varepsilon \tag{1}$$

where ε is the probability of employment in manufacturing. Equation (1) thus states that workers will move among sectoral labor markets to equate the competitive wage rate with the expected wage rate attainable through job search in manufacturing (we ignore unemployment insurance as a component of the expected income possible during the search process).

The probability of employment in manufacturing, ε, is defined to be equal to the ratio of job vacancies to the supply of workers available to fill those vacancies, or:

$$\varepsilon = \theta N_2/[L_2 - (1 - \theta)N_2] \tag{2}$$

where θ represents the fraction of the employed in manufacturing that turn-over in each time period, N_2 is equal to manufacturing employment, and L_2 depicts the labor supply available to sector 2, equal to the employed workers, N_2, plus the unemployed workers, U. The expression for ε in (2) suggests that the θN_2 slots available in manufacturing are randomly allocated among those workers available to fill them, $L_2 - (1-\theta)N_2$. Any given worker has then a probability ε of obtaining one of the openings.

Substituting equation (2) into (1), and through some manipulation, one obtains:

$$w = [\theta N_2/(U + \theta N_2)]\bar{w}. \tag{3}$$

And on the assumption that both the turnover rate and the wage rate in manufacturing remain fixed over the short-run, we can differentiate equation (3) to obtain:

$$\mathrm{d}U = -(U + \theta N_2)w^* \tag{4}$$

where we use asterisks to denote proportional changes, so that $w^* = \mathrm{d}w/w$. Equation (4) states that changes in unemployment are negatively related to changes in the wage rate available in the competitive labor market of the economy, w^*. Increases in w tend to raise the returns on employment in the service sector and in agriculture relative to manufacturing, inducing workers to offer their labor supply to the competitive market and reducing the number of unemployed laborers searching for jobs in manufacturing.

The labor force in the economy or region under consideration, $\bar{L}$, can be employed in the three sectors we have specified or be unemployed. That is:

$$a_{L1}X_1 + a_{LN}X_N + a_{L2}X_2 + U = \bar{L} \tag{5}$$

where $a_{Lj} = N_j/X_j$ is the amount of labor per unit of output employed in sector j = 1, 2, N. Note that since the use of labor in manufacturing is fixed by the rigid wage distortion, both N_2 and X_2 will remain unchanged in response to disturbances. Besides the labor force consistency equation (5), in the absence of capital market or other factor market imperfections, the following non-labor input full-employment conditions must hold:

$$a_{K1}X_1 = \bar{X}_1 \tag{6}$$

$$a_{K2}X_2 = \bar{X}_2 \tag{7}$$

$$a_{KN}X_N = \bar{X}_N \tag{8}$$

where the a_{Kj}'s represent the amount of non-labor inputs used in the production of each unit of output j, and the $\bar{K}_j$'s are the endowments of non-labor inputs used in each sector. On the assumption of constant-returns to scale, the input-output coefficients used in production are only a function of the relative factor prices facing firms in each sector, or: $a_{ij} = a_{ij}(w/r_j)$, with r_j denoting the rental rate or rate of return received by the (fixed) non-labor inputs utilized by sector j, and $i = K, L$. Note that both a_{L2} and a_{K2} are fixed.

Assuming perfect competition in product markets, producers will minimize costs by setting price equal to unit costs, or:

$$wa_{L1} + r_1 a_{K1} = P_1 \tag{9}$$

$$\bar{w}a_{L2} + r_2 a_{K2} = P_2 \tag{10}$$

$$wa_{LN} + r_n a_{KN} = P_N \tag{11}$$

where P_1 and P_2 are the prices of agricultural goods and manufacturing, respectively, and P_N the price of nontradables. Assuming that the economy or region under consideration is a small open one, P_1 and P_2 will be exogenously-determined by their values in national and international markets. The prices of nontradables, however, are determined endogenously, by the equality of demand and supply:

$$D_N = D_N(P_1, P_2, P_N, Y) = X_N \tag{12}$$

where the demand for nontradable goods, D_N, is assumed to be a function of prices and aggregate income, Y, which is defined by:

$$Y = P_1 X_1 + P_2 X_2 + P_N X_N. \tag{13}$$

This completes the basic economic structure of the model to be examined and simulated, which consists of ten equations, (3), (5)–(8) and (9)–(13) in ten variables: X_1, X_2, X_N, r_1, r_2, r_N, P_N, w, U, and

Y, with parameters $\bar{K}_1$, $\bar{K}_2$, $\bar{K}_N$, $\bar{L}$, P_1, P_2, θ, and $\bar{w}$. To examine the effects of immigration in this context we consider an exogenous inflow of labor into the economy and evaluate how this alters the model's endogenous variables. These comparative statics results are reported in the next section.

3.3 The Short-Run Impact of Immigration

Taking a short-run perspective, the use of non-labor inputs cannot be altered, implying that an inflow of labor will generate diminishing returns and therefore reduce wage rates. The magnitude of the impact on wage rates will depend on the magnitude of the immigration and on the elasticities of the marginal product of labor curves in each sector. If we define the real-wage elasticity of the marginal product of labor curve, or, in other words, the real wage elasticity of the demand for labor in each sector, by:

$$Y_{Lj} = \frac{a^*_{Kj} - a^*_{Lj}}{w^* - P^*_j} = -N^*_j/(w^* - P^*_j) > 0, \quad j = 1, \mathrm{N}$$

then, the smaller the value of the Y_{Lj}s, the stronger the negative effect of a given inflow of labor on the wage rate.

In the agricultural sector, the decline in the competitive wage rate will raise the rate of return received by employers. Differentiating equation (9) totally, and simplifying [for the details of the derivations in this paper, a mathematical appendix is available on request from the author] yields:

$$\theta_{L1}w^* + \theta_{K1}r^*_1 = P^*_1 \tag{9'}$$

where $\theta_{L1} = wN_1/P_1X_1$ and $\theta_{K1} = r_1K_1/P_1X_1$ are factor shares in agriculture. Since the small open economy assumption means that the prices of tradable goods remain unchanged in response to immigration, $P^*_1 = 0$ and, therefore:

$$r^*_1 = -(\theta_{L1}/\theta_{K1})w^* \tag{14}$$

showing the negative connection between rental rates and wage rates in agriculture. This negative link, however, is not relevant for manufacturing, whose labor force faces rigid wages and is, consequently, sheltered from the increased labor market competition introduced by immigrants. What about the nontradable goods sector? The effects of an inflow of labor on the rental rate in this sector is more difficult to discern since the result depends not only on the reduction in competitive wage rates but also on the impact of immigration on the prices of nontradables. From equation (11) above:

$$r_N^* = (P_N^* - \theta_{LN} w^*)/\theta_{KN} \tag{15}$$

with $\theta_{LN} = wN_N/P_N X_N$ and $\theta_{KN} = r_N \bar{K}_N/P_N X_N$ denoting factor shares in the service sector. Observe that the rental rate on nonlabor inputs in the service sector can increase or decrease depending on whether the price of nontradables declines or rises, and on whether this effect offsets the impact of the declining wage rate.

The reduced-form effect of immigration on the prices of nontradable goods is given by:

$$P_N^* = \frac{\theta_1(\theta_{LN} Y_{LN} - \theta_{L1} Y_{L1}) + \theta_2 \theta_{LN} Y_{LN}}{\eta_{NN} - \phi_N \theta_1 \theta_{L1} Y_{L1} - (1-\theta_N)(1-\phi_N)\theta_{LN} Y_{LN}} \phi_L L^* \tag{16}$$

where $L^* = \mathrm{d}L/L > 0$ is the proportional increase in the region's or economy's labor force due to immigration, $\eta_{NN} = (\partial D_N/\partial P_N)(P_N/D_N) < 0$ is the income-compensated price elasticity of demand for nontradables, $\theta_j = P_j X_j/Y$ is the share of the j-th sector on GNP, $\phi_N = \lambda_{LN} Y_{LN} \sum_j \lambda_{Lj} Y_{Lj} + \lambda_{L2}$, $\lambda_{L2} = (U + \theta N_2)/\bar{L}$ is the share of the labor force unemployed or searching for employment in manufacturing, $\lambda_{Lj} = L_j/\bar{L}$ is the share of the economy's labor force employed by sector $j = 1$, N, and $\phi_L = 1/(\sum_j \lambda_{Lj} Y_{Lj} + \lambda_{L2})$. Equation (16) has been derived under the implicit assumption that the income elasticity of demand for each commodity is equal to one, an assumption supported by the data [see Kravis, Heston and Summers (1983), pp. 196–200].

The explanation for the intricate expression depicted in (16) lies in that immigration shifts both the demand for and the supply of nontradables by altering not only the relative price of nontradables but also domestic income, resulting in a rather involved set of repercussions. It is clear, though, that the denominator in (16) is negative and the direction of the impact on the price of nontradables is therefore determined by the sign of the numerator. The sign of the numerator in (16), however, is not unambiguously-determined and cannot be completely specified without available numerical values on the relevant parameters involved. Still, it can be observed that, the larger the share of labor in the nontradable goods sector relative to that in agriculture (the larger θ_{LN} is relative to θ_{L1}), the more likely it is that immigration will augment the output of nontradables proportionally more than the output of agricultural goods at fixed commodity prices. The prices of nontradables would then have to decline in order to eliminate the excess supply of nontradables. If production in agriculture is relatively labor-intensive, however, then the inflow of labor will raise the output of nontradables proportionally less, resulting in an increase of their relative price. Also, the more elastic the demand for labor in the nontradable goods sector is relative to the demand for labor in agriculture (the larger Y_{LN} is relative to Y_{L1}), the more likely the prices of nontradables will decline. The reason is that the decrease in wage rates induced by immigration will then cause employment in the nontradable goods sector to increase relatively more, ceteris paribus. This is more likely to generate excess supply in the nontradable goods market and a reduction of their prices.

Whatever the effect on the prices of nontradables, it is easy to show that employment and output in the sector will always increase, independently of labor intensities. Differentiating totally equation (8), and observing that the non-labor input is sector-specific and fixed in the short-run ($\bar{K}^*_N = 0$), then:

$$X^*_N = -a^*_{KN} = -\theta_{LN} Y_{LN}(w^* - P^*_N). \tag{17}$$

Equation (17) just shows that the output of nontradables will increase only if the real wage rate facing the sector declines. Since output can be altered only through changes in the labor employed, changes in real wages stimulate changes in employment, and therefore, output. By how much a declining real wage w/P_N raises output depends, of course, on how much employment the real wage rate change induces, which depends in turn on the elasticity of demand for labor in the sector. The more elastic the demand for labor, the stronger the output expansion, ceteris paribus. Consequently, in order to determine output changes one only has to specify how the real wage rate is affected. Totally differentiating equation (5) yields:

$$L^* = \lambda_{L1}(a^*_{L1} + X^*_1) + \frac{\mathrm{d}U}{\bar{L}} + \lambda_{LN}(a^*_{LN} + X^*_N) = -\lambda_{L1}Y_{L1}(w^* - P^*_1)$$
$$-\lambda_{L2}w^* - \lambda_{LN}Y_{LN}(w^* - P^*_N) \tag{18}$$

where use has been made of equation (4). Noting that $P^*_1 = 0$ on the small open economy assumption, equation (18) can be transformed into:

$$w^* = \phi_N P^*_N - \phi_L L^*. \tag{19}$$

Substituting the expression for the change in the price of nontradables determined from equation (16) into (19), one finally obtains:

$$w^* - P^*_N = \frac{-\eta_{NN} + \theta_1\theta_{L1}Y_{L1}}{\Delta}\phi_L L^* \tag{20}$$

where Δ is equal to the denominator of equation (16). The expression in (21) shows that the real wage rate in terms of nontradables will always decline in response to immigration. Even though the prices of nontradables may decline, the nominal wage rate will drop proportionally more, thus lowering the real wage rate and raising the output of nontradables.

Since wages in manufacturing are assumed to be sheltered from the effects of immigration, the drop in the wages offered in competitive labor markets will widen the wage differential between manufacturing and the rest of the economy. This should induce some workers to quit their jobs in agriculture and in services in order to search for employment in manufacturing. But since the employment level in the latter is unresponsive to immigration, the outcome is increased unemployment. The order of magnitude of this effect depends on the turnover rate in manufacturing as well as on the extent of the reduction in the competitive wage rate. The larger the turnover rate and the stronger the drop in the competitive wage rate, the steeper the climb of the unemployment rate. Note that the increased unemployment can in principle fall equally on native and immigrant workers. In all likelihood, however, the increased unemployment can be expected to fall more heavily among native-born. The reason is that migrants tend to show a strong preference toward rapid employment rather than toward higher wages obtained at the cost of short-run unemployment. This is particularly so when it is widely known that, at least over the short-run, recent immigrants have greater difficulty obtaining access to high-wage employment in the destination. It is true, as many applied economists have noted for years now, that recent immigrants (that is, those immigrants with a short period of time since arrival in the destination) tend to be heavily employed in competitive, lower-paying labor markets and not in those sectors that can be characterized as being sheltered [see Piore (1979) and Reubens (1978)]. Since, as we noted earlier, there is a highly mobile native-born labor force responding quickly to observed wage differentials among sectors, the unemployment burden of immigration is likely to fall more heavily on those native-born workers not blessed with secure employment in manufacturing. Some simulations of the magnitude of this effect are examined in the next section.

3.4 Some Exploratory General Equilibrium Simulations

In order to provide some feeling for the numerical values involved in the present analysis, actual or estimated values for the parameters involved in the model have been utilized to simulate the effects of an inflow of immigrants of 10 percent (as a proportion of the native-born labor force). Following the model developed earlier, the parameters used are based on a disaggregation of the recipient region in the United States into three sectors: agriculture, industry and services, indexed by $j = 1$, 2 and N, respectively. The values of the parameters used in the simulation are stated in Table 3.1. The initial rate of unemployment is assumed to equal $\frac{U}{\bar{L}} = .08$ and the turnover rate $\theta = .04$, the typical for monthly turnover in U.S. manufacture.

Given the level of aggregation at which we work, extensive sensitivity analysis has been carried out. Here, we shall concentrate on reporting and comparing three basic, alternative regimes. The main difference among them lies on the values of the elasticities of the

Table 3.1. Parameters for the General-Equilibrium Simulations.

1. Parameters kept fixed among regimes.

$$\lambda_{LN} = \frac{N_N}{\bar{L}} = \left(\frac{N_N}{\bar{N}}\right)\left(\frac{\bar{N}}{\bar{L}}\right) = (0.61)(0.92) = 0.56$$

$$\lambda_{L1} = \frac{N_1}{\bar{L}} = \left(\frac{N_1}{\bar{N}}\right)\left(\frac{\bar{N}}{\bar{L}}\right) = (0.04)(0.92) = 0.04$$

$$\lambda_{L2} = \frac{(U + \theta N_2)}{\bar{L}} = \frac{U}{\bar{L}} + \theta\left(\frac{N_2}{\bar{N}}\right)\left(\frac{\bar{N}}{\bar{L}}\right)$$

$$= 0.08 + (0.04)(0.35)(0.92) = 0.093$$

$$\theta_{LN} = 0.75 \qquad \theta_{L2} = 0.69 \qquad \theta_{L1} = 0.51$$

$$\theta_1 = 0.03 \qquad \theta_2 = 0.41 \qquad \theta_N = 0.56$$

$$\eta_{NN} = -0.50 \qquad \theta = 0.04 \qquad \tfrac{U}{\bar{L}} = 0.08$$

2. Parameters subject to sensitivity analysis.

	Y_{LN}	Y_{L1}	ϕ_N	ϕ_L
Regime I	0.70	0.30	0.79	2.04
Regime II	1.00	0.50	0.83	1.51
Regime III	0.40	0.10	0.69	3.16

$\bar{N}$: Employed Labor force.

Sources: Shares of employment and sectoral income out of GNP (λ_{Lj}'s and θ_j's) taken from Stanback (1979). Shares of labor and nonlabor inputs on earnings in each sector from Stanback (1979). Elasticities of demand for labor: agriculture, Tryehniewicz and Schuh (1969); services, Hamermesh (1976). Income-compensated elasticity of demand for nontradables from Deaton and Muellbauer (1980), pp. 70–72, for travel, communications, entertainment and other services (η_{NN}).

demand for labor in each sector. Regime I utilizes the average values of these elasticities as obtained by econometric studies of the demand for labor. Regimes II and III then take more extreme values, the former specifying high elasticities while the latter considering low elasticities.

Table 3.2. The General-Equilibrium Effects of Immigration: Matrix of Results.

	Regime		
	I	II	III
P_N^*	−0.084	−0.086	−0.012
W^*	−0.270	−0.222	−0.324
$W^* - P_N^*$	−0.186	−0.136	−0.312
X_N^*	0.097	0.102	0.094
X_1^*	0.041	0.057	0.016
X_2^*	0.000	0.000	0.000
r_N^*	0.474	0.322	0.470
r_1^*	0.281	0.231	0.337
r_2^*	0.000	0.000	0.000
U^*	0.025	0.020	0.030

Notes: $U^* = \mathrm{d}U/\bar{L}$ is the change in the unemployment rate. $L^* = 0.10$ is the simulated inflow of labor.

The results of the general-equilibrium simulations of a 10 percent increase in the labor force on the various endogenous variables in the recipient region are shown in Table 3.2. The first column reports the numerical values of the response elasticities of each variable to the given change in the labor force under regime I. We look at these in detail now.

As noted in earlier sections, the prices of nontradable goods can decline or increase depending on the relative labor intensity of that sector. Given that services do tend to be labor-intensive relative to both agriculture and industry, the observed effect of a 10 percent increase in the domestic labor force through immigration would be to reduce the prices of nontradables by 8.4 percent. In addition, with diminishing returns, under regime I, the 10% inflow of labor would reduce wage rates by approximately 27 percent. As a consequence, the real wage rate in terms of nontradables declines by about 19 percent. With nominal and real wages in terms of nontradables dropping, the output of both agriculture and nontradables rises, with the nontradables sector expanding twice as much as agriculture, a result of the large labor share and high wage elasticity of demand for labor in the service sector. Given the negative connection between wages and rates of return on non-labor inputs (land, capital) in agriculture, the 10 percent inflow of labor would raise the rate of return in agriculture by approximately 28 percent. The rental rate in nontradable goods sector also rises by about 48 percent.

The drop in wage rates in competitive labor markets will induce workers to search for employment in manufacturing, raising the unemployment rate by 2.5 percentage points. As argued earlier, a large share of these 'displaced' workers will be nonimmigrants. Assuming that 60 percent of the unemployment falls on the original labor force, the unemployment of the native-born will rise by 1.5 percentage points under regime I. This does not mean, though, that employers in the service sector or in agriculture will find unemployed workers, searching for work in those sectors. On the contrary, it is unlikely that job offers made by employers in these sectors to unemployed workers will be accepted at the prevailing competitive wages. The unemployed are willing to withstand the search process for employment in higher-wage slots in manufacturing than accepting the slumping wages offered by employers in agriculture or the service sector.

Changes in the simulation regime considered alter the numerical magnitudes of these results, making the goods and factor price effects less drastic under regime II and more drastic under regime III. One overall tendency that can be derived from the simulation, then, is that the short-run effects of immigration on the prices of services, wages, rental rates or rates of return, and unemployment become stronger the more inelastic the wage elasticities of demand for labor in each sector.

3.5 Conclusions

This paper has examined and simulated the various economic effects of immigration to the U.S. on the recipient regions. Several conclusions stand out. Firstly, the numerical values of the real-wage elasticities of demand for labor in each sector of the economy or region appear to be critical in determining the magnitude of the effects of immigration. The elasticities specify by how much employment changes in response to the drop in wage rates in competitive labor markets generated by immigration. This influences, in turn, the impact on output, prices of services, unemployment, and so forth. A second conclusion evident from the simulations is the importance of the effects of immigration on the nontradable goods sector. Services are highly labor-intensive and show a relatively large labor demand elasticity, compared to other sectors in the economy. They are therefore more strongly affected by the labor inflow. Given the significance of nontradable goods sectors in most economies — composing over 60 percent of GNP in most industrial countries — an infrequently-recognized positive effect of immigration lies on the increased rates of return that the labor inflow makes possible to employers in this sector and the reduced prices of these goods and services made available to consumers. A third conclusion that can be drawn from our simulations regards the unemployment effects of immigration. A 10 percent inflow of foreign labor was found to increase the proportion of the native-born (nonimmigrant) labor force unemployed by approximately 1.5 percentage points, with the sensitivity-analysis range — connected to the span of values of the numbers are not clearly insignificant, they do suggest that the impact of immigration on the unemployment rate of nationals is not one-for-one (this conclusion is shared by the simulations of Baldwin-Grossman (1982)]. For example, in a recipient region with a labor force of 10,000 workers, an inflow of 1,000 immigrants would — under regime I simulations — raise the number of native-born unemployed by about 120–180.

Our analysis and simulation have been carried out under a number of simplifying assumptions. These include the homogeneity of the labor force — as far as skills is concerned — and the extreme wage rigidity in manufacturing, as well as the neglect of intersectoral and international capital movements, the fixed terms of trade, and the absence of migrant remittances, among others. Future research should consider examining these issues in detail.

References

Baldwin-Grossman, Jean, "Illegal Immigrants and Domestic Employment," *Industrial and Labor Relations Review* 37(2), January 1984, pp. 240–251.

———, "The Substitutability of Natives and Immigrants in Production," *Review of Economics and Statistics* 64(4), November 1982, pp. 596–603.

Chiswick, Barry, "The Impact of Immigration on the Level and Distribution of Economic Well-Being," in B. Chiswick, ed., *The Gateway: U.S. Immigration Issues and Policies*, American Enterprise Institute, Washington, D.C., 1982, pp. 289–313.

De Leew, Frank, "The Economic Effects of Immigration: Specification of a Model," Policy Discussion Paper No. 85–3, The Urban Institute, Washington, D.C., December 1985.

Deaton, A. S. and J. Muellbauer, *Economics and Consumer Behavior*, Cambridge University Press, Cambridge, 1980.

Greenwood, Michael and John McDowell, "The Potential Economic Consequences of U.S. Immigration: A Survey," Faculty Working Paper, Bureau of Business and Economic Research, College of Business Administration, Arizona State University, Tempe, Arizona, February 1985.

Hamermesh, D., "Econometric Studies of Labor Demand and Their Applications to Public Policy," *Journal of Human Resources* 11(4), Fall 1976, pp. 507–25.

Harris, John and M. P. Todaro, "Migration, Unemployment and Development: A Two-Sector Analysis," *American Economic Review* 60(1), March 1970, pp. 126–142.

Johnson, George E., "The Labor Market Effects of Immigration," *Industrial and Labor Relations Review* 33(3), April 1980, pp. 331–341.

Jones, Ronald W., "A Three-Factor Model in Theory, Trade and History," in J. N. Bhagwati, *et al.*, eds., *Trade, Balance of Payments and Growth*, North Holland and Publishing Company, Amsterdam, 1971, pp. 3–21.

———, "The Structure of Simple General Equilibrium Models," *Journal of Political Economy* 73(6), December 1965, pp. 557–572.

Kravis, Irving, A. W. Heston and R. Summers, "The Share of Services in Economic Growth," in F. Gerard Adams and Bert G. Hickman, eds., *Global Econometrics, Essays in Honor of Lawrence Klein*, MIT Press, Cambridge, 1983, pp. 188–218.

Mincer, Jacob, "Unemployment Effects of Minimum Wages," *Journal of Political Economy* 64(4), July/August 1976, Part II, pp. S87–S104.

Piore, Michael, *Birds of Passage: Migrant Labor and Industrial Societies*, Cambridge University Press, Cambridge, 1979.

———, "Notes for a Theory of Labor Market Stratification," in R. Edwards, M. Reich, and D. Gordon, eds., *Labor Market Segmentation*, D.C. Health and Company, Massachusetts, 1975, pp. 125–150.

Reder, M. W., "The Economic Consequences of Increased Immigration," *Review of Economics and Statistics* 45(3), August 1963, pp. 221–230.

Reubens, E. P., "Aliens, Jobs and Immigration Policy," *The Public Interest*, No. 51, Spring 1978, pp. 113–134.

Rivera-Batiz, Francisco, "Trade Theory, Distribution of Income and Immigration," *American Economic Review* 73(2), May 1983, pp. 183–187.

———, "The Effects of Immigration in a Distorted Two-Sector Economy," *Economic Inquiry* 19(4), October 1981, pp. 626–639.

Smith, B. and R. Newman, "Depressed Wages along the U.S.-Mexico Border: An Empirical Analysis," *Economic Inquiry* 15(1), January 1977, pp. 51–66.

Stanback, T., *Understanding the Service Economy: Employment, Productivity and Location*, Johns Hopkins University Press, Baltimore, 1979.

Tryehniewicz, E. W. and Schuh, E., "Econometric Analysis of Agricultural Labor Markets," *American Journal of Agricultural Economics* 51(4), November 1969, pp. 770–787.

Wachter, Michael L., "The Labor Market and Immigration: The Outlook for the 1980s," in Departments of Justice, Labor and State, eds., *Interagency Task Force on Immigration Policy*, Staff Report Companion Papers, August 1979, pp. 163–234.

Williamson, Jeffrey, "Immigrant-Inequality Trade-Offs in the Promised Land: Income Distribution and Absorptive Capacity Prior to the Quotas," in B. R. Chiswick, ed., *The Gateway: U.S. Immigration Issues and Policies*, American Enterprise Institute, Washington, D.C., 1992, pp. 251–288.

Wise, D. E., "The Effects of the Bracero on Agricultural Production in California," *Economic Inquiry* 12(4), December 1974, pp. 547–558.

Chapter 4

The Labor Market Effects of Immigration in the United States and Europe: Substitution vs. Complementarity*

4.1 Introduction

The effects of immigrants on the earnings and employment of resident workers has been a major policy issue in the United States and Europe for many years. In the United States the debate has been fueled recently by the large inflow of undocumented workers and the fear that immigrants have widened income inequality (see Rivera-Batiz *et al.* 1991, Borjas *et al.* 1992). In Europe the debate involves the presence of guest workers, internal migration within the European Union, and the flow of Eastern European migrants (see Layard *et al.* 1992, Burda and Wyplosz 1991a). It is also a significant issue

---

*This chapter was co-authored with Ira N. Gang and originally published in *Journal of Population Economics*, Vol. 7, No. 2 (June 1994), pp. 157–175.

This paper was presented at the Centre for Economic Policy Research Workshop, "The Economics of International Migration: Econometric Evidence", February 26 and 27, 1993, Konstanz, Germany. We benefitted from the discussion at the conference and, particularly, the comments of Anton Muscatelli. We thank three referees and the managing editor of this journal for their suggestions. We also thank Selig Sechzer for his significant contributions to the empirical analysis in this paper. Ira Gang's work was partially supported by the Rutgers University Research Council.

in the current move toward European integration: the migration of workers from less-developed to more-developed members of the European Union raises questions about their impact in both the recipient and source regions (see Krueger and Pischke 1992, Burda and Wyplosz 1991b).

The impact of immigration and immigration restrictions on the labor market outcomes of residents has a long research history in the United States; in Europe it has been a matter of growing study in recent years (see Straubhaar and Zimmermann 1993, Gordon 1989). We employ recent theoretical and empirical developments in the international and labor economics fields to examine the effects of migration flows on the wages of native-born and resident workers in the United States and Europe.

The impact of immigrants on the earnings of native-born and resident workers is closely linked to whether these groups are substitutes or complements in the production process. This topic has received substantial attention from researchers using aggregate cross-sectional data. The existing evidence from the United States is ambiguous — some studies find that immigrants and native-born workers are substitutes, others that they are complements. Recently, it has been recognized that different types of immigrants have disparate effects on the native-born. The labor market consequences of immigrants from various countries or ethnicities on native-born workers vary according to their respective skills and characteristics. Recent empirical models incorporate worker heterogeneity in estimating the effect of immigrants on wages (see, for instance, Rivera-Batiz and Sechzer 1991). We examine the impact of immigration in the United States and Europe using this latest methodology.

The next section provides a brief survey of the existing literature on the economic impact of immigration and specifies how our approach fits into — and diverges from — that literature. Section 4.3 sets up the theoretical model that describes domestic production and the determinants of wages. Section 4.4 presents the empirical model utilized to estimate the effects of immigrants, our data sources, and our estimates of the impact of different groups of immigrants on the wages of various groups of residents in the United

States and Europe. Section 4.5 discusses the implications of our analysis.

4.2 Review of the Literature

Although there is a rich European literature examining the characteristics of immigrants and the determinants of migration flows (see the surveys by Straubhaar and Zimmermann 1993, Licht and Steiner 1992), studies focusing on the estimation of the labor market impact of European migration flows is very thin (see DeNew and Zimmermann 1994). By contrast, the literature on United States immigration has examined the issue in detail (see the surveys by Rivera-Batiz and Sechzer 1991, Straubhaar and Zimmermann 1993). In particular, there is a substantial, growing, literature examining whether immigrants and the native-born are substitutes or complements.

How immigrants alter the earnings of native-born or resident workers is closely linked to whether these groups are substitutes or complements in production. There are alternative definitions of complementarity and substitutability. We employ a q-based definition in which two factor inputs are *substitutes* if an increase in the supply or endowment of one input lowers the price of the other input, and *complements* if the increased supply raises the other input's price.

The extensive empirical literature estimating the substitutability and complementarity between immigrants and native labor in the United States has yielded mixed and inconclusive results. Baldwin-Grossman (1982) provides evidence consistent with substitutability. Utilizing the 1970 Census of Population, she estimates a translog production function where immigrants, second-generation workers and natives (third-generation or beyond) enter as separate inputs in production and finds that both second-generation and foreign-born workers substitute for the native-born. Borjas (1983) uses the 1976 Survey of Income and Education in estimating a generalized Leontief production specification that incorporates Hispanic American, Black American and White American males as inputs. His results suggest that immigrants and the native-born are complements. In particular, he finds evidence that due to complementarity in production both Blacks and Whites have been helped by the presence of Hispanics in the United States labor market on this issue, see also Enchautequi (1993). Borjas (1986), using the 1970 Census of Population, reproduces his earlier results that both Hispanic and non-Hispanic immigrants are complementary to native-born male workers of all types. However, he finds that women and immigrants are substitutes. Bean *et al.* (1988) and Taylor *et al.* (1988) find legal immigrants are substitutes with respect to females and complements with respect to the male native-born, while undocumented Mexican aliens are substitutes with respect to male native-born and complements with females.

These studies consider immigrants and the native-born as separate inputs in production, i.e. nativity or ethnicity has a distinct role in production. The impact of an increased supply of immigrants on natives' wages depends on whether these inputs are substitutes or complements. However, in what sense is the labor of immigrants and native-born workers of the same sex with identical human capital characteristics (education, experience, etc.) different? Instead of concentrating on nativity, we adopt an approach more consistent with human capital theory and focus on the differences in workers due to the varying human capital endowments (education and experience) that they bring into the production process. From this perspective, ethnicity may influence the human capital characteristics of individuals (by influencing the accumulation of human capital) but not the process of producing goods and services itself. This view of ethnicity is consistent with the recent work of Borjas, whose "operational hypothesis is that ethnicity has external effects on the human capital accumulation process. This hypothesis implies that ... ethnic differences in skills are transmitted across generations" (Borjas 1993, p. 24; see also Orcutt-Duleep and Regets 1993).

Our perspective suggests that the impact of immigrants is related to the specific skills they bring to the labor market because this determines their role in the production process. A growing number of authors have followed this approach recently. Some studies make output a function of the relative supplies of highly-skilled and unskilled workers; others decompose labor into highly-educated and uneducated workers and still others disaggregate according to the age of the labor force.[1] At the root of these analyses lies the hypothesis that the impact of a labor influx on wages depends on whether the additional laborers are highly-skilled or unskilled, highly educated or not, etc., and on the substitutability or complementarity between the type of labor whose supply is increased and other types of labor. Empirical studies for the United States provide inclusive results when labor is disaggregated by education, but decompositions by age generally show younger and older workers to be complements.[2] Own-supply elasticities (measuring the price elasticity of a given factor of production with respect to a change in the endowment of that same factor) are generally found to be negative, indicating that increased supplies of a given type of labor reduce the wages of other workers in the same category.[3]

If immigrants tend to cluster into jobs requiring mostly manual work and little education or experience, and the native-born hold jobs requiring higher levels of education and/or experience, how would increased immigration affect the wages of the native-born? The answer is, of course, directly related to whether low-skilled and highly-skilled labor are substitutes or complements. Rivera-Batiz and Sechzer (1991) begin to address this issue by examining the distribution of human capital characteristics among native-born and immigrant groups, estimating the substitutability or complementarity between these characteristics.[4] Rivera-Batiz and Sechzer find that the effect of increased immigration on various groups of United States residents is small in magnitude.

4.3 The Theoretical Model

In analyzing and simulating the impact of immigration, we follow Rivera-Batiz and Sechzer (1991) in visualizing workers as supplying human capital — in the form of education and experience — as well as unskilled labor to production (see also Rosen 1983, Heckman and Sedlacek 1985). The assumption is that firms utilize as inputs a set of productive characteristics that individuals possess, i.e., unskilled labor, education (schooling) and experience. When an employer hires a laborer, he or she is actually hiring a bundle of these characteristics.

As a consequence, an individual i's earnings, W_i, are composed of returns to his/her unskilled labor supplied in the labor market as well as returns to education and experience:

$$W_i = r_u + r_e Ed_i + r_x Ex_i, \tag{1}$$

where Ed_i and Ex_i represent the endowments of education and on-the-job experience supplied by individual i in the labor market, and r_e and r_x denote the local labor market rate of return on education and experience.[5] An individual with zero education and experience earns just r_u, the rate of return to manual or unskilled labor. Our concept of unskilled labor includes all the productive inputs that a worker brings to the labor market other than human capital — where human capital is measured by education and experience.

We assume that education, experience and unskilled labor enter as inputs in production and thus receive rates of return equal to their marginal products. Consider an aggregate production function in a given labor market (e.g., country, region or city), $Y = F(L_u, L_e, L_x)$ where L_u, L_e and L_x represent the given labor market supplies of unskilled labor, education and experience.[6] If the production function exhibits standard neoclassical assumptions, the first-order conditions for profit maximization are given by:

$$r_k = \partial F/\partial L_k, \quad k = u, e, x, \tag{2}$$

where the r_k's are the remunerations to unskilled labor, education and experience, and the corresponding right-hand terms are the marginal products of these inputs.

The marginal products are a function of the endowments of the various factors used in production and, as a result, the market rates of return in (2) are a function of those endowments. How changes in the endowments of unskilled labor, education and experience affect the returns to these inputs is specified by partial elasticities of complementarity and substitutability. The partial elasticity of complementarity between inputs j and k is defined as the proportional change in factor price k given a change in the quantity of input j, $\varepsilon_{kj} = d(\ln r_k)/d(\ln L_j)$. We refer to two inputs k and j as q-substitutes if $\varepsilon_{kj} < 0$ and q-complements if $\varepsilon_{kj} > 0$.

In addition, own-price elasticities of substitution measure the elasticity of response of a factor price with respect to a change in the supply of that same factor, $\varepsilon_{kk} = d(\ln r_k)/d(\ln L_k)$. In our case, these own-price elasticities measure how changes in the endowment of each input (unskilled labor, education, experience) affect the return to that same input.

The impact of immigration on the wages of the nonimmigrant population can be specified in this framework by first determining the immigrants' endowments of unskilled labor, education and experience. One then uses (2) — as well as ε_{kj} and ε_{kk} — to specify the effects of the increased input supplies due to immigration on the remuneration rates r_k. Finally, (1) determines the effects of these changes in the rates of return on the wages of the different groups composing the nonimmigrant population, taking into account their endowments of unskilled labor, education and experience.

In this framework, the impact of alternative types of immigrants on various groups of residents can be examined by considering the different bundles of unskilled labor, education and experience supplied by both immigrants and residents. The next section describes the empirical methods we use to carry out these exercises. In general, the determination of the rates of return to education, experience and unskilled labor are a function not only of the demand functions established in (2) but also of the supply functions of each type of input. We expect, for example, that increases in the rates of return to education in a particular labor market will induce highly-schooled individuals to migrate into that area, augmenting the supply of education.[7] In the present study, however, we assume geographically distinct labor markets, i.e., the input supplies to each local labor market are exogenous. This implies that the system of equations in (2) completely specifies the determination of the rates of return to unskilled labor, education, and experience in a particular labor market. Although considering internal migration flows may alter the impact of immigration, we expect this phenomenon to be more significant in examining the long-run effects of immigration; in the short-run, the internal migration response to immigration is likely to be limited. Still, our framework can easily incorporate these induced flows. Simulations, taking into account the internal shifts in labor supply caused by immigration, could then be carried out.[8]

4.4 The Empirical Framework

For this study we use two data sources. First, we use the 1980 U.S. Census of Population 1% Public Use Micro Data Sample D (see Tolbert 1987). This data set divides the United States into 382 urban and rural labor market areas. Previously, Rivera-Batiz and Sechzer (1991) used this sample to analyze the impact of immigrants on male workers. Here we examine the effects on male and female workers. Second, for our European analysis, we rely on Euro-barometers 25, 26, 27, 29, 30 and 31 (see Rabier *et al.* 1988, 1989a, b, Reif and Melich 1990, 1991, 1992). Each of these data sets consists of a cross-section of approximately 12,000 geographically distributed randomly selected households across the twelve countries in the European Union, with about 1000 observations in each country. The main focus of the Euro-barometer series is public opinion, but the surveys contain sufficient information on household economic and demographic behavior to allow us to carry out an exploratory study of immigration. We consider 80 regions among the 12 European Community countries. In order to have enough observations in the less populated regions, we pooled the six Euro-barometer surveys completed between 1986 and 1989.

The analysis is restricted to employed civilians 16 years of age or older who reported positive income. We remove from the sample respondents who did not answer as to their occupation, age, sex, or marital status. Potential on-the-job experience is approximated by subtracting the age at which each person left school from his/her current age; education is equal to the age the person left school minus six. Both men and women are included in the sample.

Estimating the impact of various groups of immigrants on the wages of the native-born requires three steps: (1) estimating an earnings equation for each region in the sample to compute the rates of return to unskilled labor, education and experience for each region; (2) estimating a production function across regions in order to calculate partial elasticities measuring the effect of changes in the endowments of unskilled labor, education and experience on the rates of return of these factors; (3) computing the impact of shifts in rates of return caused by immigration on various groups of native-born workers. The next sub-sections carry out these empirical tasks.

Estimating Earnings Equations for Each Region

The estimation of (2) requires knowledge of the market rates of return on unskilled labor, education and experience. Since a person's earnings represent an overall reward on the bundle of unskilled labor, education and experience he or she supplies in the labor market, there is no direct measure of the market returns to each of these inputs. One can, however, impute these rates of return by estimating an equation such as (1) for various regions and using the estimates of r_u, r_e, and r_x as imputed estimates of the rates of return on unskilled labor, education and experience, respectively, in those regions. Such imputations are analogous to those obtained from hedonic price equations estimating the component of prices accounted for by non-pecuniary characteristics of commodities (see Rosen 1974). They are, in effect, what is implicitly estimated by human capital earnings functions.[9]

We estimate the following variant of a log linear version of (1) for each region, where W_i represents a person's reported income:

$$\ln(W_i) = b_u + b_e Ed_i + b_x Ex_i + b_{xsq} Ex_i^2 + \beta' X_i + U_i \qquad (3)$$

where the b_j and β are coefficients to be estimated, X_i is a vector of control and background characteristics and the shift factor or error term, U_i, can be thought of as reflecting the impact of random differences in ability among individuals on income.

For the United States, the income variable used in (3) is the annual wage and salary of the person, which we divide by the annual number of hours worked to get hourly wages. This is the measure of W_i utilized. For our European estimation, we use a different measure of W_i. The income variable contained in the Euro-barometer survey is the family income of the respondent. The b_e and b_x coefficients therefore measure how changes in the education and experience of the respondent, by influencing his or her personal income, contribute to family income. The coefficient b_u measures the contribution of a person with zero education and experience to family income.[10]

The first step in our empirical framework involves the estimation of the log linear wage equations shown in (3) by region. For the United States, we have data on the hourly wage received by individuals in the sample which we use as our dependent variable in ordinary least squares (OLS) estimation. For Europe, the information on income contained in the Euro-barometer surveys is categorical with upper and lower limit values, as in:

$$
\begin{aligned}
&\mathrm{Y} = 1 \text{ if income} < a_1\\
&\mathrm{Y} = 2 \text{ if } a_1 < \text{income} < a_2\\
&\ldots\\
&\mathrm{Y} = J \text{ if } a_\mathrm{j} < \text{income},
\end{aligned}
$$

where there are J categories for income. Comparing this structure with the standard regression model ($Y^* = \beta' X + \varepsilon$, $\varepsilon \sim N[0, \sigma^2]$), note that the dependent variable is not continuously observed and the use of OLS could result in potentially biased estimates. Given the discrete, censored dependent variable, the appropriate econometric modeling is to use a "grouped regression" model with maximum likelihood estimation (see Greene 1990, pp. 738–739). We employ the routine for completely censored group data in LIMDEP (Greene 1992, pp. 568, 598).

The estimated coefficients b_k for each region in the United States and Europe reflect the rates of return to unskilled labor, education and experience, r_u, r_e, r_x in each region.[11] Our results yield substantial differences in rates of return within particular states (in the United States) and individual European countries. This is to be expected. For instance, the existing literature shows that rates of return to education are typically higher in poorer, rural regions, even when they are geographically contiguous to richer, urban areas. The average annual rate of return to education obtained for the United States sample is 5.5%, with a high of 10.8% in suburban Philadelphia and a low of 0% in rural Wisconsin. The average annual rate of return to education in our European sample is roughly 7%, with some extremes such as the Northern region of the United Kingdom

(17%), Brabant Wallon in Belgium (14%), and Luxembourg (11%). The returns to experience and to unskilled labor also exhibit great variability in both the United States and Europe.

Estimating Production Function Equations across Regions and Calculating Partial Elasticities of Complementarity

With the imputed rates of return for each region obtained from (3), the system in (2) can then be estimated. A particular functional form must be chosen for the aggregate production function. We assume that technology is characterized by a transcendental logarithmic (translog) production function (see Christensen *et al.* 1973). This functional form can be visualized as a second-order Taylor series approximation to a concave neoclassical production function with constant returns to scale (see Burgess 1975). In the present case, it is given by:

$$\ln Y = \alpha_0 + \sum_k \beta_k \ln L_k + 1/2 \sum_k \sum_j \gamma_{kj} \ln L_k \ln L_j, \tag{4}$$

where Y is output in a given region, the L_k's and L_j's are the unskilled labor, education and experience endowments in the region (with $k, j = u, e$ and x), and the β_k and γ_{kj} are technology coefficients. Under the assumption of constant returns to scale, the following parameter restrictions obtain:

$$\sum_k \beta_k = 1 \quad \text{and} \quad \sum_k \gamma_{kj} = 0 \quad \text{for all } j.$$

Given the translog production function specification, and imposing linear homogeneity, the system in (2) becomes:

$$s_u = \partial \ln Y/\partial \ln L_u = \beta_u + \gamma_{ux} \ln L_x/L_u + \gamma_{ue} \ln L_e/L_u + V_1 \tag{5}$$

$$s_e = \partial \ln Y/\partial \ln L_e = \beta_e + \gamma_{ex} \ln L_x/L_u + \gamma_{ee} \ln L_e/L_u + V_2 \tag{6}$$

$$s_x = \partial \ln Y/\partial \ln L_x = \beta_k + \gamma_{xx} \ln L_x/L_u + \gamma_{xe} \ln L_e/L_u + V_3, \tag{7}$$

where s_k represents the share of input k in the value of output $(r_k L_k/Y)$, with the sum of the s_k's equal to 1 and where L_x/L_u

and L_e/L_u are the mean levels of experience and education in the region.[12] Note that symmetry requires cross-equation restrictions on the γ_{kj}'s, i.e., $\gamma_{ux} = \gamma_{xu}, \gamma_{ex} = \gamma_{xe}, \gamma_{ue} = \gamma_{eu}$. This, along with our assumption of homogeneity, makes one of the equations redundant. We estimate (6) and (7). This set of linear equations can be estimated using Zellner's seemingly unrelated regression technique to take into account correlation among the error terms V_1, V_2 and V_3. We use the nonlinear SURE routine available in SHAZAM (1993).

This stage of the analysis involves using the previously-estimated r_u, r_e and r_x in constructing the s_k's (the share of earnings accounted for by each input) utilized as dependent variables in (5)–(7), $s_k = r_k L_k / \sum_k r_k L_k$. We cannot discuss all of our results here. However, approximately 43% of labor income in Europe represents a remuneration to education. This compares to 44% in the United States (using 1980 Census data on men and women). Education thus plays roughly the same income generating role in the United States and across Europe. We also find that experience plays a smaller role in the income of Europeans, compared to the United States. One possible explanation is that Europe possesses, on average, a more organized, rigid labor market. More organized labor market have flatter earnings profiles, i.e., the return to experience is lower (Hamermesh and Rees 1993).

The parameter estimates γ_{kj} are directly related to the question of substitutability versus complementarity in production: it is easy to verify that the partial elasticities of factor price k with respect to a change in the quantity of input j (i.e. the partial elasticities of complementarity) are given by (Hamermesh 1986):

$$\varepsilon_{kj} = d(\ln r_k)/d(\ln L_j) = (\gamma_{kj} + s_k s_j)/s_k. \tag{8}$$

In addition, with the translog technology, the elasticity of response of a factor price with respect to a change in the supply of that same factor is given by:

$$\varepsilon_{kk} = d(\ln r_k)/d(\ln L_k) = (\gamma_{kk} + s_k^2 - s_k)/s_k. \tag{9}$$

The estimates of the γ_{kj}'s for Europe and the United States are then used to construct the q-based partial elasticities of

Table 4.1a. Estimates of Partial Elasticities of Complementarity and Own-Price Elasticities for the United States.

	$\hat{r}_x$	$\hat{r}_e$	$\hat{r}_u$
$\hat{L}_x$	−2.5550	0.6075	1.9475
$\hat{L}_e$	0.3725	−3.6124	3.2399
$\hat{L}_u$	1.7896	4.8581	−6.6477

Source: Authors' calculations from the estimation of a translog production function using data from the 1980 Census of Population-PUMS D 1070 Sample.

Table 4.1b. Estimates of Partial Elasticities of Complementarity and Own-Price Elasticities for Europe.

	$\hat{r}_x$	$\hat{r}_e$	$\hat{r}_u$
$\hat{L}_x$	−4.3039	0.2490	0.3064
$\hat{L}_e$	1.7550	−0.9765	0.6166
$\hat{L}_u$	2.5482	0.7275	−0.9231

Source: Authors' calculations from the estimation of a translog production function using data from the Eurobarometer survey series from 1988 through 1991.

complementarity, ε_{kj}, among unskilled labor, education and experience — as defined in (8) — as well as the own-supply elasticities, ε_{kk} as defined in (9). Table 4.1a, 4.1b reports our calculations of these elasticities. The signs of the own-price elasticities, ε_{kk}, are as expected: negative for both the United States and Europe. In the case of Europe, the implication is that a 1% increase in the supply of each type of input would reduce the rate of return on that input by 0.92% for unskilled labor, by 0.98% for education and 4.3% for experience. For the United States, the respective reductions in the rate of returns to unskilled labor, education and experience labor, in response to a 1% increase in input supply, are 6.6%, 3.6% and 2.6%. In addition, the figures in Table 4.1a, 4.1b indicate that in both the United States and Europe, unskilled labor, education and experience are all complements. For instance, on average, a 1% increase in the endowment of education in Europe would raise the returns to experience by 1.75% and the return to unskilled labor by a smaller 0.62%. An increase in the endowment of unskilled labor in Europe by 1% would augment the returns to education by 0.73% and raise the returns to experience by 2.55%. An increase of 1% in the endowment of experience would elevate the return to education by 0.25% and to unskilled labor by 0.31%. Similar calculations can be done for the United States.

Calculating Composite Elasticities of Complementarity

The estimated elasticities of complementarity just presented are useful in understanding the technological relationships among unskilled labor, education, and experience. Additional calculations are necessary to determine the complementarity relationship between immigrants and resident subgroups. The characteristics of both immigrants and resident groups must be specified. Once a particular group of immigrants with specific endowments of unskilled labor, education and experience is chosen, the impact of an inflow of this type of immigrant on the rates of return to unskilled labor, education and experience can be determined using the elasticities in Table 4.1a, 4.1b. One must then examine how these changes in rates of return will affect the wages of particular groups of resident workers, as is formally derived next.

The effect of an immigrant group of type on the income of residents of type t is given by a composite elasticity of complementarity (CEC), ε_{ti}, defined by:[13]

$$\varepsilon_{ti} = \hat{W}_t/\hat{L}_i = \sum_k \sum_j s_{kt}\varepsilon_{kj}\lambda_{ji}, \tag{10}$$

where a '^', *represents proportional change*, $\hat{W}_t$ denotes the proportional change in the wage of native-born group i, dW_t/W_t with W_t equal to the sample mean wage of target group t, and $\hat{L}_i = dL_i/L$, where L is the resident labor force and dL_i represents the inflow of immigrant workers of group i. To calculate the CECs the following are needed: (1) the partial elasticities of complementarity, ε_{kj}, (2) the share of each factor (unskilled labor, education and experience) in the

Table 4.2. Skill Inventory of Immigrant and Target Groups in the United States (Average Level of Skill in the Group, 1980).

Native groups			Immigrant groups		
Group	**Education**	**Experience**	**Group**	**Education**	**Experience**
US Aggregate	14.9	16.1	Africa	17.2	10.0
Prof./Tech.	17.0	15.2	North America	16.4	9.9
Service	14.4	15.9	Central/So. Am.	10.9	14.8
Farm-Craft-Oper.	13.4	17.1	Asia	15.9	12.5
White	15.0	16.2	Europe	13.5	15.4
Black	14.2	16.1	Oceania	15.9	10.4
Japanese	15.9	17.9	USSR	15.9	17.0
Chinese	15.5	16.1	70–80 Immig.	13.4	13.9
Indian	18.4	11.3	Mexico	8.8	14.3
Vietnam	14.3	13.0	Central Am.	12.0	13.3
Mexican	11.6	15.2	Caribbean	13.2	17.0
Cuban	13.3	21.0	Southea. Asia	15.9	12.4
Unskilled labor	0.0	0.0	Other Asia	16.0	12.6
Education	14.9	0.0			
Experience	0.0	16.1			

Source: US Census of Population, 1980, authors' tabulations.

income of the resident target group, s_{kt}, and (3) the mean level of each factor in the immigrant group relative to that in the target country, $\lambda_{ji} = \bar{L}_{ji}/(L_j/L)$, with $\bar{L}_{ji}$ the endowment of factor j carried into the economy by the average immigrant of group i, L_j the endowment of factor j in the economy before the labor inflow, and L the initial labor force in the economy before the labor inflow.

The matrix of CECs for a variety of immigrant and resident groups in the United States is shown in Table 4.4 and for Europe in Table 4.5. The skill inventories of each group are shown in Table 4.2 for the United States and Table 4.3 for Europe. The inherent difficulties in measuring endowments of education and experience make such estimates subject to variability and unreliability, especially for immigrants.[14] To illustrate this issue, Table 4.5 introduces two alternative sets of estimates of immigrant skills in Germany: those obtained from the immigrant samples of the Euro-barometer surveys and those reported by Licht and Steiner (1992). These estimates vary significantly.

Table 4.3. Skill Inventory of Immigrant and Target Groups in Europe (Average Level of Skill in the Group, 1988–1991).

Group	Education	Experience
EEC Average	11.8	19.9
France	12.2	18.0
Netherlands	13.1	18.3
Germany	11.2	20.5
Italy	10.8	21.6
Ireland	11.1	21.7
United Kingdom	11.2	20.0
Spain	11.1	19.1
Portugal	10.1	21.0
Other Groups in Sample		
Turks in Germany	11.2	19.8
Asians in Great Britain	11.0	14.7
Asians in France	13.5	7.0
North Africans in France	11.8	14.5
Turks in Netherlands	15.0	6.0
Surinamers in Netherlands	15.2	14.0
From Licht and Steiner		
In Germany:		
Turks	12.9	17.7
Yugoslavs	12.9	22.1
Italians	12.7	20.5
Greeks	13.0	22.9
Spaniards	12.8	21.8

Notes: For non-European immigrants, we are also looking at individuals with the average level of education and experience within that immigrant group in the target country — in other words we are asking what would be the impact of a flow of immigrants who are exactly like the immigrants already in the country. For European immigrants, we look at the mean level of characteristics in the origin country. Here we are asking what would be the impact, for example, in Germany if the average citizen from Ireland immigrated.

Source: Reif and Melich (1991), authors' calculations.

Table 4.4. Matrix of Intergroup Elasticities of Complementarity in the United States.

	Immigrant group												
Native group	Africa	North America	Central/ South A	Asia	Europe	Oceania	USSR	70–80 Immigrants	Mexico	Central America	Caribb.	Southeast Asia	Other Asia
US Aggre	0.0000	0.0000	0.0000	0.0000	0.0000	0.0000	0.0000	−0.0000	−0.0000	−0.0000	−0.0000	0.0000	0.0000
Prof-Tec	−0.0569	−0.0448	0.0547	−0.0287	0.0188	−0.0382	−0.0119	0.0146	0.0848	0.0327	0.0286	−0.0282	−0.0289
Service	0.0047	−0.0021	−0.0124	0.0018	−0.0045	0.0007	0.0034	−0.0054	−0.0189	−0.0096	−0.0047	0.0016	0.0020
Fm-Cf-Op	0.0497	0.0405	−0.0409	0.0255	−0.0139	0.0326	0.0083	−0.0091	−0.0637	−0.0225	−0.0239	0.0253	0.0256
White	−0.0016	−0.0009	0.0033	−0.0007	0.0012	−0.0005	−0.0009	0.0013	0.0050	0.0025	0.0013	−0.0006	−0.0007
Black	0.0158	0.0114	−0.0201	0.0076	−0.0071	0.0084	0.0048	−0.0067	−0.0309	0.0025	−0.0094	0.0073	0.0077
Japanese	0.0103	0.0157	0.0280	0.0079	0.0107	0.0170	−0.0095	0.0175	0.0418	0.0274	0.0060	0.0089	0.0073
Chinese	−0.0119	−0.0086	0.0153	−0.0057	0.0054	−0.0063	−0.0037	0.0051	0.0236	0.0102	0.0071	−0.0055	−0.0058
Indian	−0.1539	−0.1328	0.0895	−0.0817	0.0293	−0.1114	−0.0141	0.0086	0.1412	0.0370	0.0601	−0.0822	−0.0814
Vietnam	−0.0464	−0.0491	−0.0189	−0.0279	−0.0082	−0.0463	0.0099	−0.0217	−0.0265	−0.0291	0.0046	−0.0293	−0.0270
Mexican	0.0607	0.0389	−0.1029	0.0273	−0.0366	0.0251	0.0264	−0.0392	−0.1575	−0.0740	−0.0436	0.0257	0.0284
Cuban	0.1156	0.1056	−0.0377	0.0635	−0.0110	0.0919	0.0015	0.0092	−0.0616	−0.0019	−0.0365	0.0647	0.0627
Unskilled	0.0848	−0.2025	−1.4372	−0.0552	−0.5308	−0.3248	0.4351	−0.7399	−2.1672	−1.2390	−0.4409	−0.0930	−0.0302
Education	−0.7041	−0.5050	0.9255	−0.3364	0.3253	−0.3661	−0.2235	0.3126	1.4229	0.6225	0.4267	−0.3244	−0.3444
Experience	1.0565	1.0443	0.0540	0.6089	0.0469	0.9507	−0.1087	0.2951	0.0367	0.3326	−0.2163	0.6305	0.5947

Source: Authors' calculations.

Table 4.5. Matrix of Intergroup Elasticities of Complementarity in Europe.

Group	Average worker	Only education endowment	Only experience endowment	Only unskilled labor endowment
1. The Netherlands				
Turks	−0.0902	−0.3055	0.0390	−0.1186
Surinamers	0.0224	−0.2151	1.2889	0.0272
Portuguese	−0.0758	0.2597	−0.1037	−0.0956
Spanish	−0.0652	0.1645	−0.4736	−0.0827
Italians	−0.0428	0.2198	−1.1067	−0.0534
Irish	−0.0295	0.1965	−1.0838	−0.0364
2. France				
North African	−0.0674	−0.0147	0.7617	−0.0793
Asians	−0.1081	−0.2579	2.8169	−0.1203
Portuguese	−0.0389	0.2053	−0.1016	−0.0521
Spanish	−0.0280	0.1041	−0.4346	−0.0362
Italians	−0.0021	0.1617	−1.0809	−0.0072
Irish	−0.0127	0.1364	−1.0549	0.0110
3. United Kingdom				
Asian	−0.0806	−0.0473	1.1001	−0.0125
Portuguese	−0.0263	0.1050	−0.3723	−0.0530
Spanish	−0.0174	0.0000	1.1745	−0.0292
Italians	0.0070	2.0559	−0.4130	−0.0067
Irish	0.0205	0.0282	−0.3807	0.0127
4. Germany				
Turks	−0.0105	−0.0048	0.1360	−0.0125
Portuguese	−0.0462	0.1016	−0.2775	−0.0530
Spanish	−0.0248	−0.0026	0.2601	−0.0292
Italians	−0.0064	0.0525	−0.3153	−0.0067
Irish	0.0105	0.0249	−0.2927	0.0127
Turks (LS)	0.0440	−0.1780	0.8427	−0.0494
Yugoslavs (LS)	0.0992	−0.1245	−0.0820	0.1152
Italians (LS)	0.0696	−0.1266	0.2231	0.8029
Greeks (LS)	0.1140	−0.1235	−0.2344	0.1327
Spaniards (LS)	0.0907	−0.1195	−0.0345	0.1052

Note: (LS) refers to the Litch and Steiner mean values in Table 4.3.

Source: Authors' calculations.

We simulate the impact of various immigrant groups on target resident groups in the Netherlands, France, United Kingdom and Germany. The impact of a given immigrant flow on the income of the average native worker is computed. In addition, the last three columns of Table 4.5 show how the income due to education, experience and unskilled labor of an average person in each European country would be affected by the different immigrant groups. The last three columns are useful for measuring the effects of immigrants on residents who possess very extreme skill inventories. For example, the CEC measuring the effect of Turkish immigrants on citizens of the Netherlands with an average level of education (but, figuratively, no experience or unskilled labor) is −0.3055. This means that if the population in the Netherlands were to be augmented by 1% from an inflow of Turks (possessing the characteristics depicted in Table 4.3), the income of residents in the Netherlands due solely to education would fall by 0.31%.

Although there is variety in the signs of the composite elasticities reported in Tables 4.4 and 4.5, the simulated effects of immigrant groups on the resident groups considered are all small. Examine the European results in Table 4.5. Column 1 displays the effect of various immigrant groups on resident workers with average characteristics, as given by Table 4.3. Generally, the impact of immigrants on the average residents of the European countries considered is slightly negative. Consider a 10% increase in population due to immigration. If the inflow were to consist of Portuguese workers, then income in the Netherlands would fall by 0.76%. If instead we look at the impact of Portuguese immigrants in France, the United Kingdom and Germany, we find income declines by 0.39, 0.26 and 0.46%, respectively. An inflow of Irish workers would lower income in the Netherlands (by 0.30%) and France (0.13%), but would raise labor income in the United Kingdom (0.21%) and Germany (0.11%). Moreover, an inflow of Turks would lower German incomes (0.11%) if the Turks have the characteristics that they possess in the Eurobarometer sample, but would raise German labor incomes (0.44%) if they have the characteristics of Turks portrayed in the study by Licht and Steiner (Licht and Steiner 1992).

The last example brings out a significant point: the relative endowments of productive characteristics possessed by immigrant and target groups are important in determining the economic impact of the immigrants. Looking again at Germany, we see that while a 1% inflow of Spaniards with average characteristics would hurt the average German very little (by 0.025%), those Germans with only education would lose even less (their income would decline by 0.003%), while those with only experience would actually gain 0.26%.

Table 4.4 depicts the composite elasticities of complementarity or substitutability between immigrants and natives in the United States. Among the groups of native-born workers targeted for analysis (appearing as rows of Table 4.4), we have the overall United States population (US agg.), various occupational groups, such as professional and technical workers (Prof-tec), service workers (Service), and farm, craft and operative laborers (Fm-Cf-Op), as well as a variety of native-born ethnic/racial groups. The immigrant groups include those listed in Table 4.2. Consider the impact of Asian immigrants on various United States native groups. The effect of a 1% inflow of Asian workers on the income of the average Black American is positive, but very small (0.0076%). On the other hand, Asian immigrants lower the wages of native-born Asian Indians, but again by a small amount (−0.082%). Mexican immigrants affect Mexican-Americans negatively lowering their wages by 0.157%, but the impact on White-Americans is slightly positive (0.005%). The strongest positive impact of Mexican immigrants on any American target group is on native-born Asian Indians, but this is still negligible (0.14%). As in the European case, we find the strongest effects of immigration occur on those possessing extreme skill inventories.

The results in Tables 4.4 and 4.5 can be explained by the pattern of complementarity existing between unskilled labor, education and experience, given the relative endowments of these characteristics transferred by immigrants to receiving countries, and those of the resident groups. For instance, it can be expected that immigrant groups that have high levels of education relative to existing residents will tend to lower the wages of highly-schooled resident groups but will raise the wages of unskilled residents, especially if the latter are highly-experienced. Similarly, immigrants who are highly experienced will tend to compete with experienced native-born workers, lowering their income, but will be complementary with young workers, especially if the latter are highly educated.

From the information on Tables 4.4 and 4.5, it appears that employed United States and European workers have very little to fear from immigration. Overall, the magnitude of the effects is very small. In Europe, the largest negative effect occurs for Asian immigration in France: French income declines by 0.108% in response to a 1% Asian inflow, a very small impact. Many immigrant groups are complementary to residents, raising their wages. Target groups which are well diversified in their skills are affected less by immigrants, due to the offsetting effects of the rate of return changes that immigrants generate. On the other hand, immigrant groups with "extreme" skill inventories, that is, with skill inventories that diverge wildly from those of a given resident group, have the largest effect on that target group.

4.5 Conclusions

This paper has presented estimates of the complementarity and substitution relationship between immigrant and resident labor in the United States and the European Community. The method used relies on a theoretical model that focuses on the various inputs that individuals supply to the production process, which primarily includes unskilled labor, education and on-the-job experience. As a result, workers get rewarded for the amounts of unskilled labor, education and experience that they provide to their employers, receiving implicit rates of return on each of these inputs. The wage received by a person is an overall composite of the rewards that he/she receives for his/her unskilled labor, education and experience. In our empirical work, we use the 1980 US Census of Population and Eurobarometer surveys to estimate the implicit rates of return to unskilled labor, education and experience for men and women.

Given the amounts of unskilled labor, education and experience that a person is endowed with, a disturbance in the rates of return to these three inputs will result in a change in wages. In this framework, an inflow of immigrants affects residents by altering the returns to unskilled labor, education and experience (immigration augments the supplies of these inputs in local labor markets). By how much the rates of return are affected depends not only on the magnitude of the labor inflow and the relative endowments of education, experience and unskilled labor that the immigrants have, but also on the degree of complementarity or substitutability among the inputs. If, for instance, education and unskilled labor are complements, then an inflow of highly schooled immigrants raises the return to unskilled labor; if the two inputs are substitutes, however, the return to unskilled labor declines.

Our empirical analysis, based on the estimation of a translog production function using the 1980 US Census of Population and Eurobarometer data suggests that, in the United States and Europe, education is complementary with unskilled labor and experienced labor in production. For instance, in Europe, on average, a 1% increase in the endowment of unskilled labor — with everything else held constant — raises the returns to education by close to 3/4% and the returns to experience by 2.50%. Similarly, in Europe, a 1% increase in the endowment of education augments the returns to unskilled labor by 0.62% and raises the rate of return on experience by approximately 1.8%. Finally, an increase in the supply of experienced labor raises the remuneration of unskilled labor by about 0.31% and that of education by 0.25%. Effects of a similar magnitude are found for the United States.

The impact of immigration on the earnings of the native-born is highly complex in this framework. Immigrants with various endowments of unskilled labor, education and experience have different effects on the rates of return to these inputs in local labor markets. Given these changes in rates of return, the effects of these disturbances on the wages of natives vary according to the endowments of unskilled labor, education and experience of the different groups of residents. Using our estimates of the complementarity relationship between education, experience and unskilled labor, we have calculated the effects of a wide array of immigrant groups on a variety of residents. Although there is great diversity in the sign of the estimated impact of different immigrant groups on resident's wages, we find the absolute magnitude of the effects to be small. Broadly speaking, domestic groups with human capital endowments divergent from those of the immigrants experience wage increases as a result of immigration (because they are complements). Domestic groups with human capital endowments similar to the immigrant population experience wage reductions (since the groups are substitutes).

This paper demonstrates our initial approach to estimating the impact of various immigrant groups in Europe and America. Our results, however, must be qualified in a number of directions. The Euro-barometer data used for our European analysis is not perfectly suited for this task and our results on this account are exploratory. On the other hand, the data for the United States is for 1980. The 1990 Census data just recently released should be used to derive more updated estimates. Our theoretical framework, as used in this paper, has also its limitations. The approach makes the short-run assumption that the changes in wages that immigrants generate in different labor markets do not induce flows of migration among these markets. To the extent that we are interested in long-term effects, future work should make the supply of unskilled labor, education and experience in local labor markets endogenous. Perfect wage flexibility is assumed and, hence, no unemployment. We also represent worker characteristics by their mean levels; higher moments could be incorporated. In addition, using evidence on the time it takes to assimilate, immigrants' characteristics could be adjusted to take into account the inability to transfer skills across nations.

Our framework is flexible and can easily incorporate most of the considerations just noted. In spite of these shortcomings, we believe that the key conclusion about the minute impact of most immigrant flows on natives will withstand substantial modification. Future work should carry out this task.

Notes:

[1]See, for example, the theoretical analysis by Chiswick (1982).

[2]For a survey of this extensive literature, see Hamermesh (1993).

[3]See DeFreitas and Marshall (1983), LaLonde and Topel (1991), and Altonji and Card (1991).

[4]See also Espenshade and Goodis (1988). They analyze the impact of Mexican immigrants on the income of Black Americans in California, taking into account the issue of complementarity and substitutability.

[5]The term "rate of return" will be applied to the rates of remuneration to unskilled labor, education and experience r_k, k = u, e, x. The term "wage" will be applied only to reported composite hourly earnings.

[6]Actually, we assume $Y = F(G(L_u, L_e, L_x), K)$ where K denotes non-labor inputs. The non-labor inputs, K, may be ignored under the assumption of weak separability. Borjas (1983) and Baldwin-Grossman (1984) test and find evidence of separability.

[7]Filer (1992) and Rivera-Batiz (1981) have noted that the effects of immigration on a local labor market depend on the degree to which native-born workers emigrate from that labor market in response to worsened wages and employment opportunities.

[8]The internal migration of workers over time in response to immigration is one of a number of dynamic effects ignored by the static framework employed in this paper. In a dynamic context, one would also make endogenous the endowments of human capital of both natives and immigrants. This includes not only education but also employer investment in training, a matter of significance in Europe.

[9]See Polachek and Siebert (1993) for a survey of this literature.

[10]Estimation of b_u is somewhat complex due to the nature of the Eurobarometer data, which is family-based. After subtracting the components accounted for by the respondent's education and experience, the residual income represents the family income of a respondent with zero education and experience. To specify the share of this family income which is contributed by the unskilled labor of the respondent — versus that supplied by other adult members of the household — one must subtract the income contributed by other adults in the family. The vector Xi includes a variable intended to disentangle the contribution of other family members to income from the unskilled personal income of the respondent. We use the number of additional adults in the household as this variable. The regression coefficient on this variable represents how much additional adult family members, other than the respondent, contribute to family income. If we set this variable equal to zero (if there are no additional adult members in the family), then the remaining family income must correspond to the personal income of the respondent. There is a further issue: once we disentangle the personal income of a respondent from family income, we must still deal with the fact that different respondents supply varying amounts of hours to the labor market. This is especially so in comparing respondents who are heads of household with those who are not: heads of household usually have greater labor supply. In order to adjust for labor supply variation due to head of household status, we include a dummy variable as part of X_i equal to one if the respondent is the head of household and zero otherwise. Given these adjustments, we expect that the estimated coefficient of the constant term in (3) for the European

analysis reflects the return to unskilled labor of the average respondent in a region. It is a crude estimate, though, and our European analysis should be taken as exploratory.

[11]For a listing of the r_k's for each region, see Gang and Rivera-Batiz (1993). Our data are annual. Hence, the rates of return to education and experience represent the marginal effect of an additional year of education or experience on annual income. Alternative specifications of the earnings function were tried without significant impact on the estimated rates of return. Our results are thus robust. The r_u, r_e, r_x used in our simulations were constrained to be non-negative.

[12]The assumption is made that the technology represented by (4) is identical across regions. To adjust for possible variations in production function, our empirical analysis incorporated industrial composition as a variable in (5)–(7), but this did not have a significant impact on our estimates. Equations (5)–(7) also assume that there are no labor market imperfections and exclude wage discrimination as a factor determining earnings. To incorporate gender, racial and ethnic discrimination, the rates of return, *rk'* can be purged of any such effects by introducing gender and racial/ethnic dummy variables into the estimated earnings equations. In addition, the estimation of (5)–(7) can be carried out separately for men and women, to determine any differences in the production relationships involved. We did both types of experiments in our empirical analysis but did not find the changes had significant impact on our conclusions.

[13]For a derivation, see Gang and Rivera-Batiz (1993).

[14]The skills of immigrants and natives are assumed to be homogeneous (of the same quality) across countries. Although a simplifying assumption, one must be careful in qualifying it. The quality of education varies across countries. For instance, a year of education obtained by an immigrant from a rural area of India is unlikely to be identical to a year of schooling in a wealthy area of Brussels. In addition, skills (especially on-the-job experience) do not necessarily transfer well across countries. The experience of a legal expert in the Dominican Republic may be worthless in Spain. Our approach is flexible enough to incorporate variation in the quality of skills across countries. One would only have to adjust the skills of immigrants to reflect the effective endowments of education and experience supplied to the recipient country labor market.

References

Altonji J, Card D (1991) The effects of immigration on the labor market outcomes of less-skilled natives. In: Abowd JM, Freeman RB (eds) *Immigration, trade, and the labor market.* University of Chicago Press, Chicago, pp. 201–234.

Baldwin-Grossman J (1982) The substitutability of natives and immigrants in production. *Rev Econ Statist* 64:596–603.

Baldwin-Grossman J (1984) Illegal immigrants and domestic employment. *Indust Labor Relat Rev* 37:240–251.

Bean FD, Lowell BL, Taylor LJ (1988) Undocumented Mexican immigrants and the earnings of other workers in the United States. *Demography* 25:35–49.

Borjas GJ (1983) The substitutability of black, hispanic and white labor. *Econ Inquiry* 21:93–106.

Borjas GJ (1986) The demographic determinants of the demand for black labor. In: Freeman RB, Holzer H (eds) *The black youth employment crisis.* Univ of Chicago Press, Chicago, pp. 191–230.

Borjas GJ (1993) Immigrant skills and ethnic spillovers. CEPR workshop: The economics of international migration: econometric evidence. Konstanz, Germany, February 26/27.

Borjas GJ, Freeman RB, Katz LF (1992) On the labor market effects of immigration and trade. In: Borjas GJ, Freeman RB (eds) *Immigration and the workforce: economic consequences for the United States and source areas.* University of Chicago Press, Chicago, pp. 213–244.

Burda M, Wyplosz C (1991a) Human capital, investment and migration in an integrated Europe. CEPR Discussion Paper No. 614.

Burda M, Wyplosz C (1991b) Labour mobility and German integration: some vignettes. CEPR Discussion Paper No. 615.

Burgess DF (1975) Duality theory and pitfalls in the specification of technologies. *J Economet* 3:105–121.

Chiswick BR (1982) The impact of immigration on the level and distribution of economic well-being. In: Chiswick BR (ed) *The gateway: US immigration issues and policies.* American Enterprise Institute, Washington, DC, pp. 289–313.

Christensen L, Jorgenson D, Lau L (1973) Transcendental logarithmic production frontiers. *Rev Econ Statist* 55:28–45.

Defreitas G, Marshall A (1983) Immigration and wage growth in US manufacturing in the 1970s. AEA/IRRA Meetings, San Francisco CA.

DeNew JP, Zimmermann KF (1994) Native wage impacts of foreign labor: a random effects panel analysis. *J Popul Econ* 7:177–192.

Enchautequi M (1993) The effect of immigration on the wages and employment of black males. Urban Institute Working Paper 23.

Espenshade TJ, Goodis TA (1988) Are immigrants and native workers substitutes or complements in production? Lessons from Southern California and the American Southwest. US Dept of Labor Conf on Immigration, Sept 15–16.

Filer RK (1992) The effects of immigrant arrivals on migratory patterns of native workers. In: Borjas GJ, Freeman RB (eds) *Immigration and the work force: economic consequences for the United States and source area.* University of Chicago Press, Chicago, pp. 245–269.

Gang IN, Rivera-Batiz F (1993) Labor market effects of immigration in the United States and Europe: substitution vs. complementarity. Rutgers University Department of Economics Working Paper No. 93–18.

Gordon I (1989) The role of international migration in the changing European labour market. In: Gordon I, Thirlwall AP (eds) *European factor mobility: trends and consequences.* St. Martin's, New York, pp. 13–29.

Greene WH (1990) *Econometric analysis.* Macmillan, New York.

Greene WH (1992) Limdep: user's manual and reference guide, version 6.0. Econometric Software, Bellport NY.

Hamermesh DS (1986) The demand for labor in the long run. In: Ashenfelter O, Layard R (eds) *Handbook of labor economics*, Vol. 1. North-Holland, Amsterdam, pp. 430–471.

Hamermesh DS (1993) *Labor demand.* Princeton University Press, Princeton, NJ.

Hamermesh DS, Rees A (1993) *The economics of work and pay*, 5th edn. Harper Collins, New York.

Heckman JJ, Sedlacek G (1985) Heterogeneity, aggregation, and market wage functions: an empirical model of self-selection in the labor market. *J Polit Econ* 93:1077–1125.

Krueger A, Pischke JS (1992) A comparative analysis of East and West German labor markets: before and after unification. NBER Working Paper No. 4154.

LaLonde RJ, Topel RH (1991) Labor market adjustments to increased immigration. In: Abowd JM, Freeman RB (eds) *Immigration, trade, and the labor market.* University of Chicago Press, Chicago, pp. 167–200.

Layard R, Blanchard O, Dornbusch R, Krugman P (1992) *East-west migration: the alternatives.* MIT Press, Cambridge, MA.

Licht G, Steiner V (1992) Assimilation, labour market experience, and earnings profiles of temporary and permanent immigrant workers in Germany. Conference on mass migration in Europe: implications for east and west, Vienna, March 5–7.

Orcutt-Duleep H, Regets MC (1993) Country of origin and immigrant earnings. Middlebury College conference on immigration, Middlebury, Vermont, April.

Polachek S, Siebert WS (1993) *The economics of earnings.* Cambridge University Press, Cambridge.

Rabier JR, Riffault H, Inglehart R (1988) Euro-barometer 25. ICPSR ed., Inter-University Consortium for Political and Social Research, Ann Arbor MI.

Rabier JR, Riffault H, Inglehart R (1989a) Euro-barometer 26. ICPSR (ed) ICPSR, Ann Arbor MI.

Rabier JR, Riffault H, Inglehart R (1989b) Euro-barometer 27. ICPSR (ed) ICPSR, Ann Arbor MI.

Reif K, Melich A (1990) Euro-barometer 29. ICPSR (ed) ICPSR, Ann Arbor MI.

Reif K, Melich A (1991) Euro-barometer 30. ICPSR (ed) ICPSR, Ann Arbor MI.

Reif K, Melich A (1992) Euro-barometer 31. ICPSR (ed) ICPSR, Ann Arbor MI.

Rivera-Batiz F (1981) The effects of immigration in a distorted two-sector economy. *Econ Inquiry* 19:626–639.

Rivera-Batiz F, Sechzer SL (1991) Substitution and complementarity between immigrant and native labor in the United States. In: Rivera-Batiz FL, Sechzer SL, Gang IN (eds) *US immigration policy reform in the 1980s.* Praeger, Westport CT, pp. 89–116.

Rivera-Batiz FL, Sechzer SL, Gang IN (eds) (1991) *US immigration policy reform in the 1980s.* Praeger, Westport, CT.

Rosen S (1974) Hedonic prices and implicit prices: product differentiation in perfect competition. *J Polit Econ* 82:34–55.

Rosen S (1983) A note on aggregation of skills and labor quality: linear synthesis of skill distribution. *J Hum Resources* 18:425–431.

SHAZAM (1993) User's reference manual, version 7.0. McGraw-Hill, New York.

Straubhaar T, Zimmermann KP (1993) Towards a European migration policy. *Population Research and Policy Review*, 12(3), 225–241.

Taylor LJ, Bean FD, Rebitzer JB, Gonzalez-Baker S, Lindsay Lowell B (1988) Mexican immigrants and the wages and unemployment experience of native workers. Working Paper PRIP-Ul-1, The Urban Institute.

Tolbert CM (1987) Labor market areas for the United States. Agricultural and Rural Economic Division, Economic Research Service, US Department of Agriculture.

Part 2

The Impact of International Emigration: The Effects of the Brain Drain

Chapter 5

International Migration, Non-Traded Goods and Economic Welfare in the Source Country*

5.1 Introduction

Most of the literature on the economic effects of international migration has been undertaken under the assumption that all produced commodities are traded [see Kenen (1971), and Bhagwati and Rodriguez (1976)]. This is an extremely restrictive assumption given the fact that a substantial fraction of those workers emigrating out of less-developed countries do move out of such sectors as services, construction, transportation, etcetera, sectors which produce non-traded commodities. The case of skilled labor emigration (the so-called 'brain drain') from many LDCs is one important example, as reflected by the emigration of workers out of health service sectors (doctors, nurses), education (teachers, professors), transportation and construction (engineers, architects), etcetera. In India, for example, the Delhi Brain Drain Study concluded that 35.9% of all emigrants holding passports during the period 1960–1967 were nurses,

*This chapter was originally published in *Journal of Development Economics*, Vol. 11, No. 1 (August 1982), pp. 81–90.

The helpful comments, suggestions and encouragement of R. Baldwin, R. McCulloch and J. David Richardson and the members of seminars at Indiana University and the University of Wisconsin at Madison are gratefully acknowledged. I have also benefitted from the useful comments of a referee.

veterinarians, doctors and teachers [Institute of Applied Manpower Research (1970, table II)]. In the case of the Philippines, about 44% of all emigrants in the early 1970's consisted of emigrants with occupations associated with non-traded goods sectors, an outflow which implied an annual reduction of almost 3% in the stock of health and medical personnel alone in the country [Gupta (1973, table IX)]. This pattern of emigration can also be observed from the statistics on immigrants flowing into developed countries. Immigrant workers (legally) entering the United States in 1977 consisted of 33, whose reported occupation was related to a non-traded goods sector, such as services, construction and transportation [U.S. Immigration and Naturalization Service (1977, pp. 47–52)], a pattern which has been prevalent since the 1950's [See Watanabe (1969), and Grubel and Scott (1966)]. Similar conclusions can be derived of emigrants moving into Canada and Great Britain,[1] and of the more recent migratory flows between Arab countries [see Shaw (1979)].

This paper reconsiders the economic effects of emigration on the source country by assuming that there is a non-traded goods sector whose output and price are established endogenously in the economy. The traditional result in the literature is that, in a two-product small open economy, any given amount of emigration does not affect the welfare of the non-migrants. As Bhagwati and Rodriguez (1976) state: the presence or the absence of the migrant group in the population implies the same terms of trade, and hence the same trade opportunity, for the non-migrants. This result, of course, may not hold if there are any terms of trade effect, if there are factor specificities, or if there is any type of distortion in the economy [see Kenen (1971), Rivera-Batiz (1981a)]. It does not hold either, and this is the main point of this paper, if the economy produces non-traded goods. Assuming that the terms of trade facing the country are fixed (that is, assuming that the prices of traded goods are fixed), emigration will tend to reduce the welfare of the source country, if the economy is producing non-traded commodities. The economic intuition behind this result is that the emigration reduces the 'exchange opportunities' the non-migrants have under the presence (and with) the migrants, in terms of the exchange of traded for non-traded commodities.

5.2 The Welfare Impact of Emigration in the Source Country

We assume that the economy under consideration is a small open one producing two commodities: one traded and the other (internationally) non-traded. There are also two (freely mobile) factors of production, capital and labor, and some initial fixed endowments of these, $\bar{K}$ and $\bar{L}$ respectively. We also assume linear homogeneous production functions for both goods and perfect competition in product and factor markets.

Under these traditional assumptions,[2] we can draw an aggregate production possibilities curve for the pre-migration economy, represented in Figure 5.1 by the curve AA. We also assume that the population in the source country (including both migrants and non-migrants) has uniform preferences which, for simplicity, we assume to be homothetic, ruling out the possibility of inferiority in consumption. This gives rise to a set of social indifference curves which determine, jointly with AA, the equilibrium levels of output of traded and non-traded commodities. In Figure 5.1, this initial equilibrium is shown by point E, and the resulting equilibrium price is given by the tangent line PP. The first thing to notice about Figure 5.1 is that

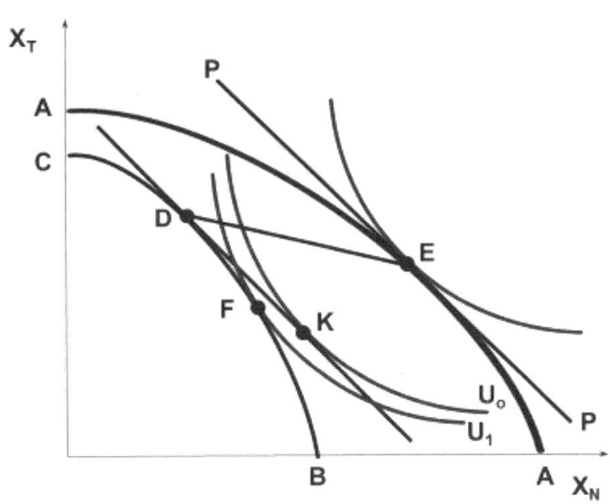

Figure 5.1. Effects of Emigration: Nontraded Goods Relatively Labor Intensive.

at point E there is balanced trade since the output and demand for traded goods are equal. In addition, there is equality of the demand and supply of non-traded goods, which also determines the endogenous price of non-traded goods (that is, disequilibria in the non-traded goods market will induce equilibrating changes in the domestic price ratio through changes in the price of non-traded goods).

We also show in Figure 5.1 the production possibilities of the non-migrants in the source economy by means of the curve CB. This production possibilities curve is a hypothetical one in the pre-migration situation since what is observed is the aggregate curve AA. It will be, however, a useful tool of analysis, given that it allows us to compare the pre- and post-migration situations of the non-migrant population [this type of framework has been formalized by Bhagwati and Brecher (1980, 1981)]. The assumption underlying the shape of the curve CB, relative to AA, is that the non-traded goods sector be comparatively labor-intensive, so that the inward shift of AA would be biased 'against' the output of non-traded goods. Given the prevailing price ratio in the economy, at PP, the non-migrants will produce at point D, in the curve CB, and consume at point K, with a level of welfare represented by U_0. Note that the line DE corresponds to the traditional Rybczynski line.

Suppose now that there is an actual emigration of labor from the economy, so that the labor force declines. On the assumption that this is the only exogenous change in the economy,[3] the production possibilities curve of the economy would shrink to the non-migrants curve, CB, and the new equilibrium would occur at point F, where trade is balanced and the market for non-traded goods is in equilibrium. A higher price of non-traded goods results and as a consequence, the non-migrants increase their production of non-traded goods, even though the aggregate (economy-wide) production of non-traded goods declines. This is reflected in Figure 5.1 by the movement from point E to point F. The reason for the increase in the price of non-traded goods lies on the fact that, under the given sectoral capital-intensity assumptions, emigration leads to a decrease in the output of non-traded goods proportionally larger than the decrease in the output of traded goods. As a consequence, at constant commodity prices, an excess demand for non-traded goods would arise. The price of non-traded goods would then increase to eliminate this disequilibrium.

As can be observed from Figure 5.1, emigration reduces the economic welfare of the non-migrants, as reflected by the movement of the social indifference curve from U_0 to U_1. It is clear from this diagrammatic representation where the decline in welfare comes from: at the initial equilibrium, the non-migrants trade with the (potential) migrants by exchanging traded for non-traded goods. In the post-emigration equilibrium, however, there is no exchange possible between migrants and non-migrants (with respect to internationally non-traded commodities), so that the welfare of the non-migrants declines. As long as there are no distortions, a disruption of the internal trade or exchange occurring in the pre-migration situation results in a loss of welfare to the non-migrants. In terms of Figure 5.1, as the migrants leave the non-migrants' consumption possibilities become circumscribed to their own production possibilities curve, *CB*, and cannot rise above it as they could when the migrant population was present (point K, for example).

Up to this point we have assumed that the production of non-traded goods is relatively labor-intensive. Our results, however, do not change if we assume instead that the traded goods sector is the relatively labor intensive one. In this case, the emigration will lead to a shift of the production-possibilities curve which is biased 'against' the traded goods sector. This is reflected in Figure 5.2 by the inward shift of the pre-migration aggregate production possibilities curve AA to *BC*, the production possibilities faced by the non-migrants. In this situation, the pre-migration equilibrium ratio would again be given by PP (the tangent to AA). At this price ratio, the non-migrants produce at point J (in their production possibilities curve) and consume at point Z, exchanging non-traded goods for traded goods with the (potential) migrant population. When the latter emigrates, however, the non-migrants' consumption possibilities become constrained by their own production-possibilities curve, *CB*, and the new equilibrium would occur at point S. Our result, as to the effect that emigration reduces the economic welfare of the non-migrants,

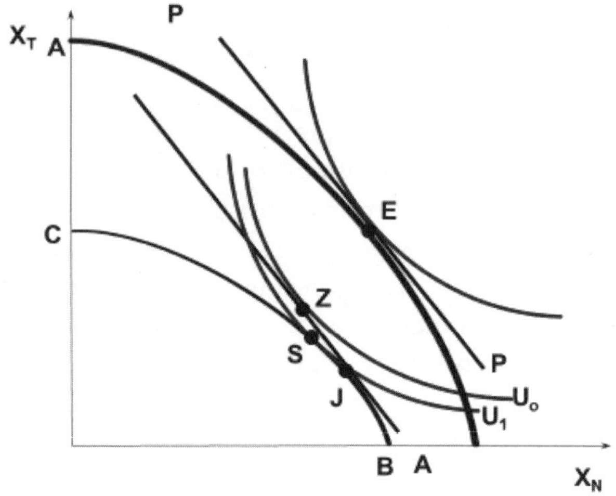

Figure 5.2. Effects of Emigration: Traded Goods Relatively Labor Intensive.

is unchanged, as is reflected in Figure 5.2 by the decrease in welfare that they suffer from U_0 to U_1. Our result, then, does not depend on the internal exchange pattern of the non-migrants with the migrants, so long as some exchange is occurring initially.

5.3 Conclusions

In this paper we have re-examined the welfare effects of emigration on the source country by introducing a dichotomy between traded and non-traded commodities. It has been shown that, in this framework, emigration always worsens the economic welfare of the non-migrants, even if there are fixed terms of trade facing the economy; changes in the price of non-traded goods give rise to the deterioration in economic welfare. Intuitively, the emigration tends to eliminate any internal exchange of traded for non-traded goods existing between migrants and non-migrants. As a result, this disruption of internal trade in (internationally) non-traded goods in the source country results in a loss of welfare.

A crucial building block of our analysis is the two-goods, two-factors (2×2) production structure utilized in modeling the introduction of non-traded goods. In this type of model, changes in factor endowments give rise to changes in the price of non-traded goods which are associated, in turn, with changes in economic welfare. These links do not necessarily hold in alternative models introducing non-traded goods. In a model with two traded goods and one non-traded good, produced through the use of two primary factors (capital and labor), the price of non-traded goods would be determined by the price of traded goods and it would be completely unresponsive to changes in factor endowments [see Komiya (1967)]. As a result, in this type of model, the economic welfare of the non-migrants in the source country would be unchanged by emigration. Actually, any model with an equal number of traded goods and factors of production would give rise to the same result. On the other hand, any model with a structure having more primary factors than traded goods (like the one we utilized here) will tend to give rise to the type of result derived in this paper [see Rivera-Batiz (1981b, 1982)].

There are a number of possibilities for further research in this area, utilizing the traded-non-traded goods dichotomy. There is a clear need for empirical research on the effects of emigration on the price and output of non-traded commodities in less developed countries (for example: what is the impact of the emigration of doctors on the price and output of health services?). There is also scope for further theoretical analysis by introducing short-run capital specificities, different types (skills) of labor, the impact of migration in an explicit two-country model, etcetera. Hopefully, this paper will serve as a stepping stone for such work.

5.4 Appendix

In this appendix we present the system of equations comprising our model and derive rigorously some of our results in the text. Following standard general-equilibrium production models, full-employment of the available capital, K, and labor, L, imply that

$$C_{LN}X_N + C_{LT}X_T = \bar{L}, \tag{A.1}$$

$$C_{KN}X_N + C_{KT}X_T = \bar{K}, \tag{A.2}$$

where X_{T} and X_N are the output of traded and non-traded goods in the economy, respectively, and where the C_{ij}'s represent the amount of input i used in the production of output j, where $i = K$, L, and $j = 1, \ldots, N$. The C_{ij}'s utilized in production are, of course, a function of the wage-rental ratio in the economy so that

$$C_{ij} = C_{ij}(\omega), \quad i = K, L, \quad j = T, N \tag{A.3}$$

where ω is the ratio of the wage rate, w, over the rental rate on capital, r.

Under perfect competition, we also know that price equals unit cost, so that

$$wC_{LN} + rC_{KN} = P_N, \tag{A.4}$$

and

$$wC_{LT} + rC_{KT} = P_T, \tag{A.5}$$

where P_j is the price of the jth commodity. The price of non-traded goods, P_N, is determined endogenously, through the interaction of demand and supply of non-traded goods. The demand for non-traded goods, which is a function of relative prices and income, must be equal to the supply of non-traded goods, in order for there to be equilibrium in that market.

Symbolically

$$D_N = D_N(P, Y) = X_N, \tag{A.6}$$

where D_N is the demand for non-traded goods, $P \equiv P_N/P_T$, and Y is national income in terms of traded goods: $Y = X_T + PX_N$. In addition, under the assumption of equilibrium in the traded goods market:

$$D_T = D_T(P, Y) = X_T, \tag{A.7}$$

where D_T is the demand for the traded commodity, and where (A.7) represents balanced trade.

The structural model of the source economy is complete, consisting of 10 equations [(A.1), (A.2), the four implied by (A.3), (A.4), (A.5), (A.6) and (A.7)] in 10 variables [C_{LN}, C_L, C_{KN}, C_{KT}, X_T,

X_N, P_N, w, r and Y]. In order to derive the effects of an exogenous change (reduction) in $\bar{L}$ on the endogenous variables of the system, one has to derive the equations of change and solve them. This is rather straightforward [see Jones (1965), Batra (1973)] and we only report our basic result in terms of the impact of a decrease in L on the price of non-traded goods.

Assuming that the only given change in the economy is an exogenous outflow of labor, and assuming fixed terms of trade and homothetic preference, the percentage change in the price of non-traded commodities is given by

$$P_N^* = L^*/|\lambda|(\sigma_D + \sigma_s), \tag{A.8}$$

The asterisks in Eq. (A.8) represent relative changes ($P_N^* = \mathrm{d}P_N/P_N$, etc.), and the following definitions apply:

$$|\lambda| \equiv (L_T L_N/LK)(k_N - k_T), \tag{A.9}$$

where $k_N = (K_N/L_N)$ and $k_T = (K_T/L_T)$ are the capital intensities in the two sectors. Also

$$\sigma_D \equiv \eta_{PN} + \eta_{PT} > 0, \tag{A.10}$$

where $\eta_{PN} \equiv -\frac{P}{D_N}\frac{\partial D_N}{\partial P}$ and $\eta_{PT} \equiv \frac{P}{D_T}\frac{\partial D_T}{\partial P}$ are elasticities of demand for non-traded: and traded commodities respectively, so that σ_D represents the so-called elasticity of demand substitution. Finally

$$\sigma_S \equiv (X_N^* - X_T^*)/(P_N^* - P_T^*) > 0 \tag{A.11}$$

which is Jones' elasticity of commodity substitution along the transformation curve.

Having determined the effect of emigration ($L^* < 0$) on the price of non-traded goods, what is its impact on the economic welfare of the non-migrants? We define the welfare of the non-migrants through the use of a standard social welfare function:

$$W = U(D_T^0, D_N^0), \tag{A.12}$$

where W is the welfare of the non-migrants and U is a concave function of their consumption of traded and non-traded goods (D_T^0 and D_N^0, respectively).

Welfare, W, is maximized subject to the budget constraint given by

$$Y = PD_N^0 + D_T^0 = PX_N^0 + X_T^0, \tag{A.13}$$

where Y is the real income of the non-migrants in terms of the traded commodity. Now, by differentiating (A.12) and (A.13) totally, and through some manipulation we can determine the factors which can give rise to a change in W:

$$\mathrm{d}W = (X_N^0 - D_N^0)\mathrm{d}P + P\mathrm{d}X_N^0 + \mathrm{d}X_T^0. \tag{A.14}$$

That is, changes in the welfare of the non-migrants can arise from change in the price ratio ($\mathrm{d}P$) and through changes in their production possibilities ($\mathrm{d}X_T^0 + p\mathrm{d}X_N^0$). But in our distortions-free framework, $\mathrm{d}X_T^0 + p\mathrm{d}X_N^0 = 0$ (along the transformation curve $\mathrm{d}X_T^0/\mathrm{d}X_N^0 = -P$) so that emigration leaves the transformation curve of the non-migrants unaltered. As a consequence, the only factor which can change W is a change in the price ratio. Since the price of traded goods is fixed (the economy is 'small'), then

$$\mathrm{d}W = P(X_N^0 - D_N^0)P_N^* \tag{A.15}$$

and substituting (A.8) into (A.15):

$$\mathrm{d}W/\mathrm{d}L = [P(X_N^0 - D_N^0)/|\lambda|(\sigma_D + \sigma_S)]L^* > 0$$

which suggests that the change in the welfare of the non-migrants, $\mathrm{d}W$, resulting from a reduction in the labor force of the economy ($\mathrm{d}L < 0$) is always negative. The reason, shown diagrammatically and verbally in the text, is that $|\lambda|$ and $(X_N^0 - D_N^0)$ are always of the opposite sign. Since σ_D, σ_S, L and P are all positive, then $\mathrm{d}W/\mathrm{d}L > 0$, giving rise to our statement that, if $\mathrm{d}L < 0$, then $\mathrm{d}W < 0$. Note finally that if $k_T > k_N$ (the non-traded is relatively labor intensive), then $|\lambda| < 0$, but $(X_N^0 - D_N^0) < 0$ also (as can be observed from Figure 5.1, the non-migrants would be exchanging traded goods for non-traded goods from the migrants). Similarly, if $k_T < k_N$, then $|\lambda| > 0$, but $(X_N^0 - D_N^0) > 0$, as can be visualized from Figure 5.2.

Notes:

[1]In 1979, for example, 22% of all emigrants from South America entering Canada reported occupations related to a non-traded goods sector, as catalogued earlier [See Manpower and Immigration Department, Canada (1979)].

[2]For a rigorous statement of our model and proofs of our results, see the appendix.

[3]This is a crucial assumption. If, for example, capital were to move out of the economy jointly with labor (as one may expect in the case of highly-skilled labor emigration but perhaps not in the case of unskilled migration), then our results below would not necessarily hold. If the capital and labor emigrate in proportion to the aggregate capital-labor ratio in the economy, then the price of non-traded goods (and, thus, the domestic price ratio) would not have to change. The economic welfare of the non-migrants would then stay unchanged.

References

Batra, R.N., 1973, *Studies in the pure theory of international trade* (St. Martin's Press, New York).

Bhagwati, J.N. and C. Rodriguez, 1976, Welfare-theoretical analyses of the brain drain, in J.N. Bhagwati, ed., *The brain drain and taxation: Theory and empirical analysis* (North-Holland, Amsterdam) 85–111.

Bhagwati, J.N. and R. Brecher, 1980, "National welfare in an open economy in the presence of foreign-owned factors of production," *Journal of International Economics* 10, 100–115.

Bhagwati, J.N. and R. Brecher, 1981, "Foreign owner hip and the theory of trade and welfare," *Journal of Political Economy* 89, 497–511.

Grubel, H. and A. Scott, 1966, "The immigration of scientists and engineers to the United States, 1949–61," *Journal of Political Economy* 74, 368–378.

Gupta, M.L., 1973, "Outflow of high-level manpower from the Philippines," *International Labor Review* 107, 167–191.

Institute of Applied Manpower Research, 1970, "The brain drain study," Report No. 4 (New Delhi).

Jones, R.W., 1965, "The structure of simple general equilibrium models," *Journal of Political Economy* 73, 557–572.

Kenen, P.R., 1971, Migration, the terms of trade and economic welfare in the source country, in: J.N. Bhagwati *et al.*, eds., *Trade, balance of payments and growth* (North-Holland, Amsterdam) 238–260.

Komiya, R., 1967, "Non-traded goods and the pure theory of international trade," *International Economic Review* 8, 132–152.

Manpower and Immigration Department, 1979, Immigration Statistics, Immigration and Demographic Policy Group, Canada.

Rivera-Batiz, F., 1981a, "The effects of immigration in a distorted two-sector economy," *Economic Inquiry* 19, 626–639.

Rivera-Batiz, F., 1981b, "Technological change, factor endowments and the pure theory of international trade with non-traded goods," Department of Economics Discussion Paper No. 81–11 (Indiana University, Bloomington, IN).

Rivera-Batiz, F., 1982, "Non-traded goods and the pure theory of international trade with equal numbers of goods and factors," *International Economic Review* 23, 401–409.

Shaw, R.P., 1979, "Migration and employment in the Arab world: Construction as a key policy variable," *International Labour Review* 118, 589–605.

United States Department of Justice, 1977, Annual Report, United States Immigration and Naturalization Service.

Watanabe, S., 1969, "The brain drain from developing to developed countries," *International Labour Review* 99, 401–429.

Chapter 6

International Migration, Remittances and Economic Welfare in the Source Country*

6.1 Introduction

One of the key, but often overlooked, aspects of international migration is the flow of remittances sent by emigrants back to source countries. The traditional neglect of these flows in economic analysis is unfortunate since, for some developing countries, they constitute a major source of foreign exchange. Table 6.1 displays the net workers' remittances received by a sample of major labour-exporting countries, reported as a fraction of merchandise exports. For some countries (e.g. Jordan, Pakistan and the Yemen Arab Republic) workers' remittances even exceed the value of merchandise exports. If anything, these figures derived from official balance of payments statistics, are likely to understate the inflows of remittances and, therefore, their significance for most of these countries.[1]

Recent work on the theory of international migration has started to examine the role of remittances on the impact of emigration in

*This chapter was originally published in *Journal of Economic Studies*, Vol. 13, No. 3 (October 1986), pp. 3–19. © 1986 Emerald Group Publishing Ltd.

This paper was written while I was a Visiting Associate Professor in the Department of Economics at the University of Pennsylvania. I have benefitted from the comments of the participants of a seminar at the Department of Economics of the University of Southern California in Los Angeles and two anonymous referees.

Table 6.1. Net Workers Remittances Expressed as a Fraction of Merchandise Exports.

Country	1983	1984
Antigua-Barbuda	0.33	0.30
Bangladesh	0.88	0.34
Dominica	0.30	0.36
Dominican Republic	0.35	NA
Egypt	0.87	NA
Greece	0.22	0.20
Haiti	0.34	0.21
India	0.27	NA
Jamaica	0.10	NA
Jordan	1.91	1.64
Morocco	0.43	0.39
Pakistan	1.02	1.01
Portugal	0.40	0.38
Sudan	0.48	0.42
Syrian Arab Republic	0.24	NA
Tunisia	0.26	0.17
Turkey	0.26	0.17
Yemen Arab Republic	122.07	NA

Note: NA: Not Available.

Source: International Monetary Fund, Yearbook of Balance of Payments Statistics, Vol. 35, October 1985.

source countries. Djajic (1986), in particular, discusses the welfare impact of the remittances made by permanent migrants, defined as those migrants whose production and consumption occurs in the destination country and whose welfare, therefore, constitutes part of the recipient country's welfare. Kirwan and Holden (1986), on the other hand, look at the welfare effects of temporary emigrants, where the temporary migrant "produces in the host country but consumes in the source country with remittances linking both activities".[2] Both of these studies consider only the impact of remittances that are completely allocated to consumption spending.[3] This is restrictive assumption as, often, migrants will invest rather than consume their remittances in the source country. In some Mexican regions, for example, the remittances of migrants to the US are heavily channeled into investment. As Piore (1979, pp. 124 –125) remarks of the influential fieldwork of Juan Diez-Canedo on Mexican remittances:

> Diez-Canedo sees the major function of [Mexican-US] migration in the development of Jalisco [Mexico] as that of providing scarce capital... the outstanding example of the contribution of migration to industrial development is a study of a town in Jalisco, Mexico, where an extensive textile industry has grown up from nothing, financed by immigrant remittances. The industry began when one returning migrant invested his savings in a single piece of machinery, which he operated in his home. Since that time, the original entrepreneur has expanded substantially. He has also been imitated by most of his neighbors. Diez-Canedo found a number of other examples of the investment of remittances in small-scale enterprises in agriculture, in commerce and in services of one kind or another.[4]

Cornelius (1979, p. 47) finds that 16 per cent of the illegal [Mexican] migrants he interviewed "invested most of their US earnings in capital goods". The fraction of remittances allocated to investment, however, is dependent on the type of migration (temporary *versus* permanent) and on the country, region or even community involved. Research on the remittances of emigrants in some areas of the world (e.g., such as the Middle East and the Caribbean) shows an insignificant fraction of remittances dedicated to investment spending.[5]

What is the impact of emigration on the source country when a fraction of remittances is invested? This article provides an analytical answer to this question. We develop a model that distinguishes between the impact of temporary and permanent migration, thus integrating and comparing the previous work of Djacic and Kirwan and Holden. In addition, we look not only at net welfare aspects but also at the impact of remittances on income distribution and domestic prices. In the next section we set up the model of the source country and of remittances and report our results on the impact of temporary and permanent emigration. In the third section we examine the welfare effects of emigration and in the final section we summarize our conclusions.

6.2 The Basic Model

Following Rivera-Batiz (1982) and a growing literature based on it,[6] we assume the source country is a small open economy producing non-traded goods and a composite of traded goods. Each sector uses two factors of production, capital and labour, so that, with full employment,

$$a_{LN}X_N + a_{LT}X_T = \bar{L} \quad (1)$$

$$a_{KN}X_N + a_{KT}X_T = \bar{K} \quad (2)$$

where $\bar{K}$ and $\bar{L}$ are the economy's initial endowments of capital and labour, X_j is the output of sector j (with $j = N$, T indexing non-traded and traded goods, respectively, and the a_{ij}'s represent the quantity of input i used in production of a unit of output j, where $i = K$, L indexes capital and labour inputs). On the assumption of constant returns to scale and cost minimization, the a_{ij}'s are strictly a function of the wage rental ratio in the economy,

$$a_{ij} = a_{ij}(\omega) \quad i = K, L; \;\; j = T, N \quad (3)$$

where $\omega = W/r$ represents the ratio of the wage rate, W, to the rental rate on capital, r. Under the additional assumption of perfect competition, prices will equal unit costs so that:

$$Wa_{LN} + ra_{KN} = P_N \quad (4)$$

$$Wa_{LT} + ra_{KT} = P_T \quad (5)$$

with P_j depicting the price of the jth commodity. Although the price of traded goods, P_T, is assumed to be exogenously determined in world markets, the price of non-traded goods, P_N, is an endogenous variable influenced by demand and supply. Equilibrium in that market thus required that the demand for non-traded goods, D_N, be equal to the supply of non-traded goods, or:

$$D_N = D_N(P, Y) = X_N \quad (6)$$

where $P = P_N/P_T$, and Y is real income, deflated by the price of traded goods, that is:

$$Y = D_T + PD_N \quad (7)$$

with D_T depicting the demand for traded goods. In addition, under the assumption that the economy starts from a position of balanced trade, the demand for and supply of traded goods are initially

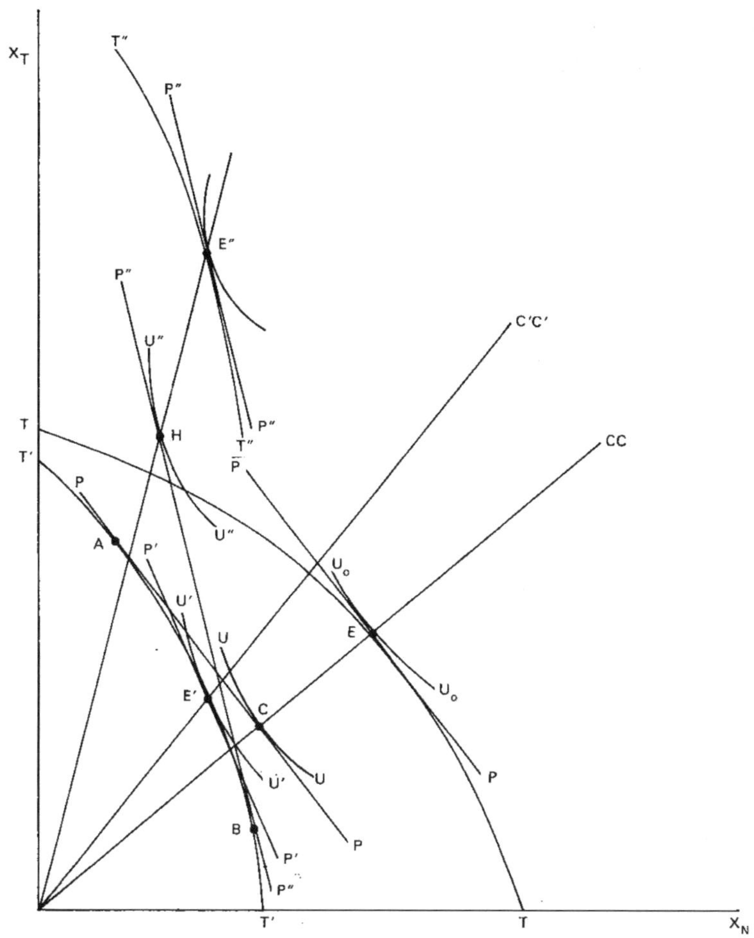

Figure 6.1. The Effects of Remittances.

equalized, or:

$$D_T = D_T(P, Y) = X_T. \tag{8}$$

This completes the model of the economy, whose initial equilibrium is depicted by point E in Figure 6.1, showing the intersection of the economy's production-possibilities curve, TT, with the income-consumption line CC, which is linear on the assumption of homothetic preferences. The equilibrium price of non-traded goods in terms of traded goods, $\bar{P} = \bar{P}_N/P_T$, corresponds to the absolute value of the slope of the PP line.

The next step is to examine the impact of emigration. As noted in the introduction, international migration can be temporary or permanent. Temporary migration is associated with production abroad and consumption at home, with remittances closely reflecting the total income received by the migrants[7]; permanent migration implies both production and consumption abroad, with remittances reflecting a pure transfer of the emigrants to the non-migrants in the source country. Since only a minor fraction of their total income is usually sent back by permanent migrants to the source country, the remittances of permanent migrants are less than those of temporary migrants. If we denote the fraction of income remitted to the source country by γ_R^k where $k = t$, p for temporary and permanent migration, respectively, then $\gamma'_R > \gamma_R^P$.

Remittances can be in the form of consumption transfers, that take place through traded goods remitted by the migrants to the source country, or in the form of investment transfers, which are associated with an increase in the supply of capital goods (instead of final traded goods) in the source country. More formally, suppose there is an outflow of labourers from the economy that reduces the domestic (source country) labour force by $\hat{L}$ in proportional terms (we shall always use a circumflex, '^', to denote proportional changes, so that $\hat{L} = d\bar{L}/\bar{L}$). Associated with this labour outflow is, first, an inflow of remittances in the form of an increase in the domestic capital stock. The distribution of remittances between consumption and investment purposes is reflected by the parameter Ω, which is the fraction of remittances allocated to consumption (traded goods) remittances; $(1-\Omega)$ remittances are then allocated to raise the source country capital stock.[8]

Consumption remittances will directly alter the traded goods market equilibrium condition in (8) in the following way:

$$\hat{D}_T = \hat{X}_T + \hat{R} \tag{9}$$

where $\hat{R}$ denotes emigrants' consumption (traded goods) remittances, R, as a proportion of the economy's supply of traded goods,

X_T. But it is easy to derive (see the appendix) that:

$$\hat{R} = \frac{R}{X_T} = -\Omega\frac{\theta_{LY}}{\theta_{TY}}\gamma_R^k(1+\hat{W}^*)\hat{L}. \tag{10}$$

Equation (10) stages that, everything else constant, the flow of remittances will be higher, the larger the proportion of the labour force that emigrates, $-\hat{L}$, the larger the proportional real income boots received by these migrants, $\hat{W}^*$ (defined by the differential between foreign real wages, W^*/P_T, and source country real wages, W/P_T, as a proportion of the latter) and the larger the fraction of their income that emigrants remit back to the source country, γ_R^k.[9] Also, *ceteris paribus*, the larger the share of labour on national income, $\theta_{LY} \equiv W\bar{L}/P_T Y$, the larger the remittances of a given *proportion* of the labour force that emigrates; and, the smaller the share of traded goods on national income, $\theta_{TY} \equiv X_T/Y$, the higher the remittances as a *proportion* of the output of traded goods in the economy.

In addition, remittances might occur in the form of an increase in the economy's supply of capital, $\hat{K} \equiv d\bar{K}/\bar{K}$. These remittances are allocated to investment and modify directly the capital endowment equation (2) above. If we denote by r^* the rental rate at which units of capital acquired in international markets,[10] then investments remittances will increase the domestic capital stock by:

$$\hat{K} = -(1-\Omega)\frac{W^*}{r^*}\frac{\bar{L}}{\bar{K}}\gamma_R^k\hat{L} \tag{11}$$

with all variables as defined above. Equation (11) equates an increase in investment remittances with greater labour outflows, larger fractions of income remitted, and higher wage-rental ratios in the host country (which improve the terms at which migrants can trade their labour for capital abroad). The *proportional* impact of a given labour outflow on the source country capital stock depends on the absolute size of the initial labour force, $\bar{L}$, and capital stock $\bar{K}$. Finally, the capital inflow will be determined by the share of remittances allocated to investment purposes, $1-\Omega$.

To specify the general-equilibrium effects of emigration in the presence of remittances, one only has to differentiate totally the system embedded in equations (1)–(8), taking into account (9)–(11), and solve for the effects of a reduction in the labour force. We carry out the derivations in an appendix and report here our results. The first variable whose impact we want to look at is the price of home (non-traded) goods. The reduced form expression for the effect of an outflow of labour from the economy on the price of non-traded goods is given by:

$$\hat{P}_N = \frac{1 - |\lambda|\Omega\frac{\theta_{LY}}{\theta_{TY}}\gamma_R^k(1+\hat{W}^*) + (1-\Omega)\frac{W^*}{r^*}\frac{\bar{L}}{\bar{K}}\gamma_R^k}{|\lambda|(\sigma_D + \sigma_s)}\hat{L} \qquad (12)$$

where $|\lambda| \equiv (L_T L_N/\overline{LK})(k_N - k_T)$, with $k_N = K_N/L_N$ and $k_T = K_T/L_T$ equal to capital-labour ratios in the non-traded and traded goods sectors, $\sigma_D \equiv \eta_{PN} + \eta_{PT} > 0$ depicts the elasticity of commodity substitution in demand with $\eta_{PN} \equiv -(P/D_N)(\delta D_N/\delta P)$ and $\eta_{PT} \equiv (P/D_T)(\delta D_T/\delta P)$ equal to price elasticities of demand for non-traded and traded goods, respectively, and σ_s is the elasticity of commodity substitution in production (along the transformation curve), defined by $\sigma_S \equiv (\hat{X}_N - \hat{X}_T)/\hat{P}_N > 0$.

Equation (12) states that a reduction in the labour force of the economy, $\hat{L} < 0$, will result in an increase of non-traded goods prices ($\hat{P}_N > 0$) so long as the non-traded goods sector is labour-intensive ($k_N < k_T$), which the evidence seems to support and is therefore assumed throughout the paper.[11] Note that the effect of remittances is to magnify the inflationary impact of emigration. Algebraically, in the absence of remittances, $\gamma_R^k = 0$. Therefore, if we denote the changes in the price of non-traded goods in the absence of remittances by $\hat{P}_N^0$, one can obtain from equation (12) that:

$$\hat{P}_N - \hat{P}_N^0 = -\frac{\Omega|\lambda|\frac{\theta_{LY}}{\theta_{TY}}\gamma_R^k(1+\hat{W}^*) - (1-\Omega)\frac{W^*}{r^*}\frac{\bar{L}}{\bar{K}}\gamma_R^k}{|\lambda|(\sigma_D + \sigma_s)}\hat{L} \qquad (13)$$

which is positive whenever $\hat{L} < 0$ (there is emigration) and $k_N < k_T$ (non-traded goods are relatively labour-intensive). Intuitively, the first term in the numerator of the right-hand side of equation (13) reflects the inflationary impact of consumption remittances. Since the transfer of traded goods represents a rise in real income, it spills over into an excess demand for non-traded goods, at given prices. This excess demand is eliminated through an upsurge of non-traded goods prices. In the case of investment remittances, on the other hand, the impact is represented by the second term in the right-hand side of equation (13). The increase in the economy's capital stock tends to raise the supply of the relatively capital-intensive traded goods at the expense of the relatively labour-intensive non-traded goods. An excess demand for non-traded goods emerges, with a consequent inflationary impact.

Equation (12) can be used to integrate previous work on the theory of international migration. The papers by Rivera-Batiz (1982, 1984) and Thompson (1984) ignore remittances,[12] implying that $\gamma_R^k = 0$ in equation (12). The work of Djacic (1985), on the other hand, considers only the consumption remittances of permanent migrants, which in equation (12) would be associated with $\gamma_R^k = \gamma_R^P$ and $\Omega = 1$. The paper by Kirwan and Holden (1986) finally, assumes $\gamma_R^k = \gamma_R'$ and $\Omega = 1$, that is, it examines the consumption remittances of temporary migrants.[13] As far as we know, there exists in the literature no analytical examination of the impact of emigration in the presence of investment remittances. Therefore, in Figure 1 we pursue the diagrammatics of this case in detail.

The immediate impact of emigration is to reduce the source country labour force, shifting the production possibilities curve from TT to T′T′. In the absence of remittances, equilibrium would be re-established at point E', with a rise in the price of non-traded goods, as reflected in the more steeply-negative slope of the line $P'P'$ relative to that of PP. This, however, is not the end of the story. An inflow of investment remittances would augment the economy's capital stock, pushing out the production possibilities curve of the source country from T′T′ to T″T″ (the latter is not drawn in its entirety, for diagrammatical simplicity). Note that this shift is biased in favour of the relatively capital-intensive traded goods sector, increasing its output while reducing that of non-traded goods at constant non-traded goods prices. This is, of course, another application of the Rybczinski Theorem. As a consequence of the biased growth of traded-goods production, an excess demand for non-traded goods arises at constant prices. Non-traded goods prices must increase further, as is reflected by the more steeply-negative slope of the line P″P″ relative to T′T′.

In other words, the investment remittances reinforce the impact of emigration in raising the relative price of non-traded goods.

What is the impact of emigration-cum-remittances on income distribution? The analysis in this article indicates that emigration tends to raise real wage rates and reduce real rates of return on capital, an impact that is reinforced by remittances, no matter whether they are used for consumption or investment purposes. The economic intuition explaining this particular influence of remittances is straightforward. Consumption remittances, firstly, raise the demand for relatively labour-intensive, non-traded goods, increasing the aggregate demand for labour and, therefore, real wages. Investment remittances, on the other hand, augment the economy's capital stock, shifting upwards the marginal productivity of labour and real wages. The reduced form for the impact of emigration on real wages and real rental rates on capital are:

$$\hat{W} - \hat{P}_N = -\frac{\theta_{KN}}{|\theta||\lambda|(\sigma_D + \sigma_S)} \times \left[1 - |\lambda|\Omega\frac{\theta_{LY}}{\theta_{TY}}\gamma_R^k(1 + \hat{W}^*) + (1 - \Omega)\frac{W^*}{r^*}\frac{\bar{L}}{\bar{K}}\gamma_R^k\right]\hat{L} \tag{14}$$

$$\hat{r} - \hat{P}_N = \frac{\theta_{KN}}{|\theta||\lambda|(\sigma_D + \sigma_S)} \times \left[1 - |\lambda|\Omega\frac{\theta_{LY}}{\theta_{TY}}\gamma_R^k(1 + \hat{W}^*) + (1 - \Omega)\frac{W^*}{r^*}\frac{\bar{L}}{\bar{K}}\gamma_R^k\right]\hat{L} \tag{15}$$

where $|\theta| \equiv \frac{W_r L_T L_N}{P_T X_T P_N X_N}(k_N - k_T)$, $\theta_{LN} \equiv \frac{WL_N}{P_N X_N}$ and $\theta_{KT} \equiv \frac{rK_T}{P_T X_T}$. As before, we assume $k_N < k_T$, implying $\hat{W} - \hat{P}_N > 0$ and $\hat{r} - \hat{P}_N < 0$, if $\hat{L} < 0$.

6.3 The Welfare Impact of Emigration in the Source Country

In this section we examine how the economic changes triggered by emigration (summarized in the previous section) affect national welfare in the source country. National welfare is composed of the welfare of two groups. The first group consists of the migrants themselves (assuming they are temporary migrants; permanent migrants, as noted earlier, can be considered to become part of the host country) plus the beneficiaries of the migrants' transfers, which would include mainly relatives in the source country. We refer to these as migrants-cum-relatives. The second group consists of that portion of the population that is not directly connected to the migratory process. This includes non-migrants not receiving transfers from abroad. We shall refer to them simply as non-migrants. Although it is apparent that remittances will influence positively the welfare of the first group, it is not clear how they will influence the welfare of non-migrants. It is the purpose of the following discussion to clarify the issue analytically.

We define welfare through the use of a standard social welfare function,

$$U^e = U^e(D_T^e, D_N^e) \tag{16}$$

where $e = 1, 2$ indexes the two groups whose welfare we are interested in: the migrants-cum-relatives ($e = 1$) and the non-migrants ($e = 2$), respectively. U^e is the welfare of group e, which is a concave function of its consumption of traded and non-traded goods, D_T^e and D_N^e, respectively, with positive partial derivatives, $U_1^e = \delta U^e/\delta D_T^e$ and $U_2^e = \delta U^e/\delta D_N^e$. Welfare is maximized subject to the budget constraint that each group faces, given by:

$$Y^e = PD_N^e + D_T^e = PX_N^e + X_T^e + R_e \tag{17}$$

where the remittances received by non-migrants are zero: $R_2 = 0$.

Differentiating totally the welfare function in (16), the result is:

$$dU^e = U_1^e dD_T^e + U_2^e dD_N^e. \tag{18}$$

Assuming that welfare is maximized, so that, from the usual first-order conditions, the marginal rate of substitution in consumption is set equal to the equilibrium price ratio, P:

$$\frac{U_2^e}{U_1^e} = P \tag{19}$$

and setting $P = \bar{P}$ and $U_1 = 1$ initially (without loss of generality) equation (19) can be substituted into (18) to yield:

$$dU^e = dD_T^e + \bar{P}dD_N^e. \tag{20}$$

Differentiating equation (17) totally, and simplifying, one obtains:

$$dD_T^e = dX_T^e + \bar{P}dX_N^e + X_N^e dP - D_N^e dP - \bar{P}dD_N^e + R_e \tag{21}$$

where $dR_e = R_e$ on the assumption that $R_e = 0$ initially. Substitution of (21) into (20) then yields:

$$dU^e = (dX_T^e + \bar{P}dX_N^e) + \bar{P}(X_N^e - D_N^e)\hat{P}_N + X_T^1\hat{R}_e. \tag{22}$$

By setting $e = 1$, equation (22) shows explicitly that the welfare of migrants-cum-relatives is most likely to rise with emigration since $(dX_T^1 + \bar{P}dX_N^1) > 0$, representing the gain in output obtained from the capital accumulated through investment remittances, and $\hat{R}_1 > 0$, depicting the emigrants' consumption remittances. The second term in (22) is: $-\bar{P}D_N^1\hat{P}_N < 0$ (since $X_N^1 = 0$ for migrants-cum-relatives, on the assumption that the migrants' relatives do not engage in production in the source country) and shows that the real income gains of migrants are trimmed-down by the impact of emigration in raising non-traded goods prices. Whatever the nominal gains obtained by migrants-cum-relatives in the form of remittances, their real value is reduced by the non-traded goods inflation.

The impact of emigration on non-migrant welfare can be determined from (22) by setting $e = 2$. Note that $\hat{R}_2 = 0$ and $dX_T^2 + \bar{P}dX_N^2 = 0$, on the definition that non-migrants are that part of the population not receiving remittances, whether of the consumption or the investment type. This yields:

$$dU^2 = \bar{P}(X_N^2 - D_N^2)\hat{P}_N \tag{22'}$$

showing that non-migrant welfare can be affected by emigration only in so far as it changes non-traded goods prices. To specify more clearly the overall impact of emigration on non-migrant welfare we decompose the effects into those occurring in the absence of remittances, $d\bar{U}^2$, and those connected to remittances, $d\tilde{U}^2$. The welfare effects in the absence of remittances are determined by setting

$\hat{P}_N = \hat{P}_N^0$ in equation (22′), with $\hat{P}_N^0$ as determined in the preceding section above. We obtain:

$$d\bar{U}^2 = \bar{P}(\bar{X}_N^2 - \bar{D}_N^2) = \frac{\bar{P}(\bar{X}_N^2 - \bar{D}_N^2)}{|\lambda|(\sigma_D + \sigma_s)}\hat{L} < 0 \tag{23}$$

where $\bar{X}_N^2$ and $\bar{D}_N^2$ are the output of and demand for non-traded goods on the part of non-migrants in the pre-migration regime. Note that $|\lambda| < 0$ and $(\bar{X}_N^2 - \bar{D}_N^2) < 0$ on the assumption that non-traded goods are relatively labour-intensive. Therefore, as Rivera-Batiz (1982) has noted, emigration reduces the welfare of non-migrants. This is illustrated in Figure 6.1, where T′T′ depicts the transformation curve facing non-migrants in the source country. The consumption and production points are C and A in the pre-migration regime, implying that the non-migrants are importing non-traded goods from the potential (future) emigrants. Of course, with emigration (and in the absence of remittances) this internal trade disappears and the non-migrant equilibrium must then lie at point E′, with equality of their demand for and supply of non-traded goods. The reduction in non-migrant welfare is depicted by the shift of the social indifference curve from UU to U′U′. Of course, what we are interested in this article is how remittances alter this result.

Since non-migrants do not receive transfers from abroad ($R_2 = 0$), the channel through which remittances would affect non-migrant welfare is by altering prices in the economy. Therefore, let us suppose that there were no remittances and that we compare welfare without remittances with that obtained with remittances. What would be the difference? As specified in the last section, the change in non-traded good prices implied by remittances is $(\hat{P}_N - \hat{P}_N^0)$. Therefore, from (22′), the change in non-migrant welfare would be:

$$\begin{aligned} d\tilde{U}^2 &= \bar{P}(\tilde{X}_N^2 - \tilde{D}_N^2)(\hat{P}_N - \hat{P}_N^0) \\ &= -\bar{P}(\tilde{X}_N^2 - \tilde{D}_N^2)\frac{\Omega|\lambda|\frac{\theta_{LY}}{\theta_{TY}}\gamma_R^k(1+\hat{W}^*) - (1-\Omega)\frac{W^*}{r^*}\frac{\bar{L}}{\bar{K}}\gamma_R^k}{|\lambda|(\sigma_D + \sigma_S)}\hat{L} > 0 \end{aligned} \tag{24}$$

where $\tilde{X}_N^2$ and $\tilde{D}_N^2$ represent the output of and demand for non-traded goods on the part of non-migrants when the economy's equilibrium with remittances is achieved. These are specified by points B and H in Figure 6.1 for the particular case of investment remittances, although the same type of impact could be discerned if consumption remittances were also included. Equation (24) suggests that remittances increase non-migrant welfare. This might sound implausible given that non-traded goods' prices rise with remittances, which (by itself) tends to reduce the real income of non-migrants. What must be understood, however, is that the migratory process makes non-migrants net "exporters" of non-traded goods within the economy. The rising non-traded goods prices induce non-migrants to raise their production, and reduce their consumption, of non-traded goods. The net "exports" of non-traded goods on the part of non-migrants ($\tilde{X}_N^2 - \tilde{D}_N^2 > 0$) represent internal trade that the non-migrants engage in with the migrants-cum-relatives in the presence of remittances. The migrants-cum-relatives trade part of their traded goods remittances (or part of the traded goods they earn from the use of their capital goods remittances) in exchange for an "import" of non-traded goods from the non-migrants. This internal trade raises the welfare of non-migrants and is what equation (24) represents; it is depicted by the gain in non-migrant welfare implied by U″U″ relative to U′U′ in Figure 6.1.

The conclusion is that, under the assumptions, non-migrants welfare is raised by emigrants' remittances and, as a consequence, the net welfare impact of emigration on non-migrants might be positive, as the case shown in Figure 6.1. The exact expression for the net change in non-migrant welfare is:

$$dU^2 = d\tilde{U}^2 + d\bar{U}^2$$

$$\bar{P}(\bar{X}_N^2 - \bar{D}_N^2) - \bar{P}(\tilde{X}_N^2 - \tilde{D}_N^2)$$

$$= \frac{\left[|\lambda|\Omega\frac{\theta_{LY}}{\theta_{TY}}\gamma_R^k(1+\hat{W}^*) - (1-\Omega)\frac{W^*}{r^*}\frac{\bar{L}}{\bar{K}}\gamma_R^k\right]}{|\lambda|(\sigma_D + \sigma_s)}\hat{L} \qquad (25)$$

whose sign is dependent on an array of parameters relating to the volume and type of remittances, the internal trade pattern of non-migrants, and the effect of emigration on non-traded goods prices. It is the task of future work to specify the actual values of the parameters involved in equation (25) with respect to particular cases of emigration from developing countries.

Notice that the gain obtained by non-migrants through the increase in non-traded goods prices is closely connected to the loss in real income that this change in prices causes the migrants-cum-relatives. In other words, part of the real income gains obtained by emigrants abroad and spent in the source country end up in the hands of non-migrants through the non-traded goods price hike mechanism. It should be emphasized, though, that associated with these gains is a major shift of the internal trade pattern of non-migrants, transforming them from net buyers to net sellers of non-traded goods within the economy. The social implications of this transformation and of the conflicts involved in local consumption spending have often been noted in the sociological literature on return migration.

6.4 Conclusions

This article has examined the effects of emigration in the source country, integrating the analysis of permanent and temporary migration and of consumption and investment remittances. Notwithstanding the particular differences in quantitative impact that we have found, there are some general conclusions that tend to hold independently of the particular type of migratory process considered. First, emigration tends to raise home (non-traded) goods prices and remittances reinforce this impact. Secondly, emigration turns income distribution in favour of labour and against capital; remittances (whether intended for consumption or investment purposes) again reinforce this pattern. Finally, although remittances provide a net gain to migrants and their relatives, their real impact is diminished by the home goods' price increase they ignite. The net balance of remittances on non-migrant welfare is positive, as they generate internal trade (within the economy) between migrants and non-migrants; the mechanism through which non-migrants benefit is the increase in the relative price of non-traded goods, which redistributes real income from the migrants to non-migrants.

The framework developed in this article to analyze emigration and emigrants' remittances is a simplified one, intended to illustrate some basic aspects of emigration. And additional issue not discussed in the present article (or in the literature noted in the introduction, for that matter) is the increased variability of income that emigration imposes on the source country. When a significant fraction of the labour force is working abroad and a substantial amount of national income is derived from this migration, source country income becomes subject to the vagaries of labour market behavior in the host countries. Not only does a large fraction of source country income become dependent on employment and income conditions in the host countries but it also becomes subject to the uncertainty of immigration policy changes in those countries and/or the risk that exchange controls on the outflow of remittances might be imposed. Drastic, rapid changes in immigration policy have been repeatedly observed during the history of the industrialized countries. In the US, the sudden end of the Bracero program of temporary Mexican-US migration in 1964 imposed massive adjustments costs along Mexico's border areas and stimulated illegal flows of migrants to the US.[14] But when illegal immigration is difficult (as in some West European countries), the shock of immigration policy changes on source countries can be even more severe. For instance, the boom in the guest worker population in Europe during the 1960s and early 1970s became a bust in the mid- and late-1970s. From September 1973 to September 1978 alone, there was a decline in the number of foreign workers in Germany of 661,000 and 234,000 in Switzerland.[15] Such fluctuations in the foreign demand for labour (and in the associated remittances) raise the variability of real income in source countries, imposing adjustment costs not reflected in figures showing average income gains.[16] Future work must incorporate an evaluation of these costs into the analysis of the welfare impact of emigration.[17]

6.5 Appendix

This appendix sketches the derivations behind the main algebraic results in the text. Firstly, to derive equation (10) note that:

$$\hat{R} = \frac{R}{X_T} = \frac{\Omega\gamma_R^k(W^*/P_T)d\bar{L}}{X_T} = -\Omega\gamma_R^k\frac{\theta_{LY}}{\theta_{TY}}(1+\hat{W}^*)\hat{L}.$$

To derive equation (12), differentiate equations (1), (2), (4) and (5) totally:

$$\lambda_{LN}\hat{X}_N + \lambda_{LT}\hat{X}_T = \hat{L} - [\lambda_{LN}\hat{a}_{LN} + \lambda_{LT}\hat{a}_{LT}] \qquad (1A)$$

$$\lambda_{KN}\hat{X}_N + \lambda_{KT}\hat{X}_T = \hat{K} - [\lambda_{KN}\hat{a}_{KN} + \lambda_{KT}\hat{a}_{KT}] \qquad (2A)$$

$$\theta_{LN}\hat{w} + \theta_{KN}\hat{r} = \hat{P}_N - [\theta_{LN}\hat{a}_{LN} + \theta_{KN}\hat{a}_{KN}] \qquad (3A)$$

$$\theta_{LT}\hat{w} + \theta_{KT}\hat{r} = \hat{P}_T - [\theta_{LT}\hat{a}_{LT} + \theta_{KT}\hat{a}_{KT}] \qquad (4A)$$

with λ_{ij} equal to the proportion of the ith factor employed in the jth commodity (so that $\lambda_{iN} + \lambda_{iT} = 1$), and θ_{ij} is the share of the ith factor in the total earnings of the jth commodity (so that $\theta_{Lj} + \theta_{Kj} = 1$). Also, costs are minimized if the first derivative of unit costs is set equal to zero, so:

$$wa_{LN}\hat{a}_{LN} + ra_{KN}\hat{a}_{KN} = 0$$

$$\text{and} \quad wa_{LT}\hat{a}_{LT} + ra_{KT}\hat{a}_{KT} = 0.$$

Dividing the equations by P_j:

$$\theta_{LN}\hat{a}_{LN} + \theta_{KN}\hat{a}_{KN} = 0 \qquad (5A)$$

$$\theta_{LT}\hat{a}_{LT} + \theta_{KT}\hat{a}_{KT} = 0 \qquad (6A)$$

where $\hat{a}_{ij} = \frac{da_{ij}}{a_{ij}} = \frac{1}{a_{ij}}\frac{\delta a_{ij}}{\delta\omega}d\omega$, so that the elasticity of factor substitution in the jth sector is given by:

$$\sigma_i = \frac{\hat{a}_{Kj} - \hat{a}_{ij}}{\hat{w} - \hat{r}} \qquad (7A)$$

and, substituting (7A) into (5A) and (6A):

$$\hat{a}_{Lj} = -\theta_{K_j}\sigma_j(\hat{w} - \hat{r}), \quad j = N, T \qquad (8A)$$

$$\hat{a}_{Kj} = \theta_{L_j}\sigma_j(\hat{w} - \hat{r}), \quad j = N, T \qquad (9A)$$

The relationships in (8A) and (9A) can then be substituted into (1A)–(4A) to obtain:

$$\lambda_{LN}\hat{X}_N + \lambda_{LT}\hat{X}_T = \hat{L} + \beta_L(\hat{w} - \hat{r}), \qquad (10A)$$

$$\lambda_{KN}\hat{X}_N + \lambda_{KT}\hat{X}_T = \hat{K} + \beta_K(\hat{w} - \hat{r}), \qquad (11A)$$

$$\theta_{LN}\hat{w} + \theta_{KN}\hat{r} = \hat{P}_N \tag{12A}$$

$$\theta_{LT}\hat{w} + \theta_{KT}\hat{r} = \hat{P}_T \tag{13A}$$

where

$$\beta_L = \lambda_{LN}\theta_{KN}\sigma_N + \lambda_{LT}\theta_{KT}\sigma_T$$

$$\beta_K = \lambda_{KN}\theta_{LN}\sigma_N + \lambda_{KT}\theta_{LT}\sigma_T.$$

Differentiating totally the demand functions in equations (6) and (7) of the text yields:

$$\hat{D}_N = -\eta_{PN}(\hat{P}_N - \hat{P}_T) + \eta_{YN}\hat{Y} \tag{14A}$$

$$\hat{D}_T = \eta_{PT}(\hat{P}_N - \hat{P}_T) + \eta_{YT}\hat{Y} \tag{15A}$$

where $\eta_{PN} \equiv -\frac{P}{D_N}\frac{\delta D_N}{\delta P}$ and $\eta_{PT} \equiv -\frac{P}{D_T}\frac{\delta D_T}{\delta P}$, are the price elasticities of demand, and $\eta_{Yj} \equiv \frac{Y}{D_j}\frac{\delta D_j}{\delta Y}$ are the income elasticities of demand for the jth commodity (with $j = T,\, N$).

Now, subtracting (15A) from (14A) gives us:

$$\hat{D}_N - \hat{D}_T = -\sigma_D(\hat{P}_N - \hat{P}_T) + (\eta_{YN} - \eta_{YT})\hat{Y} \tag{16A}$$

where $\sigma_D \equiv \eta_{PN} + \eta_{PT}$, which is the so-called elasticity of demand substitution (which has to be positive since both η_{PN} and η_{PT} are positive).

Subtracting (10A) from (11A) and (13A) from (12A) we obtain:

$$|\lambda|(\hat{X}_N - \hat{X}_T) = \hat{K} - \hat{L} - (\hat{W} - \hat{r})(\beta_k + \beta_L) \tag{17A}$$

$$\text{and} \quad |\theta|(\hat{W} - \hat{r}) = \hat{P}_T - \hat{P}_N \tag{18A}$$

where

$$|\lambda| = \lambda_{LT}\lambda_{KN} - \lambda_{LN}\lambda_{KT} = \frac{L_T L_N}{\bar{L}\bar{K}}(k_N - k_T)$$

and where $k_N = K_N/L_N$, $k_T = K_T/L_T$, and $|\theta|$ is given by

$$|\theta| = \theta_{LT}\theta_{KN} - \theta_{LN}\theta_{KT} = \frac{wrL_T L_N}{P_T X_T P_N X_N}(k_N - k_T).$$

Substituting (18A) into (17A) we get:

$$\hat{X}_N - \hat{X}_T = \frac{\hat{K} - \hat{L}}{|\lambda|} + \sigma_s(\hat{P}_N - \hat{P}_T) \tag{19A}$$

where:

$$\sigma_s \equiv \frac{\hat{X}_N - \hat{X}_T}{\hat{P}_N - \hat{P}_T} = \frac{\beta_K + \beta_L}{|\lambda||\theta|},$$

which is the Jones' elasticity of commodity substitution along the transformation curve. Noting that, from equations (6) and (9):

$$\hat{D}_N - \hat{D}_T = \hat{X}_N - \hat{X}_T - \hat{R} \tag{20A}$$

and using equations (16A) and (19A):

$$-\sigma_D(\hat{P}_N - \hat{P}_T) + (\eta_{YN} - \eta_{YT})\hat{Y} = \frac{\hat{\bar{K}} - \hat{\bar{L}}}{|\lambda|} + \sigma_s(\hat{P}_N - \hat{P}_T) - \hat{R}. \tag{21A}$$

For simplicity, our analysis in the second section of this article assumes that traded goods price are fixed ($\hat{P}_T = 0$), and that both emigrants and non-migrants have identical, homothetic preferences, so that $\eta_{YN} = \eta_{YT}$. Equation (21A) can therefore be simplified to

$$\begin{aligned}\hat{P}_T &= \frac{\hat{L} - \hat{K}}{|\lambda|(\sigma_D + \sigma_s)} + \frac{\hat{R}}{\sigma_D + \sigma_s} \\ &= \frac{\left[1 - \Omega|\lambda|\frac{\theta_{LY}}{\theta_{TY}}\gamma_R^k(1 + \hat{W}^*) + (1 - \Omega)\frac{W^*}{r^*}\frac{\bar{L}}{\bar{K}}\gamma_R^k\right]\hat{L}}{|\lambda|(\sigma_D + \sigma_s)}\end{aligned} \tag{22A}$$

where use has been made of equations (10) and (11).

Using equations (12A) and (13A), we can derive the effects of emigration on income distribution:

$$\hat{W} = -\frac{\theta_{KT}\hat{P}_N}{|\theta|} \tag{23A}$$

$$\hat{r} = \frac{\theta_{LT}\hat{P}_N}{|\theta|} \tag{24A}$$

$$\hat{W} - \hat{P}_N = -\frac{\theta_{KN}}{|\theta|}\hat{P}_N \tag{25A}$$

$$\hat{r} - \hat{P}_N = \frac{\theta_{LN}\hat{P}_N}{|\theta|}. \tag{26A}$$

Substitution of (22A) into (23A)–(26A) determines the corresponding equations in the text.

Notes:

[1]The figures in Table 6.1 measure only cash remittances reported through official channels. Many migrants, however, transfer their remittances in kind, in the form of merchandise goods. For instance, World Bank estimates for Pakistan indicate that as much as 17 per cent of migrants' remittances are in kind (Chandavarkar, 1980, p. 37); and a recent study of Caribbean cane cutters in Florida indicates that 24 per cent of total remittances is repatriated directly in the form of merchandise (Wood and McCoy, 1985, p. 274). In addition, a large fraction of cash remittances usually goes unreported. This is so, first, because many countries do not require that cash remittances below specified limits be reported, but a large share of remittances is sent back to source countries precisely in the form of relatively small, but frequent, periodical sums. Secondly, in countries like the Dominican Republic and Mexico, the illegal flow of labour and goods to and from the United States does not permit accurate reporting of remittances. In these cases, estimates of the value of remittances will be highly unreliable. For example, estimates of the number of illegal aliens in the United States range from 2 to 11 million. Based on these differences, and on an array of other parameters that influence remittances, guesses about the value of the annual remittances of illegal Mexican migrants in the US ranges from $1.5 billion (North and Houstoun, 1976) up to $4 billion (Johnson, 1984).

[2]Kirwan and Holden (1986, p. 3).

[3]See also the work of Lundahl (1985).

[4]Piore (1979, p. 124).

[5]See Chandarvakar (1980), Serageldin *et al.* (1983, Chapter 9) and Richards and Martin (1983, pp. 467–468) for a discussion of remittances in the interregional flow of migrants in the Middle East. In their recent study of English Caribbean temporary migration to the US, Wood and McCoy (1985, p. 274) report that "remittances are used primarily for consumption purposes".

[6]See Thompson (1984), Rivera-Batiz (1984), Djacic (1986), Kirwan and Holden (1986), and Lundahl (1985).

[7]The remittances of temporary migrants are equal to their total income abroad minus that share of income allocated to subsistence consumption expenditures in the host country.

[8]For simplicity, we assume that the fraction of remittances allocated to investment spending is fixed. To endogenise it would require an inter-temporal framework, with parameters such as the inter-temporal rate of substitution in consumption and the real interest rate determining Ω.

[9]Although in the present article we are not concerned with the explicit factors influencing γ'_R and γ_R^P, in a more specialized setting one would like to look further to examine how the altruistic behavior of the emigrants and/or the implicit inter-temporal contractual arrangements between emigrants and their families in the source country determine them; for a discussion and evidence on this issue, see Stark and Bloom (1985), and Lucas and Stark (1985).

[10]To simplify, it is assumed that the remittances are used to purchase capital goods in international markets; an alternative is to consider a gestation period through which a process of domestic capital accumulation occurs. Note also the implicit assumption of zero international capital mobility. Though capital controls and equity restrictions do impose severe constraints on direct foreign investment in some developing countries, this assumption should be relaxed in future work.

[11]A large share of non-traded goods production consists of services. Available evidence indicates that, particularly in developing countries (from which the emigration analyzed in this article occurs) services are relatively labour-intensive. See Kravis, Heston and Summers (1983, Table 12).

[12]See equation (A.8) in Rivera-Batiz (1982, p. 88) for comparison purposes.

[13]We should note that neither Djajic nor Kirwan and Holden derive reduced-form expressions for the impact of emigration, on any variables, in the source country. Kirwan and Holden provide, however, a partial analysis of the welfare impact of temporary migration, and Lundahl (1985) examines the impact of consumption remittances on home goods prices and income distribution.

[14]See Cornelius (1979, p. 8).

[15]See Bohning (1979).

[16]The marked variability of emigrants' remittances in the Middle East and the fall in the flow from Europe to some Mediterranean countries in the late 1970s is noted by Serageldin *et al.* (1983, p. 91).

[17]For a discussion of the issues regarding fluctuations in the demand for temporary migrant workers from a host-country perspective, see Ethier (1985).

References

Birks, J. S. and Sinclair, C. A., *International Migration and Development in the Arab Region*, International Labour Office, Geneva, 1980.

Bohning, W. B., "International Migration in Western Europe: Reflections on the Past Five Years", *International Labour Review*, 118, No. 4, 1979, pp. 401–414.

Chandarvakar, A. G., "Uses of Migrants' Remittances in Labor-Exporting Countries", *Finance and Development*, 17, No. 2. 1980, pp. 36–39.

Cornelius, W., "Mexican Migration to the United States: Causes, Consequences and U.S. Responses", MIT Migration and Development Study Group, Discussion Paper No. C178–9, Massachusetts Institute of Technology, 1979.

Diez-Canedo, J., "Migration, Return and Development in Mexico," Ph.D. thesis, Department of Economics, Massachusetts Institute of Technology, 1980.

Djajic S., "International Migration, Remittances and Welfare in a Dependent Economy", *Journal of Development Economics*, 21, No. 2, 229–234, 1986.

Ethier, W., "International Trade and Labor Migration", *American Economic Review*, 75, No. 4, 1985, pp. 691–707.

Johnson, K. F., *Mexican Democracy: A Critical View*, New York, Praeger Special Studies, 1984.

Kirwan, F. and Holden, D., "Emigrants Remittances, Non-traded Goods and Economic Welfare in the Source Country," *Journal of Economic Studies*, 13, 1986.

Kravis, I., Heston, A. and Summers, R., "The Share of Services in Economic Growth", in Adams, F. G. and Hickman, B. (Eds.), *Global Econometrics: Essays in Honour of Lawrence R. Klein*, Cambridge, Massachusetts, MIT Press, 1983.

Lucas, R. E. B. and Stark, O., "Motivations to Remit: Evidence from Botswana," *Journal of Political Economy*, 93, No. 5, 1985, pp. 901–918.

Lundahl, M., "International Migration, Remittance and Real Incomes: Effects on the Source Country," *Scandinavian Journal of Economics*, 87, No. 4, pp. 647–657, 1985.

Mines, R. C., "Network Migration and Mexican Rural Development: A Case Study", in Jones, R. C. (Ed.), *Patterns of Undocumented Migration, Mexico and the United States*, New Jersey, Rowman and Allanheld, 1984.

North, D. and Houstoun, M., *The Characteristics and Role of Illegal Aliens in the U.S. Labor Market: An Exploratory Study*, Washington, DC, Linton and Company, Inc., 1976.

Papademetriou, D. G., "Issues and Reality in International Migration: Migration and Development in PostWorld War II Greece", *International Migration*, 23, No. 3/4, 1985, pp. 211–223.

Piore, M., *Birds of Passage, Migrant Labor and Industrial Societies*, Cambridge, Cambridge University Press, 1979.

Richards, A. and Martin, P. L., "The Laissez-Faire Approach to International Labor Migration: The Case of the Arab Middle East", *Economic Development and Cultural Change*, 31, No. 3, 1983.

Rivera-Batiz, F., "International Migration, Non-traded Goods and Economic Welfare in the Source Country", *Journal of Development Economics*, 11, No. 1, 1982, pp. 81–90.

Rivera-Batiz, F., "International Migration, Non-traded Goods and Economic Welfare in a Two-Class Economy", *Journal of Development Economics*, 16, No. 3, 1984, pp. 325–330.

Serageldin, I., Socknat, J. A., Birks, S., Li, B. and Sinclair, C., *Manpower and International Labor Migration in the Middle East and North Africa*, Oxford, Oxford University Press, 1983.

Stark, O. and Bloom, D. E., "The New Economics of Labor Migration", *American Economic Review*, 75, No. 2, 1985, pp. 173–178.

Thompson, H., "International Migration, Non-traded Goods and Economic Welfare in the Source Country: Comment", *Journal of Development Economics*, 16, No. 3, 1984, pp. 321–325.

Wood, C. H. and McCoy, T., "Migration, Remittances and Development: A Study of Caribbean Cane Cutters in Florida", *International Migration Review*, 19, No. 2, 1985, pp. 251–277.

Chapter 7

International Migration, Non-Traded Goods and Economic Welfare in a Two-Class Economy: A Reply*

7.1 Introduction

In his comment on my international migration paper, Professor Thompson has extended my analysis in Rivera-Batiz (1982) to encompass the effects of emigration on the real income of source-country capital and labor. The two factors of production are considered to be separate groups, each consuming different fractions of traded and nontraded goods. As a result, Thompson argues that emigration may actually reduce real labor income in the source country, in spite of the fact that labor outflows tend to raise domestic nominal wage rates. This is because in the framework considered, emigration also leads to increases in the prices of nontraded goods thus causing a possible reduction in real wages. Still, Thompson's comment appears only to scratch the surface of the issues it raises, which regard the problem of the impact of emigration in a multiple agent situation. It

*This chapter was originally published in the *Journal of Development Economics*, Vol. 16, No. 3 (December 1984), pp. 325–330.

This paper was written while I was a Visiting Post-Doctoral Fellow in International Economics at the Department of Economics of the University of Chicago. The support of a grant from the National Research Council of the National Academy of Sciences is gratefully acknowledged.

is the purpose of this reply to develop a more general approach to the problem, to put some flesh on its bare bones, so to speak.

7.2 Modeling a Two-Class Economy

The basic consideration to be examined surrounds the presence of differences in tastes and/or endowments among agents in the economy, a matter usually shoved under the rug by the one-consumer assumption implicit in the use of aggregate utility functions. To capture this type of effect, a model of emigration is developed below for an economy in which two classes of individuals exist. This is clearly the simplest model in which multiple agent considerations can be analyzed, but as Mirrlees notes, it 'is sufficiently rich in possibilities to be worth examining, for it captures in a crude way many of the two-way distinctions that strike one as interesting and relevant — rich and poor, capitalists and workers, urban and rural dwellers, etc'.[1]

Before anything else, it should be clear that both Thompson's and the following model are built on the implicit assumption that the economy is originally at a locally stable equilibrium and that the comparative statics undertaken are in the form of small, local variations in the neighborhood of this equilibrium. This is not trivial since the model under consideration does not guarantee the uniqueness of competitive equilibrium. The reason is because, instead of an aggregate concave utility function from which nicely behaved demand functions can be obtained, the two-agent economy presumes the presence of two sets of preferences whose aggregation does not preclude the crisscrossing of aggregate excess demand and excess supply functions and, thus, multiple equilibria.[2]

The main component of my 1982 paper to be revised involves the demand functions for traded and non-traded goods. Instead of there being an aggregate demand function for each commodity [Eqs. (A.6) and (A.7) in my earlier article], there are now two demand functions corresponding to each of the two classes under consideration. These differing demand functions generate differences in the proportion of each commodity consumed by each class. Assuming homothetic utility functions, the demand functions for non-traded and traded goods of each class $m (m = 1, 2)$, D_N^m and D_T^m respectively, are given by

$$P_N D_N^m = \theta_N^m(P) Y_m, \quad (1)$$

and

$$D_T^m = [1 - \theta_N^m(P)] Y_m, \quad (2)$$

where θ_N^m represents the fraction of the mth class income spent on non-traded goods, which is a function of $P \equiv P_N/P_T$, the ratio of non-traded to traded goods prices; and where Y_m equals each class' nominal income. The nominal income of each class is generally composed of both wage and capital income, or

$$Y_m = rK_m + WL_m, \quad (3)$$

with r and W the factor prices on capital and labor, and (K_m/L_m) the factor endowments of class m. Observe that Thompson's framework forms a special case of the present approach with the two classes being capitalists (with $K_1 = \bar{K}$, $L_1 = 0$) and workers (with $K_2 = 0$, $L_2 = \bar{L}$), where $\bar{K}$ is the economy-wide capital endowment and $\bar{L}$ is labor's.

Combining Eqs. (1) and (2) for each class, the aggregate demand for each commodity is then given by

$$P_N D_N \equiv P_N(D_N^1 + D_N^2) = \theta_N^1(P) Y_1 + \theta_N^2(P) Y_2 \quad (4)$$

and

$$D_T \equiv (D_T^1 + D_T^2) = \theta_T^1(P) Y_1 + \theta_T^2(P) Y_2. \quad (5)$$

Equations (4) and (5) can be differentiated totally, and the second one subtracted from the first, to obtain:

$$D_N^* - D_T^* = -\sigma_D P_N^* + \left(\frac{D_N^1}{D_N} - \frac{D_T^1}{D_T}\right)(Y_1^* - Y_2^*), \quad (6)$$

where $\sigma_D \equiv 1 - (Y/D_T)(D_N^1 \varepsilon_{N1}/D_N + D_N^2 \varepsilon_{N2}/D_N) > 0$ is the aggregate elasticity of commodity substitution, representing the substitutability between traded and non-traded goods in consumption given fixed levels of income and its distribution. As observed the value of σ_D in a two-class framework is dependent on the price elasticities of the non-traded goods consumption share of each class, defined by $\varepsilon_{Nm} = (\partial\theta_N^m/\partial P)(P/\theta_N^m)$, which are assumed to be negative. The more price elastic the non-traded goods shares are, the more responsive the demand for non-traded goods will be and the larger the resulting value of the aggregate elasticity of substitution. In addition, the larger the fraction of non-traded goods demanded by the class with relatively high elasticity, the more elastic the aggregate commodity substitution elasticity. As a result, in the present framework, the aggregate elasticity of substitution in consumption will depend on the distribution of tastes in the economy, as represented by the differences between the two classes considered.

From the income expressions represented by Eq. (3), it is easy to show that:

$$Y_m^* = \theta_K^m r^* + \theta_L^m W^*, \tag{7}$$

where $\theta_K^m \equiv rK_m/Y_m$ is the share of class m's income received from its earnings on capital, and $\theta_L^m \equiv WL_m/Y_m$ is labor's share on the income of class m.

Substitution of (7) into (6) results in:

$$D_N^* - D_T^* = -\sigma_D P_N^* + \left(\frac{D_N^1}{D_N} - \frac{D_T^1}{D_T}\right)(\theta_K^1 - \theta_K^2)(r^* - W^*). \tag{8}$$

Equation (8) shows how changes in income distribution will affect relative aggregate demands in the economy. For instance, if there is a decrease in the wage-rental ratio, and if the share of class 1's capital income on its total income is larger than class 2's, then this will tend to increase the total income of class 1 relative to the income of class 2. If the proportion of non-traded goods relative to traded goods consumed by class 1 is larger than the economy's (if $D_N^1/D_T^1 > D_N/D_T$), then the shift in income distribution towards class 1 will tend to induce a relative increase in the demand for non-traded goods in the economy, independently of the direct effects of any change in the price of non-traded goods. The overall implication is that the distributional effects of disturbances to the economy, such as emigration, will have to be explicitly taken into account in the comparative statics exercises. Observe that were individuals in the economy to have the same preferences and factor endowments, then the distributional effects would not arise. In terms of Eq. (8), if $D_N/D_T = D_N^1/D_T^1$, and $\theta_K^1 = \theta_K^2$, then the second term disappears. Note also that Thompson's analysis assumes the two classes considered own only capital or labor and, as a result, if class 1 refers to capitalists, then $\theta_K^1 \equiv rK_1/Y_1 = r\bar{K}/Y_1$, and $\theta_K^2 = 0$. The distributional effects of emigration on demand must thus be incorporated into his framework too.

The production structure of the model stays basically unchanged from the one discussed in my earlier paper. As a result, and as is easily shown, emigration of individuals from the economy will cause the following change in the price of non-traded goods:

$$P_N^* = \frac{L^* - K^*}{|\lambda|(\sigma_D + \sigma_S - \sigma_K/|\theta|)}, \quad \text{with } \sigma_S \equiv \frac{X_N^* - X_T^*}{P_N^* - P_T^*} > 0 \tag{9}$$

along the transformation curve,

$$\sigma_K \equiv \left(\frac{D_N^1}{D_N} - \frac{D_T^1}{D_T}\right)(\theta_K^1 - \theta_K^2),$$

$$|\lambda| \equiv \frac{L_T L_N}{LK}(k_N - k_T).$$

$$|\theta| \equiv \frac{wL_N L_T}{P_T X_T P_N X_N},$$

and σ_D as defined above. Equation (9) can be compared with Eq. (A.8) in my earlier paper in this *Journal*. Following Thompson, it is assumed that the non-traded goods sector is relatively labor-intensive and thus $k_T \equiv K_T/L_T$ exceeds $k_N \equiv K_N/L_N$ implying $|\lambda|$ and $|\theta|$ are both negative. In addition, it is assumed individuals of class 1 are capital-rich relative to those of class 2, so that $\theta_K^1 > \theta_K^2$. In this case, the term σ_K is positive if class 1 consumes relatively more non-traded goods than class 2 and negative if less. Observe how the response of the price of non-traded goods to the emigration depends on the distributional effects represented by σ_K. For the present purposes, though, the term $(\sigma_D + \sigma_S - \sigma_K/|\theta|)$ will be assumed to be positive.

7.3 International Migration in a Two-Class Economy

Emigration in the present framework may be of individuals of class 1 or 2, that is, of capital-rich or labor-rich individuals. If labor-rich individuals emigrate (and they take both their capital and labor with them), then the economy's labor endowment will decline proportionally more than its capital endowment. Symbolically, L^* will be larger in absolute value than K^*. The result is a reduction in the economy's aggregate labor-capital ratio ($L^* - K^* < 0$), which causes a Rybczinski-type decline in the output of the labor-intensive non-traded goods, an excess demand for these commodities and a consequent rise in their prices. If emigration of capital-rich individuals occurs, however, the results are exactly the opposite. In this situation, the economy's endowment of capital is reduced proportionally more than the endowment of labor and, as a result the economy's aggregate capital-labor ratio declines ($L^* - K^* > 0$). The effect is a decline in the prices of non-traded goods. Finally, if the migrants abandon the economy but leave their capital behind, such as in the case of temporary migrants planning to return to the source country some time in the future, then the prices of non-traded goods would increase, even if the migrants are members of the capital-rich class (symbolically: $L^* < 0$, but $K^* = 0$).

The impact of emigration on the real income of the non-emigrants must be subdivided into its impact on the two classes in the economy. The real income of class m, y_m is equal to its nominal income, Y_m, divided by an index of the prices of the commodities it consumes, denoted by P_m. Consequently

$$y_m = \frac{Y_m}{P_m} = \frac{rK_m + WL_m}{\theta_N^m P_N + (1 - \theta_N^m)P_T}. \tag{10}$$

Totally differentiating this expression, one obtains:

$$\begin{aligned} y_m^* &= \theta_k^m r^* + (1 - \theta_k^m)W^* - \theta_N^m P_N^* \\ &= [\theta_k^m \beta_{KN} + (1 - \theta_k^m)\beta_{LN} - \theta_N^m]P_N^*, \end{aligned} \tag{11}$$

where $r^* = \beta_{KN} P_N^*$ and $W^* = \beta_{LN} P_N^*$, with $\beta_{KN} = -\theta_{LT}/|\theta| < 0$ and $\beta_{LN} = \theta_{KT}/|\theta| > 0$, and where $|\theta|$ is as defined above, P_N^* is given by Eq. (9), $\theta_{LT} \equiv WL_T/P_TX_T$ and $\theta_{KT} = rK_T/P_TX_T$. The sign of y_m^* clearly depends on the sign of the changes in the prices of non-traded goods and factor prices as well as on the shares of the capital and labor earnings on the income of a given class and the share of a class' income spent on non-traded goods. One special case is the one picked by Thompson, in which one class in the economy owns only capital and the other only labor. With class 1 denoting the 'capitalist' class and class 2 the 'working' class, then $\theta_k^1 = 1$, $\theta_L^1 = 0$, $\theta_k^2 = 0$, and $\theta_L^2 = 1$. From Eq. (11):

$$y_m^* = (\beta_{mN} - \theta_N^m)P_N^*,$$

where $\beta_{mN} = \beta_{KM}$ or β_{LN} if $m = 1$ or 2 respectively. Assuming labor emigrates, then the prices of non-traded goods increase, implying $y_1^* < 0$ but according to Thompson, $y_2^* \lesseqgtr 0$, which are Thompson's results in his Eq. (8). More generally, however, emigration will consist of individuals owning both capital and labor. In this situation, if the emigrants form part of a class 1 endowed with a relatively large fraction of capital — which they take with them — then the prices of the labor-intensive non-traded goods would decline. As a result, the real income of the non-emigrants forming part of the capital-rich class would unambiguously improve, while the impact on the real income of the non-emigrants composing class 2, with relatively larger labor-capital endowments, is ambiguous and may actually decline if the fraction of non-traded goods they consume is small enough.

Notes:

[1]Mirrlees (1975, pp. D–28).

[2]For an example of the resulting multiple equilibria in a two-agent pure exchange economy, see Shapley and Shubik (1977). See also Atkinson and Stiglitz (1980, pp. 188–189).

References

Atkinson, A.B. and J.E. Stiglitz, 1980, *Lectures on public economics* (McGraw-Hill, New York).

Mirrlees, J.A., 1975, "Optimal commodity taxation in a two-class economy," *Journal of Public Economics* 4, 27–33.

Rivera-Batiz, F., 1982, "International migration; non-traded goods and economic welfare in the source country," *Journal of Development Economics* 11, 81–90.
Shapley, L.S. and M. Shubik, 1917, "An example of a trading economy and three competitive equilibria," *Journal of Political Economy* 85, 873–875.
Thompson, H., 1984, "International migration, non-traded goods and economic welfare in the source country: A comment," *Journal of Development Economics*, 16(3), 321–324.

Chapter 8

The Impact of International Migration on Real Wages: Another Look*

8.1 Introduction

In 1982 I wrote a paper in the *Journal of Development Economics* looking at the impact of emigration within a trade-theoretic framework incorporating the economy's nontraded goods — or service — sector. I showed that, assuming nontraded goods are relatively labor-intensive, labor emigration raises nominal wages and lowers the rental rate on capital but reduces the overall economic welfare of those left behind. In his 1984 paper, Thompson postulated that, even though under my assumptions nominal wages would rise with labor emigration, the impact on the real income of labor was ambiguous since nontraded goods prices also increase. In a reply to Thompson, I presumed his conclusion to be correct and questioned instead his modeling of real income considerations in a two-class economy. I proceeded

*This chapter was originally published in the *Journal of Development Economics*, Vol. 31, No. 1 (July 1989), pp. 185–192.

An extended version of section 3 of this paper was presented at the University of Chicago, Indiana University-Bloomington, the University of Texas at Austin and the University of Wisconsin-Madison. The author is grateful to the participants of these seminars for their comments.

to develop a more complete framework, describing explicitly the factor ownership and demand functions of each class and how their introduction alters the discussion.

In his paper, Quibria (1988) reexamines in an innovative way Thompson's analysis concluding that 'there is no ambiguity in the link between emigration and real wages', and that 'the result appears quite robust to different production-side specifications'. Although Quibria is correct in showing that Thompson's argument is defective and that, under the assumptions utilized in that paper, real wages always rise with emigration, I believe that he paints with a broad brush when he extends his criticisms to my 1984 article. Within the framework of my 1984 paper, the conclusion that real wages can decline with emigration continues to hold, as is shown in the next section. In addition, I believe that the connection between emigration and real wages is closely dependent on the production-side specifications of the model utilized. If those specifications are altered to incorporate, for instance, increasing returns, emigration can reduce real wages. It is the purpose of section 3 to prove this point.

8.2 Emigration and Real Wages in a Two-Class Economy

In my 1984 paper, I state a model that explicitly distinguishes between two kinds of individuals, or classes, on the basis of differences in demand patterns and ownership of factors of production. One class (class 1) is assumed to possess a ratio of capital to labor higher than the average while the other class (class 2) has a lower ratio. If we denote the economy's endowments of capital and pure labor by K and L, then the assumption made is that $K_1/L_1 > K/L > K_2/L_2$. In addition, for simplicity, the capital-rich class is assumed to spend a larger proportion of their income on non-traded goods. Within this context, emigration can either raise or lower real wages or real income, depending on what type of individual emigrates and on whether they take away all the factors they own when they migrate.

Consider the impact of emigration on the real income of a given class, m Within the model established in my 1984 paper [see its

Eqs. (9) and (11)], this is given by

$$y_m^* = [\theta_k^m \beta_{kN} + (1 - \theta_k^m)\beta_{LN} - \theta_N^m] P_N^*$$
$$y_m^* = \frac{\theta_k^m \beta_{kN} + (1 - \theta_k^m)\beta_{LN} - \theta_N^m}{|\lambda|(\sigma_D + \sigma_S - \frac{\sigma_k}{|\theta|})}(L^* - K^*), \qquad (1)$$

where

y_m = real income of class m,
P_N = the price of non-traded goods,
L = the economy's supply of pure labor,
K = the supply of capital,
θ_k^m = the share of income received by class m on its holdings of capital,
θ_N^m = the fraction of income that class m spends on non-traded goods,
$|\lambda| = (L_T L_N / LK)(k_N - k_T)$, with $k_j = K_j/L_j$, where L_j and K_j denote the labor and capital used in sector j.
$|\theta| = (WrL_N L_T / P_T X_T P_N X_N)(k_N - k_T)$, where P_j and X_j are the price and output of good j, W and r are wage and rental rates, and $\sigma_k = [(D_N^1/D_N) - (D_T^1/D_T)](\theta_k^1 - \theta_k^2)$, with D_j^1 denoting the demand for sector-j goods, and 0; the demand for sector-j goods on the part of class 1

and σ_D and σ_S are the aggregate elasticities of substitution in consumption and production [as defined by Jones (1965) and applied in the present model by Rivera-Batiz (1984)]. Asterisks denote proportional changes. Note that

$$|\theta| < 0, \quad |\lambda| < 0, \quad \sigma_D < 0, \quad \sigma_s > 0, \quad \sigma_K > 0$$
$$\beta_{LN} = -rK_T/P_T X_T |\theta| > 0, \quad \text{and} \quad \beta_{KN} = WL_T/P_T X_T |\theta| < 0$$

under standard, neoclassical assumptions regarding production, and given the restrictions placed earlier on the distribution of tastes and factor endowments and on relative factor intensities.

Both Thompson and Quibria examine the effects of pure labor emigration on the real income of labor, in which case, in Eq. (1): $m = 2$, $\theta_k^2 = 0$, $L^* < 0$, and $K^* = 0$. The impact of emigration then hinges on the sign of the term $(\beta_{LN} - \theta_k^2)$. The confusion in Thompson's paper — that I transmitted into my paper — can be traced algebraically to his assumption that the parameter β_{LN} could be less than one. If that were so, emigration of pure labor ($L^* < 0$, $K^* = 0$), could result in lower real wages ($y_2^* < 0$). As Quibria correctly notes, β_{LN} is always larger than one. Emigration of pure labor then always raises real wages.

Note, however, that both Quibria and Thompson assume that each class owns only labor or capital but not both. Emigration reduces the economy's labor force but not its capital endowment. High-income emigrants, though, often withdraw their wealth from the country from which they migrate. In addition, if one thinks of capital as including human capital, the emigration of skilled workers implies a joint flight of labor and human capital from the economy. The brain drain can thus be visualized as consisting of the emigration of labor and human capital bundled together. Analyzing this issue was indeed the purpose of my 1984 paper. But, within its context, emigration may or may not raise real income, as Eq. (1) clearly shows. Suppose, for example, that capital-rich individuals (that is, persons in class 1) emigrate. This lowers the economy's capital-labor ratio, and pulls down the wage-rental ratio. As a result, the real income of labor-rich individuals can decrease with the emigration [in terms of Eq. (1), if $L^* - K^* > 0$, and θ_k^2 is small enough, then, $y_2^* < 0$]. An extreme example of this occurs when class 1 is assumed to own only capital and class 2 only pure labor [$\theta_k^2 = 0$ in Eq. (1)]. If members of class 1 emigrate, then $L^* = 0$ and $K^* < 0$ and, given that the denominator in Eq. (1) is negative and $(\beta_{LN} - \theta_k^2)$ is positive, the effect on real wages (the real income of class 2) is unambiguously negative, that is, $y_2^* < 0$.

Summarizing, I have shown that, in contrast to Thompson's paper, my 1984 model can sustain a negative connection between emigration and real wages. There is, therefore, nothing wrong in the way the problem was posed or analyzed in my paper. There is, however, in my explanation of Thompson's results an error in assuming that this ambiguity extends to the particular case discussed by Thompson. It does not, as Quibria clearly shows.

8.3 Increasing Returns, Emigration and Real Wages

In his paper, Quibria states that the positive connection between emigration and real wages that he obtains would withstand production side modifications. It is argued here that, if the supply side of his model is modified to incorporate increasing returns, real wages can be negatively related to emigration.

We introduce increasing returns into the production side of the non-traded goods sector. Given the standard assumption — followed by all the papers mentioned earlier — that non-traded goods are relatively labor-intensive, we simplify by assuming that firms in this sector use only labor as an input. The labor requirements of each firm k producing non-traded goods, L_{KN}, given by

$$L_{KN} = \gamma + \beta X_{kN}, \tag{2}$$

where γ represents a fixed labor requirement and β is equal to a variable unit labor requirement. For simplicity, it is assumed that all firms use the same technology (identical γ and β parameters).

With the labor requirements depicted by (2), each firm's total costs are equal to WL_{KN}. Average costs are then given by $AC_k = W\beta + W\gamma/X_{kN}$, which decline with output reflecting the presence of internal economies of scale [this follows the structure of the monopolistic competition model developed by Krugman (1979)]. Note also that marginal costs are equal to $W\beta$.

Each non-traded goods producer maximizes profits by setting marginal cost equal to marginal revenue. Marginal revenue is given by

$$MR_k = P_{kN}[1 - (1/\varepsilon_k)], \tag{3}$$

where $\varepsilon_k = -(P_{kN}/C_k)(\partial C_k/\partial P_{kN})$ is the price elasticity of demand facing firm k, P_{kN} is the price it sets, and C_k is the aggregate demand for the firm's product.

To determine the elasticity of demand, ε_k, one must specify the preferences of consumers towards non-traded goods as well as the market structure in that sector. With respect to the latter, it is assumed that firms supply differentiated products in a market structure of free-entry oligopoly or oligopolistic competition [see Hart (1985)]. Each oligopolistic producer is also considered to act strategically in a Cournot–Nash fashion, conjecturing that other firms will not alter their output in response to changes in the firm's own price.

Utility functions are assumed to be of the following form:

$$U_j = \alpha_{1j} \ln C_{jT} + (1 - \alpha_{ij}) \ln V_j, \tag{4}$$

where U_j aggregates the utility of individuals in class j(j could be set equal to 1 and 2, following our earlier dichotomy), α_{1j} represents the fraction of income that individuals in class j allocate to traded goods, C_{jT} denotes the consumption of traded goods by class j, and V_j is a sub-utility function of class j's consumption of non-traded goods. Following Dixit and Stiglitz (1977), the function V_j is considered to be concave and, for expositional convenience, of the CES form

$$V_j = \left(\sum_{k=1}^{n} C_{kj}^{\theta} \right)^{1/\theta}, \tag{5}$$

where C_{kj} denotes the demand for each non-traded good k by households in class j, the number of differentiated goods is equal to n, and $0 < \theta < 1$ is a parameter representing the strength of preferences toward product variety. This last parameter is assumed, for simplicity, to be identical for all individuals in the economy. Observe that, as θ approaches a value of one, non-traded goods tend to become perfect substitutes and product variety loses value; as θ approaches zero, on the other hand, the utility function in (5) becomes more concave, and increased product variety provides a stronger effect on utility.

Demand functions are determined by the maximization of the utility function in (4) subject to the budget constraint

$$P_T C_{jT} + \sum_{k=1}^{n} P_{kN} C_{kj} = I_j, \tag{6}$$

where I_j denotes the income of individuals in class j. For expositional brevity, we reproduce here only the final expression we obtain for the demand for a single non-traded good [for more details, see Rivera-Batiz (1988)]:

$$C_{kj} = \left[\frac{(1-\alpha_{1j})I_j}{P_{kN}V_j^{\theta}}\right]^{1/(1-\theta)}, \tag{7}$$

whose price elasticity is given by

$$\varepsilon_k = \frac{-P_{kN}}{C_{kj}}\frac{\partial C_{kj}}{\partial P_{kN}} = \frac{1}{1-\theta[1-(1/n)]}. \tag{8}$$

Observe that this elasticity is the same independently of whose class' demand curve it represents ($j = 1$ or 2). It, therefore, also constitutes the elasticity of the demand curve for a non-traded good k on the part of the aggregate economy. This elasticity is always greater than one and increases with the number of firms in the non-traded goods sector. Equation (8) thus embodies the fact that a larger number of firms cause each single producer to lose some of its influence on the aggregate demand for non-traded goods, making the industry more competitive. Each supplier faces this increased competition through higher price elasticity of demand for its product.

Substituting the expression we obtain for the price elasticity in (8) into marginal revenue [see Eq. (3)], and equating to marginal cost yields the profit-maximizing price set by each firm:

$$P_{kN} = \frac{\varepsilon_k}{\varepsilon_k - 1}\beta W = (\beta/\theta\sigma)W, \tag{9}$$

where $\sigma = [1-(1/n)] = \sigma(n)$, with $\sigma' > 0$ and $\sigma'' < 0$. Equation (9) can be interpreted as stating that each firm sets a price at a markup over unit variable costs, βW. This markup is inversely related to the parameter σ. Thus, if the number of firms in the non-traded goods market decreases, σ declines and the markup increases. The reduced competition enhances the monopoly power of the remaining producers allowing them to charge a higher markup above unit variable costs. Note that, with all suppliers utilizing the same technology and facing identical demand conditions, their prices are also identical, so that $P_{kN} = P_N$.

Entry of firms into the non-traded goods sector will guarantee that the industry's long-run equilibrium is one with no unexploited profit opportunities. This occurs at the equilibrium output level:

$$X_{kN} = \frac{\gamma\theta\sigma}{\beta(1-\theta\sigma)}. \tag{10}$$

Since the parameter σ is positively related to the number of producers in the non-traded goods sector, a drop in the latter will reduce the scale of each firm in the sector. The explanation is that, with fewer competitors, the remaining firms will have a larger degree of monopoly power that induces them to contract output.

Consider an economy composed of individuals owning only labor or capital, as in Thompson and Quibria's discussion. Suppose that an economy of the type just described undergoes an emigration of pure labor. The emigration would push upwards nominal wages, raising unit labor costs and, thus, the prices of non-traded goods. In addition, some non-traded goods producers exit the market, which results in greater monopoly power for those firms that remain. These firms raise their price markups and the prices of non-traded goods end-up increasing proportionally more than nominal wages. Symbolically, when the number of producers, n, declines in the non-traded goods sector, the parameter σ drops in value, with the remaining firms exerting their increased monopoly power and raising P_N relative to W. Alternatively, one can visualize the impact of emigration as lowering the own-price real wage W/P_N. As derived from Eq. (9),

$$W/P_N = (\theta\sigma/\beta). \tag{11}$$

Given that W/P_N drops, it can be concluded that the impact of emigration on real wages can be negative in the presence of increasing returns. Algebraically, since $W^* = \eta P_N^*$, where $\eta < 1$, the effect of a reduction in the labor force on real wages will hinge on the sign of $(\eta - \theta_N^m)$, which is ambiguous. By reducing the number of domestic producers and their scale of operations, emigration can lower labor productivity and, thus, depress real wages.

8.4 Concluding Remarks

It has been the purpose of this paper to show, first, how my 1984 article can sustain an ambiguous (possibly negative) relationship between emigration and real wages and, secondly, to suggest how alterations of the supply side assumptions in the neoclassical model can also support such ambiguity. More specifically, in the presence of increasing returns, the effects of labor emigration on real wages can be negative.

References

Dixit, A.K. and J. Stiglitz, 1977, "Monopolistic competition and optimum product diversity," *American Economic Review*, 67, 297–308.

Hart, O., 1985, "Monopolistic competition in the spirit of Chamberlin: A general model," *Review of Economic Studies*, 52, 529–546.

Jones, R.W., 1965, "The structure of simple general equilibrium models," *Journal of Political Economy*, 73, 557–572.

Krugman, P., 1979, "Increasing returns, monopolistic competition, and international trade," *Journal of International Economics*, 9, 469–479.

Quibria, M.G., 1989, "International migration and real wages: Is there any neoclassical ambiguity?," *Journal of Development Economics*, 31 (1), 177–183.

Rivera-Batiz, F., 1982, "International migration, nontraded goods and economic welfare in the source country," *Journal of Development Economics*, 11, 81–90.

Rivera-Batiz, F., 1984, "International migration, nontraded goods and economic welfare in a two-class economy: A reply," *Journal of Development Economics*, 16, 325–330.

Rivera-Batiz, F., 1988, "Increasing returns, imperfect competition, and the welfare impact of international migration," Mimeo. (Department of Economics, Rutgers University, New Brunswick, NJ).

Thompson, H., 1984, "International migration, nontraded goods and economic welfare in the source country: A comment," *Journal of Development Economics*, 16, 321–324.

Chapter 9

The Service Sector, Monopolistic Competition and the Impact of Emigration*

9.1 Introduction

A substantial fraction of emigrants from developing countries move out of the production of service-sector commodities. The emigration of some types of highly-qualified workers (such as doctors, nurses, etc.) as well as of many unskilled workers (employed in the traditional service sector) follows this pattern. The question asked here is: what impact do these emigrants have on the economic welfare of those left behind?

In general, the geographical movement of service-sector goods tends to involve high transport costs and, as a result, they are usually lumped under the category of (internationally) non-traded goods. The standard models of open economies producing non-traded goods imply emigration should not affect at all the economic welfare of the non-migrants. This is because, when three commodities (exportables, importables and non-traded) are produced by means of two inputs (capital and labor), factor prices and the prices of

---

*This chapter was originally published in *Economics Letters*, Vol. 12, No. 3 (June 1983), pp. 327–332.

This paper was written while I was a Post-Doctoral Fellow in the Department of Economics at the University of Chicago. The support of a grant from the National Research Council of the National Academy of Sciences is gratefully acknowledged.

nontraded goods are completely determined by the exogenous traded goods prices [Komiya (1967, p. 134)]. As a result, 'when migration occurs, the migrants essentially disappear with their constant marginal product and, at the unchanged commodity price ratio, the nonmigrants are left as well off as before' [Bhagwati and Rodriguez (1976, p. 92)]. One crucial assumption in this analysis is that non-traded goods are homogeneous commodities produced under conditions of perfect competition and constant returns to scale. Many service-sector goods, however, may best be characterized as being slightly-differentiated commodities, produced under conditions of monopolistic competition and increasing returns to scale. One reason is because non-traded goods depend on local (home market) demand and cannot rely on international trade to attain some eventual minimum average cost. In addition, many services involve a close interaction between producer and consumer (as in the case of health services, restaurants, etc.) and they are thus more subject to the product differentiations arising from such interaction. In this note we show that, in a framework where service-sector goods are produced under conditions of monopolistic competition and product differentiation, emigration will tend to have a negative effect on the economic welfare of those left behind, even when factor and product prices remain unchanged.

9.2 The Model

Exportables and importables are assumed to be produced under constant returns to scale and perfect competition [our model may thus be more applicable to developing countries, whose international trade tends to be more of the inter-industry (rather than intra-industry) type]. The implication is that their prices will equal unit costs:

$$P_1 = Wa_{L1} + ra_{K1}, \tag{1}$$

$$P_2 = Wa_{L2} + ra_{K2}. \tag{2}$$

With P_1 and P_2 equal to the prices of exportables and importables (exogenous in a small economy), W is the wage rate, $r$is the rental rate, and the a_{ij}'s represent the requirement of the ith input

($i = K, L$) per unit of the jth good. The a_{ij}'s are a function only of input prices (under CRS), and (1) and (2) thus constitute a system of two equations in two endogenous variables, W and r. Consequently, for a small open economy, factor prices would be unaffected by emigration. This result remains the same as in the existing literature.

The service sector's market structure is assumed to follow the Dixit-Stiglitz (1977)-Krugman (1979, 1980) framework of monopolistic competition. There are n service-sector commodities, indexed by k, each of which is produced through the use of labor, L_s^k, according to

$$L_s^k = \gamma + \beta X_s^k, \tag{3}$$

where X_s^k is the output of the kth service, γ is a fixed labor requirement, and β is a variable labor requirement. Each service-sector firm is assumed to use the same technology [given by (3)]. Note that, since firms can differentiate their products costlessly, it will pay each producer to specialize in a single differentiated product.

The economy's utility function is given by

$$U = \sum_{j=1}^{3} \alpha_j \log D_j, \quad j = 1, 2, 3, \tag{4}$$

where α_j is a parameter representing the share of commodity j on income (so that $\sum_{j=1}^{3} \alpha_j = 1$), D_1 and D_2 are the aggregate demand for exports and imports, and D_3 is a sub-utility function of the service-sector goods, assumed to be of the CES type:

$$D_3 = \left(\sum_{k=1}^{n} C_k^\theta \right)^{1/\theta}, \tag{5}$$

where C_k is equal to the aggregate demand for the kth service, and $0 < \theta \leq 1$ is a parameter representing the preference for product variety. When $\theta = 1$, service-sector goods become perfect substitutes and no utility is derived from product variety; if $\theta < 1$, variety is valued positively.

Service-sector firms are assumed to choose their own price, P_k^s, to maximize profits (following, of course, the Chamberlinian premise that the firm cannot itself affect in any significant way the demand for other services or the overall aggregate demand for service-sector goods). With technology as specified by (3), and consumer preferences by (4) and (5), the profit-maximizing price of a service-sector commodity can be easily shown to be determined (see Krugman (1980)] by

$$P_s^k = \theta^{-1}\beta W \tag{6}$$

which shows the price set by a service-sector firm, P_s^k, as a markup over the wage rate. Since θ, β and W are the same for all firms, the prices of all the firms producing services would be the same ($P_s = P_s^k$ for all k). Each firm would also produce the same amount of output, implying that changes in the output of services would arise from new entrants into the sector. The zero-profit entry condition would then determine the number of firms, n. Given that the wage rate is unaffected by changes in factor endowments [from (1) and (2)], then P_s, would also be fixed; that much of the standard trade-theoretical framework introducing non-traded goods remains.

9.3 The Impact of Emigration in the Presence of Product Diversity

The economic welfare of the non-migrants (the population which stays behind), U^0, is given by

$$U^0 = \sum_{j=1}^{3} \alpha_j^0 \log D_j^0, \quad j = 1, 2, 3 \tag{7}$$

with α_j^0 equal to the share of income non-migrants allocate to the consumption of jth-sector goods, D_1^0 and D_2^0 are the amounts of traded goods the non-migrants consume, and D_3^0 is a sub-utility function of the non-migrants' consumption of services, given by

$$D_3^0 = \left(\sum_{k=1}^{n} C_{k0}^\theta\right)^{1/\theta} = (nC_{k0}^\theta)^{1/\theta} = n^{(1-\theta)/\theta} C_s^0, \tag{8}$$

where C_{k0} is equal to the demand of the non-migrants for a single service, $C_s^0 = nC_{k0}$ represents their consumption of all service-sector goods.

Differentiating Eq. (7) totally:

$$\mathrm{d}U^0 = \alpha_1^0 \hat{D}_1^0 + \alpha_2^0 \hat{D}_2^0 + \alpha_3^0 \hat{D}_3^0, \tag{9}$$

where caps, '^' represent proportional changes ($\hat{D}_1^0 \equiv \mathrm{d}D_1^0/D_1^0$, etc.). $D_1^0 = \alpha_1^0 I^0$, $D_2^0 = \alpha_2^0 I^0/P_2$, $D_3^0 = \alpha_3^0 I^0/P_s$, and I^0 represents the income of the non-migrants. Emigration leaves factor and product prices unchanged. As a result, non-migrant income would not change either, leaving the total amounts of goods the non-migrants consume unaffected ($\hat{D}_1^0 = \hat{D}_2^0 = \hat{D}_3^0$). From Eq. (8): $\hat{D}_3^0 = \hat{C}_s^0 + (1 - \theta/\theta)\hat{n}$. Even though the aggregate amount of services consumed by the non-migrants is unchanged ($\hat{C}_s^0 = 0$), the variety of these products available to them decreases when the migrants leave ($\hat{n} < 0$). This reduction is caused by the overall decreased demand for services in the economy. With reduced population, the monopolistically competitive service sector will not be able to support as many firms, and some will have to exit. Consequently, the expression for the change in non-migrant welfare in (9) becomes: $\mathrm{d}U^0 = \alpha_3^0 \hat{D}_3^0 = (1-\theta/\theta)\alpha_3^0 \hat{n}$. We have to specify $\hat{n}$.

The aggregate demand for services in the economy, C_s, is a function of relative prices and income, or: $C_s = C_s(P_2, P_s, I)$, with I equal to aggregate income. When emigration occurs, income declines from I to I^0, and C must decline to C_s^0. Assuming migrants and non-migrants have the same preferences, and differentiating the function C_s totally, we obtain $\hat{C}_s = \eta_s \sigma_L \hat{L}$, where $\eta_s \equiv (\partial C_s/\partial I)(I/C_s)$ is the income elasticity of demand for services, $\sigma_L \equiv WL/I$ is the contribution of labor to income, and $\hat{L}$ is the percentage reduction in the economy's labor force due to emigration. Since demand and supply of non-traded goods must remain equal: $\hat{C}_s = \hat{X}_s = \hat{n}$, and we can substitute the corresponding expression for $\hat{n}$ into $\mathrm{d}U^0$ to obtain

$$\mathrm{d}U^0 = \alpha_3^0 \eta_s \sigma_L \frac{1-\theta}{\theta} \hat{L}. \tag{10}$$

Emigration ($\hat{L} < 0$) thus tends to reduce the economic welfare of the non-migrants in the source country. As the economy's labor force decreases, factor prices remain unchanged, but the total output of service-sector commodities decreases. As a consequence, the number of services in the source country declines, reducing the variety of these products available, and, thus, the welfare of those left behind. In a certain sense, the emigration imposes a negative externality on the non-migrants by reducing the extent of the market and, thus, the variety of service-sector goods available.

Various factors are shown by (10) to affect this result. First, if product variety is not positively valued, there would be no loss in welfare. And, as product variety is valued more highly, the loss gets more significant. Secondly, as the aggregate income elasticity of the demand for services declines, the impact of emigration on non-migrant welfare decreases. The smaller the income elasticity, the smaller the reduction in the economy's total demand for services and, consequently, the smaller the decrease in their variety. A third factor regards the share of labor on income. The larger this share, the stronger the impact on welfare. This is because the proportional impact of labor emigration on the demand (and output) of service-sector commodities would increase. Finally, the smaller the share of income non-migrants spend on services, the smaller the impact of the emigration on their welfare.

9.4 Concluding Remarks

There are a number of qualifications and extensions to the present analysis. First, we have assumed the elasticity of substitution in consumption between service-sector goods is fixed. In general, as the number of products decreases, this elasticity should increase. If this happens, the welfare loss to the non-migrants from emigration would increase [as can be discerned from (10)]. In a sense, as the variety of products available decreases, the welfare loss from emigration becomes more acute. The monopoly power of the remaining producers would also increase significantly. This seems especially applicable to the emigration of doctors, nurses and other qualified personnel, whose numbers are quite limited in many developing countries.

Our model has the expositionally convenient result that the output of each service remains fixed in spite of a decrease in the aggregate demand for services. In a more general setting, emigration may tend to reduce both the number of firms and the output of each firm. Given the presence of (internal) economies of scale, emigration, in this case, may lead to increases in the prices of services, causing a further deleterious effect on non-migrant welfare. Finally, the losses in welfare discussed above may be affected by the presence of unemployment, complete specialization, remittances, terms of trade effects, taxation and public goods use effects, etc. [see Rivera-Batiz (1981 and 1982), and Bhagwati and Rodriguez (1976)]. The present framework may be extended to apply to cases of rural–urban migration, and may describe some of the aspects of rural decline in the presence of emigration. We should end by noting that the present approach to monopolistic competition is one among various alternatives [see Lancaster (1979) and Helpman (1981)].

References

Bhagwati, J.N. and C. Rodriguez, 1976, "Welfare-theoretical analyses of the brain drain," in: J.N. Bhagwati, ed., *The brain drain and taxation: Theory and empirical analysis* (North-Holland, Amsterdam) 85–111.

Dixit, A. and J. Stiglitz, 1977, "Monopolistic competition and optimum product diversity," *American Economic Review* 67, 297–308.

Ethier, W., 1972, "Nontraded goods and the Hecksher-Ohlin model," *International Economic Review* 13, 132–147.

Helpman, E., 1981, "International trade in the presence of product differentiation, economies of scale and monopolistic competition: A Chamberlin-Hecksher-Ohlin approach," *Journal of International Economics* 11, 305–340.

Komiya, R., 1967, "Nontraded goods and the pure theory of international trade," *International Economic Review* 8, 132–152.

Krugman, P., 1979, "Increasing returns, monopolistic competition and international trade," *Journal of International Economics* 9, 469–479.

Krugman, P., 1980, "Scale economies, product differentiation and the pattern of trade," *American Economic Review* 70, 950–959.

Lancaster, K., 1979, "Intra-industry trade under perfect monopolistic competition," *Journal of International Economics* 10, 151–175.

Rivera-Batiz, F., 1981, "The effects of immigration in a distorted two-sector economy," *Economic Inquiry* 19, 626–639.

Rivera-Batiz, F., 1982, "Nontraded goods and the pure theory of international trade with equal numbers of goods and factors," *International Economic Review* 23, 401–409.

Chapter 10

International Migration, the Brain Drain and Economic Development*

10.1 Introduction

International migration flows have expanded by historical proportions in recent years. In 1960, there was a stock of slightly over 75 million people residing in countries other than their country of birth. By 2005, this number had grown to 190 million. For many developing countries, international labor flows have become a natural outcome of the globalization process, as much as trade and investment flows. The money the migrants send back home has become a major source of income for families in developing countries. In 2005, migrant remittances amounted to $600 billion. For some countries, the income received from the services of workers abroad is now a major item of the balance of payments.

But international migration flows are not without their costs. For many years, the issue of the brain drain has been studied by international economists. From software engineers in India to doctors in the Philippines and nurses in sub-Saharan Africa, the exodus of skilled migrants has been a policy concern for many developing countries. The impact on the skilled labor forces of some countries has been substantial, especially in sub-Saharan Africa. In Ghana, for

*This chapter was originally published in Amitava Krishna Dutt and Jaime Ros, eds., *International Handbook of Development Economics*, Cheltenham: Edward Elgar, 2008, pp. 119–136.

example, over 40 percent of persons with a college degree or more have migrated to other countries. In Gambia, the corresponding proportion is close to 65 percent, and in Somalia it is 59 percent. What are the consequences of these labor outflows? What benefits or costs do they impose in the sending nations?

This paper provides an analysis and survey of the key recent trends in international migration, their determinants and major consequences. Section 10.2 presents data on the growth of global migration flows in the last few decades. Section 10.3 then proceeds to examine the causes of these migration flows, focusing on the main economic factors involved. Section 10.4 concludes with an analysis of the consequences of international migration for source countries.

10.2 Trends in International Migration Flows

International migration refers to the movement of people across national borders. Data on migration is available directly from national immigration authorities in recipient countries. However, the data available for many countries is sketchy and difficult to compare with data for other countries due to differences in migration policies, definitions of what constitutes immigrants, the presence of undocumented migration, etc. Some international organizations gather cross-country data on migration and seek to provide more uniform, comparable statistics. The Organization for Economic Cooperation and Development (OECD) has for many years collected information on the migration of OECD countries and has an extensive database for these countries [see, for example, OECD (2006)]. The United Nations has the most comprehensive worldwide database on the number of migrants residing in different countries [United Nations (2007)]. There are also data collection efforts supported by the World Bank [Docquier and Marfouk (2006)], the International Monetary Fund [Carrington and Detragiache (1998)], and other institutions, such as the Development Research Centre on Migration, Globalisation and Poverty at the University of Sussex [see Parsons *et al.* (2005)].

Table 10.1 shows the massive growth in the estimated number of international migrants in the world over the last 45 years. In 2005,

Table 10.1. Estimates of the Stock of International Migrants in the World, 1960–2005.

Year	Stock of migrants	Change between years
1960	75,463,352	
		2,980,581
1965	78,443,933	
		2,891,846
1970	81,335,779	
		5,453,525
1975	86,789,304	
		12,486,594
1980	99,275,898	
		11,737,332
1985	111,013,230	
		43,932,103
1990	154,945,333	
		10,134,902
1995	165,080,235	
		11,655,537
2000	176,735,772	
		13,897,792
2005	190,633,564	

Source: United Nations (2007).

there were 190 million people residing in countries other than their country of birth, up from 75 million in 1960. Most of these migrants originated in developing countries: it is estimated that 123 million migrants, or 65 percent of the total, were born in developing countries. Mexico had the highest number of persons residing abroad, equal to over 10 million in 2000, largely in the United States. This was followed by India, which had close to 9 million persons residing abroad in 2000, with the country's diaspora spread all over the world. Other countries with mass emigration include Bangladesh (6.6 million emigrants), the Philippines (3.4 million), Pakistan (3.4 million), Turkey (3.0 million), Afghanistan (2.7 million), Morocco (2.6 million), Egypt (2.5 million) and Algeria (2.1 million), among others.

The destination of emigrants from developing countries is evenly split between high-income and developing countries. In 2005, close to 62 million people born in developing countries were residing in high-income economies, but 61 million resided in other developing nations. Among high-income countries, those with the largest number of immigrants included the United States (38.4 million), Germany (10.1 million), France (6.4 million), and Canada (6.1 million). Developing countries with the highest immigrant populations included Russia (12.1 million, who moved mostly from elsewhere in the former Soviet Union), Ukraine (6.8 million), Saudi Arabia (6.4 million), India (3.3 million) and the United Arab Emirates (3.2 million).

The emigration of skilled workers is one of the major concerns relating to migration flows in developing countries. To measure the magnitude of skilled emigration or brain drain, a country's labor force is divided into those who are skilled — generally considered to be those who have some tertiary education, that is, 13 years of schooling or more — and those who are less-skilled, who have achieved less than tertiary education. The emigration of the skilled has been rising, just as global migration flows have increased in general. In OECD countries, for example, there were 12.5 million skilled immigrants of working age in 1990, but by 2000 the number had risen to 20.4 million, equal to 34.6 percent of the total number of immigrants in these countries.

The skilled emigration rate is defined as the stock of skilled migrants from a country (all persons with tertiary education living abroad) calculated as a percentage of the total skilled labor force in the source country augmented by the skilled migrants themselves. This shows the percentage of workers with tertiary education who were born in a country but is residing outside its borders. Hence, it is a measure of the relative impact of the emigration on the sending country's skilled labor market. The highest skilled emigration rates in the world prevail in the Caribbean, where in 2001 as much as 42.8 percent of the region's tertiary labor force resided outside its borders [Docquier and Marfouk (2006)]. Skilled emigration has also been enormous for a number of countries in Africa. In East Africa, the skilled emigration rate was close to 20 percent in 2001.

10.3 The Determinants of International Migration Flows

What has caused the mass migration documented in the previous section? There is a massive literature examining the determinants of migration flows. This section presents the main forces and conceptual approaches that seek to explain migration flows.

The Economic Approach to Migration: Costs and Benefits

At the theory level, the classical economic model of the decision to migrate was formalized by Sjaastad (1962) and has been extended in a number of directions [see, for example, Lucas (1985) and Borjas (1999)]. In this approach, the decision to migrate is seen as an investment decision that depends on individual assessments of the net balance of the present and future costs and benefits of migration. For a worker i, the net gain from migration, G_i, is equal to the present discounted value of the benefits minus the costs of migrating:

$$G_i = \sum_{t=1}^{T} \left[\frac{B_{\mathrm{t}}^i}{(1+r)t} - \frac{C_{\mathrm{t}}^i}{(1+r)t} \right], \qquad (1)$$

where T is the lifespan of the worker, r is a discount rate, B_{it} are the benefits received by a worker i at any given time t, generally in the form of higher wages or improved employment opportunities in the destination country, and the costs, C_{it}, include the direct costs of the move (transportation costs), the foregone earnings when the individual migrates, and any utility losses associated with leaving the homeland.

Note that different individuals will face varying costs and benefits and the probability of a person migrating from an origin to a destination area will vary. Older workers, for example, may suffer the greatest net losses in foregone earnings and may also face higher psychic costs of leaving the source country. As a result, the likelihood of migration declines with age. Location also matters. Indeed, most migration flows occur among geographically-close, often neighboring, countries, where the costs of migration are lower. Empirically, the role of geographical and cultural proximity in determining migration movements has been emphasized by the so-called *gravity model of migration flows*, for which there is ample supporting evidence [see Karemera *et al.* (2000), and Hatton and Williamson (2005)].

Labor Markets and the Returns to International Migration

Due to the difficulties of estimating future costs and benefits, most studies examining the decision to migrate focus on the current labor market gains from migrating, $\mathrm{I_i}$, given by:

$$\mathrm{I_i} = \log W_{iD} - \log W_{iO} \tag{2}$$

where W_{iD} is the wage rate that individual i can obtain in the destination and W_{iO} is the equivalent wage at home. These wage rates are influenced by the various characteristics of workers, including their schooling, Ed_i, their on-the-job experience, Ex_i, their motivation, M_i, health, marital status, number of children, etc. Suppose, for simplicity, that the following characterizes the wages of individual i in the destination and origin regions:

$$\log W_{iD} = \alpha_D + \alpha_{1D} Ed_i + \alpha_{2D} Ex_i + \alpha_{3D} M_i \tag{3}$$

$$\log W_{iO} = \alpha_O + \alpha_{1O} Ed_i + \alpha_{2O} Ex_i + \alpha_{3O} M_i \tag{4}$$

where the α's represent how the various individual characteristics (education, experience, etc.) are rewarded in each country. The net gain from migration is thus:

$$I_i = \log W_{iD} - \log W_{iO}$$

$$= (\alpha_D - \alpha_O) + (\alpha_{1D} - \alpha_{1O})Ed_i + (\alpha_{2D} - \alpha_{2O})Ex_i + (\alpha_{3D} - \alpha_{3O})M_i. \quad (5)$$

For any individual, the incentive to migrate will vary on the basis of the skills (education, experience, etc.) that the worker is endowed with, his or her motivation, and how skills as well as motivation are rewarded in relative terms in the source and destination countries.

A large body of research has now accumulated studying the labor market outcomes of developing country emigrants in their destinations (see, for example, the collection of research in Zimmermann and Constant, 2004, as well as the surveys by Borjas, 1999, and Hanson, 2006). This literature suggests that the economic returns to migrating are substantial for most workers.

But the economic progress of migrants varies according to the characteristics of the migrants themselves (age, schooling, immigration status, etc.), the timing of the migration, and the country of destination. In some European countries, for instance, immigrants have substantially lower rates of labor force participation as well as higher unemployment rates than the native-born population. The relatively poor labor market outcomes of some immigrants are partly related to lack of skills, but they also depend on labor market conditions in — and time spent in — recipient countries [Fertig and Schmidt (2002), Rivera-Batiz (2007)].

Migrant Selectivity

One of the most discussed issues in the international migration literature is whether emigrants are the most qualified, skilled workers in the origin economy or not. If migrants are positively selected, then they will be more likely to succeed abroad, but their exit from the source country will drain the most-capable, most-skilled population from the nation, with a potentially negative impact on its economy and society.

What determines whether migrants are positively or negatively selected? There are forces that favor a positive selectivity and others that encourage a negative selectivity. The best-known hypothesis is that emigrants tend to be positively selected because in order to compensate for the substantial costs of migration, only those who have the strongest drive and motivation — and the expectations of great rewards — will actually undertake the migration process (see Chiswick, 1978, 1999). Of course, if costs of migration decline, then this aspect of selectivity will tend to become less significant. In addition, as equation (5) suggests, the impact of motivation on migration depends on whether motivational skills are more strongly rewarded in the destination region. Indeed, one suspects that holding constant the distribution of motivational skills in a population, if these skills are poorly rewarded at home but richly rewarded abroad, the incentives to migrate from source to destination regions will increase.

A second hypothesis (referred in the literature as the *Roy model*) is that, if those with greater skills or abilities are rewarded more highly compared to the less-skilled in the origin area when compared to the destination region, this will generate less incentives for those at the top of the skills or ability distribution to emigrate compared to those at the bottom of the distribution, causing a negative selectivity of migrants. Therefore, the emigrant contingent will be positively or negatively selected depending on the relative inequality of the distribution of income at home and abroad. For instance, the more unequal the income distribution in the origin area as compared to the destination, the lower the incentives for the highly skilled to emigrate relative to the less skilled. This result is easily obtained from equation (5). Since $\partial \mathrm{I_i}/\partial \mathrm{Ed_i} = (\alpha_{\mathrm{iD}} - \alpha_{\mathrm{iO}})$, if greater inequality in the source country is associated with a rate of return to education in the origin area that exceeds the rate of return in the destination country, then $(\alpha_{\mathrm{iD}} - \alpha_{\mathrm{iO}}) < 0$. This implies that, as the education of the prospective migrant rises, the incentives to migrate tend to decline. Note also that under asymmetric information, employers in the destination region may not be able to accurately assess the skills of the migrants and they may offer lower wages to the highly-skilled migrants, when compared to employers in the source country, that are able to assess more accurately the potential migrants' skills and pay them wages more consonant with their skills. This will again reduce the rate of return to education received by the emigrants in the destination region relative to the source country $[(\alpha_{\mathrm{iD}} - \alpha_{\mathrm{iO}})$

will decline], shrinking the incentive to migrate of the highly-skilled relative to the unskilled [see Stark and Taylor (1991)].

Some evidence appears to support the implications of the Roy model [see Borjas (1987, 2006)]. For instance, recent research finds a negative selectivity in the migrant contingent from Mexico to the United States (that is, the emigrant group tends to have lower average skills than the population left behind), as would be expected from the relatively more unequal distribution of income in Mexico relative to the United States [see Fernandez-Huertas Moiraga (2007) for this analysis and Chiquiar and Hanson (2005) for alternative results].

Income Differences and International Migration

Overall, the evidence on the importance of economic factors in motivating migration flows, as presented in equations (1)–(4) is extensive. Both documented and undocumented migration flows have been found to be strongly correlated to the relative economic conditions in recipient and source countries [see, for example, Hanson and Spilimbergo (1999), Drinkwater (2003), Castaldo *et al.* (2005), Hanson (2006)].

But despite the widespread support for the hypothesis that increased income differentials between recipient and source countries stimulates migration, there is also ample support for the view that this connection does not always work and may actually hold in reverse [see Hatton and Williamson (1998) and the review by Waddington and Sabates-Wheeler (2003)]. For instance, in recent research seeking to determine the impact of differences in income per-capita on migration flows in the world, Hatton and Williamson (2005, p. 240) find that in sub-Saharan Africa, increases in income at home *increase* migration. Indeed, the evidence suggests that the relationship between income per-capita in source countries and emigration has an inverted-U shape. For poor countries, as income rises, migration actually *increases*. But as the wealth of a country grows, at some point, further increases in income per capita actually reduce emigration.

One explanation for this behavior is the fact that, at low levels of income per-capita, a large part of the population just simply cannot afford the monetary costs of migrating. However, as per-capita income in a country rises, this allows some people to save enough to pay for the transport and other costs of migration, thus increasing migration flows [see Hatton and Williamson (2005)]. An additional explanation is that the massive structural changes occurring in the early industrialization of an economy (the shift from agriculture to industry and services, from urban to rural areas, etc.) leads to a dislocation of the population that fosters international migration. As the economic development process matures, however, these changes diminish and migration declines. A third hypothesis for the paradoxical rise of migration flows as income increases in many economies is based on *relative deprivation theory*. It suggests that, as inequality rises in the early years of economic development (a trend first noted by economist Simon Kuznets), those who become relatively poor will become increasingly dissatisfied with their relative standing in the community. This will stimulate them to emigrate in order to improve their standard of living [see Stark and Taylor (1991)].

Families and the Decision to Migrate

Despite its powerful role in explaining migration flows, another problem of using a simple economic approach based on income differences across countries is that it cannot explain temporary migration. If there is a significant and persistent wage and employment differential between origin and destination regions, why do so many migrants wish to stay in the destination only for short periods of time?

One explanation is offered by the so-called new economics of labor migration [see Stark and Bloom (1985)]. In this approach, it is understood that migration decisions are often made by families and households, not individuals. In contrast to the analysis in equations (1)–(4), the decision-making is not in the hands of an individual who maximizes his or her utility. Rather, migration decisions are made by families or households that maximize household utility over time. This utility, U, is derived from a stream of consumption by family members located in the home and/or destination regions, C_D and C_O, added all the way up to the time horizon of the family, T, and discounted to the present time, t:

$$U = \left[\sum_{j=1}^{T} \beta^{t+j} \{ (1-\theta) \log (C_{D,t+j}) + \theta \log (C_{O,t+j}) \} \right] \tag{6}$$

where β is a time discount rate and θ is a parameter reflecting the relative weight of persons located in the origin and destination areas within the overall family utility function.

Equation (6) is maximized subject to a budget constraint establishing that the present discounted value of income earned in the source and destination areas is equal to or greater than the present discounted value of family consumption spending.

Visualizing migration as an intertemporal family/household decision can help understand that the migration of some household members may be part of the savings and investment decisions of a family. The idea is that, if low-income households encounter capital market imperfections at home, which exclude them from access to the financing of investments in housing, durable goods, or in self-employed businesses, migration abroad may lead to the accumulation of remittances that can then be used to finance those purchases and investments. Migration becomes a short-term activity needed by households to raise funds in the absence of local financing. Another application of this approach is that the migration of one household member may reduce the costs of migration for other household members. This is what *network or chain migration theory* suggests [see Piore (1979) and Bauer, Gang and Epstein (2000)].

The Political Economy of Immigration Policy

The discussion so far has described the wide array of forces that may generate a supply of potential migrants. However, in an international context, destination country governments exert an enormous force in restricting immigration flows. As a result, the volume of migration between developing countries and high-income economies is often determined by the immigration policies imposed by the latter.

Research on the determinants of immigration policies follows a growing literature in political economy that seeks to answer the question of how the policies of a country are generated through the interaction of economic, political and social forces (Mayda and Patel, 2006). A wide array of economic forces may lie behind the setting of immigration policies. For instance, if immigration reduces wages and raises the profits of employers and owners of capital, then persons who own firms or farms or own relatively large amounts of capital will be in favor of immigration but those who do not have wealth and only have their labor will be against immigration [see Benhabib (1996)]. But if the distribution of capital in a country is highly concentrated, with a great part of the workforce laboring at low wages, then there may be very few persons supporting immigration and many opposing it. If immigration policy is determined by influence of voters, immigration policy restrictions may be high. This force is magnified if the immigrants are unskilled since in this case the immigrants may be perceived as competing with the poor, generating stronger cries for immigration restrictions [Hatton and Williamson (2005)].

The available evidence confirms the role that economic forces play in affecting the immigration attitudes of natives in recipient countries [see Gang, Rivera-Batiz and Yun (2002, 1999), Scheve and Slaughter (2001), and Mayda (2006)]. But economic factors are not the only ones affecting attitudes towards immigrants. Social phenomena, such as xenophobia and bias against foreigners, can have a major influence on immigration policies [see Gang and Rivera-Batiz (1994) and Gang, Rivera-Batiz and Yun (2002) for analyses of the determinants of attitudes towards immigrants].

10.4 International Migration and Economic Development

What are the economic consequences of mass migration for the developing world? What changes in the source countries are generated by migrants? The following sections examine the existing theory and evidence on how emigration affects developing nations.

The Distributional and Welfare Impact of Emigration

The simplest theoretical framework that can be used to examine the effects of international migration is one that focuses on the aggregate

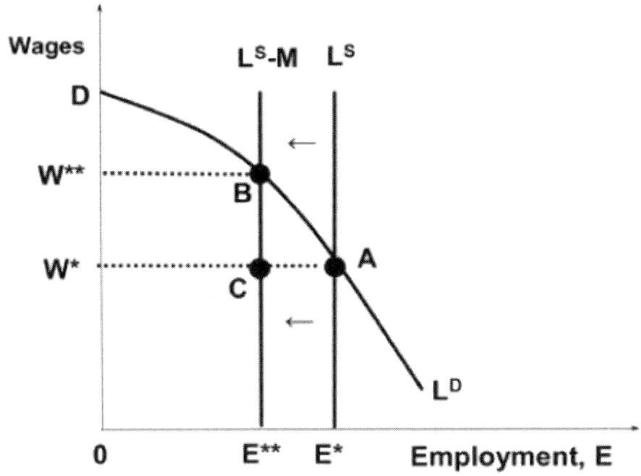

Figure 10.1. The Effects of Emigration on the Source Country.

economy, within a simplified setting where there are only two inputs: capital and labor [see Bhagwati and Rodriguez (1975), Borjas (1999) and Mishra (2006)]. Figure 10.1 shows the labor market in the source country before and after emigration. The demand for labor (the economy's marginal value product curve) is L^D and the supply of labor before emigration is depicted by L^S, where it is assumed that there is an inelastic supply of labor given by the country's labor force. Under the assumption that the labor market is perfectly competitive and generates full-employment, the equilibrium before emigration is at point A, with a wage rate equal to W* and employment E*. If the number of emigrant workers is given by M, the labor force declines, shifting the aggregate supply of labor to the left, to L^S-M. The equilibrium after migration occurs at point B. The shortage of labor induced by emigration, reduces employment from E^* to E^{**}, and raises wages rates from W^* to W^{**} (this assumes that the domestic capital stock is unaffected by emigration).

The impact of emigration can be depicted in Figure 10.1 by noting first that national income is given by $Y = WL + rK$, with K equal to the economy's capital stock and r the rate of return to capital. Diagrammatically, after emigration, the income received by the workers that remain in the economy is equal to $W^{**}E^{**}$, as represented by $0W^{**}BE^{**}$. This rises compared to the situation before emigration, when the income of these workers was W^*E^{**}. The gain in income by labor is $(W^{**} - W)E^{**}$. But although labor gains by emigration, capital is hurt by it. The income received by capital is given by $Y - WL$. Diagrammatically, the value of national income, Y, is equal to the area below the demand for labor curve up to the level of employment. After emigration, the value of national income is $DBCE^{**}O$. As a result, after emigration, the income received by capital is $Y - WL = DBCE^{**}O - W^{**}E^{**} = DBW^{**}$. The income derived by capital before the emigration was $DBACW^*$. Hence, the income of capital declines by $DBACW^* - DBW^{**} = W^{**}BAW^*$.

In this context, emigration results in a redistribution of income from capital to labor. But the emigration has also a net, overall negative impact on the income of those left behind. Adding the loss of capital and the gain to labor leaves a net loss represented diagrammatically by the area BAC. Algebraically, this loss can be approximated by:

$$\frac{\Delta Y}{Y} = -\left(\frac{1}{2}\right)\left(\frac{\Delta W}{Y}\right)M = -\left(\frac{1}{2}\right)S_L\eta_L\left(\frac{M}{E}\right)^2 \tag{7}$$

where Y is the initial level of national income in the economy, ΔY is the change in national income due to the emigration, ΔW is the change in wages ($\Delta W = W^{**} - W^*$), M is the loss of labor ($M = -\Delta E = E^* - E^{**}$), $S_L = (WE/Y)$ and $\eta_L = -(\partial W/\partial E)(E/W)$ is the negative of the elasticity of the labor demand curve with respect to wages.

Although in this simplified setting emigration results in a gain to labor (the mobile factor), a loss to capital (the fixed factor) and a net loss to the overall economy, these conclusions can be reversed in more complex frameworks. First of all, the model is a partial-equilibrium, closed-economy model but most modern economies are both highly diversified and engage in substantial international trade. In a general equilibrium framework with trade, such as the Hecksher-Ohlin-Samuelson model, emigration has no lasting impact on the source country, whether on income distribution or in terms of the net impact on economic welfare. The explanation is that the emigrants themselves induce a reduction in the demand for labor in the source country. As the migrants leave, they do place upward pressure on wages, as noted in the earlier model. But this makes employment in capital-intensive sectors, such as heavy manufacturing, more profitable. As production shifts away from labor-intensive products and into capital-intensive sectors, the overall demand for labor in the economy shrinks. This puts downward pressure on wages, reversing the initial impact of the emigration. This result, where an outflow of labor leads to no change in wages, is based on the Rybczyinski effect in the trade literature [see Bhagwati and Rodriguez (1975) and Rivera-Batiz (1983)].

But the assumptions of the HOS model under which this result is derived are stringent. Besides the assumptions of perfect competition and no distortions, the framework assumes the absence of externalities and increasing returns. In addition, the model does not distinguish between skilled and unskilled labor emigration. Once these assumptions are relaxed, the theoretical analysis may yield complex and ambiguous effects of emigration [see, for example, Dutt (2005)]. Furthermore, when considering costs and benefits from migration one should consider as well the overall, global impact of migration flows. If there are net world gains, there are then strong reasons for governments in recipient and destination areas to coordinate their migration policies, so that both developing countries and high-income economies can profit from the migration flows [see Pritchett (2005) and Kapur and McHale (2005)].

The empirical evidence on the welfare and distributional effects of emigration on source countries is scant (the analysis of the impact of immigration has been more extensive). Recently, however, some studies have utilized Census data over time to examine the issue. Mishra (2006) examines emigration from Mexico to the U.S., concluding that the outflow of Mexican workers to the United States between 1970 and 2000 has increased worker earnings in Mexico worker by 5.9 percent of GDP and has reduced the income of the owners of fixed factors by 6.4 percent of GDP, with a small, negative net impact on overall economic welfare of those left behind [see also Borjas (2006)]. On the other hand, there are other potential impacts of emigration to consider that are not examined in this literature, as discussed next.

Remittances and the Impact of Emigration

One of the most visible impacts of the migrants on source countries is connected to the remittances that they send back home. These flows of resources have grown exponentially in recent decades. Measured in 2000 international PPP dollars, developing countries received $50 billion in migrant remittances in 1980, but by 2005 this had multiplied to $605 billion [World Bank (2007)]. The regions receiving the most remittances were East Asia and Pacific and South Asia (each receiving about $171 billion in 2005), followed by Latin America and the Caribbean (with $86 billion), Europe and Central Asia ($78 billion), the Middle East and North Africa ($75 billion) and sub-Saharan Africa ($24 billion).

The significance of remittances in many developing countries can be seen by comparing the value of remittances with the value of the merchandise goods exported by the source countries. Table 10.2 shows how significant migrant remittances can be, rising in some countries to over 100 or 300 percent of exports.

Remittances clearly constitute an improvement in the standard of living for family members who are recipients of such income. And recent evidence suggests that remittances are connected to lower poverty levels (see Acosta *et al.*, 2006, Adams, 2007). Some questions have been raised as to the extent to which the remittances simply raise current consumption instead of stimulating investment and future economic growth. Recently, however, a number of studies have documented that, first, a significant portion of so-called consumption spending consists of household investments in housing, automobiles and durable goods, whose long-term wealth-raising capacities are substantial; second, the use of remittances for community investment projects is not insignificant and also acts to stimulate local development; and, third, the multiplier effects of the increased consumption spending in generating local economic activity may be substantial (see, for example, de la Garza and Lowell, 2002 and Adams, 2007).

On the other hand, remittances do tend to be spent largely on internationally non-tradeable goods, which can result in rising prices of these goods compared to internationally traded goods, generating

Table 10.2. Migrant Remittances in Developing Countries, Largest Recipients, 2005.

Country/Region	Remittances in current $	Remittances in PPP-adjusted $	Remittances as a % of merchandise exports
Developing Countries	179,425	605,678	6.0%
Mexico	21,772	32,222	10.3
India	19,843	105,564	26.2
Philippines	11,634	45,605	29.2
Lebanon	5,722	5,493	335.3
Morocco	4,221	12,325	42.5
Serbia/Montenegro	4,129	9,868	103.8
Pakistan	3,955	14,277	29.5
Bangladesh	3,583	15,407	43.1
Brazil	3,540	7,682	3.0
Colombia	3,345	10,704	15.8
Egypt	3,341	8,018	43.5
Guatemala	2,592	5,962	88.2
El Salvador	2,564	5,718	77.8
Dominican Republic	2,471	6,671	43.0
Algeria	2,460	7,577	7.9
Jordan	2,288	5,010	58.9

Source: Data for remittances in current $ are taken from World Bank (2007); other indicators are author's calculations using PPP adjustments and exports from World Bank (2007).

an appreciation in the value of the domestic currency, which adversely affects domestic export sectors [Rivera-Batiz (1986)]. Evidence of this, Dutch-disease type effect has emerged recently [see Amuedo-Orantes and Pozo (2004) and Acosta *et al.* (2007)]. A vicious cycle may develop, where emigration leads to remittances that then deteriorate domestic competitiveness and growth, leading to further emigration, and so on.

The Impact of the Brain Drain

The contribution of migrant remittances for economic development must be weighted against any externalities generated by the migration flows. In countries where emigration leads to the loss of the most talented and skilled, the so-called brain drain, migration could result in significant negative externalities [see Bhagwati (1979), Bhagwati and Rodriguez (1974)].

If the emigration of skilled labor is substantial and these workers are employed in local service sectors, the result can be acute shortages in the supply of essential services, from school teachers and nurses to professors and nurses. Note that the emigration of workers employed in sectors that produce exports and imports is not subject to these effects because local consumers can import these products from abroad when the laborers leave the country. But when the workers are employed in service sectors that produce internationally-nontraded goods, the impact of emigration is more significant and potentially disastrous because domestic consumers can only obtain those services locally [see Rivera-Batiz (1982)]. If doctors and nurses emigrate, the supply of health services can collapse, resulting in higher prices and acute shortages. A brain drain can therefore reduce sharply the economic welfare of those left behind.

On the other hand, there may be positive externalities of skilled emigration on source countries. First of all, some researchers have recently suggested that a brain drain may actually raise the level of schooling of the population in the source country, at least in the long-run. There are several reasons for this. One hypothesis is that the brain drain will raise the rate of return to education and, as a result, more young people in the country will decide to pursue higher education, thus raising educational attainment. Indeed, the point that the emigration of skilled workers may lie behind the rising relative wages of skilled labor in many developing countries has been frequently made. However, evidence that these changes have stimulated local investments in human capital has not been produced yet [see Schiff (2005)].

Another possible positive externality associated with the brain drain relates to the fact that emigrants may generate international networks that could enhance the scientific and technological capacities at home. One example is the role that has been played by the Indian diaspora in Silicon Valley and elsewhere on the growth of India's information technology sector. By generating greater flow of skills and information among countries, and by raising the reputation of a domestic sector internationally, this type of emigration can have significantly positive effects at home [see Kapur and McHale (2005)].

10.5 Implications for Future Research

Both the theory and empirical evidence on the determinants and consequences of international migration have grown enormously in recent years. This research matches the growing importance of migratory flows. But despite the progress, the literature so far has generally failed to consider the dynamic effects of emigration, focusing instead on analyzing — and estimating — static models. This is an especially relevant issue to discuss in relation to the brain drain since there are a number of possible mechanisms through which the emigration of the skilled can affect a country's economic growth.

First of all, the mainstream analysis of economic growth, as developed by Solow and Swan, suggests that a drop in population growth should lead to an economic expansion for those left behind since the steady-state amount of capital per worker in the economy would rise, increasing per-capita income. But there are a number of caveats to this story. First, the emigration of working-age people means that the dependency rate in the economy rises, which tends to absorb resources that would otherwise be dedicated to the accumulation of capital and economic growth. The working-age skilled emigrants are also more likely to have higher savings rates than the rest of the population. Indeed, the empirical evidence available is consistent with a negative impact of a brain drain due to these demographic effects [Bloom and Williamson (1988)].

Another issue is that the emigration of skilled labor may reduce the human capital available to those left-behind. This can potentially have a devastating effect on economic growth. One of the main sources of economic growth is technological change, which depends to a large extent on human capital [Rivera-Batiz and Romer (1990)]. But if human capital flees a country, then the ability of those left behind to sustain innovation and technical change may be compromised, thus reducing an economy's economic growth [Rivera-Batiz (1996)].

On the other hand, a growing literature suggests that in countries where the quality of the public sector governance is low, many educated workers tend to be employed in activities that are not necessarily high-productivity activities. In other words, in economies where the government is highly bureaucratic, where corruption is rampant, and the rule of law does not apply, many highly-educated workers will not be able to be gainfully employed [see Rivera-Batiz (2002)]. In this case, the potentially negative impact of the brain drains on technological change and, therefore, on economic growth diminishes. It is a matter for future research to examine theoretically and empirically in greater detail how emigration is connected to technical change and economic growth.

References

Acosta, P., E. Lartey and F. Mandelman (2007) "Remittances and the Dutch Disease," Working Paper No. 2007–8 (Atlanta: Federal Reserve Bank of Atlanta).

Acosta, P., C. Calderón, P. Fajnzylber and H. Lopez (2006) "Remittances and Development in Latin America," *World Economy*, 30: 957–987.

Amuedo-Dorantes, C. and S. Pozo (2004) "Workers' Remittances and the Real Exchange Rate: A Paradox of Gifts," *World Development*, Vol. 32: 1407–1417.

Adams, R. (2007) 'International Remittances and the Household: Analysis and Review of Global Evidence,' Policy Research Working Paper No. 4116 (Washington, D.C.: The World Bank).

Bauer, T., I. N. Gang and G. Epstein (2000) "What are Migration Networks?," IZA Discussion Paper No. 200 (Bonn: Institute for the Study of Labor).

Benhabib, J. (1996) "On the Political Economy of Immigration." *Economic European Review* 40, No. 9: 1737–1743.

Bhagwati, Jagdish N. (1979) "International Migration of the Highly Skilled: Economics, Ethics and Taxes," *Third World Quarterly*, Vol. 1(3): 17–30.

Bhagwati, Jagdish N. and Carlos Rodriguez (1975) "Welfare-Theoretical Analyses of the Brain Drain," *Journal of Development Economics*, Vol. 2: 195–221.

Bloom, David E. and Jeffrey Williamson (1998) "Demographic Transitions and Economic Miracles in Emerging Asia," *World Bank Economic Review*, Vol. 12, No. 3: 419–55.

Borjas, G. (1987) "Self-Selection and the Earnings of Immigrants," *American Economic Review*, 77: 531–553.

Borjas, G. (1999) "The Economic Analysis of Immigration," in O. Ashenfelter and R. Freeman (eds.), *Handbook of Labor Economics* (Amsterdam: North Holland).

Borjas, G. (2006) "Labor Outflows and Labor Inflows in Puerto Rico," Working Paper (Cambridge, Mass.: Harvard University).

Carrington, W. and E. Detragiache (1998) "How Big is the Brain Drain?," IMF Working Paper No. 98/102 (Washington, D.C.: International Monetary Fund).

Castaldo, A., J. Litchfield and B. Reilly (2005) "Who is Most Likely to Migrate from Albania? Evidence from the Albania Living Standards Measurement Study," Working Paper No. T-11 (Sussex: Sussex Centre for Migration Research).

Chiquiar, D. and G. Hanson (2005) "International Migration, Self-Selection and the Distribution of Wages: Evidence from Mexico and the United States," *Journal of Political Economy*, Vol. 113, No. 2, April, 239–281.

Chiswick, B. (1978) 'The Effects of Americanization on the Earnings of the Foreign-Born,' *Journal of Political Economy*, 86: 897–922.

Chiswick, B. (1999) 'Are Immigrants Favorably Selected?,' *American. Economic. Review*, 89: 181–185.

de la Garza, R. and B. Lindsay Lowell (2002) *Sending Money Home: Hispanic Remittances and Community Development* (London: Rowman & Littlefield).

Drinkwater, S. (2003) "Estimating the Willingness to Move from Central and Eastern European Countries," Working Paper (Surrey: University of Surrey).

Docquier, Frederic and Abdeslam Marfouk (2006) "International Migration by Educational Attainment: 1990–2000," in Caglar Ozden and Maurice Schiff, eds., *International Migration, Remittances and the Brain Drain* (Washington, D.C.: The World Bank), 151–199.

Dutt, A.K. (2005) "Globalization, South-North Migration and Uneven Development," in P. Gangopadhy and M. Chatterji, eds., *Economics of Globalization* (Aldershot: Ashgate), 115–129.

Fernandez-Huertas Moraga, Jesus (2007) "New Evidence on Emigrant Selection," Ph.D. Dissertation, Department of Economics (New York: Columbia University).

Fertig, Michael and Christoph Schmidt (2002) "First and Second-Generation Migrants in Germany: What Do We Know and What Do People Think?" In R. Rotte and P. Stein, eds. *Migration Policy and the Economy: International Experiences* (Muenchen, Germany: Hanns-Seidel Foundation).

Gang, Ira N., Francisco L. Rivera-Batiz and Myeong-Su Yun (2002) "Economic Strain, Ethnic Concentration and Attitudes towards Foreigners in the European Union," IZA Discussion Paper No. 578 (Bonn: Institute for the Study of Labor).

Gang, Ira N., Francisco L. Rivera-Batiz and Myeong-Su Yun (1999) "Immigrants and Unemployment in the European Community: From the Eyes of Natives," IZA Discussion Paper No. 70 (Bonn: Institute for the Study of Labor).

Gang, Ira N. and Francisco L. Rivera-Batiz (1994) "Unemployment and Attitudes towards Foreigners in Germany," in Gunter Steinmann and Ralf Ulrich, eds., *The Economics of Immigration in Germany* (Berlin: Springer – Verlag) 121–154.

Hanson, Gordon (2005) 'Emigration, Labor Supply and Earnings in Mexico.' Working Paper No. 11412 (Cambridge, Mass.: National Bureau of Economic Research).

Hanson, Gordon (2006) 'Illegal Migration from Mexico to the United States,' *Journal of Economic Literature* 44: 869–924.

Hanson, Gordon and Antonio Spilimbergo (1998) 'Illegal Immigration, Border Enforcement, and Relative Wages: Evidence from Apprehensions at the U.S.-Mexico Border,' *American Economic Review* 89: 1337–1357.

Hatton, Timothy and Jeffrey G. Williamson (1998) *The Age of Mass Migration: Causes and Economic Impact* (New York: Oxford University Press).

Hatton, Timothy and Jeffrey Williamson (2005) *Global Migration and the World Economy: Two Centuries of Policy and performance* (Cambridge, Mass.: The MIT Press).

Kamemera, D., Oguledo, V. I. and Davis, B. (2000), "A Gravity Model Analysis of International Migration to North America," *Applied Economics* 32(13), pp. 1745–55.

Kapur, D. and J. McHale (2005) *Give Us Your Best and Brightest: The Global Hunt for Talent and its Impact on the Developing World* (Washington, D.C.: Brookings).

Lucas, R. E. B. (1985), "Migration among the Batswana," *Economic Journal* 95 (June), 358–82.

Mayda, Anna Maria and Krishna Patel (2006) "International Migration Flows: The Role of Destination Countries' Migration Policies," Working Paper (Washington, D.C.: Center for Strategic and International Studies).

Mayda, Anna Maria (2006). "Who Is Against Immigration? A Cross Country Investigation of Individual Attitudes towards Immigrants." *Review of Economics and Statistics.*

McKenzie, David J. (2006) "A Profile of the World's Young Developing Country Migrants," Policy Research Working Paper 4021 (Washington, D.C.: The World Bank).

Mishra, P. (2006) 'Emigration and Wages in Source Countries: Evidence from Mexico.' Working Paper No. WP/86/06 (Washington, D.C.: International Monetary Fund).

Organization for Economic Cooperation and Development (2006) Trends *in International Migration* (Paris: OECD).

Ortega, F. (2005) "Immigration Quotas and Skill Upgrading." *Journal of Public Economics* 89, No. 9–10: 1841–1863.

Parsons, Christopher, R. Skeldon, T. Walmsley, and L. Alan Winters (2005) "Quantifying the International Bilateral Movements of Migrants," Development Research Centre on Migration, Globalization and Poverty Working Paper T-13 (Brighton: University of Sussex).

Piore, Michael J. (1979) *Birds of Passage: Migrant Labor and Industrial Societies* (New York: Cambridge University Press).

Pritchett, Lant (2005) *Let Their People Come: Breaking the Gridlock on Global Labor Mobility* (Washington, D.C.: Center for Global Development).

Rivera-Batiz, Francisco L. (1982) "International Migration, Nontraded Goods and Economic Welfare in the Source Country," *Journal of Development Economics,* Vol. 11: 81–90.

Rivera-Batiz, Francisco L. (1983) "Trade Theory, Distribution of Income, and Immigration," *American Economic Review*, Vol. 73, No. 2, May, 183–187.

Rivera-Batiz, Francisco L. (1986) "International Migration, Remittances and Economic Welfare in the Source Country," *Journal of Economic Studies*, Vol. 13, No. 3, October, 3–19.

Rivera-Batiz, Francisco L. (1996) "The Economics of Technological Progress and Endogenous Growth in Open Economies," in H. Scharrer, ed. *The Economics of High Technology Competition and Cooperation in Global Markets*, Institut für Wirtschaftsforschung, Hamburg, 31–62.

Rivera-Batiz, Francisco L. (2002) "Democracy, Governance and Economic Growth: Theory and Evidence," *Review of Development Economics*, Vol. 6, No. 2, June, 225–247.

Rivera-Batiz, Francisco L. (2007) "How Do Migrants from Latin America and the Caribbean Fare in the U.S. Labor Market?," *World Economy*, Vol. 30, No. 9: 1399–1429.

Rivera-Batiz, Luis A. and Paul M. Rower (1991) "Economic Integration and Economic Growth," *Quarterly Journal of Economics*, Vol. 106, No. 21, 531–555.

Scheve, K., and M. Slaughter (2001) "Labor Market Competition and Individual Preferences Over Immigration Policy." *Review of Economics and Statistics* 83, No. 1: 133–145.

Schiff, Maurice (2005) "Brain Gain: Claims about its Size and Impact on Welfare and Growth are Greatly Exaggerated," in C. Ozden and M. Schiff, *International Migration, Remittances and the Brain Drain* (Washington, D.V.: The World Bank).

Sjaastadt, Larry (1962), "The Costs and Returns of Human Migration," *Journal of Political Economy* 70(5, Part 2), pp. S80–S93.

Stark, Oded and David E. Bloom (1985) "The New Economics of Labor Migration." *American Economic Review*, 75(2): 173–178.

Stark, Oded and J. Edward Taylor (1991) "Migration Incentives, Migration Types: The Role of Relative Deprivation." *Economic Journal*, 101(408): 1163–78.

United Nations (2007) "International Migration Estimates," Demographic Estimates, Population Division, Department of Economic and Social Affairs (New York: United Nations).

Waddington, Hugh and R. Sabates-Wheeler (2003) "How Does Poverty Affect Migration Choice?" Development Research Centre on Migration, Globalization and Poverty Working Paper (Sussex: University of Sussex).

World Bank (2007) *World Development Indicators* (Washington, D.C.: The World Bank).

Zimmermann, K. and A. Constant (2004) eds. *How Labor Migrants Fare* (Berlin: Springer-Verlag).

Part 3

How Do Migrants Fare?

Chapter 11

English Language Proficiency and the Economic Progress of Immigrants*

11.1 Introduction

The vast majority of immigrants to the U.S. come from countries whose native language is other than English. As a result, the nature of their participation in the U.S., labor market is closely mediated by English language proficiency. Although there are employment opportunities — in the garment industry, agriculture and in ethnic enclaves — that do not require extensive use of English for their performance, one expects English language deficiency to block successful entry into mainstream U.S. labor markets, impeding upward labor mobility and constraining earnings. The ability of immigrants to receive compensation in the U.S. commensurate with their education and skills should thus be closely related to English language proficiency.

*This chapter was originally published in *Economics Letters*, Vol. 34, No. 2, November 1990, pp. 295–300.

This paper was written while I was a National Assessment of Educational Progress Post-Doctoral Fellow at Educational Testing Service in Princeton, New Jersey. The author is thankful to William H. Angoff, Kyle Johnson, and the participants of seminars at Educational Testing Service and the Bureau of International Labor Affairs, U.S. Department of Labor for useful comments. The financial assistance of grants from the U.S. Department of Labor and the Rutgers University Research Council is gratefully acknowledged.

The existing research examining the role played by English language proficiency on labor market outcomes shows mixed results. In his study of Hispanic earnings, Borjas (1984) examined the issue using the 1976 Survey of Income and Education (SIE), finding that a variable measuring English proficiency was not statistically significant in influencing hourly wages for any of the various Hispanic groups he examined. Borjas concluded: 'This finding raises important questions about the role of language acquisition in determining earnings' [Borjas (1984, p. 77)]. These results are generally shared by Reimers (1983, 1985) for males and females in the SIE data set, and by Gwartney and Long (1978) and Carliner (1980) using Census data. On the other hand, research by Grenier (1984), McManus *et al.* (1983), Kossoudji (1988), and Tainer (1988) has found significant positive effects of English language proficiency on earnings.

All of the existing studies use data from surveys asking individuals to specify qualitatively how well they speak/understand English, with responses such as very well, well, not well, etc. They thus provide information only on oral or spoken English proficiency, ignoring the role played by reading and writing. They are also based on subjective, self-reported assessments that can be subject to personal bias and are difficult to quantify. In this paper, we reexamine the issue of the impact of English language proficiency on wages using a data set that provides test-based measurements of individual English language proficiency. The data set used is the 1985 National Assessment of Educational Progress (NAEP) Young Adult Literacy Assessment survey [for details on this survey, see Kirsch and Jungeblut (1987)]. This nationally representative household survey of persons 21 to 25 years old provides scores on a reading proficiency test administered to each individual sampled in addition to the usual background information. Through the use of these test-based, rather than self-assessed, English reading proficiency measurements, this paper intends to sketch a more reliable picture of the role played by language on wages. The study estimates human capital wage equations for male and female immigrants and second-generation individuals (persons whose mother and/or father are foreign-born) using

English reading proficiency scores as one of a set of explanatory variables.

11.2 The Empirical Model

Following the literature mentioned earlier, we estimate the following empirical human capital model separately for men and women in our sample:

$$\log W_{ij} = \beta' X_{ij} + U_{ij}, \tag{1}$$

where W_{ij} is the hourly wage rate received by individual i of sex j, β is a vector of coefficients to be estimated, x_{ij} is a vector of human capital and demographic characteristics affecting wages, and U_{ij} is a stochastic disturbance.

Variables in the vector X_{ij} include, firstly, years of schooling, introduced to reflect the impact of academic skills on earnings. To differentiate between the returns to high school and college education, schooling is entered into the wage equation through two dummy variables: *HSEDUC*, which equals 1 if the person has 12–15 years of schooling, that is, a high school diploma but not a college degree, and zero otherwise, and *COLLEDUC*, which equals one if the individual has a college degree or more and zero otherwise. Years of on-the-job experience, proxied by the variable *EXPER* (measured as age minus maximum years of schooling minus six), and vocational training (*VOCAT*, measured in weeks of participation) incorporate the effects of non-academic skills on wages. Region of residence is added to acknowledge the presence of geographical wage differentials due to labor market disequilibria. We include the variables *NORTHEAST*, *SOUTHEAST* and *CENTRAL* as dummy variables equal to one if the person resides in the northeastern, southeastern or central U.S., respectively, and zero otherwise.

Given the limited job opportunities available to non-English speakers in U.S. labor markets, we expect English language proficiency to be positively correlated with wages. We introduce the scores received by individuals in the survey's English reading proficiency test as the variable *ENGLISH*. The scores are based on a scale of 0 to 500, with higher scores indicating improved levels of English reading proficiency. As standardized by *NAEP*, a score of 150 indicates very rudimentary reading skills, a score of 200 indicates basic reading skills, 250 shows intermediate reading proficiency, 300 reflects adept reading skills, and 350 advanced reading proficiency. It is to be emphasized that *NAEP* tests are explicitly developed to measure English reading proficiency and are administered to students nationwide as part of periodic assessments of reading skills among the U.S. student population.

Previous literature has found that, perhaps because of an initial lack of familiarity with the U.S. labor market, immigrant earnings rise with time in the U.S. independently of other factors [see Chiswick (1978, 1979)]. We thus add the variable *TIMEUS*, equal to the number of years the person has been residing in the U.S. (the age of the individual for second-generation persons) to our human capital equations.

The U_{ij}'s in Eq. (1) represent an error term that is usually assumed to be randomly distributed among the population. However, the group of individuals for whom wages are observed, and which is thus used for purposes of estimating Eq. (1), is not randomly selected from the population since it only includes individuals who have non-zero wages and excludes those who are not participating in the labor market (in the present sample most of the latter are in school). There is thus a possible selectivity bias problem. We follow the two-stage sample selection bias correction procedure postulated by Heckman (1979). Mainly, we first estimate a binary probit model, where the dependent variable is one if the person is an employee in the wage sample and zero otherwise. The results are used to find inverse Mills' ratios that are then introduced into the original regression Eq. (1) to adjust for the sample selection bias. In this second stage of the estimation procedure, we define the variable $MILLS_{ij}$ to identify the inverse Mills' ratio computed for person i of sex j. With $MILLS_{\mathrm{ij}}$, included as an independent variable, the wage equations can be estimated using ordinary least squares, providing consistent estimates. Since the specification and results of the first stage of the estimation method are not of our particular interest in this paper, they are not reported here, but can be requested from the author [Rivera-Batiz (1988)].

11.3 English Reading Proficiency and Wages: Results

There are a total of 241 foreign-born and second-generation persons (with foreign-born mother and/or father) in our wage sample. Of these, 93 were second-generation individuals and 148 were immigrants. Most of the latter were from Spanish-speaking countries (a total of 88). On average, these Spanish-speaking immigrants received lower wages than immigrants from English-speaking and other countries, a result shared with previous studies [see Chiswick (1979, p. 376), and Tainer (1988, Table 1)]. Among Spanish-speaking immigrants, the average wage rate was \$5.78, compared to \$7.63 received by English-speaking immigrants and \$6.85 received by other immigrants. The shortfall in the wages of immigrants from Spanish-speaking countries appears to be correlated with the sharply lower English proficiency exhibited by this group, which scored an average of 208 in the reading proficiency test, as compared to a 284 average score for immigrants from English-speaking countries and 274 among other immigrants. Whether this positive correlation between wages and English proficiency is sustained in our multivariate analysis of earnings is discussed next.

Table 11.1 depicts the sample means for the variables included in our analysis. Table 11.2 shows our results, with Table 11.2-A depicting the estimated coefficients for men and Table 11.2-B those for women. For purposes of comparison, Eq. (1) presents the estimated coefficients when the English proficiency variable, *ENGLISH*, is excluded from the wage equation. Equation (2) then shows the results with the English proficiency variable included.

The adjusted R^2 rises substantially when *ENGLISH* is added — from 0.12 to 0.15 among men and from 0.25 to 0.31 among women — reflecting the relevance of English proficiency in explaining the variance of wages among immigrants and second-generation individuals. In addition, the value of the coefficient on the *TIMEUS* variable diminishes substantially. This suggests that higher English proficiency is a major explanation for the growth of earnings among immigrants as their stay in the U.S. prolongs. Indeed, in our sample,

Table 11.1. Sample Means for Wage Equations, by Sex.

	Males		Females	
Variable	**Mean**	**SD**	**Mean**	**SD**
HOURLY WAGE (Dollars)	6.95	3.22	5.87	2.60
ENGLISH (Test-based reading proficiency, 0–500)	256.55	73.93	258.98	76.78
SECEDUC (Proportion with 0–11 years of schooling completed)	0.31	—	0.23	—
HSEDUC (Proportion with 12–15 years of schooling completed)	0.50	—	0.52	—
COLLEDUC (Proportion with 16 years of schooling completed)	0.19	—	0.25	—
EXPER (Years of on-the-job experience=age-schooling-6)	5.02	2.38	5.07	2.60
VOCAT (Weeks of vocational training)	5.07	14.0	10.7	20.9
NORTHEAST (Proportion of sample residing in the Northeast)	0.21	—	0.23	—
SOUTHEAST (Proportion residing in the Southeast)	0.10	—	0.20	—
CENTRAL (Proportion residing in the Central U.S.)	0.09	—	0.11	—
WEST (Proportion residing in the Western U.S.)	0.60	—	0.46	—
TZMEUS (Number of years of residence in the U.S.)	15.4	8.0	15.7	8.0
MILLS	0.63	0.29	0.62	0.30
Number of observations	122	—	119	—

the average wage of immigrants who had resided in the U.S. for less than 5 years was equal to \$5.36 and their reading proficiency 192; for immigrants who had resided in the U.S. between 6 to 10 years the wage rate was equal to \$6.24 and reading proficiency 202; for immigrants with over 10 years of residence, the wage was \$7.03 and English proficiency 288.

The increase in immigrant English proficiency as time in the U.S. accumulates may result from assimilation and the acquisition of English as a second language. An alternative explanation is that more recent cohorts of immigrants have lower human capital endowments than previous cohorts [see Borjas (1985)]. If this is so, then

Table 11.2. Estimated Coefficients, Human Capital Wage Equations[a].

	Dependent variable: Natural logarithm of hourly wage rate					
	(1)			**(2)**		
Independent variable	**Parameter estimate**	**t-statistic H_0: $\beta = 0$**	**Prob $> \|t\|$**	**Parameter estimate**	**t-statistic H_0: $\beta = 0$**	**Prob $> \|t\|$**
A. Men						
INTERCEPT	1.4324	6.12	0.0001	1.1853	5.49	0.0001
HSEDUC	0.2783	2.85	0.005	0.2047	2.01	0.05
COLLEDUC	0.5194	3.73	0.0003	0.4126	2.86	0.005
ENGLISH	—	—	—	0.0020	2.11	0.03
EXPER	0.0328	1.55	0.12	0.0400	1.90	0.06
VOCAT	0.0024	0.97	0.33	0.0019	0.75	0.45
NORTHEAST	−0.1573	−1.81	0.07	−0.1709	−2.00	0.05
SOUTHEAST	−0.0709	−0.59	0.55	−0.0942	−0.80	0.43
CENTRAL	−0.0505	−0.41	0.68	−0.0700	−0.58	0.56
TIMEUS	0.0028	0.55	0.58	−0.0071	−1.02	0.31
MILLS	−0.0027	−0.01	0.98	−0.1225	−0.67	0.50
ADJUSTED R^2	0.12			0.15		
Dependent variable mean: 1.854, Number of observations: 122						
B. Women						
INTERCEPT	1.7458	7.86	0.0001	1.1910	5.67	0.0001
HSEDUC	0.1031	1.03	0.30	0.0553	0.57	0.57
COLLEDUC	0.3102	2.24	0.03	0.2164	1.60	0.11
ENGLISH	—	—	—	0.0030	4.06	0.0001
EXPER	−0.0229	−1.22	0.22	−0.0084	−0.45	0.65
VOCAT	0.0012	0.78	0.44	0.0010	0.67	0.50
NORTHEAST	−0.0665	−0.83	0.41	−0.1116	−1.43	0.15
SOUTHEAST	−0.1457	−1.71	0.09	−0.2150	−2.56	0.01
CENTRAL	0.0374	0.35	0.73	−0.0570	−0.54	0.59
TIMEUS	0.0113	2.70	0.008	0.0004	0.09	0.93
MILLS	−0.3393	−2.27	0.02	−0.4361	−2.93	0.004
ADJUSTED R^2	0.25			0.31		
Dependent variable mean: 1.690, Number of observations: 119						

[a]Adjusted for sample selection bias.

one would expect to see immigrants who have resided in the U.S. for a longer period of time to have higher English proficiency levels because of their belonging to a 'higher quality' cohort, not necessarily because of their acquisition of English skills over time in the U.S.

Equation (2) in Table 11.2 shows that English reading proficiency is a major determinant of earnings in our sample. Among men, the

English proficiency variable is statistically significant at the 5 percent confidence level while among women the variable is statistically significant at the 0.01 percent confidence level. The absolute value of the coefficient — 0.0020 among men and 0.0030 among women — can be transformed into elasticity form (evaluated at the sample mean) to yield a value of 0.54 for men and 0.82 for women. This suggests that an improvement in English proficiency scores of one standard deviation (74–76 points) would raise wages by 13.5 percent among men and 20.5 percent among women, holding other things constant. These are significant wage changes, changes which would substantially diminish the wage premium received by immigrants from English speaking countries relative to other immigrants (the average wage among English-speaking male immigrants in the sample is 27% higher than that of Spanish-speaking immigrants; among females, the wage of English-speaking immigrants is 41.7% above that of Spanish-speaking immigrants).

11.4 Conclusions

This paper has made use of a test-based measure of English language proficiency to estimate the role played by such proficiency in explaining the earnings of immigrants and second-generation persons in the U.S. This contrasts with the previous literature in this field, which has used self-assessed, non-test measures of English language proficiency. Our analysis unequivocally suggests that English reading deficiency is a major factor constraining the wage opportunities of immigrants and may explain a substantial fraction of the relatively lower wages received by non-English speaking immigrants in the U.S.

References

Borjas, G., 1984, The economic status of male Hispanic migrants and natives in the United States, in: R. Ehrenberg, ed., *Research in labor economics* (JAI Press, Greenwich) 65–122.

Borjas, G., 1985, "Assimilation, changes in cohort quality, and the earnings of immigrants," *Journal of Labor Economics*, 3, 463–489.

Carliner, G., 1980, "Wages, earnings and hours of first, second, and third generation American males," *Economic Inquiry*, 18, 87–102.

Chiswick, B.R., 1978, "The effects of Americanization on the earnings of foreign-born men," *Journal of Political Economy*, 86, 897–921.

Chiswick, B.R., 1979, "The economic progress of immigrants: Some apparently universal patterns," in: W. Fellner, ed., *Contemporary economic problems* (American Enterprise Institute, Washington, DC) 357–399.

Grenier, G., 1984, "The effects of language characteristics on the wages of Hispanic-American males," *Journal of Human Resources*, 19, 35–52.

Gwartney, J.D. and J.E. Long, 1978, "The relative earnings of blacks and other minorities," *Industrial and Labor Relations Review*, 31, 336–346.

Heckman, J.J., 1979, "Sample selection bias as a specification error," *Econometrica*, 47, 153–162.

Kirsch, I. and A. Jungeblut, 1987, *Literacy: Profiles of America's young adults* (Educational Testing Service, Princeton, NJ).

Kossoudji, S.A., 1988, "English language ability and the labor market opportunities of Hispanic and East Asian immigrant men," *Journal of Labor Economics*, 6, 205–228.

Long, J.E., 1980, "The effect of Americanization on earnings: Some evidence for women," *Journal of Political Economy*, 88, 620–629.

McManus, W., W. Gould and F. Welch, 1983, "Earnings of Hispanic men: The role of English language proficiency," *Journal of Labor Economics*, 1, 101–130.

Reimers, C., 1983, "Labor market discrimination against Hispanic and black men," *Review of Economics and Statistics*, 65, 570–579.

Reimers, C., 1985, "A comparative analysis of the wages of Hispanics, blacks and non-Hispanic whites," in: G. Borjas and M. Tienda, eds., *Hispanics in the U.S. economy* (Academic Press, Orlando, FL) 27–76.

Rivera-Batiz, F., 1988, "English language proficiency and the economic progress of immigrants in the U.S.," Research report (Division of Immigration Policy and Research, Bureau of International Labor Affairs, U.S. Department of Labor, Washington, DC).

Shapiro, D., 1984, "Wage differentials among black, Hispanic, and white young men," *Industrial and Labor Relations Review*, 37, 570–581.

Tainer, E., 1988, "English language proficiency and the determination of earnings among foreign-born men," *Journal of Human Resources*, 23, 108–122.

Chapter 12

How Do Migrants from Latin America and the Caribbean Fare in the U.S. Labor Market?*

12.1 Introduction

Migration from Latin America and the Caribbean (LAC) to the United States has accelerated in recent years. Since 1990, over 10 million migrants from the region have become residents of the United States, with three million of these settling in the country just in the period of 2000 to 2005. Inflows of legal immigrants have been at record levels, with an average of over 400,000 persons born in LAC admitted to the US each year as legal permanent residents over the last 15 years. To these, one must add the hundreds of thousands of undocumented workers — mostly from Mexico and Central America — who have successfully crossed the border. Estimates are that in recent years over 300,000 undocumented workers from the region have entered the United States on a net basis each year.

The money these migrants send to the region has become a major source of income for families back home. According to the World Bank (2007), more than $87 billion were received by Latin American

*This chapter was originally published in *The World Economy*, Vol. 30, No. 9, September 2007, pp. 1399–1429. © 2007 Blackwell Publishing Ltd.

The author is grateful for the comments of the participants of the Economics of Education workshop at Columbia University. The efficient research assistance of Veronica Cabezas is also acknowledged.

and Caribbean countries in 2004 in the form of migrant remittances.[1] For some countries, the income received from the services of workers abroad (mostly in the US) is now a major item of the balance of payments. For El Salvador, for example, migrant remittances are equal to 78 per cent of merchandise exports. In Guatemala, the corresponding amount is 93 percent, in the Dominican Republic it is 44 per cent and in Mexico nine per cent. The country with the heaviest reliance on income received from their migrant employment abroad is Haiti, where migrant remittances are equal to 242 per cent of merchandise exports!

How much Latin America and the Caribbean earns from the globalization of labor flows depends on the success of the migrants in the recipient countries. How do migrant workers from LAC fare in the United States? What is their labor market performance compared to that of migrants from other parts of the world? And how has that performance changed over time? It is the purpose of this paper to examine the latest evidence available on these questions.

A large body of research has now accumulated studying the labor market outcomes of immigrants (see, for example, the collection of research in Zimmermann and Constant, 2004; as well as Borjas, 1999b; Borjas and Katz, 2005; and Hanson, 2006). In the United States, the evidence appears to suggest that the economic outcomes of immigrants relative to natives have generally deteriorated since the 1960s. But there are differences among immigrant groups. On average, LAC immigrants have substantially lower earnings than those from other parts of the world. Furthermore, their economic outcomes have sharply deteriorated relative to other immigrants in recent decades. In 1980, Latin American and Caribbean migrants on average earned 76.1 per cent of the weekly wages received by other immigrants. By 2005, the corresponding percentage was 54.7 per cent, a drop of over 20 percentage points.

Why have the labor market outcomes of LAC migrants deteriorated relative to other migrants? Explanations vary but they include lower educational attainment among LAC migrants compared to other migrants, the presence of a larger cohort of recent lower-paid immigrants in the LAC migrant population, changes in US labor markets that have resulted in a reduction of the wages paid to the relatively unskilled workers sent by LAC to the United States, and the expansion of undocumented migration from that region, among other factors.

Which of these factors, then, is the most significant in explaining the trends in the economic outcomes of migrants from Latin America and the Caribbean in the United States? This paper examines the alternative explanations behind those changes, providing evidence on their relative importance. Section 12.2 presents the key trends in LAC migration to the US, as well as the changes in the economic outcomes of the migrants over time. Section 12.3 provides a discussion of the factors that may explain the changes in the economic performance of LAC migrants when compared to other migrants. Sections 12.4 and 12.5 then present estimates of the relative importance of these factors. Section 12.6 provides a set of conclusions.

12.2 Trends in Latin American and Caribbean Migration to the United States

The migration from LAC to the US over the last century has been massive, although it has had its ups and downs. Table 12.1 shows the number of migrants from the region legally admitted to the US in the period of 1900 to 2005. The figure increases sharply in the first three decades of the twentieth century, but drops precipitously in the decade of the 1930s and the 1940s. Since then, emigration from LAC has gradually increased to become, by far, the largest migrant group entering the US every year. The migration flow peaked in the 1990s, when close to half a million immigrants from the region were accepted to the US as legal permanent residents on average each year. The figure declined to 390,172 per year in the period of 2000–2005, still a massive migration flow by historical standards.

Legal Migration Flows from LAC to the United States

The gyrations in the migration flows between LAC and the United States depicted by Table 12.1 have followed socioeconomic conditions in the two regions as well as the migration policies established

Table 12.1. Migrants from LAC Admitted to the US as Legal Permanent Residents.

Decade	All immigrants	Immigrants from Latin America and Caribbean	Percentage of total
1900–09	8,202,388	154,742	1.9
1910–19	6,347,380	361,824	5.7
1920–29	4,295,510	641,992	14.9
1930–39	699,375	67,616	9.6
1940–49	856,608	167,524	19.6
1950–59	2,499,268	568,441	22.7
1960–69	3,213,749	1,241,044	38.6
1970–79	4,248,203	1,725,088	40.6
1980–89	6,244,379	2,539,016	40.7
1990–99	9,775,398	4,942,955	50.6
2000–05	5,743,058	2,341,036	40.8

Source: US Department of Homeland Security (2006).

by both the recipient and the sending countries. Migration to the US from LAC countries was virtually unimpeded until the 1920s. Very few restrictions on immigration were introduced until that time. Recorded migration statistics show that Latin American and Caribbean migration to the US expanded rapidly in the 1910s and 1920s. Most of this migrant flow originated in Mexico, where almost 700,000 people moved to the US between 1910 and 1929. This mass migration partly responded to the social turmoil and economic distress generated by the Mexican revolution in the period of 1910 to 1917, as well as its chaotic aftermath (Gamio, 1930). But it was also motivated by the expansion of labor demand in the US. With no effective restrictions on immigration across the Southwest border at the time, hundreds of thousands of Mexican workers made their way to the US, lured by recruiters and contractors offering employment in labor-short farms, mining operations and railroad construction.

The onset of the Great Depression in the 1930s ended the first mass migration from Latin America to the US. The rising unemployment and declining wages in the US led many to seek easy scapegoats for the socioeconomic ills of the country. A popular target was the recently-arrived Mexican immigrant population, which was accused of taking jobs away from US citizens. As a result of pressures by nativists and various interest groups, severe restrictions on Mexican migration to the US were imposed. Furthermore, a policy of 'repatriation' of Mexican workers who had legally migrated to the United States in previous years was instituted. Approximately 500,000 Mexicans were deported from the US in the 1930s (Sanchez, 1993).

Migration from LAC to the US began to grow back in the 1940s and 1950s. Responding to pressures from agricultural growers and a wide range of industrialists facing labor shortages due to the expansion of the military during World War II, the US Congress began a reversal of its restrictive immigration policies towards Mexico. In August 1942, the two countries signed a bilateral agreement that allowed for the legal immigration of temporary Mexican laborers (called in Spanish *braceros*) into the country. By 1952, close to 200,000 Mexican laborers were contracted for work in the US and the numbers rose in the mid-1950s. The bracero program peaked in 1959 but was sharply curtailed in the following years and terminated unilaterally by the US Congress in December 1964. The end of the bracero program responded in part to a growing perception among policymakers that there was rampant exploitation and violation of the civil rights of the braceros (Craig, 1971).

The demise of the bracero program did not end legal migration flows to the US but instead replaced what was effectively a guest worker program with a growing immigration of legal permanent residents. The 1965 amendments to the 1952 Immigration and Nationality Act — which eliminated stringent quotas imposed on non-European countries — set the background for this switch. This immigration policy shift generated a process through which the composition of US legal permanent immigrant admissions shifted from one originating mainly in European countries to one dominated by Latin American and Caribbean (as well as Asian) nations. But the immigration policy shift was also helped by social and economic forces that have been intimately connected to the rising tide of LAC migrants entering the US.

Consider migration from the Caribbean to the United States, which took off on a massive scale in the 1960s. Cuban migration had already started to grow in the 1950s, as closer economic relations between the US and Cuba had risen in that decade. But it was the social and political upheaval of the Cuban revolution that led to a massive exodus that raised the number of Cubans entering the US from 73,221 in the 1950s to 202,030 in the 1960s, and 256,497 in the 1970s. These flows have abated since that time, but continue to be substantial even to the present day. In the Dominican Republic, the restrictive migration policies of dictator Rafael Leónidas Trujillo, who ruled the country from 1930 to 1961, prevented any significant migration to the US. After Trujillo's death, Dominican migration began to rise at a gradual, but explosive growth. Motivated first by government policies that actively encouraged migration to the US, and later by economic stagnation that led to negative income growth between the late 1970s and the early 1990s, Dominican migration to the US grew from 83,552 in the decade of the 1960s to 139,249 in the 1970s, 221,552 in the 1980s and 359,818 in the 1990s (see Hernandez and Rivera-Batiz, 1997).

The rise of Central and South American migration to the US in recent decades has also been marked by social and economic upheavals. To some extent or another, from El Salvador and Guatemala to Colombia and Peru, persistent insurgencies, internal social conflicts or economic crises have plagued countries in the region since the late 1970s. In Central America, the migration of legal permanent residents to the US rose from 40,201 in the 1950s to 120,274 in the 1970s, 339,376 in the 1980s and 610,189 in the 1990s. For South America, the corresponding out-migration increased from 78,418 in the 1950s to 250,754 in the 1960s, 273,608 in the 1970s, 398,862 in the 1980s and 570,624 in the 1990s.

The Rise of Undocumented Migration

Up to this point, trends in the migration of legal permanent residents to the US have been presented. But equally important has been the rise of undocumented migration. By definition, the number of migrants moving from LAC to the US without legal documents is unknown. However, a rough picture of the ups and downs in these flows can be made on the basis of the migrants who are caught

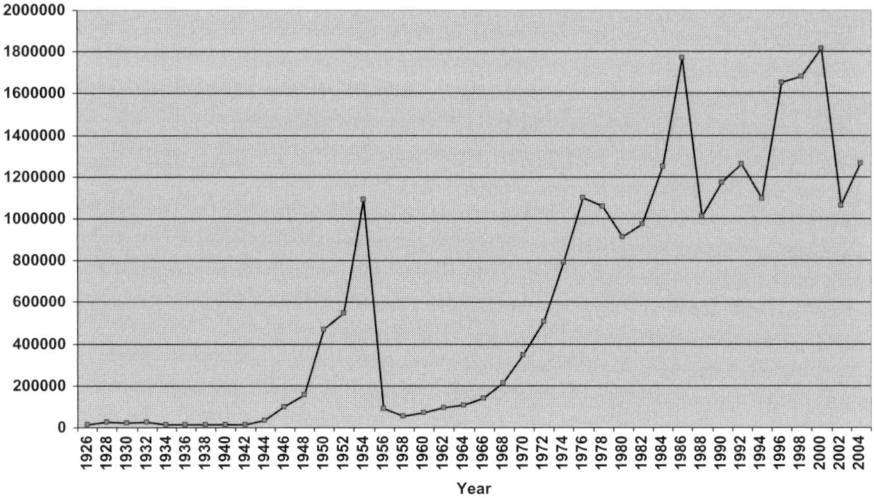

Figure 12.1. Apprehended Undocumented Immigrants in the US, 1926–2004.

by authorities entering the US.[2] This is especially illuminating for LAC flows since most of the apprehended undocumented workers are detained crossing the Mexican border and are largely born in the region (96 per cent in fiscal year 2005).

Figure 12.1 plots the number of undocumented workers apprehended in the US from 1926 to 2004. The first period of rising undocumented migration to the US occurred in the 1940s and 1950s, when hundreds of thousands of migrants from LAC were attracted by a labor shortage in agriculture, construction and other sectors during World War II and its aftermath. However, the start of the bracero program, combined with stringent border enforcement and interdiction policies, led to a sharp drop of undocumented migration in the following years.

The end of the bracero programme then marked the start of a long-term, secular rebound of undocumented migration from Latin America to the US. In the 1960s, the average annual number of undocumented worker apprehensions was approximately 160,000. By the 1980s, the average number of immigrants apprehended each year had increased to 1,188,000, and in the 1990s, the annual apprehensions rose even more, to about 1,215,000. After 11 September, 2001, apprehensions have dropped, but continue at levels of over one million a year.

Although historically a large fraction of undocumented workers from LAC would stay in the US only temporarily, returning home after a certain period of time, the 1990s saw a major turnaround of this pattern. Paradoxically, the stricter border enforcement policies adopted by the US under the 1986 Immigration Reform and Control Act and especially the 1996 Illegal Immigration Reform and Responsibility Act have acted to increase the undocumented migrant population that stays across the border.[3] By increasing the difficulty of back-and-forth movements across the border, the policies have acted to reduce the likelihood of return migration to LAC. Indeed, the probability of return migration of the typical undocumented worker may have dropped to 10 percent in the 1990s (see Massey *et al.*, 2002).

The lower probability of return migration has acted to increase the net flow of undocumented migrants from LAC to the US, leading to an unprecedented rise in the number of these immigrants residing in the United States. It is estimated that 10.5 million undocumented immigrants resided in the US in 2005, up from 3.5 million in 1990.[4] The majority of these migrants are from LAC. Estimates are that 5,970,000 undocumented Mexican immigrants resided in the US in 2005, 470,000 from El Salvador, 370,000 from Guatemala, 180,000 from Honduras and 170,000 Haitians.

Mass Migration and Its Consequences

The increased migration of legal permanent residents to the US, combined with a rise of the number of undocumented workers who remain as long-term residents in the US, has led to a massive increase of Latin American and Caribbean immigrants residing in the US. Table 12.2 shows that this number rose from 4,543,700 in 1980 to 19,671,641 in 2005, with the percentage of immigrants residing in the US accounted for by LAC climbing from 29.7 per cent in 1980 to 51.5 percent in 2005.

The largest immigrant group from LAC residing in the US is from Mexico: there were 11,258,554 Mexican migrants in the US in

Table 12.2. Changes in the Number of Immigrants from LAC Residing in the United States, 1980–2005.

	1980	1990	2000	2005
All Immigrants	15,260,400	21,595,271	32,922,052	38,292,252
LAC	4,543,700	8,760,664	16,336,554	19,671,641
Mexico	2,254,800	4,442,054	9,318,787	11,258,554
Caribbean	1,293,300	1,996,130	2,993,655	3,286,047
Central America	388,100	1,175,340	2,065,607	2,585,628
South America	607,500	1,147,140	1,958,445	2,541,422
El Salvador	95,500	453,745	833,803	1,001,180
Cuba	625,700	749,953	892,566	940,972
Dominican Republic	173,600	350,586	724,719	881,266
Guatemala	63,700	234,611	477,836	658,197
Jamaica	207,600	354,194	525,959	608,827
Colombia	159,000	298,806	513,397	574,720
Haiti	96,200	229,060	417,190	497,024
Peru	50,800	161,578	276,981	385,014
Honduras	36,300	110,838	258,065	397,094

Source: US Census of Population and American Community Survey data for various years; author's tabulations.

2005. In addition, there were 1,001,180 from El Salvador, 940,972 from Cuba, 881,266 from the Dominican Republic, 658,197 from Guatemala, 608,827 from Jamaica, 574,720 from Colombia, 497,024 from Haiti, 397,794 from Honduras and 385,014 from Peru.

Although US immigration policy changes and the social and political situations in many countries have been partly linked to the mass migration that we have just documented, the stronger, underlying force is economic. Both documented and undocumented migration flows have been found to be strongly correlated with the relative economic conditions in the US and in LAC (see, for instance, Passel and Suro, 2005; and Hanson and Spilimbergo, 1999). Figure 12.2 shows the behavior of GDP per capita for the US relative to GDP per capita for LAC between 1980 and 2005. As can be seen, there has been a divergence of income per capita levels between the US and the region. In 1980, the ratio of GDP per capita of the US relative to LAC overall was 3.43. By 2005, this ratio had risen to 4.94. The greatest divergence is that of Haiti: the GDP per capita of the US

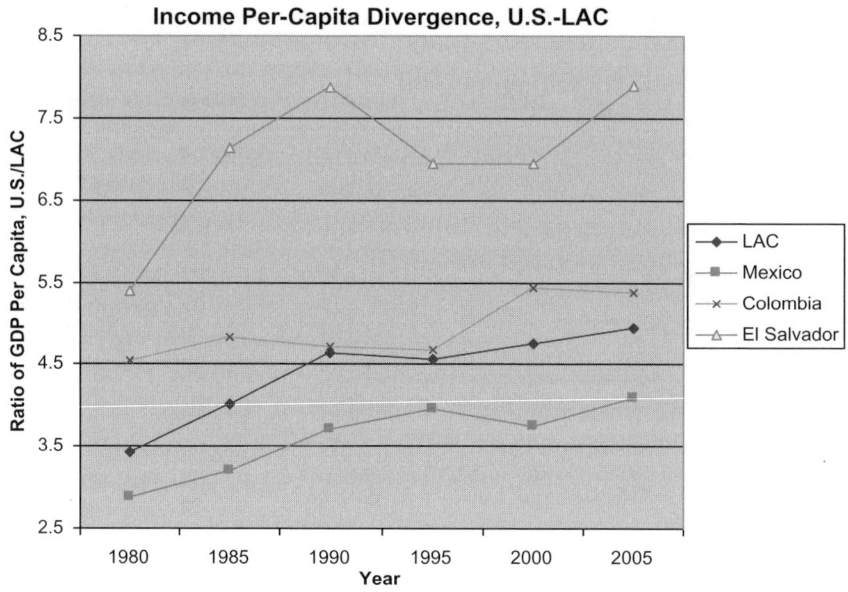

Figure 12.2. The Growing Income Gap between the US and LAC.

Notes: The ratio in the vertical axis is that of gross domestic product (GDP) per capita in the US divided by the equivalent for countries in LAC (LAC), where the source data are PPP-adjusted, expressed in constant 2000 international dollars.

Source: World Bank (2007).

relative to Haiti rose from 7.18 in 1980 to 22.8 in 2005. The US-Mexico ratio of GDP per capita also increased, from 2.87 in 1980 to 4.09 in 2005.

These trends are a consequence of sluggish economic growth in LAC. For some countries, such as Haiti, GDP per capita has declined almost continuously since 1980. For others, stagnation was almost uniform in the 1980s (the so-called 'lost decade' in the region) and in the second half of the 1990s. This was despite the implementation of drastic neoliberal economic policies across the region, which had the goal of revitalizing economic growth. In Mexico, for instance, major structural changes in the economy in the 1980s and 1990s — including privatization, trade liberalization, etc. — have not been associated yet with an expansion of long-term economic growth, while igniting increased income and regional inequalities that may have heightened emigration (see Massey *et al.*, 2002; and Cornelius and Marcelli, 2000).

The divergence in economic progress between LAC and the United States was also fueled by the US economic boom of the 1980s and 1990s. While many countries in the region struggled through the two decades, the United States sailed through it (only temporarily interrupted by the 1989–1992 recession), with an average growth rate of real GDP per capita of 2.5 per cent per year in the period of 1980 to 2005.

The broad — and widening — gap in employment opportunities and wages between the US and the LAC region lies behind the continuous expansion of migration flows from the latter to the former over the last 25 years. And the most visible impact of the migrants south of the border is connected to the remittances that they send back home. Table 12.3 presents the value of these remittances in

Table 12.3. Migrant Remittances to LAC, 2004 (in Millions of US Dollars).

Country/Region	**Remittances in current $**	**Remittances in PPP-adjusted $**	**Remittances as a percentage of merchandise exports**
Overall Latin American and the Caribbean	$41,042	$87,328	9
Mexico	16,613	23,533	9
Brazil	3,576	9,281	4
Colombia	3,190	10,877	20
Guatemala	2,592	5,037	93
El Salvador	2,564	5,432	78
Dominican Republic	2,471	8,019	44
Ecuador	1,610	2,725	21
Peru	1,440	3,276	12
Honduras	1,142	3,004	73
Haiti	876	3,773	242

Source: Data for remittances in current $ are taken from World Bank (2007); other indicators are author's calculations using PPP adjustments and exports from World Bank (2007).

2004. That year, Latin American and Caribbean countries received \$41 billion in remittances from their migrants abroad, up from \$4.5 billion in 1980 (adjusted for inflation and expressed in 2000 dollars). But the real value of these remittances is greater since each dollar buys much more in LAC than in the US. Therefore, when one adjusts the \$41 billion for differences in purchasing power, one obtains that the value of the remittances in 2004 was \$87 billion. This was equal to nine per cent of the value of merchandise exports that the region produced that year. But for some countries, remittances are even more significant. The PPP-adjusted value of remittances received by Colombia in 2004 was \$10.9 billion, or 20 per cent of merchandise exports, for Guatemala remittances were equal to 93 per cent of exports, for El Salvador it was 78 percent, for the Dominican Republic 44 per cent and for Haiti, 242 per cent.

Remittances clearly constitute an improvement in the standard of living for family members who are recipients of such income. And recent evidence suggests that remittances are connected to lower poverty levels in LAC (see Acosta *et al.*, 2006; and Adams, 2007). Some questions have been raised over the years as to the extent to which the remittances simply raise current consumption instead of stimulating investment and future economic growth (see, for example, Reichert, 1982). Recently, however, a number of studies have documented that, first, a significant portion of so-called consumption spending consists of household investments in housing, automobiles and durable goods, whose long-term wealth-raising capacities are substantial; second, the use of remittances for community investment projects is not insignificant and also acts to stimulate local development; and, third, the multiplier effects of the increased consumption spending in generating local economic activity may be substantial (see, for example, De la Garza and Lowell, 2002; Parrado, 2004; and Adams, 2007).

The positive contribution of migrant remittances for economic development must be weighed against any negative consequences of the migration flows. Because the process of migration is costly and sometimes dangerous, migrants have been known to be positively selected from the general population in the source country, having above-average motivation and/or skills (Chiswick, 1999). The loss of such a group of workers can result in negative externalities for those communities suffering from substantial emigration. In addition, local labor shortages may result in rising local wages, increased prices of services, and a growing spiral of dependency on migration as a source of income (see Rivera-Batiz, 1982 and 1986; Hanson, 2005b; and Mishra, 2006). Remittances may or may not offset these potentially negative effects.

How Have LAC Migrants Fared in the US Labor Markets?

The volume of remittances received by sending countries partly depends on the economic success of the migrants across the border. How have migrant workers from LAC fared?

Table 12.4 shows the labor force participation rate of migrants from LAC in the United States, in 1980 and in 2005. This rate has increased from 66.2 to 70.4 per cent and it is higher than that prevailing among other immigrants in the US and the native population. Table 12.4 also presents unemployment rates. As can be seen, Latin American and Caribbean immigrants do display higher unemployment rates than other immigrants and natives. In 1980, migrants from the region had unemployment rates of 8.5 per cent in 1980,

Table 12.4. Labor Market Status of LAC Migrants (Persons 16 Years of Age or Older).

	In the labour force (Per cent)		**Unemployment rate (Per cent)**	
Category	**1980**	**2005**	**1980**	**2005**
Immigrants from Latin America and the Caribbean	66.2	70.4	8.5	7.5
Other Immigrants	53.3	63.5	5.8	5.6
Non-immigrants in the US	63.5	65.7	6.4	6.9

Source: Data from 1980 US Census of Population and 2005 American Community Survey; author's tabulations.

Table 12.5. The Wages of Immigrants from LAC in the US, 1980–2005 (Persons 18 to 64 Years of Age with Positive Wages and Hours of Work).

	Weekly wage		Hourly wage	
Category	**1980**	**2005**	**1980**	**2005**
Overall Immigrant Population	$626	$767	15.9	18.6
Immigrants from Latin America and the Caribbean	521	565	13.3	14.0
Other Immigrants	684	1,002	17.3	24.0
Non-immigrants in the US	644	850	16.1	20.4
Ratio of Wages in Per Cent LAC Immigrants/Other Immigrants	76.1	54.9	76.9	58.3
Ratio of Wages in Per Cent LAC Immigrants/Non-immigrants	80.9	66.5	82.6	68.6

Note: The wages for 1980 have been adjusted for inflation and expressed in 2005 dollars.

Source: Data from 1980 US Census of Population and 2005 American Community Survey; author's tabulations.

compared to 5.8 per cent among other immigrants and 6.4 per cent for non-immigrants. Note, however, that unemployment rates for Latin American and Caribbean migrants have declined over time, approaching the levels prevailing among non-immigrants. In 2005, migrants from the region had an unemployment rate of 7.5 percent while non-immigrants had unemployment of 6.9 per cent.

Table 12.5 focuses on the wages received by employed workers. Immigrants from LAC earn substantially less than other immigrants in the US, whether one measures wages by the week or on an hourly basis. In 2005, for example, migrants from the region earned an average hourly wage rate of $14, compared to $24 among other immigrants, and $20.4 for non-immigrants. Furthermore, when one examines wage trends over time, one finds that the earnings of Latin American and Caribbean migrants have been sharply declining relative to the earnings of other immigrants as well as natives. In 1980, the hourly wage rate received by the region's immigrants was equal to 76.9 per cent of the average wage of other immigrants and 82.6 per cent of the wage rate of non-immigrants. By 2005, this ratio had declined to 58.3 per cent relative to other immigrants and 68.6 per cent when compared to non-immigrants. In fact, the absolute value of the wages received on average by immigrants from LAC in the US hardly increased at all between 1980 and 2005, when measured in real terms.

In 1980, migrants from the region earned an average of $13.3 per hour (measured in 2005 dollars) while in 2005 it was $14.0, an increase of just five per cent in 15 years! During the same time period, the average wages received by immigrants from other regions rose by close to 40 per cent and among natives by 27 percent.

What explains the relative shortfall in the labor market outcomes of Latin American and Caribbean migrants in the US, compared to other immigrants? Why have the relative wages of migrants from the region deteriorated so sharply over the last 25 years compared to other migrants in the US? The next sections seek to answer these questions.

12.3 Explaining the Labor Market Outcomes of Latin American and Caribbean Migrants

There are a number of forces that can explain the relative deterioration in the labor market outcomes of Latin American and Caribbean immigrants. These range from demographic factors and changes in the characteristics of the migrants to changes in the structure of the US economy and the economic opportunities it offers Latin American migrants relative to other migrants.

Cohort Effects

It is clear that because of the drastic increase in migration flows since the 1960s, there is a larger cohort of recent Latin American and Caribbean immigrants when compared to other immigrants. In 1980, for example, only 17.3 per cent of immigrants 16 years of age or older from the region had been in the US for more than 20 years. Among other immigrants, the equivalent percentage was 49.1 per cent. This pattern was still maintained in 2005, but it was not as sharp as before: 32.6 per cent of immigrants from LAC had been in the US for more than 20 years, compared to 44 per cent of other immigrants.

The presence of a cohort of immigrants that has been in the US for a shorter period of time tends to push down average wages. The research of Chiswick (1978 and 1999) and Duleep and Regets (1999) has suggested that immigrants face an initial shortfall or dip in their labor market performance after they arrive in the country. This dip is the result of the adjustment costs that immigrants suffer as they enter the US. With limited knowledge about labor market institutions in the US — and a compelling need to obtain employment — recent migrants may accept jobs with wage offers lower than those they would otherwise accept given their skills. As their stay increases and they are able to search for better-paying jobs, earnings will rise and they will be paid wages that correspond more closely to their skill endowments.

The comparatively poorer labor market performance of recent immigrants may be compounded by another phenomenon. Because of the effort required by — and the costs involved in — the process of migrating from one country to another, migrants tend to be a favorably selected group of people. They tend to be highly-motivated people who are willing to face great challenges and make great efforts to improve their well-being and that of their families. One expects the first newcomers in any migration process to be the most motivated and driven of all the persons willing to leave their homeland to seek better opportunities abroad. As a result, one would also expect these migrants to perform at a very high level in their destinations, perhaps even eventually obtaining better labor market outcomes than natives (see Chiswick, 1978). But as the migration process of a country grows, especially in situations of mass migrations, as in the case of LAC migrations to the US, the positive selectivity of migrants relative to the rest of the population in the home country may decline. As a result, over time, recent migrants may not perform as well as their earlier cohorts (see Borjas, 1987 and 1995; Chiquiar and Hanson, 2005; and Hernandez-Huertas, 2007). If this phenomenon does affect Latin American and Caribbean migrants, it would also contribute to their lower wages compared to those of other regions who have not displayed mass migration to the US.

Declining Relative Educational Attainment

A second hypothesis that could potentially explain the relative deterioration of the earnings of Latin American and Caribbean immigrants is if their skills, particularly educational attainment, have declined over time relative to other immigrants and natives (see Borjas, 1999a and 2000). Indeed, the relative educational attainment of immigrants from LAC has dropped sharply. Table 12.6 shows the distribution of educational attainment for persons aged 25 or older residing in the US in 1980 and 2005. It is clear that migrants from LAC have

Table 12.6. The Comparative Educational Attainment of Latin American and Caribbean Migrants, 1980–2005.

Group	**Less than high school (Per cent)**	**High school (Per cent)**	**Some college (Per cent)**	**College or more (Per cent)**
1980				
Immigrants from Latin America and the Caribbean	58.3	21.2	11.3	9.3
Other Immigrants	41.4	26.1	13.7	18.9
Overall Immigrants	45.9	24.7	13.0	16.3
Non-immigrants	31.9	35.7	16.0	16.3
2005				
Immigrants from Latin America and the Caribbean	43.3	29.6	15.6	11.5
Other Immigrants	12.2	23.3	21.8	42.7
Overall Immigrants	27.7	26.5	18.7	27.1
Non-immigrants (Natives)	10.7	32.9	29.7	27.2

Source: Data from 1980 US Census of Population and 2005 American Community Survey; author's tabulations.

lower educational attainment than other immigrants and natives. In 1980, 58.3 per cent of all immigrants from the region had less than a 12th-grade (high school) education, compared to 41.4 per cent among other immigrants and 31.9 per cent among natives. In 2005, 43.3 per cent of Latin American and Caribbean immigrants had less than a high school education, compared to 12.2 per cent among other immigrants and 10.7 per cent among non-immigrants.

Although schooling is rising for all groups being considered, including Latin American and Caribbean immigrants, it is also clear that these figures show a deterioration of the relative educational attainment of the latter. In 1980, for example, the percentage of migrants from LAC with less than a 12th-grade (high school) education was almost twice the corresponding figure for natives in the US and 140 percent when compared to immigrants from other regions. By 2005, the percentage of immigrants from the region with less than a 12th-grade schooling was about four times the equivalent percentage for natives and 3.5 times the percentage for other immigrants. Since greater schooling is richly rewarded in the labor market, this relative decline of educational attainment could explain the comparatively sluggish increase in earnings of Latin American and Caribbean immigrants relative to other migrants.

Changes in US Labor Markets

Changes in US labor markets have been postulated as another possible factor explaining the deteriorating economic outcomes of Latin America and Caribbean immigrants relative to other immigrants. Since the early 1980s, rates of return to education have skyrocketed in the US while the employment opportunities and wages of workers with relatively lower skills have worsened in relative terms (see, for example, the surveys by Katz and Autor, 1999; and Acemoglu, 2002). This trend continues to the present time, although some research finds that in recent years the demand for workers at the very lowest levels and the very highest levels of the educational distribution may be increasing relative to workers in the middle, thus still maintaining the rising trend in inequality but now also leading to a polarization of the labor market (see Autor *et al.*, 2006).

There are a number of hypotheses seeking to explain these changes. The most popular is that skill-biased technical change has increased the relative demand for highly-educated workers. Since the introduction of computers in the early 1980s coincides with the trend towards higher demand for skilled labor, some research suggests that the growing use of computers in the workplace may have been connected to the rising demand for skilled labor (see, for instance, Krueger, 1993; and Levy and Murnane, 2004). There are other hypotheses as well, including the decline of high-paying manufacturing jobs in the US, de-unionization and a collapse in the real value of minimum wages (see Bernard and Bradford Jensen, 2000).

Whatever the nature of the processes that have led to a rising rate of return to education, the growing skill premium would have impacted more forcefully immigrants from LAC, who — as noted earlier — tend to have lower schooling than other immigrants. The clustering of many Latin American immigrants in relatively unskilled jobs in agriculture, construction and service industries would mean that they have borne a disproportionate burden of the impact of the lower relative wages of less-skilled workers. For example, in the late 1990s, close to 90 per cent of California's farm labor force was Mexican-born. Although not as high, the Mexican presence in California's highly-unskilled occupations such as gardening, restaurant cook, household childcare, electronics assembling and construction laborer all hovered above 50 per cent in the late 1990s (Cornelius and Marcelli, 2000).

Undocumented Migration

Another factor that may account for the deterioration of the relative economic status of Latin American and Caribbean immigrants in the US is the expansion of undocumented migration from that region. Over 70 per cent of undocumented workers residing in the US in 2005 were born in LAC. These migrants often operate in underground labor markets that yield employment opportunities offering lower wages and limited upward mobility. For instance, Rivera-Batiz (1999 and 2001) analyzed the earnings of Mexican undocumented immigrants in the US labor market using a nationally-representative sample of these immigrants obtained from the 1989/1992 Legalized Population Survey (LPS). This research confirms that Mexican undocumented workers receive substantially lower earnings relative to legal immigrants in the US. Comparing data on legal immigrants with data on undocumented immigrants for 1987/1988, the study shows that, on an hourly basis, male Mexican legal immigrants in the US earned 41.8 percent more than undocumented workers while female legal immigrants earned 40.8 percent more. Undocumented immigrants have lower average educational attainment than legal immigrants, lower English-language proficiency and a smaller number of years of residence in the US, all of which reduce their relative wages. There is also evidence consistent with exploitation of the migrants, meaning that they receive substantially lower wages when compared with other workers who have the same productive characteristics, such as schooling, age, etc.[5]

Since undocumented immigrants have expanded within the Latin American and Caribbean immigrant contingent in the US, particularly since 1990, they are an increasingly significant factor in determining the overall characteristics of the migrants from the region. The lower wages of the undocumented migrants may have pulled down the overall relative socioeconomic status of the Latin American and Caribbean immigrant population in the US.

Which of the factors discussed in this section, then, is the most significant in explaining the trends in the economic outcomes of migrants from LAC in the United States? The next sections develop an empirical framework that studies the factors that explain the relative wages of immigrants and how these have changed over time, determining their importance in accounting for the deterioration in the relative wages of Latin American and Caribbean immigrants in the United States.

12.4 The Earnings of Immigrants: An Empirical Analysis

The framework adopted in this paper to examine the determinants of wages follows the standard empirical human capital literature in postulating that the natural logarithm of the wage rate of a worker i of sex j is given by:

$$\log W_{ij} = \beta' X_{ij} + U_{ij}, \tag{1}$$

where W_{ij} is the hourly wage rate received by the worker, β is a vector of coefficients to be estimated, X_{ij} is a vector of individual human capital, occupational and demographic characteristics affecting wages, and U_{ij} is a stochastic disturbance term.

Explanatory Variables Included

The human capital variables in the vector X_{ij} include, first of all, years of schooling, represented by the dummy variables HIGHSC, equal to 1 if the person has 12 years of schooling (a high school education) and 0 otherwise, SOMECO, equal to 1 if the worker has between 13 and 15 years of schooling (some college education) and 0 otherwise, and COLLEGE, equal to 1 if the person has 16 or more years of schooling and 0 otherwise. In addition, English language proficiency has been found to be a key human capital variable influencing the earnings of immigrants. Employment opportunities may be severely limited if the immigrant's knowledge of the English language is not sufficient. On the other hand, ethnic enclaves can allow broad leeway for immigrants to find jobs even if their English proficiency is absent. The measure of English proficiency utilised in this paper is symbolised by the variable ENGLISH, which is an index that ranges from 0 to 4, where the value of 0 means the worker does not speak English at all, a value of 4 means the worker only speaks English, and the intermediate values, 1 to 3, imply the person knows English 'not well', 'well' and 'very well', respectively. The existing research examining the role played by English-language proficiency on labour market outcomes generally finds a positive impact of English proficiency on earnings (see, for example, Rivera-Batiz, 1990; and Chiswick and Miller, 2004).

To reflect the skills acquired by the worker through seniority and ageing in the labour market, the equation includes years of on-the-job experience, proxied by the variable EXPER (measured as age minus years of schooling completed minus six). The variable

EXPERSQ, equal to the square of years of on-the-job experience, is also introduced in the equation to reflect variable returns to experience. On the assumption of positive, but diminishing, returns to on-the-job experience, it is anticipated that the variable EXPER would have a positive coefficient and EXPERSQ a negative coefficient in the earnings equation.

Workers supply various amounts of hours per week on their jobs. Labor supply can influence earnings, not only because increasing the number of hours worked per week, at a given hourly wage rate, will increase weekly earnings, but also because the hourly rate for overtime work may be higher than for the regular workday. To incorporate this, the analysis includes a variable denoted by HOURS, equal to the number of hours per week that the person supplies in the labor market. It can be expected that, holding other things constant, increased hours of work per week will be associated with higher weekly wages.

As discussed earlier, the longer immigrants reside in a country, the higher their earnings. To incorporate the impact of recency of immigration into the analysis, we define a set of dummy variables: COHORT1, equal to one if the immigrant moved to stay as a resident of the US in the five years previous to interview, and zero otherwise, COHORT2, equal to one if the immigrant moved between 6 and 10 years before the interview, COHORT3, equal to one if the migrant moved between 11 and 20 years before, and COHORT4, equal to one if the immigrant arrived in the US more than 20 years before the sampling. One expects the coefficients on the variables COHORT1, COHORT2 and COHORT3 to be negative, reflecting lower earnings relative to COHORT4.

The presence of undocumented workers is expected to generate a strong, negative impact on the wages of immigrants, as was discussed earlier. The data used in this research are based on US Census survey data that include all US residents — including undocumented workers — but do not identify the latter. As a proxy, since undocumented immigrants have a greater concentration among Mexican immigrants, the equation introduces a dummy variable MEXICAN, equal to one if the immigrant was born in Mexico and zero otherwise. The coefficient on this variable is expected to be negative.

The discussion so far suggests that the wage equation to be estimated should be given by

$$\begin{aligned}\log W_{ij} = {} & \beta_0 + \beta_1 MEXICAN_{ij} + \beta_2 HIGHSC_{ij} + \beta_3 SOMECO_{ij} \\ & + \beta_4 COLLEGE_{ij} + \beta_5 ENGLISH_{ij} + \beta_6 EXPER_{ij} \\ & + \beta_7 EXPERSQ_{ij} + \beta_8 COHORT1_{ij} + \beta_9 COHORT2_{ij} \\ & + \beta_{10} COHORT3_{ij} + \beta_{11} HOURS_{ij} + U_{ij}, \qquad (2)\end{aligned}$$

where all the variables are as defined above.

The empirical model in equation (2) is applied to examine separately the weekly wages of immigrants from LAC and those of other immigrants in the United States. The analysis is carried out separately for male and female workers. The data sets used are the 1980 US Census of Population's one percent PUMS and the 2005 American Community Survey, as distributed by IPUMS. Individuals with no responses on the relevant questions used to determine individual characteristics (such as earnings, educational attainment, etc.) were eliminated from the analysis. In addition, following the custom in the literature, the sample was circumscribed to persons 18 to 64 years of age, the age group most likely to be fully involved in the labor market.

The surveys utilized in this research provide information on the annual wages of persons in the year before they were sampled as well as the average number of weeks they worked during the year and the usual hours worked per week. The annual wages were divided by the number of weeks worked to obtain weekly wages. The data for weekly wages in 1980 were then adjusted for inflation and converted to 2005 constant dollars. Only workers with positive hours of work in the year before the sample was taken were considered in the analysis.

Sample Means

Tables 12.7 and 12.8 present the sample means for the variables introduced in the wage equations, by immigrant origin (place of birth) and

Table 12.7. Sample Means for Immigrants from LAC and Other Immigrants, Males.

	LAC immigrants		Other immigrants	
	1980	**2005**	**1980**	**2005**
Weekly Wage Mean	610.8	624.2	870.6	1,217.5
Log of Weekly Wage	6.1670	6.2135	6.5062	6.7647
HIGHSCH (If person has 12 years of schooling)	0.210	0.319	0.257	0.206
SOMECO (If person has 13–15 years of schooling)	0.134	0.146	0.184	0.229
COLLEGE (If person has 16 years of schooling or more)	0.099	0.097	0.306	0.499
ENGLISH (Index of English proficiency from 0 to 4)	1.99	1.81	2.95	2.84
EXPER (Age minus years of schooling minus 6)	19.7	20.0	20.3	20.4
EXPERSQ (EXPER squared)	551.1	536.2	593.3	551.1
COHORT1 (If has resided in US for 5 years or less)	0.246	0.235	0.201	0.177
COHORT2 (If has resided in US between 6 and 10 years)	0.254	0.190	0.150	0.167
COHORT3 (If has resided in US between 11 and 20 years)	0.334	0.303	0.245	0.274
HOURS (Weekly hours of work)	41.5	42.2	42.3	43.2
MEXICAN (If person was born in Mexico)	0.529	0.618	—	—
Number of observations	13,369	51,249	23,226	47,901

Note: The wages for 1980 have been adjusted for inflation and expressed in 2005 dollars.

Source: Data from 1980 US Census of Population and 2005 American Community Survey; author's tabulations.

gender. The first row shows the average values for weekly wages and the second row presents the average value of the dependent variable, the logarithm of the weekly wage. As noted earlier, the average weekly wages of Latin American and Caribbean migrants are substantially lower than those received by other immigrants, both in 1980 and in 2005. In addition, the weekly wages of men are

Table 12.8. Sample Means for Immigrants from LAC and Other Immigrants, Females.

	LAC immigrants		Other immigrants	
	1980	**2005**	**1980**	**2005**
Weekly Wage Mean	420.7	502.9	479.3	816.0
Log of Weekly Wage	5.8047	5.9570	5.9247	6.3567
HIGHSCH (If person has 12 years of schooling)	0.275	0.313	0.337	0.215
SOMECO (If person has 13–15 years of schooling)	0.162	0.218	0.206	0.450
COLLEGE (If person has 16 years of schooling or more)	0.086	0.148	0.202	0.450
ENGLISH (Index of English proficiency from 0 to 4)	2.12	2.06	2.96	2.84
EXPER (Age minus years of schooling minus 6)	19.5	20.9	20.2	20.6
EXPERSQ (EXPER squared)	545.8	577.5	594.1	565.4
COHORT1 (If has resided in US for 5 years or less)	0.192	0.165	0.174	0.154
COHORT2 (If has resided in US between 6 and 10 years)	0.253	0.162	0.152	0.155
COHORT3 (If has resided in US between 11 and 20 years)	0.391	0.329	0.262	0.283
HOURS (Weekly hours of work)	38.0	37.9	36.7	38.3
MEXICAN (If person was born in Mexico)	0.376	0.480	—	—
Number of observations	9,285	34,701	19,132	43,478

Note: The wages for 1980 have been adjusted for inflation and expressed in 2005 dollars.

Source: Data from 1980 US Census of Population and 2005 American Community Survey; author's tabulations.

substantially higher than those received by women, for both LAC and other immigrants.

The lower wages received by immigrants from LAC compared to other immigrant workers may be a reflection of mean differences in the characteristics of the two groups. Tables 12.7 and 12.8 document some of these key differences.

The main difference in characteristics between LAC and other immigrants is that the former have substantially lower levels of education than the latter. For instance, the sample means for the variable COLLEGE show that 9.9 per cent of Latin American and Caribbean immigrant male workers had 16 years of schooling or more in 1980 and 9.7 percent in 2005. By comparison, male immigrants from other regions had a substantially higher proportion of college graduates, equal to 30.6 per cent in 1980 and 49.9 per cent in 2005. Similar gaps hold for female workers.

Tables 12.7 and 12.8 confirm that although schooling has increased for all groups, the relative educational attainment of immigrants from LAC has been lagging relative to other immigrants. For males, for example, the proportion with a college degree stayed basically unchanged between 1980 and 2005 at slightly less than 10 per cent. By comparison, the corresponding proportion for other male immigrants rose from 30.6 per cent in 1980 to close to 50 per cent in 2005. Among women, the proportion of college graduates among LAC immigrants rose from 8.6 per cent to 14.8 percent between 1980 and 2005, but for other immigrants it climbed from 20.2 to 45.0 percent.

The data on educational attainment are consistent with the sample means for English-language proficiency, which show much lower proficiency levels among immigrants from LAC. In an index that ranges from 0 to 4, with 0 implying no knowledge of English at all and 4 only knowledge of English, immigrants from LAC had a value of around 1.8 to 2.1, depending on gender and the year, but for other immigrants, the values range from 2.8 to 3.0.

Results

Tables 12.9 and 12.10 present the key results of the empirical analysis. Table 12.9 shows the OLS coefficients of the estimated wage regression equations for men while Table 12.10 depicts the results for women. Note that the signs of the regression coefficients on the explanatory variables are generally identical in the four equations. Furthermore, the signs are in line with the theoretical expectations, as stated earlier. On the other hand, there are some significant differences in the magnitude of the coefficients across equations.

Table 12.9. Regression Estimates, Male Wage Equations.

	Equations for LAC		Equations for Non-LAC	
Independent variable	1980 parameter estimate (*s.e.*) t-statistic	2005 parameter estimate (*s.e.*) t-statistic	1980 parameter estimate (*s.e.*) t-statistic	2005 parameter estimate (*s.e.*) t-statistic
INTERCEPT	5.0626* (0.0433) 116.8	5.0071 (0.0188) 265.8	4.8893* (0.0288) 169.8	4.5175* (0.0244) 184.9
MEXICAN	0.0258 (0.0138) 1.9	−0.0247* (0.0059) −4.2	—	—
HIGHSC	0.1671* (0.0169) 9.9	0.1170* (0.0067) 17.5	0.1103* (0.0131) 8.4	0.0535* (0.0161) 3.3
SOMECO	0.2558* (0.0206) 12.4	0.2637* (0.0087) 30.4	0.2163* (0.0146) 14.8	0.2157* (0.0161) 13.4
COLLEGE	0.5122* (0.0228) 22.4	0.6266* (0.0098) 63.7	0.4862* (0.0132) 36.9	0.7337* (0.0155) 47.4
ENGLISH	0.0641* (0.0059) 10.9	0.0727* (0.0026) 27.7	0.0869* (0.0050) 17.4	0.1224* (0.0040) 31.0
EXPER	0.0390* (0.0016) 23.7	0.0356* (0.0008) 43.1	0.0577* (0.0012) 47.1	0.0571* (0.0011) 52.0
EXPERSQ	−0.00066* (0.00003) −19.8	−0.00061* (0.00002) −38.7	−0.00092* (0.00003) −35.5	−0.00099* (0.00002) −41.2
COHORT1	−0.2755* (0.0219) −12.6	−0.2537* (0.0092) −27.7	−0.1830* (0.0139) −13.1	−0.1570* (0.0111) −14.1

(*Continued*)

Table 12.9. (*Continued*)

Independent variable	Equations for LAC 1980 parameter estimate (*s.e.*) t-statistic	Equations for LAC 2005 parameter estimate (*s.e.*) t-statistic	Equations for Non-LAC 1980 parameter estimate (*s.e.*) t-statistic	Equations for Non-LAC 2005 parameter estimate (*s.e.*) t-statistic
COHORT2	−0.1716*	−0.1858*	−0.0671*	−0.0415*
	(0.0205)	(0.0089)	(0.0139)	(0.0107)
	−8.4	−20.9	−13.2	−3.9
COHORT3	−0.0638*	−0.1257*	−0.0025	−0.0544*
	(0.0188)	(0.0072)	(0.0118)	(0.0089)
	−3.4	−17.5	−0.2	−6.1
HOURS	0.0137*	0.0158*	0.0134*	0.0122*
	(0.0007)	(0.0003)	(0.0004)	(0.0003)
	20.5	57.0	30.8	66.9
R-SQ	0.18	0.28	0.26	0.34

Notes: * = Statistically significant at the 99 per cent confidence level.

Tables 12.9 and 12.10 show rates of return to a college education that have been increasing at a very sluggish rate among immigrants from LAC when compared to other immigrants. In fact, the rate of return to a college degree in 1980 was higher among LAC male immigrants than among other immigrants. But this gap turns around by 2005, when the rate of return to a college education was lower among male immigrants from LAC. Among women, immigrants from the region had lower rates of return to a college education both in 1980 and 2005, and the increase in rates of return between 1980 and 2005 again lags behind that displayed by other immigrants.

These differences in the behavior of rates of return to schooling may be connected to a wide array of factors. Quality of schooling can influence rates of return to education and it is possible that reductions in the quality of schooling of Latin American and Caribbean migrants relative to that of other immigrants (mostly European and Asian) is the factor that lies behind their lower rates of return to

Table 12.10. Regression Estimates, Female Wage Equations.

	Equations for LAC		Equations for Non-LAC	
Independent variable	**1980 parameter estimate (*s.e.*) t-statistic**	**2005 parameter estimate (*s.e.*) t-statistic**	**1980 parameter estimate (*s.e.*) t-statistic**	**2005 parameter estimate (*s.e.*) t-statistic**
INTERCEPT	4.7721*	4.4385	4.4276*	4.3253*
	(0.0471)	(0.0224)	(0.0302)	(0.0242)
	101.3	198.3	146.5	178.9
MEXICAN	−0.0263	−0.0809*	—	—
	(0.0156)	(0.0073)		
	1.7	−11.1		
HIGHSC	0.1286*	0.0919*	0.1360*	0.0681*
	(0.0183)	(0.0092)	(0.0133)	(0.0160)
	7.1	10.0	10.3	4.4
SOMECO	0.2413*	0.2712*	0.2933*	0.2656*
	(0.0227)	(0.0106)	(0.0152)	(0.0161)
	10.7	25.6	19.4	16.5
COLLEGE	0.4639*	0.5917*	0.5512*	0.7176*
	(0.0274)	(0.0118)	(0.0153)	(0.0158)
	17.0	50.0	36.1	45.5
ENGLISH	0.0518*	0.0991*	0.0153*	0.0661*
	(0.0062)	(0.0033)	(0.0052)	(0.0040)
	8.3	30.5	2.9	16.7
EXPER	0.0221*	0.0250*	0.0244*	0.0359*
	(0.0019)	(0.0010)	(0.0012)	(0.0010)
	12.0	25.9	19.8	34.7
EXPERSQ	−0.00044*	−0.00042*	−0.00039*	−0.00066*
	(0.00004)	(0.00002)	(0.00003)	(0.00002)
	−11.5	−21.5	−14.8	−28.9
COHORT1	−0.2141*	−0.2236*	−0.1048*	−0.2727*
	(0.0252)	(0.0117)	(0.0155)	(0.0117)
	−8.5	−19.1	−6.8	−23.4

(*Continued*)

Table 12.10. (*Continued*)

Independent variable	Equations for LAC		Equations for Non-LAC	
	1980 parameter estimate (*s.e.*) t-statistic	2005 parameter estimate (*s.e.*) t-statistic	1980 parameter estimate (*s.e.*) t-statistic	2005 parameter estimate (*s.e.*) t-statistic
COHORT2	−0.1113* (0.0231) −4.8	−0.1798* (0.0110) −16.4	−0.0172 (0.0154) −1.1	−0.1431* (0.0111) −12.9
COHORT3	−0.0718* (0.0207) −3.5	−0.1276* (0.0085) −15.1	0.0026 (0.0122) 0.2	−0.0835* (0.0088) −9.5
HOURS	0.0191* (0.0007) 24.8	0.0259* (0.0003) 76.5	0.0269* (0.0005) 57.3	0.0297* (0.0003) 98.9
R-SQ	0.15	0.35	0.26	0.36

Notes: * = Statistically significant at the 99 per cent confidence level.

education.[6] These differences in quality do not need to be associated exclusively with characteristics of schools but could also be due to socioeconomic differences between the families of the immigrants (with migrants from LAC on average coming from families with lower socioeconomic status).

An alternative explanation is that the sluggish increase of the rate of return to education among Latin American and Caribbean immigrants reflects a lower level of schooling within the COLLEGE category. Since this category includes college graduates only, it is possible that immigrants from outside the region have an increasing proportion of master's and doctorates when compared to immigrants from LAC. Since greater levels of schooling would result in higher earnings, this discrepancy would result in higher observed rates of return among immigrants from outside LAC.

Another trend that can be discerned from Tables 12.9 and 12.10 is that the rate of return to a high school education has been sharply declining for all groups analyzed. Among immigrants from LAC, the rate of return to a high school education declines from 16.7 per cent in 1980 to 11.7 percent in 2005 for men and from 12.9 per cent to 9.2 per cent among women. For other immigrants, the decline is from 11.0 per cent to 5.3 per cent for men and from 13.6 per cent to 6.8 per cent among women. These changes are consistent with a US labor market that is becoming increasingly polarized. In this case, the wages of workers with very low levels of schooling would rise relative to workers with average levels of schooling. In the analysis above, the rates of return have as a basis of comparison workers with less than a high school education (the excluded dummy variable in equation (2)). Hence, when the rate of return to a high school education declines, it means that salaries of these workers have dropped relative to workers with less than a high school education. Since the rates of return to college graduates are also rising in relation to high school graduates, the implication is that it is those at the middle of the educational distribution (those with a high school education) that are exhibiting slower wage growth relative to those at the extremes (those with less than a high school education and those with a college education). This is precisely what a polarized labor market looks like.

The economic returns to labor market experience also vary across the various groups considered. Women tend to have lower rates to return to experience than men, a pattern that is obtained for non-immigrants in the US economy as well. Also, as with the rates of return to education, the rate of return to experience among both men and women is substantially lower for LAC immigrants. To understand this result, note that the years of residence in the US, as represented by the COHORT dummy variables, is being held constant while changes in EXPER and EXPERSQ are considered. Given the number of years that an immigrant has been residing in the US, changes in the EXPER variable are directly related to changes in the number of years of experience the worker has had abroad. One way to interpret the higher EXPER coefficient in the non-LAC equation is that it shows that the returns in the US labor market of an increase in years of experience abroad are proportionally higher for these workers than for LAC migrants. This pattern, in turn, may be determined by the relative success of immigrants from other parts of the world in matching their occupational experience abroad with that in the United States.

The results in Tables 12.9 and 12.10 confirm that, holding other things constant, Mexican immigrants tend to have lower wages than other immigrants. This effect, however, has been emerging over time and was not significant back in 1980. In fact, at that time, Mexican male immigrants had higher wages than other immigrants from LAC (other things held constant), but this result was not statistically significant. By 2005, the negative sign on the Mexican dummy variable is statistically significant, for both men and women. These results are consistent with the hypothesis stated earlier, to the effect that a greater presence of undocumented workers will be associated with lower immigrant wages, all else held constant. Undocumented migration to the US has been particularly important among Mexican migrants and such migration exploded after 1980, particularly in the 1990s.

Tables 12.9 and 12.10 show that more recent immigrants face a substantial penalty in wages relative to earlier immigrants. In 2005, male immigrants from LAC who had been in the US for five years or less had 25.4 per cent lower wages while female immigrants from that region had 22.4 per cent lower wages. For other immigrants, the most recent cohort had 15.7 per cent lower wages for men and 27.3 per cent lower wages for females. But the results in Tables 12.9 and 12.10 do not confirm any systematic changes in the costs of recency of migration, whether for Latin American and Caribbean immigrants or other migrants. For Latin American and Caribbean immigrants, the penalties of being a recent migrant actually decline between 1980 and 2005 for men, but they slightly rise for women. For other immigrants, men also appear to face lower costs from being a recent immigrant, but women face substantially greater penalties.

Ability to speak English, as reflected by the variable ENGLISH, has a consistently positive influence on earnings, for all groups examined. And as was the case with rates of return to a college education, rates of return to English-language skills have also risen sharply between 1980 and 2005. Furthermore, the rates of return to English proficiency are lower among immigrants from LAC. Hours worked are also significantly related to weekly earnings.

12.5 Accounting for the Decline in Relative Wages of LAC Migrants

Having examined the factors determining the earnings of LAC and other immigrants, what does this analysis suggest are the main factors that have been connected to the deterioration of the earnings of LAC immigrants relative to other migrants? In order to calculate the relative weight of the various factors explaining wages, labor economists utilize a so-called Blinder-Oaxaca wage decomposition (see Blinder, 1973; Oaxaca, 1973; and Oaxaca and Ransom, 1996).

The Blinder-Oaxaca wage decomposition for the case of immigrants from LAC and other immigrants is based on a comparison of the means of the log-wages for these two groups of workers. Using Equation (1) yields the following equations for the means of the log-wages of LAC and other immigrants:

$$\overline{\log W}_L = \beta_L' \overline{X}_L \tag{3}$$

$$\overline{\log W}_O = \beta_O' \overline{X}_O, \tag{4}$$

where the subscript L represents LAC immigrants, O denotes other immigrants, and bars over variables denote mean values. Subtracting equation (4) from (3) results in:

$$\begin{aligned} \overline{\log W}_L - \overline{\log W}_O &= \beta_L' \overline{X}_L - \beta_O' \overline{X}_O \\ &= (\overline{X}_L - \overline{X}_O)(\beta_L' + \beta_O')/2 \\ &\quad + (\beta_L' - \beta_O')(\overline{X}_O + \overline{X}_L)/2. \end{aligned} \tag{5}$$

Equation (5) decomposes the log-wage difference between LAC and other immigrants (equal to the percentage difference in the geometric means of the observed wage rates for the two groups) into two components: (1) a part due to differences in the average characteristics of LAC and other immigrants, as represented by the vectors of human capital and demographic variables in X_L and X_O, shown in the second row of equation (5); and (2) a part due to differences in the parameters of the wage equations for the two groups (such as differences in rates of return to education), as symbolized by β'_L and β'_O, shown in the third row of equation (5).

An analysis of the differences in the wages of LAC and other immigrants was carried out for both 1980 and 2005. As was examined earlier, the log-wage difference in wages between these two immigrant groups widened during this time period, with the shortfall in the wages of LAC migrants growing from −0.34 in 1980 to −0.55 in 2005 for men, and from −0.12 to −0.40 for women. By determining the relative weight of the factors that explain these wage gaps for each year, one can then determine what factors account for the expansion of the relative wage shortfall facing LAC migrants in 2005 compared to 1980.

This analysis shows that the lower relative wages of LAC migrants are largely explained by the sluggish rise in the educational attainment of these migrants compared to other immigrants. For instance, the proportion of college graduates in the LAC immigrant contingent rose between 1980 and 2005, but it increased much more among other immigrants. For men, this deterioration of the supply of college graduates among LAC migrants compared to other migrants explains as much as 45 per cent of the deterioration in the relative wages of LAC workers. For women, the relative deterioration in the supply of college graduates explains 50 per cent of the relative wage loss of LAC migrants.

The second major factor accounting for the comparative earnings losses of LAC migrants is the relative decline in English-language proficiency of LAC workers when compared to other immigrants. A third force that is also significant for both men and women is the tepid increase in the rates of return to a college education and to English proficiency among LAC immigrants when compared to other immigrants. Other factors, such as cohort and time-in-the-US effects, differences in experience and/or rates of return to experience, the greater proportion of Mexican workers (as a proxy for undocumented workers), differences in hours of work, etc., just do not explain a significant fraction of the deteriorating relative wages.

12.6 Conclusions

The last 25 years have seen a marked increase in the migration of people from LAC to the United States, both documented and undocumented. As a result, the number of Latin America and Caribbean immigrants residing in the US rose from 4,543,700 in 1980 to 19,671,641 in 2005, and the percentage of all immigrants residing in the US accounted for by LAC countries leaped from 29.7 percent in 1980 to 51.5 percent in 2005.

This paper has discussed the forces behind this mass migration, including the most significant US immigration policy changes over time as well as the social and economic forces connected to some of the most significant migration bursts. Underlying the migration process is the growing divergence between the per capita income of most LAC countries and that of the United States. Between 1980 and 2005, the ratio of GDP per capita of the US relative to LAC overall rose from 3.43 to 4.94.

How do migrants from LAC fare in US labor markets? The evidence presented in this paper shows that LAC migrants have substantially lower wages than other migrants. In 2005, for instance, migrants from the region earned an average hourly wage rate of \$14, compared to \$24 among other immigrants, and \$20.4 for non-immigrants. Furthermore, the earnings of LAC migrants have been sharply declining relative to the earnings of other immigrants as well as natives. In 1980, the hourly wage rate received by the region's immigrants was equal to 76.9 per cent of the average wage of other immigrants and 82.6 per cent of the wage rate of non-immigrants. By 2005, this ratio had declined to 58.3 per cent relative to other immigrants and 68.6 per cent when compared to non-immigrants. In fact, the absolute value of the wages received on average by immigrants from LAC in the US hardly increased at all between 1980 and 2005, when measured in real terms, but the average wages received by immigrants from other regions rose by close to 40 per cent and among natives the increase was equal to 27 per cent.

The empirical work presented in this paper shows that the most significant factor explaining both the lower relative wages of LAC migrants and the deterioration of those wages relative to other migrants is the comparatively low — and declining — educational attainment of these migrants relative to other immigrants and natives in the US. In 1980, for example, the percentage of migrants from LAC with less than a 12th-grade (high school) education was equal to 58.3 per cent, which was almost twice the corresponding figure for natives in the US and 140 per cent higher than for immigrants from other regions. By 2005, the percentage of Latin America and Caribbean immigrants with less than a 12th-grade schooling was 43.3 per cent, which was about four times the equivalent percentage for natives and 3.5 times the percentage for other immigrants. This relative skill deterioration among LAC migrants accounts for 45 percent of the relative wage loss of these migrants between 1980 and 2005 for men and 50 percent of the loss for women.

Compounding the declining relative skills of LAC migrants are changes in US labor markets since the early 1980s that have made rates of return to education skyrocket while the wages of workers with relatively lower skills have worsened. The research presented in this paper also shows that rates of return to education among LAC migrants are lower than those of other migrants and have not increased in line with those of other immigrant groups.

English-language proficiency was found to be another important force explaining the declining wages of LAC migrants relative to other migrants. Indeed, immigrants from LAC countries tend to have substantially lower English-language proficiency. In addition, rates of return to English-language skills have risen sharply between 1980 and 2005.

The paper also presents evidence examining the role played by cohort effects in explaining the lower wages of LAC migrants. There is a substantial penalty in wages paid by recent LAC migrants. In 2005, male immigrants from LAC who had been in the US for five years or less had 25.4 percent lower wages while female immigrants from that region had 22.4 percent lower wages. But the data do not confirm any systematic changes in the costs of recency of migration, whether for LAC migrants or other immigrants. This factor does not appear to be significant in explaining the declining relative wage of LAC migrants.

These issues have significant policy relevance. In absolute magnitude, migration to the US will continue to provide massive economic rewards for LAC in the foreseeable future. But if migrants were to lose some of their economic power, their benefits to sending countries may eventually stagnate. Given the reliance of many countries on the income that migrants provide to supplement their own income, the social and economic ripples of such a trend could be significant.

But even more importantly, if migrants from LAC were to become an underclass of workers in the United States, with persistently low earnings, lack of upward mobility and rising poverty rates, perceptions about the economic benefits of these migrants among natives in the US may turn against them. The result could be a rise of anti-immigrant feelings that could have a negative impact on US immigration policies towards the region (see Hanson, 2005a). In the past, US immigration policies have in fact followed perceptions (or misperceptions) about the economic effects of immigrants. As noted in this paper, massive deportations of both legal and undocumented Mexican immigrants were undertaken by the United States in the midst of the Great Depression in the 1930s, in response to the popular perceptions among policymakers and the public that the migrants were taking jobs away from natives. It is hard to avoid the implication that the relative success of the migrants themselves may determine the future of migration policies towards them.

Notes:

[1]This figure is expressed in PPP-adjusted international dollars.

[2]Undocumented worker apprehensions is only a rough estimate of undocumented migration flows since it depends also on enforcement and interdiction efforts.

[3]IRCA introduced employer-sanctions for employers that knowingly hire undocumented workers, allocated greater resources for border enforcement, and provided for an amnesty of undocumented immigrants who had been continuously residing in the US since 1 January, 1982. The Illegal Immigration Reform and Immigrant Responsibility Act of 1996 further extended the scope of IRCA by

providing additional resources for border control, increasing penalties for illegal entry, reforming exclusion and deportation procedures, and placing restrictions on the public benefits available to immigrants; see Hoefer (1991) and Rivera-Batiz (2002).

[4]Estimates of the undocumented immigrant population are constructed using the so-called residual methodology, which calculates this population as the difference between the total number of immigrants who are counted in the US at any given moment in time (through census-type surveys) and the number of legal immigrants residing in the US at that time (determined from US immigration data); see Hoefer *et al.* (2006) and Pew Hispanic Centre (2006).

[5]See Valenzuela and Melendez (2003) and Rivera-Batiz (2004), for a discussion of this issue in relation to undocumented Mexican immigrants in New York City.

[6]Hanushek and Kimko (2000) have calculated differences in quality of schooling among various countries, based on the results of international educational assessments that test students in maths and science at a certain grade level in various countries. The average index of school quality calculated by these authors for LAC in the period of 1965 to 1991 was substantially below that of the world average. The world mean index was 48.6 while it was 35.4 for LAC, more than a full standard deviation below the mean.

References

Acemoglu, D. (2002), "Technical Change, Inequality and the Labor Market," *Journal of Economic Literature*, 40, 1, 7–72.

Acosta, P., C. Calderón, P. Fajnzylber and H. López (2006), "Remittances and Development in Latin America," *The World Economy*, 29, 7, 957–87.

Adams, R. (2007), "International Remittances and the Household: Analysis and Review of Global Evidence," Policy Research Working Paper No. 4116 (Washington, DC: The World Bank).

Autor, D., L. Katz and M. Kearney (2006), "The Polarization of the U.S. Labor Market," Working Paper No. 11986 (Cambridge, MA: National Bureau of Economic Research).

Bernard, A. and J. Bradford Jensen (2000), "Understanding Increasing and Decreasing Wage Inequality," in R. C. Feenstra (ed.), *The Impact of International Trade on Wages* (Chicago: University of Chicago Press).

Blinder, A. S. (1973), "Wage Discrimination: Reduced Form and Structural Estimates," *Journal of Human Resources*, 8, 4, 436–55.

Borjas, G. (1987), "Self-selection and the Earnings of Immigrants," *American Economic Review*, 77, 4, 531–53.

Borjas, G. (1995), "Assimilation and Changes in Cohort Quality Revisited: What Happened to Immigrant Earnings in the 1980s?," *Journal of Labor Economics*, 13, 2, 201–45.

Borjas, G. (1999a), "The Economic Analysis of Immigration," in O. Ashenfelter and R. Freeman (eds.), *Handbook of Labor Economics* (Amsterdam: North Holland).

Borjas, G. (1999b), *Heaven's Door: Immigration Policy and the American Economy* (Princeton, NJ: Princeton University Press).
Borjas, G. (2000), "The Economic Progress of Immigrants," in G. Borjas (ed.), *Issues in the Economics of Immigration* (Chicago: University of Chicago Press).
Borjas, G. and L. Katz (2005), "The Evolution of the Mexican-born Workforce in the United States," Working Paper No. 11281 (Cambridge, MA: National Bureau of Economic Research).
Card, D. and E. Lewis (2005), "The Diffusion of Mexican Immigrants in the 1990s: Patterns and Impacts," Working Paper (Berkeley, CA: UC Berkeley Center for Labor Economics).
Cerrutti, M. and D. Massey (2004), "Trends in Mexican Migration to the United States, 1965 to 1995," in J. Durand and D. Massey (eds.), *Crossing the Border: Research from the Mexican Migration Project* (New York: Russell Sage Foundation).
Chiquiar, D. and G. Hanson (2005), "International Migration Selection and the Distribution of Wages: Evidence from Mexico and the United States," *Journal of Political Economy*, 113, 2, 239–81.
Chiswick, B. (1978), "The Effects of Americanization on the Earnings of the Foreign-born," *Journal of Political Economy*, 86, 5, 897–922.
Chiswick, B. (1999), "Are Immigrants Favorably Selected?," *American Economic Review*, 89, 2, 181–85.
Chiswick, B. and P. Miller (2004), "Language Skills and Earnings among Legalized Aliens," in K. Zimmermann and A. Constant (eds.), *How Labor Migrants Fare* (Berlin: Springer-Verlag).
Cornelius, W. and E. Marcelli (2000), "The Changing Profile of Mexican Migrants to the United States: New Evidence from California and Mexico," Discussion Paper No. 220 (Bonn: Institute for the Study of Labor).
Craig, R. B. (1971), *The Bracero Program: Interest Groups and Foreign Policy* (Austin, TX: University of Texas Press).
De la Garza, R. and B. Lindsay Lowell (2002), *Sending Money Home: Hispanic Remittances and Community Development* (London: Rowman & Littlefield).
Duleep, H. and M. Regets (1999), "Immigrants and Human-capital Investment," *American Economic Review*, 89, 2, 186–91.
Gamio, M. (1930), *Mexican Immigration to the United States: A Study of Human Migration and Adjustment* (Chicago: University of Chicago Press).
Hanson, G. (2005a), Why Does Immigration Divide America? Public Finance and Political Opposition to Open Borders (Washington, DC: Institute of International Economics).
Hanson, G. (2005b), "Emigration, Labor Supply and Earnings in Mexico," Working Paper No. 11412 (Cambridge, MA: National Bureau of Economic Research).
Hanson, G. (2006), "Illegal Migration from Mexico to the United States," *Journal of Economic Literature*, 44, 4, 869–924.
Hanson, G. and A. Spilimbergo (1999), "Illegal Immigration, Border Enforcement, and Relative Wages: Evidence from Apprehensions at the U.S.-Mexico Border," *American Economic Review*, 89, 5, 1337–57.

Hanushek, E. and D. Kimko (2000), "Schooling, Labor Force Quality and the Growth of Nations," *American Economic Review*, 90, 5, 1184–208.

Hernandez, R. and F. Rivera-Batiz (1997), *Dominican New Yorkers: A Socio-economic Profile*, Dominican Research Monographs (New York: Dominican Studies Institute).

Hernandez-Huertas, J. (2007), "New Evidence on Emigrant Selection," Mimeo (New York: Columbia University Economics Department).

Hoefer, M. (1991), "Background of U.S. Immigration Policy Reform," in F. Rivera-Batiz, S. Sechzer and I. Gang (eds.), *U.S. Immigration Policy Reform in the 1980s: A Preliminary Assessment* (New York: Praeger).

Hoefer, M., N. Rytina and C. Campbell (2006), *Estimates of the Unauthorized Immigrant Population Residing in the United States: January 2005* (Washington, DC: United States Department of Homeland Security, Office of Immigration Statistics).

Immigration and Naturalization Service (1999), "Illegal Alien Resident Population" (Mimeo, Washington, DC: United States Department of Justice).

Katz, L. and D. Autor (1999), "Changes in the Wage Structure and Earnings Inequality," in O. Ashenfelter and D. Card (eds.), *Handbook of Labor Economics* (Amsterdam: North Holland).

Krueger, A. (1993), "How Computers Have Changed the Wage Structure: Evidence from Microdata 1984–1989," *Quarterly Journal of Economics*, 108, 1, 33–60.

Levy, F. and R. Murnane (2004), *The New Division of Labor: How Computers Are Creating the Next Job Market* (Princeton, NJ: Princeton University Press).

Massey, D. (1987), "Do Undocumented Immigrants Earn Lower Wages than Legal Immigrants? New Evidence from Mexico," *International Migration Review*, 21, 2, 236–74.

Massey, D., J. Durand and N. Malone (2002), *Beyond Smoke and Mirrors: Mexican Immigration in an Era of Economic Integration* (New York: Russell Sage Foundation).

Mishra, P. (2006), "Emigration and Wages in Source Countries: Evidence from Mexico," Working Paper No. WP/86/06 (Washington, DC: International Monetary Fund).

Oaxaca, R. (1973), "Male-Female Wage Differentials in Urban Labor Markets," *International Economic Review*, 14, 3, 693–709.

Oaxaca, R. and M. Ransom (1994), "On Discrimination and the Decomposition of Wage Differentials," *Journal of Econometrics*, 61, 1, 5–21.

Parrado, E. (2004), "U.S. Migration, Home Ownership and Housing Quality," in J. Durand and D. Massey (eds.), *Crossing the Border: Research from the Mexican Migration Project* (New York: Russell Sage Foundation).

Passel, J. and R. Suro (2005), *Rise, Peak and Decline: Trends in U.S. Immigration, 1992–2004* (Washington, DC: Pew Hispanic Centre).

Pew Hispanic Centre (2006), *The Foreign-born at Mid Decade* (Washington, DC: Pew Hispanic Centre).

Reichert, J. (1982), "A Town Divided: Economic Stratification and Social Relations in a Mexican Migrant Community," *Social Problems*, 29, 4, 413–23.

Rivera-Batiz, F. (1982), "International Migration, Nontraded Goods and Economic Welfare in the Source Country," *Journal of Development Economics*, 11, 1, 81–90.

Rivera-Batiz, F. (1986), "International Migration, Remittances and Economic Welfare in the Source Country," *Journal of Economic Studies*, 13, 3, 3–19.

Rivera-Batiz, F. (1990), "English Language Proficiency and the Economic Progress of Immigrants," *Economics Letters*, 34, 2, 295–300.

Rivera-Batiz, F. (1999), "Undocumented Workers in the Labor Market: An Analysis of the Earnings of Legal and Illegal Mexican Immigrants in the United States," *Journal of Population Economics*, 12, 1, 91–116.

Rivera-Batiz, F. (2001), "Illegal Immigrants in the U.S. Economy: A Comparative Analysis of Mexican and Non-Mexican Undocumented Workers," in S. Djajic (ed.), *International Migration: Policy and Economic Impact* (London: Routledge).

Rivera-Batiz, F. (2002), "The International Migration Experience of Mexico: Socioeconomic Aspects," in R. Rotte and P. Stein (eds.), *Migration Policy and the Economy* (Muenchen, Germany: Hanns-Seidel Foundation).

Rivera-Batiz, F. (2004), "NewYorktitlán: The Socioeconomic Status of Mexican New Yorkers," *Regional Labor Review*, 6, 1, 33–45.

Sanchez, G. (1993), *Becoming Mexican American: Ethnicity, Culture and Identity in Chicano Los Angeles, 1900–1945* (New York: Oxford University Press).

Trejo, S. (1997), "Why Do Mexican Americans Earn Low Wages?," *Journal of Political Economy*, 105, 6, 1235–68.

Trejo, S. (2003), "Intergenerational Progress of Mexican-origin Workers in the U.S. Labor Market," *Journal of Human Resources*, 38, 3, 467–89.

United States Department of Commerce (1993), *1990 U.S. Census of Population and Housing 5% Public Use Microdata Sample* (Washington, DC: US Department of Commerce).

United States Department of Labour (1996), *Legalized Population Survey Public Use File* (Washington, DC: Bureau of International Labour Affairs, Washington, DC).

US Department of Homeland Security (2006), *Yearbook of Immigration Statistics 2005* (Washington, DC: US Department of Homeland Security, Office of Immigration Statistics).

US Immigration and Naturalization Service (2001), *Estimates of the Unauthorized Immigrant Population in the United States: 1990 and 2000* (Washington, DC: US Immigration and Naturalization Service, Office of Policy and Planning).

Valenzuela, A. and E. Melendez (2003), "Day Labor in New York: Findings from the NYDL Survey," Community Development Research Centre (New York: New School University).

World Bank (2007), *World Development Indicators* (Washington, DC: The World Bank).

Zimmermann, K. and A. Constant (eds.) (2004), *How Labor Migrants Fare* (Berlin: Springer-Verlag).

Part 4

Undocumented Workers and Immigration Policy

Chapter 13

Undocumented Workers in the Labor Market: An Analysis of the Earnings of Legal and Illegal Mexican Immigrants in the U.S.*

13.1 Introduction

Illegal immigration has become a topic of worldwide controversy in recent years. Whether it is concerned with the migration of Bangladeshis to India, Albanians to Greece, North Africans to Italy, or Mexicans to the United States, host country governments are rushing to define policies intended to curtail illegal immigration. In the United States, a prolonged debate over the issue has led to two major immigration policy initiatives: the 1986 Immigration Reform and Control Act (IRCA), and the 1996 Illegal Immigration Reform and Immigrant Responsibility Act. Despite this legislation, the debate

---

*This chapter was originally published in *Journal of Population Economics*, Vol. 12, No. 1, February 1999, pp. 91–116.

This paper was prepared for the conference on The Economics of Illegal Immigration sponsored by the Centre for Economic Policy Research held in Athens during February 14–15, 1997. The author is thankful to the participants of that conference for useful comments. The author also acknowledges the valuable suggestions of Jagdish N. Bhagwati, Ira N. Gang, Todd Idson, and two anonymous referees.

on the role of undocumented workers in the American labor market rages on.

One of the key issues surrounding undocumented workers is the extent to which they are exploited, or discriminated against, in host country labor markets by being paid wages that are substantially below those paid to legal workers with identical characteristics. The view that the exploitation of illegal immigrants is rampant in U.S. labor markets has been the landmark of many popular accounts that have surfaced in the press, although it also appears in some academic studies. For instance, the following August 1995 case involving Thai and Hispanic undocumented garment workers received broad attention in the American press: "The workers were forced to toil in a compound ringed with barbed wire for less than $1 an hour [when the minimum wage was $4.25]. The workers' plight was discovered when sweatshops were raided in El Monte, California" (Reuters 1996). The sweatshop owners were later forced to pay their employees the legal minimum retroactively. Similarly, in a detailed 1995 exposé of sweatshops in New York City, the *New York Times* concluded "Sweatshops... are flourishing... nearly 2,000 sweatshops operate openly throughout New York City... They generally employ 20 to 50 workers, many of them illegal immigrants, willing to suffer long hours, low pay and miserable working conditions just to have a job" (Finder 1995, p. B4).

Even in working environments other than sweatshops, illegal immigrants have been documented to receive lower pay compared to similar legal workers. In an account of the lives of illegal immigrant workers in California, *New York Times* contributor Richard Rayner joined a Mexican illegal immigrant, Ruben, in his morning trip to work in a construction site, reproducing some of the worker's comments along the way. One of these comments is on the issue of wages: "... the truck heads out again, up into Topanga Canyon. "There's a lot of construction up there," says Ruben. "Many rich people. But they use legal workers. Those guys will get $20 an hour. I'm looking to get $7, $8 an hour. Sometimes, however, he has to take $4" (Rayner 1996, p. 31).

On the surface, existing surveys of illegal immigrants in the United States appear to support these observations, finding that many undocumented workers receive wages that are generally lower than those prevailing in the labor market. For instance, one of the earliest, and best-known, surveys of illegal immigrants consists of a 1975 sample of 793 illegal immigrants apprehended by the Immigration and Naturalization Service (INS), analyzed by David North and Marion Houstoun. The average hourly wage received by the illegal workers was 37% lower than the average wage received by all workers in the same industry (North and Houstoun 1976, p. S-11). An identical wage gap between legal and illegal immigrants is obtained by Douglas Massey, in his own 1987 survey of Mexican immigrants.

Despite the broad evidence showing that many undocumented workers receive lower wages than other workers in the U.S. economy, many of the leading economists in this field do not share the believe that illegal immigrants are exploited. As Barry Chiswick clearly notes: "There is no denying that illegal aliens are paid low wages relative to the average U.S. worker. But the low wages of illegal aliens do not appear to be the result of employer exploitation. Rather, they appear to be the result of low skill levels. Most illegal aliens have low levels of schooling, limited fluency in English, and are relative newcomers in the U.S. labor market" (Chiswick 1988, p. 143). A similar opinion is voiced by George Borjas: "... the empirical evidence, limited as it is, provides little support to the proposition that American employers take advantage of illegal aliens... Illegal aliens in the United States have lower wages than legal immigrants not because they are illegal, but because they are less skilled. In other words, if one compares two persons who are demographically similar (in terms of education, age, English proficiency, years on the job, and so on), legal status has no direct impact on the wage rate" (Borjas 1990, p. 72).

All the studies quoted so far have relied for their conclusions on individual observations or comparatively small surveys that are not necessarily representative of the illegal immigrant population in the United States. For instance, the 1975 sample mentioned earlier consisted of 793 illegal immigrants apprehended by the INS; Chiswick uses a survey of 292 illegal immigrants, and Massey's results are based on a sample of 232 Mexican illegal immigrants interviewed in their region of origin in Mexico. Borjas' comments, on the other hand, are based on the results of these studies. Therefore, all the statements made earlier on the exploitation or lack of exploitation of illegal immigrants are subject to the limited data available on the issue.

The paucity of research on the labor market performance of illegal immigrants is mostly due to the absence of substantial information sources. Data collected by the U.S. Department of Commerce, through its decennial Census and the annual Current Population Surveys, do not generally identify illegal immigrants. The latter are also likely to be underrepresented in the samples gathered by official government surveys. The fact is that, although there exists now a vast literature examining the earnings of legal immigrants in the United States, including analyses of the role played by education, English language proficiency, quantitative skills, national origin, propensities for return migration, and cohort effects,[1] little systematic research exists on the labor market status of illegal immigrants.

This paper examines the earnings of illegal Mexican immigrants in the United States using information provided by a national sample of illegal immigrants surveyed by the U.S. Department of Labor. The data set used is the 1989–1992 Legalized Population Survey (LPS). The persons surveyed by the LPS include a random sample of 6,193 illegal immigrants who were residing in the United States in 1987/1988 when they sought legal permanent residence through the Immigration Reform and Control Act of 1986 (IRCA). IRCA constituted the major illegal immigration reform legislation of the 1980s in the United States, introducing sanctions for employers knowingly hiring undocumented workers, increasing the resources of the INS, and introducing an amnesty program through which illegally resident persons could obtain lawful permanent resident status.

The legalization component of IRCA consisted of two programs. The first one, the regular program, applied broadly to any illegal immigrant who could document that he or she had continuously resided in the United States since the end of 1981. This program allowed about 1.6 million undocumented workers to become legal residents. The second program, the Special Agricultural Worker

Program, was more specialized and applied only to illegal immigrants who had performed field labor in perishable agricultural commodities in the United States for at least 90 days during the year ending May 1, 1986. This program was included in IRCA due to the pressure of agricultural producers concerned about the possible emergence of farm labor shortages in response to the legislation (for more details, see Rivera-Batiz *et al.* 1991). The LPS survey provides a random sample of illegal immigrants seeking legalization under the regular program. It does not include illegal immigrants legalized under the Special Agricultural Worker program.

The sample of legalized illegal aliens examined in this study was interviewed first in 1989 and then in 1992. An extensive set of information was collected from the migrants in 1989 relating to their labor market and general socioeconomic experience at the time that they applied for legalization. In 1992, follow-up interviews examined their experience in the United States after legalization. Not all previously-undocumented workers were re-interviewed since some changed residence after 1989 and could not be found in 1992. As a consequence, out of the 6,193 respondents in 1989, 4,012 were re-interviewed in 1992. Note also that the LPS sample is representative of all illegal immigrants in the United States who came forward with the necessary documentation to seek legalization. Although most observers agree that a large portion of the illegal alien population residing in the United States in 1987 and 1988 was reached by IRCA's amnesty program, it is also likely that short-term, temporary workers were not as widely reached by the program. It may be safer to think of the analysis in this paper as applying to those illegal aliens who intended to remain permanently in the United States, and not to temporary migrants (for more details on the LPS data, see Tienda *et al.* 1991, Smith *et al.* 1996).

The LPS data provide the most extensive information available yet on the experiences of illegal immigrants in the United States. This paper makes use of the LPS, combining it with data from the 1990 U.S. Census of Population to provide (1) a cross-sectional, comparative analysis of the earnings of legal and illegal immigrants in the United States in the late 1980s; and (2) a longitudinal examination of the changes in the earnings of undocumented immigrants after legalization, determining the nature of the earnings changes of these workers between 1987–1988, when they were undocumented, and 1992, when they had been legalized under the IRCA provisions. Because close to 70% of the LPS sample consists of Mexican illegal immigrants — with small sample sizes for immigrants from other countries — the paper focuses on Mexican immigrants exclusively.

Section 13.2 summarizes the main labor market issues discussed in the paper and specifies the empirical model to be estimated to examine the differences in earnings between legal and illegal immigrants. Section 13.3 presents the results of the empirical analysis using the cross-section of illegal immigrants provided by the LPS data set, compared with a sample of Mexican immigrants from the 5% Public Use Microdata Sample (PUMS) of the 1990 U.S. Census of Population. Section 13.4 examines the extent to which the earnings shortfall of undocumented workers relative to legal immigrants can be explained by differences in the characteristics of these two groups of migrants. Section 13.5 then presents the empirical model used to examine the changes in the earnings of undocumented immigrants over time, before and after legalization, as well as the results of this analysis. Section 13.6 provides an overview of our main conclusions.

13.2 The Empirical Model

The first objective of this paper is to provide a comparative analysis of the earnings of Mexican legal and illegal immigrants in the U.S. labor market. Differences in earnings between legal and illegal immigrants can be related to (1) differences in the characteristics of the two types of workers, and/or (2) variation in the rewards the labor market offers to the two types of workers, given their characteristics. As the existing literature has amply noted, a shortfall in the earnings of undocumented workers may be explained by their weaker educational attainment, lower on-the-job experience, more limited English proficiency, or by other gaps in skills relative to those of legal immigrants. The wage gap may also be related to the particular occupations and industries where illegal immigrants cluster. Because of their need to be sheltered from detection, undocumented workers are often employed in marginal jobs or in declining industries that offer comparatively low pay. In New York City, for example, *The New York Times* reports, that many Mexican undocumented workers, have carved a niche as flower vendors; selling flowers on the street may be illegal and unpredictable, the logic goes, but it is better than punching a clock at a factory, where workers are quick bait for immigration agents (Alvarez 1996, p. B7). In the restaurant industry, where many illegals are employed, legal immigrants may be employed as waiters or waitresses dealing directly with customers while illegals are hired as dishwashers or helpers inside the kitchen, away from the limelight.

Even after taking into account measured differences in demographic, occupational, and human capital characteristics between legal and illegal immigrants, there may still be a gap in wages among them. This may be the result of unmeasured differences between the two types of workers. For example, if undocumented workers have lived for a longer period of time in their country of origin than legal immigrants, their labor market experience may not be as valuable in the U.S. labor market, when compared to that of legal immigrants, who have worked for a longer period of time in the United States. However, since explicit information on the personal labor market history of immigrants in the United States and in their country of origin is rarely available (neither the Census nor the Legalized Population Survey provide these data), this difference in characteristics between the two groups remains unmeasured and may account for unexplained gaps in wages between them.

Any remaining gaps in earnings between legal and illegal immigrants may be due to wage discrimination against undocumented workers. In examining this issue, we adopt the well-known definition of labor market discrimination, which is said to occur when individual workers who have identical productive characteristics are treated differently because of the demographic groups to which they belong (Ehrenberg and Smith 1994, p. 402). Based on this definition, if illegal and legal immigrants with identical demographic, occupational and human capital characteristics are compared, and the wages of the latter exceed those of the former, then the evidence would be consistent with discrimination against illegal immigrants.

The key theoretical hypothesis explaining discrimination against undocumented workers is that illegality allows employers to exert monopsonistic power over these workers because of their great fear of being reported to immigration authorities, which would lead to immediate deportation. Such is the case of immigrant smuggling networks. These transport thousands of undocumented workers to the United States and force them to labor under conditions of servitude or indentured labor until each immigrant repays the smuggler for the cost of the trip (which may be as high as $30,000). For instance, *The New York Times* reports that "The swarms of illegal Chinese immigrants being smuggled into the United States on the promise of a bountiful life all too often find themselves in a bleak existence under the watchful eyes of criminals ready to resort to brutality against those who don't pay their full fare" (Kleinfeld 1993, p. A1).

In general, however, the monopsonistic power of employers over undocumented workers lies somewhere in-between this extreme and that of a competitive labor market. Hence, the extent to which illegal immigrants are subject to this type of discrimination or exploitation depends on the degree to which illegality: (1) restricts the employment choices available to undocumented workers to one or a few illegal employers, and/or (2) makes risky and difficult the process of searching for alternative wage offers, inducing illegals to lower their reservation wages to levels sharply below those of legal immigrants, possibly below the minimum wage. Although these conditions have been observed by journalists and ethnographers, the extent to which they characterize the typical illegal immigrant is open to question. One key factor here is whether the illegal immigrants can easily obtain fake documents — social security cards, driver's licenses, etc. — that make them appear indistinguishable from legal immigrants. In cases where illegals have such documents, they can disguise as legal workers, allowing them to seek employment outside the segmented illegal labor market, eliminating the source of bias against them. A second factor determining the extent of wage discrimination against illegals is the availability of information networks. As Bailey

(1987, p. 132) observes: "Although legal vulnerability undoubtedly influences the search for employment and the willingness to bargain for higher wages, the strength of this effect depends largely on the information available to the immigrant. An illegal alien who is isolated and has contact with only one or two employers is more likely to end up in a job with unusually low wages than one who is integrated into a network of family and friends with experience and contacts in the labor market."

Summarizing: although there are reasons to suspect that illegality is associated with wage discrimination, there is no a-priori presumption that all, or even most of, illegal immigrants are discriminated against or exploited. One must resort to empirical evidence to illuminate the issue. For these purposes, we will estimate human capital earnings functions separately for a sample of Mexican illegal immigrants interviewed in 1989, as supplied by the LPS data, and for a random sample of Mexican immigrants counted in the 1990 Census, who are predominantly legal immigrants. Since the experiences of men and women in the labor market diverge considerably, we carry out separate analyses on the basis of gender. The earnings of both legal and illegal immigrants are gross earnings, on an hourly basis, expressed in 1989 dollars.[2]

The natural logarithm of the wage rate of a person i of sex j is given by:

$$\log W_{ij} = \beta X_{ij} + U_{ij} \tag{1}$$

where W_{ij} is the hourly wage rate received by the individual, β is a vector of coefficients to be estimated, X_{ij} is a vector of human capital, occupational and demographic characteristics affecting wages, and U_{ij} is a stochastic disturbance term.

The variables in the vector X_{ij} include, first of all, two schooling dummy variables introduced to reflect the impact of skills learned in school on earnings. These are: INTERM, equal to one if the person completed between 6 and 9 years of schooling and zero otherwise, and HIGHSC, equal to one if the person completed 10 or more years of schooling and zero otherwise. Both INTERM and HIGHSC are expected to have positive coefficients in the earnings equation.

Secondly, we include years of on-the-job experience, proxied by the variable EXPER (measured as age minus years of schooling completed minus six), intended to reflect the skills acquired by the person through seniority and aging in the labor market. The variable EXPERSQ, equal to the square of years of on-the-job experience, is also introduced in the equation to reflect diminishing returns to experience. On the assumption of positive, but diminishing, returns to on-the-job experience, it is anticipated that the variable EXPER would have a positive coefficient and EXPERSQ a negative coefficient in the earnings equation.

English language proficiency is another key variable influencing earnings. Given the wide usage of Spanish as the main language among Mexican immigrants, employment opportunities may be severely limited if the immigrant's knowledge of the English language is not sufficient. On the other hand, ethnic enclaves can allow broad leeway for immigrants to find jobs, even if their English proficiency is absent. The measure of English proficiency utilized in this paper is symbolized by the variable NOENGLISH, which is equal to one if the person does not know how to speak English at all, and zero otherwise. The existing research examining the role played by English language proficiency on labor market outcomes generally finds a positive impact of English proficiency on earnings (see, for example, Bloom and Grenier 1993; Carliner 1995; Chiswick and Miller 1996; and Rivera-Batiz 1990, 1992, 1996).

The presence of disequilibria in the labor market, as well as the existence of compensating wage differentials, implies that different occupations may be endowed with different wages, holding individual characteristics constant. As a result, our wage equations introduce a set of occupational dummy variables. These are: PROFTC, equal to one if the person was employed in managerial, professional, technical, sales and administrative occupations, and zero otherwise; FARMING, equal to one if the immigrant was employed in agricultural occupations, and zero otherwise; OPERAT, if the worker was an operator, fabricator or laborer, and zero otherwise; and PRODUCT, if the person was in precision production, craft and repair occupations, and zero otherwise. The excluded, baseline, occupations are service occupations. Since the baseline service jobs generally offer comparatively lower wages in the American economy, we expect the occupational dummy variables to be positively associated with earnings, perhaps with the exception of FARMING.

In examining the labor market performance of immigrants, it is important to realize that a large share of immigrants make migratory decisions on basis of family considerations. A higher level of effort, and higher earnings, may be associated with marriage, especially if the family has children. In addition, if spouses are residing in Mexico, married Mexican immigrants will have an incentive to increase their effort levels, to receive higher weekly earnings, in order to increase the amount of remittances they can send their spouses. A dummy variable, SINGLE, is included in the analysis to reflect possible differences in earnings between single and married persons. The variable is equal to one if the person is single and zero otherwise.

The longer immigrants have stayed in a country, the higher their earnings. There are two explanations for this connection. Firstly, as postulated by Chiswick (1978), the greater knowledge of local labor market institutions gained over time by immigrants in their host countries provides improved job search efficiency, allowing immigrants to find higher-paying job offers. Alternatively, Borjas (1994, 1987) has suggested that, more recent immigrant cohorts in the United States have lower quality than previous ones, thus also receiving lower wages, holding everything else constant. Therefore, the longer an immigrant has been in the United States, the older the immigrant cohort with which he or she is associated, and the lower the earnings. To incorporate the impact of recency of immigration into the analysis, we define a dummy variable RECENT to be equal to one if the immigrant moved to stay as a resident of the United States in the 1980s, and zero otherwise. Note that, whether because of assimilation or because of cohort effects, one expects the variable RECENT to have a negative impact on immigrant earnings.

Another explanatory variable utilized in the wage equations is location, which is represented by the variable CALIF, a dummy variable equal to one if the migrant resided in California and zero otherwise. Since the largest share of both legal and illegal Mexican immigrants locates in California, the agglomeration of these migrants can be expected to generate ethnic enclaves and networks that could exert a positive impact on earnings. Portes and Bach (1985) have explained the superior economic performance of the Mariel Cuban immigrants relative to that of Haitian immigrants in the 1980s as deriving from the employment opportunities available to the Cuban immigrants in the Cuban-American ethnic enclave of the Miami area. Given the higher concentration of Mexican immigrants in California, it can be expected that, holding other things constant, Mexican immigrants will be more likely to find jobs, and higher-paying employment opportunities, in California than elsewhere. On the other hand, the effects of immigrant networks operate at the local level and may not be well-defined by a state-wide variable. Depending on the local neighborhood, location in New York City may provide a stronger Mexican immigrant network than location in a small town in California.

The discussion so far suggests that the wage equation to be estimated should be given by:

$$\begin{aligned}\log W_{ij} = \beta_0 &+ \beta_1 INTERM_{ij} + \beta_2 HIGHSC_{ij} + \beta_3 EXPER_{ij}\\ &+ \beta_4 EXPERSO_{ij} + \beta_5 NOENGLISH_{ij} + \beta_6 PROFTC_{ij}\\ &+ \beta_7 FARMING_{ij} + \beta_8 OPERAT_{ij} + \beta_9 PRODUCT_{ij}\\ &+ \beta_{10} SINGLE_{ij} + \beta_{11} RECENT_{ij} + \beta_{12} CALIF_{ij} + U_{ij},\end{aligned} \tag{2}$$

where all the variables are as defined above.

The U_{ij} variable in equation (2) represents an error term that is usually assumed to be randomly distributed among the population. Note, however, that the group of individuals for whom wages are observed, and which is thus used for purposes of estimating equation (2), is not randomly selected from the population since it only includes individuals who are in the labor force. There is thus a possible sample selection bias problem. Traditionally, studies in this area adjusted for this selectivity bias using the "Heckit" method proposed by Heckman (1979). In recent years, however, the selectivity bias adjustment has come under attack due to its lack of robustness (see, for instance, Manski 1989). For this reason, the recent literature examining wage differences among labor market participants has not used the technique (see, for instance, Blau and Kahn 1997; Trejo 1997). It is not employed in this paper either.

13.3 The Earnings of Legal and Illegal Immigrants: Results

The empirical model discussed in the last section was applied to illegal and legal Mexican immigrants in the United States. The information for illegal immigrants was taken from the 1989 LPS random sample of illegal immigrants applying for legalization. The information for legal immigrants was obtained from the 1990 U.S. Census of Population by selecting a 10% random sample out of the 5% Public Use Microdata Samples (PUMS). Note that, in principle, the 1990 U.S. Census counted legal as well as illegal immigrants. However, there are two major reasons why the illegal immigrant population counted in the 1990 Census was a small fraction of the total foreign-born population. First of all, by 1990 a large fraction of the illegal immigrant population residing in the country in the 1980s had been legalized under the provisions of IRCA (see, for instance, Gonzalez-Baker (1990), chapter 5). As a result, the Urban Institute estimates that the 1990 illegal immigrant population was at the most 13% of all the foreign-born in the United States at the time. Secondly, many undocumented workers avoid Census enumerators for fear of being identified by the INS. The Census thus undercounts the undocumented. Given these considerations, for purposes of the discussion below, we will assume that the sample of immigrants from the 1990 Census constitute legal immigrants, although in reality it consists *predominantly* of legal immigrants.

Individuals with no responses on the relevant questions used to determine individual characteristics (such as earnings, educational attainment, etc.) were eliminated from the analysis. In addition, following the custom in the literature, the sample was circumscribed to persons 18 to 64 years of age. Also, as noted earlier, only Mexican immigrants were considered. With these restrictions, the samples utilized in the wage equations estimated in this paper include 2,035 legal Mexican immigrants and 2,163 illegal Mexican immigrants.

The LPS sample provides information on the hourly wages of illegal immigrants in the week before they applied for legalization. Since the window for applications was from May 5, 1987 to May 4, 1988, the data available on wages for illegal immigrants corresponds to either 1987 or 1988. The 1990 Census data, on the other hand, supplies hourly wages earned on average during the year preceding the Census, that is, 1989. In order to adjust for inflation, the 1987–1988 wage data for illegal immigrants were converted into 1989 dollars by using the change in the consumer price index between 1987–1988 and 1989. The illegal immigrant earnings have thus been revised to ensure comparability with the legal immigrant sample. It is these adjusted, real wages (expressed in 1989 dollars) that are discussed throughout the following analysis and compared to the wages of legal immigrants.

Table 13.1 presents the sample means for the variables introduced in the wage equations, by immigrant status and gender. Note first that the average hourly wage for men is substantially higher than for women. This pattern is consistent for both legal and illegal immigrants. For both samples, men have approximately 36% higher earnings. At the same time, the wages of illegal immigrants are significantly lower than those of legal immigrants. This gap holds for both men and women, with legal immigrant men receiving 41.8% higher earnings than illegals, on average, and legal immigrant women receiving 40.8% higher wages than illegals. These wage gaps are consistent with the previous evidence on the wage gaps between legal and illegal immigrants. Both Massey (1987), and North and Houstoun, in their study quoted earlier, found a 37% wage gap (see also Chiswick 1984).

Although the substantial gap between the earnings of legal and illegal immigrants could reflect exploitation and labor market discrimination against illegals, it could also be simply the reflection of differences in the characteristics of the two groups of workers. Table 13.1 documents some of these key differences. Illegal immigrants have substantially lower levels of education than legal

Table 13.1. Sample Means, Cross-Sectional Data, by Immigrant Group and Sex.

	Legal immigrants		**Illegal immigrants**	
Variable	**Male**	**Female**	**Male**	**Female**
Hourly wage (1989 Dollars)	9.561	7.022	6.742	4.986
Log hourly wage	1.962	1.766	1.824	1.506
ELEM (Proportion of sample with less than 6 years of schooling)	0.207	0.167	0.336	0.299
INTERM (Proportion of sample with 6 to 9 years of schooling)	0.408	0.354	0.410	0.465
HIGHSC (Proportion of sample with 10 or more years of schooling)	0.385	0.479	0.254	0.236
EXPER (Years of experience)	18.9	19.2	18.7	19.0
EXPERSQ (Experience squared)	500.6	529.0	465.0	480.0
NOENGLISH (Proportion of sample who cannot speak English at all)	0.144	0.170	0.314	0.411
PROFTC (Proportion of sample employed in professional, technical, sales and managerial occupations)	0.132	0.308	0.068	0.126
FARMING (Proportion employed in agricultural occupations)	0.161	0.084	0.127	0.037
OPERAT (Proportion employed as operators, fabricators and laborers)	0.359	0.300	0.391	0.379
PRODUCT (Proportion employed as precision production, craft and repair workers)	0.193	0.067	0.193	0.050
SERVICE (Proportion employed in services)	0.155	0.241	0.221	0.408
SINGLE (Proportion never married)	0.319	0.274	0.392	0.320
RECENT (Proportion who migrated to the United States in the 1980s to stay)	0.474	0.361	0.703	0.571
CALIF (Proportion residing in California)	0.577	0.577	0.603	0.652
Number of observations	1,425	610	1,484	679

immigrants. The sample means for the variable HIGHSC show that the proportion of male Mexican illegal immigrant workers in the LPS sample with 10 years of schooling or more was on average equal to 25.4%, compared to 38.5% among legal Mexican immigrants. There is an even greater educational gap among women. For female Mexican illegal immigrant workers, the proportion with 10 or more years of schooling was 23.6%, compared to 47.9% among legal immigrants.

Another major difference between legal and illegal workers is their English language proficiency. As Table 13.1 depicts, the proportion of illegal immigrants who expressed that they could not speak English at all was 31.4% among men and 41.1% among women. By comparison, the equivalent percentages for the legal immigrant worker population was 14.4% for men and 17% for women.

There are also major differences in the length of time that immigrants have been in the United States. Since Mexican undocumented immigration in the United States began to grow rapidly only after the mid-1970s, while Mexican legal immigrants have arrived in significant numbers to the United States for many decades, one can expect illegal immigrants to have resided in the United States for a shorter period of time. Indeed, among Mexican illegal immigrants, 70.3% of all men and 57.1% of all women arrived in the United States during the decade of the eighties. On the other hand, among the overall Mexican immigrant group, 47.4% of all men and 36.1% of all women declared that they had arrived in the United States during the eighties. If recency of immigration is negatively related to earnings, then this gap could partly explain the lower earnings of undocumented workers relative to legal immigrants.

The distribution of employment by sector also varies by immigrant status. Both legal and illegal immigrants are employed predominantly in blue-collar occupations, but the undocumented workers are almost exclusively blue-collar workers. Indeed, 93.2% of the male sample of Mexican illegal immigrants was employed in blue-collar occupations and 87.4% of the female sample was. By comparison, among the overall Mexican immigrant population, 86.8% of all male workers and 69.2% of all female workers were employed in blue-collar occupations.

There is also a big difference between legal and illegal immigrants in terms of the distribution of their employment among the various blue-collar occupations. As Table 13.1 shows, both for men and women, undocumented workers tend to be sharply overrepresented in service occupations. These occupations include many of the jobs traditionally associated with illegal immigrants, such as housekeepers, household workers, food service workers, janitors and cleaners (all of which are service occupations). In addition, illegals are heavily represented in the operators, fabricators and laborers categories, which include many of the textile jobs taken by females and the helper jobs taken by male workers. As many as 74.8% of all undocumented Mexican male workers and 78.7% of female workers were employed in these two categories. By contrast, the legal immigrant population has much greater representation in the group of occupations catalogued as professional, technical, managerial, sales and administrative support. For men, 13.2% of all immigrant workers were employed in these occupations, as compared to only 6.8% among illegal immigrant men. For women, 30.8% of the legal Mexican immigrant population was employed as professional, technical, managerial, sales and administrative support workers compared to only 12.6% among illegals.

The majority of Mexican immigrants in the data resided in California. Close to 58% of legal immigrants and about 62% of illegal immigrants were located in California. Given the geographical proximity to Mexico, and the fact that the comparatively large Mexican ethnic enclave in Los Angeles and other parts of California provides a comparative advantage for the employment of legal and illegal immigrants, it is not surprising that most Mexican immigrants locate in that state. Finally, in terms of marital status, there is a greater proportion of single men and women among undocumented workers, and for years of on-the-job experience (as estimated in this paper), the average value is similar among legal and illegal immigrants.

Tables 13.2 and 13.3 present the key results of our empirical analysis. Table 13.2 shows the coefficients of the estimated wage equations for men while Table 13.3 depicts the results for women. Note that the signs of the coefficients for all the variables are identical in the legal and illegal immigrant equations, except for the INTERM variable, which has a negative (although statistically insignificant) sign for female legal immigrants and a positive one for all other groups. Furthermore, the signs of the coefficients in the two equations are largely as expected. There are some significant differences among the various equations, though, in the absolute value of the coefficients.

Table 13.2. Regression Estimates, Cross-Sectional Analysis, Male Wage Equation.

	Legal immigration equation		Illegal immigrants equation	
Independent variable	**Parameter estimate (s.e.)**	**T-statistic**	**Parameter estimate (s.e.)**	**T-statistic**
INTERCEPT	1.5956* (0.1023)	36.81	1.5129* (0.0620)	24.40
INTERM	0.0142 (0.0461)	0.31	0.0628 (0.0251)	2.50
HIGHSC	0.2329* (0.0553)	4.22	0.1446* (0.0342)	4.23
EXPER	0.0156* (0.0054)	2.87	0.0192* (0.0037)	5.21
EXPERSQ	−0.0002* (0.0001)	−2.21	−0.0004* (0.0001)	−5.53
NOENGLISH	−0.0874 (0.0613)	−1.87	−0.0702* (0.0219)	−3.21
PROFTC	0.2553* (0.0601)	4.25	0.1488* (0.0424)	3.51
FARMING	−0.0335 (0.0565)	−0.59	−0.0215 (0.0343)	−0.63
OPERAT	0.1125** (0.0534)	2.35	0.0904* (0.0255)	3.54
PRODUCT	0.2699* (0.0534)	5.05	0.2657* (0.0298)	8.90
SINGLE	−0.1042* (0.0401)	−2.60	−0.0963* (0.0283)	−4.11
RECENT	−0.1544* (0.0381)	−4.05	−0.0512** (0.0215)	−2.38
CALIF	0.1501* (0.0308)	4.69	0.0996* (0.0200)	4.80
R-SQ	0.14	—	0.15	—

* = Statistically significant at the 99% confidence level.
** = Statistically significant at the 95% confidence level.

Table 13.2 shows that for male undocumented workers the rate of return to education for intermediate schooling (6 to 9 years of schooling completed) is higher than for legal immigrants. However, the rate of return to completing at least some high school education

Table 13.3. Regression Estimates, Cross-Sectional Analysis, Female Wage Equation.

	Legal immigration equation		**Illegal immigrants equation**	
Independent variable	**Parameter estimate (s.e.)**	**T-statistic**	**Parameter estimate (s.e.)**	**T-statistic**
INTERCEPT	1.3425* (0.1317)	10.20	1.1838* (0.0978)	12.11
INTERM	−0.0200 (0.0670)	−0.30	0.1281* (0.0447)	2.87
HIGHSC	0.1745** (0.0706)	2.22	0.2297* (0.0637)	3.61
EXPER	0.0239* (0.0069)	3.45	0.0111 (0.0061)	1.81
EXPERSQ	−0.00047* (0.00013)	−3.46	−0.00023** (0.00012)	−1.99
NOENGLISH	−0.0522 (0.0634)	−0.87	−0.0995* (0.0385)	−2.59
PROFTC	0.2866* (0.0647)	4.39	0.2623* (0.0576)	4.55
FARMING	0.0466 (0.0886)	0.53	0.1197 (0.0924)	1.30
OPERAT	0.1588* (0.0598)	2.65	0.1839* (0.0399)	4.61
PRODUCT	0.3229* (0.0934)	3.43	0.2850* (0.0805)	3.54
SINGLE	−0.0967 (0.0541)	−1.79	−0.1026* (0.0387)	−2.65
RECENT	−0.1482* (0.0742)	−2.93	−0.0994* (0.0349)	−2.85
CALIF	0.1084* (0.0436)	2.46	0.1795 (0.0366)	4.91
R-SQ	0.13	—	0.18	—

* = Statistically significant at the 99% confidence level.
** = Statistically significant at the 95% confidence level.

(10 or more years of schooling), as reflected by the HIGHSC coefficient, is much higher for male legal immigrants than for the illegals. Perhaps because of the limited job opportunities that they can find, male undocumented workers with greater educational attainment

are severely constrained in their earnings opportunities compared to legal immigrants. On the other hand, Table 13.3 suggests that more educated female illegal immigrants do not encounter the same type of restriction, with the coefficient on HIGHSC higher in the illegal immigrant equation. In contrast to men, undocumented female workers with greater schooling can find jobs offering substantially higher compensation.

The economic returns to labor market experience also vary across the various groups considered. Among men, the rate of return to experience is higher for illegal immigrants than for legal immigrants. Among women, the opposite holds: the returns to experience are higher for the legal migrants. To understand these relationships, note that the variable RECENT, associated with years of residence in the United States, is being held constant while we consider changes in EXPER. Given the number of years that a Mexican immigrant has been residing in the United States, changes in the EXPER variable are directly related to changes in the number of years of experience the worker has had abroad, in Mexico. One way to interpret the higher EXPER coefficient in the male undocumented worker equation is that it shows that the returns in the U.S. labor market of having greater years of experience in Mexico are proportionally higher for the undocumented male worker than for the legal immigrant. For male legal immigrants, greater experience in Mexico provides fewer gains in the U.S. labor market than for male illegals. Among women, on the other hand, the results in Table 13.3 suggest that greater years of experience in the Mexican labor market are associated with higher earnings gains for legal immigrants. Female undocumented workers do not gain as much from having greater years of on-the-job experience in Mexico.

These differences in the experiences of male and female immigrants in the U.S. labor market may be explained by differences in the extent to which undocumented male and female workers can match their occupational experience in Mexico with that in the United States. The LPS data set does include information on the occupations held by undocumented workers in their countries of origin just before moving to the United States. When one compares the occupations held by illegals in the United States with those they held in Mexico before, 19.2% of the male workers had jobs in the same occupational category while only 11.8% of females had matching jobs. For male un-documented workers, then, their labor market experience in Mexico is more valuable in the United States because they have an easier time finding jobs in the U.S. labor market similar to those they held in Mexico. For female undocumented workers the opposite is true: finding jobs in the United States similar to those held before in Mexico is less likely.

Lack of ability to speak English, as reflected by the variable NOENGLISH, has a consistently negative influence on earnings, for both legal and illegal immigrants.

The occupational dummies are generally positive in Tables 13.2 and 13.3 suggesting that the various categories, including professional, technical, managerial, sales and administrative support workers, operators, fabricators and laborers, all tend to have higher earnings than service sector occupations, a pattern that holds for both legal and illegal immigrants. This positive association of certain occupational categories with higher earnings is quantitatively important. For instance, illegal immigrant workers employed in professional, technical, managerial or administrative support occupations can earn on average between 15 and 26% higher earnings, whether it is women or men, respectively.

Single workers earn substantially less than married workers, both among men and women and among legal and illegal immigrants. In addition, residence in California is linked to greater earnings, everything else held constant.

13.4 Accounting for Legal–Illegal Wage Differences

The previous section established that there is a substantial premium in the earnings received by legal immigrants when compared to undocumented workers. One possibility is that these wage differences reflect discrimination against illegal immigrants by U.S. employers. On the other hand, the wage differences may be due to the higher educational attainment of the legal workers, their greater English proficiency, or other average differences in characteristics between legal and illegal immigrants. To determine whether the data are consistent with the presence of exploitation or discrimination, it must be shown that there is a significant wage gap between legal and illegal workers even after holding constant the characteristics of the two groups. This is precisely what the well-known Blinder–Oaxaca wage decomposition seeks to establish (see Blinder 1973; Oaxaca 1973; Oaxaca and Ransom 1996). This section uses the regression coefficients presented in Tables 13.2 and 13.3 to carry out a Blinder–Oaxaca decomposition for the wage gap between legal and illegal immigrants in the United States.

The Blinder–Oaxaca wage decomposition for the case of legal and illegal immigrants is based on a comparison of the means of the log-wages for these two groups of workers. Using equation (1) yields the following equations for the means of the log-wages of legal and illegal immigrants:

$$\overline{\log W_L} = \beta_L' \bar{X}_L, \tag{3}$$

$$\overline{\log W_I} = \beta_I' \bar{X}_I, \tag{4}$$

where the subscript L represents legal immigrants, I denotes undocumented workers, and bars over variables denote mean values. Substracting equation (4) from (3) results in:

$$\begin{aligned} \overline{\log W_L} - \overline{\log W_I} = \beta_L' \bar{X}_L - \beta_I' \bar{X}_I &= (\bar{X}_L - \bar{X}_I)(\beta_L' + \beta_I')/2 \\ &+ (\beta_L' - \beta_I')(\bar{X}_I - \bar{X}_L)/2 \end{aligned} \tag{5}$$

Equation (5) decomposes the log-wage difference between legal and illegal immigrants (equal to the percentage difference in the geometric means of the observed wage rates for the two groups) into two components: (1) a part due to differences in the average characteristics of legal and illegal immigrants, as represented by the vectors of human capital and demographic variables in X_L and X_I, shown in the second row of equation (5); and (2) a part due to differences in the parameters of the wage equations for the two groups, as symbolized by β_L' and β_I', shown in the third row of equation (5).

The first component of the wage decomposition reflects the extent to which differences in wages between legal and illegal workers can be explained by mean differences between the two groups in educational attainment, English proficiency, sector of employment, experience, and other measured characteristics.

The second component of the wage decomposition reflects the extent to which wage differences between legal and illegal immigrants cannot be explained by differences in the measured characteristics of workers in the two groups. It is this component that would reflect labor market discrimination against illegal immigrants. However, it could also reflect the presence of differences in unmeasured characteristics of workers in the two groups. Still, if this second component constitutes a substantial proportion of the wage gap, it is unlikely that it could be due solely to unmeasured characteristics. Instead, it would strongly suggest the presence of some degree of discrimination against undocumented workers.

Table 13.4 presents the various components of the Blinder–Oaxaca decomposition for the wage gap between legal and illegal workers. Note first that the observed log-wage gap between the two groups is substantially higher (almost twice as big) among women than among men. Secondly, the portion of the log-wage difference that is due to differences in measured characteristics leaves unexplained a large fraction of the log-wage differential. For males, 51.3%

Table 13.4. Accounting for Wage Differentials between Legal and Illegal Immigrants.

	Male	**Female**
Observed log-real wage difference between legal and illegal immigrants (in 1989 dollars)	0.1385	0.2600
Log-wage difference		
due to differences in characteristics between legal and illegal immigrants	0.0674	0.1119
due to differences in ability to speak English	0.0134	0.0187
due to differences in recency of immigration	0.0236	0.0310
due to differences in other characteristics	0.0058	0.0191
Percentage of observed log-wage difference explained by differences in characteristics	48.7%	43.0%
Percentage of observed log-wage differential unexplained by differences in characteristics	51.3%	57.0%

of the wage premium received by legal immigrants over illegals cannot be explained by differences in measured characteristics. For women, the unexplained part of the log-wage difference is 57%. The most important characteristics in explaining the wage gap are: schooling, English proficiency, and recency of immigration. Overall, however, the joint effect of differences between legal and illegal immigrants in these and other measured characteristics leaves a large portion of the wage gap unexplained.

The substantial unexplained gap in wages between legal and illegal immigrants suggests the presence of discrimination against undocumented workers. On the other hand, the evidence is also consistent with the presence of differences in characteristics that have not been measured and could not therefore be included in the regressions in Tables 13.2 and 13.3. Ultimately, then, the cross-sectional analysis presented in this section, comparing legal and illegal immigrants at a given point in time, is only suggestive and cannot fully resolve the issue of the extent to which the residual wage premium of legals over illegals is due to discrimination/exploitation or differences in unmeasured characteristics.

An analysis that can provide stronger evidence on the extent to which illegals are subject to discrimination or exploitation is a longitudinal one, comparing the wages received by a given group of undocumented workers before and after legalization. Since the LPS data set does include a sample of workers for which these data is available, the next section sets out to examine whether the earnings of undocumented workers rise after legalization, and the forces behind such gains.

13.5 A Longitudinal Analysis of the Earnings of the Undocumented

The LPS survey first interviewed undocumented workers applying for legalization in 1989. It then re-interviewed a sample of these immigrants in 1992, after they had been fully legalized. This section examines the changes in the earnings of illegal workers after legalization, and the factors explaining these changes. Note that not all undocumented immigrants sampled by LPS in 1989 were re-interviewed in 1992. Because many of the respondents changed addresses, the Department of Labor could not locate them. As a result, out of 6,193 applicants for legalization sampled in 1989, a total of 4,012 were re-interviewed in 1992. Among these individuals, only those who were employed in 1987–1988 (before legalization) and in 1992 (after legalization) were used in the analysis. In addition, persons for which data were not available on educational attainment, age, sector of employment, etc., were excluded from the analysis. The remaining sample consists of 1,103 immigrants.

The longitudinal data allows an analysis of the determinants of the earnings of undocumented workers before and after legalization. Similarly to equation (2), the following human capital wage equation is estimated:

$$\begin{aligned}\log W_{ij} = {} & \beta_0 + \beta_1 INTERM_{ij} + \beta_2 HIGHSC_{ij} + \beta_3 EXPER_{ij} \\ & + \beta_4 EXPERSO_{ij} + \beta_5 NOENGLISH_{ij} + \beta_6 PROFTC_{ij} \\ & + \beta_7 FARMING_{ij} + \beta_8 OPERAT_{ij} + \beta_9 PRODUCT_{ij} \\ & + \beta_{10} SINGLE_{ij} + \beta_{11} RECENT_{ij} + \beta_{12} CALIF_{ij}, \qquad (6)\end{aligned}$$

where i denotes a specific male or female immigrant, and $j = 88$ and 92, denoting whether the data are for the undocumented worker before legalization (1987–1988) or after legalization (1992). All the symbols in equation (6) are as defined earlier.

Table 13.5 presents the sample means for the variables used in the analysis. The average hourly wage received by illegal immigrants rose significantly after the workers were legalized. Among men, the hourly wage rose from \$6.902 before legalization to \$7.933 after legalization (where the wages before and after legalization are both converted into 1989 dollars). Among women, the hourly wage increased from \$4.968 to \$5.995. Although it could be presumed that this rise in wages is due to the shift from illegality to legality, one also consider the fact that the measured characteristics of illegal immigrants also changed between 1987/1988, when they first applied for legalization, and 1992, when they were legal immigrants.[3]

Table 13.5. Sample Means, Longitudinal Data, before and after Legalization.

Variable	Before legalization		After legalization	
	Male	Female	Male	Female
Hourly wage (1989 Dollars)	6.902	4.968	7.933	5.995
Log hourly wage	1.846	1.509	1.983	1.682
ELEM (Proportion of sample with less than 6 years of schooling)	0.328	0.315	0.282	0.273
INTERM (Proportion of sample with 6 to 9 years of schooling)	0.418	0.465	0.398	0.428
HIGHSC (Proportion of sample with 10 or more years of schooling)	0.254	0.220	0.320	0.299
EXPER (Years of experience)	18.4	19.0	22.7	22.8
EXPERSQ (Experience squared)	441.0	471.0	625.0	632.0
NOENGLISH (Proportion of sample who cannot speak English at all)	0.299	0.399	0.153	0.280
PROFTC (Proportion of sample employed in professional, technical, sales and managerial occupations)	0.059	0.113	0.095	0.160
FARMING (Proportion employed in agricultural occupations)	0.128	0.025	0.103	0.022
OPERAT (Proportion employed as operators, fabricators and laborers)	0.399	0.418	0.394	0.406
PRODUCT (Proportion employed as precision production, craft and repair workers)	0.178	0.044	0.203	0.053
SERVICE (Proportion employed in services)	0.236	0.400	0.205	0.359
SINGLE (Proportion never married)	0.284	0.327	0.155	0.195
RECENT (Proportion who migrated to the United States in the 1980s to stay)	0.701	0.528	0.701	0.528
CALIF (Proportion residing in California)	0.615	0.638	0.610	0.638
Number of observations	787	317	787	317

The differences in the characteristics of illegal immigrants before and after legalization are presented in Table 13.5. The educational attainment of the immigrants is greater, as reflected in an increase in the proportion of workers with 10 or more years of schooling, from 25.4% to 32.0% among men and from 22% to close to 30% among women. Also, since the workers were significantly older after legalization, their on-the-job experience rose on average by about 4 years, for both men and women. There was also a substantial improvement in English language proficiency. The proportion of men who could not speak English at all declined from 29.9% to 15.3%, and among women the change was from 39.9% before legalization to 28% after. There were also significant sectoral changes. The proportion employed in the service sector dropped after legalization, from 23.6% to 20.5% among men and from 40% to 35.9% among women. In addition, the proportion of immigrants employed in professional, technical, sales, managerial and administrative support occupations rose, from 5.9% to 9.5% among men, and from 11.3% to 16% among women. Finally, due again perhaps to the older age of the immigrants after they were re-interviewed in 1992, a much greater proportion of men and women had been married after legalization.

Equation (6) was estimated separately for males and females using the LPS data before and after legalization. The results of this analysis, for males and females, are presented in the Appendix. In order to isolate the direct impact of legalization on earnings, independent of the changes in the characteristics of the immigrants over time, we again use Blinder–Oaxaca decompositions. The Blinder–Oaxaca wage decomposition for the case of illegal immigrants before and after legalization is based on a comparison of the means of the log-wages for these two groups of workers. The means of the log-wages of illegal immigrants before and after legalization are:

$$\overline{\log W_{92}} = \beta_{92}' \bar{X}_{92} \tag{7}$$

$$\overline{\log W_{88}} = \beta_{88}' \bar{X}_{88}, \tag{8}$$

where the subscript 92 represents the values of the variables for illegal immigrants in 1992, after they were legalized, and 88 denotes their values in 1987/1988, when the workers were still undocumented.

As before, bars over variables denote mean values. Subtracting equation (8) from (7) results in:

$$\begin{aligned}\overline{\log W_{92}} - \overline{\log W_{88}} &= \beta'_{92}\bar{X}_{92} - \beta'_{88}\bar{X}_{88} \\ &= (\bar{X}_{92} - \bar{X}_{88})(\beta'_{92} + \beta'_{88})/2 \\ &\quad + (\beta'_{92} - \beta'_{88})(\bar{X}_{92} + \bar{X}_{88})/2. \qquad (9)\end{aligned}$$

Equation (9) decomposes the log-wage gain of immigrants after they were legalized (equal to the percentage difference in the geometric means of the observed wage rates after and before legalization) into two components: (1) a part due to changes in the average measured characteristics of the immigrants in 1992 and 1987/1988, as represented by the vectors of human capital and demographic variables in X_{92} and X_{88}, shown in the second row of equation (9); and (2) a part due to differences in the parameters of the wage equations in 1992 and 1987/1988, as symbolized by β'_{92} and β'_{88}, shown in the third row of equation (9).

The first component of the wage decomposition reflects the extent to which the wage gains of workers after legalization can be explained by mean changes in educational attainment, English proficiency, sector of employment, experience, and other measured characteristics. The second component displays the extent to which the wage gains after legalization cannot be explained by changes in the measured characteristics of workers over time. This may be because labor market discrimination or exploitation of illegal workers diminished due to legalization. It could also reflect any changes in unmeasured characteristics of workers between 1987/1988 and 1992. However, it is the same group of workers that is being examined over time, and it is therefore unlikely that major changes in unmeasured characteristics have occurred. For instance, one unmeasured variable is the quality of the educational background of the worker before coming to the United States. This unmeasured variable could explain differences in the wages of a cross-section of illegal immigrants at a given point in time, but it *cannot* explain the *change* in wages of the immigrants between 1988 and 1992 because the variable has not changed between 1987 and 1992. With longitudinal data, then, the presence of

Table 13.6. Accounting for Wage Differentials of Immigrants before and after Legalization.

	Male	**Female**
Observed log-real wage difference between legal and illegal immigrants (in 1989 dollars)	0.1376	0.1723
Log-wage difference		
due to differences in characteristics between legal and illegal immigrants	0.0602	0.0649
due to gains education	0.0103	0.0156
due to gains in spoken English language proficiency	0.0067	0.0101
due to gains on-the-job experience	0.0158	0.0010
due to change in marital status	0.0145	0.0201
due to differences in other characteristics	0.0129	0.0025
Percentage of observed log-wage difference explained by differences in characteristics	43.7%	37.7%
Percentage of observed log-wage differential unexplained by differences in characteristics	56.3%	62.3%

a significant unexplained residual wage growth would strongly suggest that legalization has acted to diminish discrimination against undocumented workers.

Table 13.6 presents the various components of the Blinder–Oaxaca decomposition for the wage gains of the sample of legalized immigrants. Note first that the log-wage increase between 1987/1988 and 1992 was greater among women than among men. Since the wage shortfall of undocumented workers relative to legal immigrants in 1987/1988 was greater for women, the greater female wage gains obtained from legalization are not surprising. Secondly, the portion of the log-wage gain that is due to changes in the measured characteristics of the sample of illegal immigrants between 1987/1988 and 1992 still leaves unexplained a large fraction of the log-wage differential. For males, 56.3% of the wage gain between 1987/1988 and 1992 cannot be explained by differences in measured characteristics. For women, the unexplained part of the log-wage gain is 62%. The changes in the characteristics of immigrants that do help account the most for the wage gap include greater schooling, higher English proficiency, greater marriage rates, and more on-the-job experience.

The large proportion of the wage gain of illegal immigrants between 1987/1988 and 1992 that remains unexplained after changes in individual characteristics have been taken into account strongly suggests that the change in the legal status of illegal immigrants had a strong positive effect on their earnings. This is also consistent with the earlier evidence that we have presented on the substantial unexplained shortfall in the wages of undocumented workers relative to legal immigrants. It all suggests that legalization has a direct positive effect on the earnings of illegal immigrants, whether by eliminating the monopsonistic power that some employers exert over them or by allowing immigrants greater access to the labor market. This is not, of course, the only impact of legalization. Some of the changes in the characteristics of the sample of illegal immigrants examined here between 1987/1988 and 1992 are probably also indirectly related to the change in immigration status. The greater educational attainment and English proficiency of workers after legalization may have not been achieved if the workers had remained illegally in the United States instead of applying for legalization.

13.6 Conclusions

This paper has examined the earnings of Mexican illegal immigrants in the U.S. labor market. A cross-sectional analysis was carried out first of the determinants of the wage gap between Mexican legal and illegal immigrants. In addition, longitudinal information was utilized to examine the changes in the earnings of illegal immigrants before and after they were legalized. In contrast to the previous literature in the field, the paper uses nationally-representative data for illegal immigrants, obtained from the 1989/1992 Legalized Population Survey (LPS), released for public use in 1996.

Our findings confirm that Mexican undocumented workers receive substantially lower earnings relative to legal immigrants in the United States. Comparing data on legal immigrants with data on illegal immigrants for 1987/1988, the paper shows that, on an hourly basis, male Mexican legal immigrants in the United States earned 41.8% more than undocumented workers while female legal immigrants earned 40.8% more. At the same time, the paper also shows that there are substantial differences in the main human capital, occupational and demographic characteristics influencing the earnings of legal and illegal Mexican immigrants. We find that illegal immigrants have lower average educational attainment than legal immigrants, lower English language proficiency, and a smaller number of years of residence in the United States.

Some of the literature on illegal immigrants has suggested that differences in the characteristics of legal and illegal immigrants essentially explain the lower wages received by the undocumented, leaving little room, if any, for exploitation or discrimination as a factor determining the earnings of these workers. This paper has examined this issue in detail. The paper finds that differences in the measured human capital, occupational, and demographic characteristics of legal and illegal immigrants — such as the lower educational attainment of illegals, their more limited knowledge of spoken English, and their shorter time of residence in the United States — do not explain most of the observed wage gap between the two groups, whether for males or females. Indeed, differences in measured characteristics explain only 48.7% of the observed log-wage gap between legal and illegal male immigrants, and 43% of the observed log-wage gap for women. The characteristics that do help account the most for the wage gap include schooling, English proficiency, and recency of immigration.

The large proportion of the gap in wages between legal and illegal immigrants unexplained by differences in the measured characteristics of these two groups strongly suggests the presence of systematic discrimination against undocumented workers. It is still possible, though, that the gap in wages is related to the presence of differences in unmeasured characteristics of legal and illegal workers, such as employment instability. In order to provide an answer to the question of whether illegal status itself, and not individual characteristics, is the culprit behind the lower wages of illegals when compared to legal immigrants, this paper carried out an analysis of longitudinal data for undocumented workers before and after legalization. Since unmeasured characteristics are likely to remain constant for any particular individual before and after legalization, this analysis is less subject to the criticism leveled against the cross-sectional analysis. Using the LPS data set, which includes a sample of workers for which these data is available, this paper examined whether the earnings of Mexican undocumented workers rise after legalization, and whether such a rise is due to changes in characteristics, like greater education or experience, or whether it is associated directly to the change in legal status.

Our analysis shows that the gain in real hourly earnings of illegal immigrants in the United States between 1987/1988, when they were undocumented, and 1992, when they had been legalized, was 15% for men and 21% for women. However, the illegal immigrants also changed some of their measured characteristics after legalization, including greater educational attainment, improved English proficiency, higher marriage rates, and more experience. In order to determine the extent to which the change in illegal immigrant status itself, versus the changes in measured characteristics, explains the wage gains, an analysis of the determinants of the wage growth after legalization was carried out. We find that the portion of the wage gain that is due to changes in measured characteristics between 1987/1988 and 1992 still leaves unexplained a large fraction of the log-wage differential. For males, 56.3% of the wage gain between 1987/1988 and 1992 cannot be explained by differences in measured characteristics. For women, the unexplained part of the log-wage gain is 62%.

The substantial fraction of the wage gains of illegal immigrants between 1987/1988 and 1992 that cannot be explained by changes in individual characteristics strongly suggests that the change in the legal status of illegal immigrants had a strong positive effect on their earnings. Legalization had a positive effect on the earnings of illegal immigrants, whether by eliminating the monopsonistic power that some employers exert over them, or by allowing immigrants greater access to the labor market. Taken together, the cross-sectional and longitudinal analyses presented in this paper imply that (1) the lower wages of Mexican illegal immigrants in the United States are partly associated with exploitation or discrimination based on their illegal status, and (2) legalization of undocumented workers provides substantial direct positive effects on the earnings of these immigrants.

13.7 Appendix

Table 13.A-1. Regression Estimates, Longitudinal Data, Male Wage Equation.

	Immigrants before legalization		**Immigrants after legalization**	
Independent variable	**Parameter estimate (s.e.)**	**t-statistic**	**Parameter estimate (s.e.)**	**t-statistic**
INTERCEPT	1.5225* (0.0855)	17.79	1.17553* (0.1070)	16.42
INTERM	0.0749** (0.0344)	2.17	0.0270 (0.0361)	0.75
HIGHSC	0.1782* (0.0471)	3.78	0.1433* (0.0509)	2.81
EXPER	0.0208* (0.0053)	3.87	0.0074 (0.0060)	1.23
EXPERSQ	−0.0004** (0.0001)	−3.83	−0.0002 (0.0001)	−1.57
NOENGLISH	−0.0457 (0.0305)	−1.50	−0.0731* (0.0317)	−2.30
PROFTC	0.1464** (0.0619)	2.36	0.1403* (0.0542)	2.59
FARMING	−0.0452 (0.0461)	−0.98	−0.0978 (0.0343)	−1.88
OPERAT	0.0529 (0.0343)	1.54	0.0624 (0.0371)	1.68
PRODUCT	0.2885* (0.0534)	6.97	0.2012* (0.0425)	4.72
SINGLE	−0.1189* (0.0327)	−3.42	−0.0781** (0.0394)	−1.98
RECENT	−0.0664** (0.0294)	−2.25	−0.0375 (0.0302)	−1.24
CALIF	0.0865* (0.0276)	3.12	0.1634* (0.0200)	5.79
R-SQ	0.17	—	0.14	—

* = Statistically significant at the 99% confidence level.
** = Statistically significant at the 95% confidence level.

Table 13.A-2. Regression Estimates, Longitudinal Data, Female Wage Equation.

	Immigrants before legalization		Immigrants after legalization	
Independent variable	**Parameter estimate (s.e.)**	**t-statistic**	**Parameter estimate (s.e.)**	**t-statistic**
INTERCEPT	1.1920* (0.1327)	8.98	1.3501* (0.1648)	8.19
INTERM	0.0524 (0.0590)	0.89	0.0736 (0.0635)	1.16
HIGHSC	0.2217** (0.0875)	2.53	0.1653** (0.0842)	1.96
EXPER	0.0172** (0.0084)	2.04	0.0177 (0.0095)	1.87
EXPERSQ	−0.0004* (0.0001)	−2.64	−0.0004* (0.0002)	−2.63
NOENGLISH	−0.0845 (0.0525)	−1.61	−0.1032** (0.0524)	−1.97
PROFTC	0.3792* (0.0844)	4.49	0.2773* (0.0762)	3.64
FARMING	0.0984 (0.1504)	0.64	−0.1666 (0.1643)	−1.01
OPERAT	0.2026* (0.0535)	3.79	0.0933 (0.0561)	1.66
PRODUCT	0.3330* (0.1165)	2.86	0.2067 (0.1106)	1.87
SINGLE	−0.1525* (0.0520)	−2.93	−0.1357** (0.0614)	−2.21
RECENT	−0.0787* (0.0466)	−1.69	−0.0034 (0.0478)	−0.07
CALIF	0.1580* (0.0497)	3.12	0.1635* (0.0503)	3.25
R-SQ	0.24	—	0.20	—

* = Statistically significant at the 99% confidence level.
** = Statistically significant at the 95% confidence level.

Notes:

[1]See, for example, Borjas (1994, 1992), Bloom and Grenier (1993), Carliner (1995), Chiswick (1978), Orcutt Duleep and Regets (1996a,b), and Rivera-Batiz (1996, 1992, 1990), among many others.

[2]Note that if there are systematic differences in the extent to which illegal and legal immigrants pay taxes, this might generate differences in net earnings even if there are no differences in gross earnings; since we do not have data on the payment of taxes by immigrants, the significance of this issue cannot be assessed.

[3]In principle, one should also consider changes in the economy over time in explaining the rising real wages of illegal immigrants. In the present context, the U.S. economy was booming at the time that the illegal immigrants applied for legalization in 1987 and 1988. However, when they were re-interviewed in 1992, the American economy was just beginning a recovery from a severe recession. As a result, average hourly earnings in U.S. private nonagricultural industries declined by 4% in real terms between 1987 and 1992. If anything, then, the gains in the earnings due to legalization documented in this paper may be a conservative estimate of such gains. If the U.S. economy had been at the same level of activity in 1992 as it was in 1987, the estimated earnings gains from legalization would have been somewhat higher.

References

Alvarez L (1996) Down from Poverty: Mexico to Manhattan. *The New York Times*, October 9: pp A1–B7.

Bailey TR (1987) *Immigrant and Native Workers: Contrasts and Competition.* Westview Press, Boulder, Colorado.

Blinder AS (1973) Wage Discrimination: Reduced Form and Structural Estimates. *Journal of Human Resources* 8, 436–455.

Blau F, and Kahn L (1997) Swimming Upstream: Trends in the Gender Wage Differential in the 1980s. *Journal of Labor Economics* 15, 1–42.

Bloom D, Grenier G (1993) Language, Employment and Earnings in the United States: Spanish-English Differentials from 1970 to 1990. National Bureau of Economic Research Working Paper No. 4584, Cambridge.

Borjas GJ (1994) Assimilation and Changes in Cohort Quality Revisited: What Happened to Immigrant Earnings in the 1980s? National Bureau of Economic Research Working Paper No. 4866, Cambridge, Massachusetts.

Borjas GJ (1992) National Origin and the Skills of Immigrants in the Postwar Period. In: Borjas G, Freeman R (eds). *Immigration and the Workforce.* University of Chicago Press, Chicago, 17–47.

Borjas GJ (1990) *Friends or Strangers: The Impact of Immigrants on the U S Economy.* Basic Books, New York.

Borjas GJ (1987) Self-Selection and the Earnings of Immigrants. *American Economic Review* 77, 531–553.

Borjas GJ, Tienda M (1993) The Employment and Wages of Legalized Immigrants. *International Migration Review* 27, 712–747.

Carliner G (1995) The Language Ability of U.S. Immigrants: Assimilation and Cohort Effects. National Bureau of Economic Research Working Paper No. 5222, Cambridge, Massachusetts.

Chiswick B (1988) *Illegal Aliens: Their Employment and Employers.* Upjohn Institute for Employment Research, Kalamazoo, Michigan.

Chiswick B (1984) Illegal Aliens in the United States Labor Market: An Analysis of Occupational Attainment and Earnings. *International Migration Review* 18, 714–732.

Chiswick B (1978) The Effects of Americanization on the Earnings of Foreign-Born Men. *Journal of Political Economy* 86, 897–921.

Chiswick B, Miller P (1996) Language Skills and Earnings among Legalized Aliens. Paper presented at the 1997 American Economic Association Meetings, New Orleans, mimeo.

Ehrenberg R, Smith RS (1994) *Modern Labor Economics: Theory and Public Policy*. Harper Collins, New York.

Finder A (1995) Despite Tough Laws, Sweatshops Flourish. *The New York Times* February 6: p. A1.

Gonzalez-Baker S (1990) *The Cautious Welcome: The Legalization Programs of the Immigration Reform and Control Act*. University Press of America, Lanham, Maryland.

Heckman J (1979) Sample Selection Bias as Specification Error. *Econometrica* 47:153–162.

Juhn C, Murphy K, Pierce B (1991) Wage Inequality and the Rise in Returns to Skill. *Journal of Political Economy* 101, 410–442.

Kleinfeld NR (1993) Immigrant Dream of Plenty Turns to Misery and Regret. *The New York Times* June 8: A1–B2.

Manski CF (1989) Anatomy of the Selection Problem. *Journal of Human Resources* 24, 343–360.

Massey D (1987) Do Undocumented Immigrants Earn Lower Wages than Legal Immigrants: New Evidence from Mexico. *International Migration Review* 21, 236–274.

North DS, Houston M (1976) The Characteristics and Role of Illegal Aliens in the United States Labor Market: An Exploratory Study. Mimeo, Linton and Co., Washington, D.C.

Oaxaca R (1973) Male–Female Wage Differentials in Urban Labor Markets. *International Economic Review* 14, 693–709.

Oaxaca R, Ransom M (1994) On Discrimination and the Decomposition of Wage Differentials. *Journal of Econometrics* 61, 5–21.

Orcutt Duleep H, Regets MC (1996a) Admission Criteria and Immigrant Earnings Profiles. *International Migration Review* 30, 571–590.

Orcutt Duleep H, Regets MC (1996b) The Elusive Concept of Immigrant Quality: Evidence from 1970–1990. Mimeo, Program for Research on Immigration Policy, The Urban Institute, Washington, D.C.

Portes A, Bach R (1985) *Latin Journey: Cuban and Mexican Immigrants in the United States*. University of California Press, Berkeley.

Ranney S, Kossoudji S (1993) Profiles of Temporary Mexican Labor Migrants to the United States. *Population and Development Review* 9, 475–493.

Rayner R (1996) What Immigration Crisis? *The New York Times Magazine* January 7, 1996.

Reichert J, Massey D (1979) "Patterns of US Migration from a Mexican Sending Community: A Comparison of Legal and Illegal Immigrants," *International Migration Review* 13, 599–623.

Reimers CW (1985) A Comparative Analysis of the Wages of Hispanics, Blacks and Non-Hispanic Whites. In: Borjas G, Tienda M (eds) *Hispanics in the US Economy.* Academic Press, Orlando, 27–76.

Reuters L (1996) Sweatshop Workers Share $1.1 Million. *The New York Times* March 9, 1996, p. A12.

Rivera-Batiz FL (1996) English Language Proficiency, Quantitative Skills and the Economic Progress of Immigrants. In: Orcutt Duleep H, Wunnava P (eds) *Immigrants and Immigration Policy: Individual Skills, Family Ties and Group Identities.* 1AI Press, Greenwich, Connecticut.

Rivera-Batiz FL (1992) "English Language Proficiency and the Earnings of Young Immigrants in U.S. Labor Markets," *Policy Studies Review* 11, 262–274.

Rivera-Batiz FL (1990) English Language Proficiency and the Economic Progress of Immigrants. *Economics Letters* 34, 295–300.

Rivera-Batiz FL, Sechzer S, Gang I (eds) (1991) *U S Immigration Policy Reform in the 1980s: A Preliminary Assessment.* Praeger Publishers, New York.

Smith S, Kramer R, Singer A (1996) *Characteristics and Labor Market Behavior of the Legalized Population Five Years Following Legalization.* Immigration Policy and Research Division, Bureau of International Labor Affairs, U.S. Department of Labor, Washington, D.C.

Taylor 1E (1985) Selectivity of Undocumented Mexico-US Migrants and Implications for U.S. Immigration Reform. The Urban Institute, Working Paper No. PDS–85–4.

Tienda M, Borjas G, Cordero-Guzman H, Neuman K, Romero M (1991) The Demography of Legalization: Insights form Administrative Records of Legalized Aliens. NORC, University of Chicago, Chicago.

Trejo S (1997) Why Do Mexican Americans Earn Low Wages? *Journal of Political Economy* 105,1235–1268.

United States Department of Commerce (1993) *1990 U S Census of Population and Housing 5% Public Use Microdata Sample.* Bureau of the Census, Washintgon, D.C.

United States Department of Labor (1996) *Legalized Population Survey Public Use File.* Bureau of International Labor Affairs, Washington, D. C.

Chapter 14

Illegal Immigrants in the U.S. Economy: A Comparative Analysis of Mexican and Non-Mexican Undocumented Workers*

14.1 Introduction

The prevailing image of undocumented workers in the United States is that of a population with low levels of educational attainment, employed in sectors supplying low-skilled jobs. This stereotypical view is reinforced by the frequent images portrayed in the press of the millions of unskilled Mexican immigrants who illegally cross the border with the U.S. every year. It is a perception that is shared by most migration scholars. For example, in an analysis of a sample of illegal immigrants in Chicago, Illinois, Chiswick (1988: 143) concludes that "most illegal aliens have low levels of schooling." Similarly, a recent report from the National Academy of Sciences (1997: 7) observes that, compared to legal immigrants: "illegal immigrants...are generally more poorly educated." And in a recent book, Borjas refers to the employers of illegal immigrants in the U.S. as "large agricultural enterprises, sweatshops, and native households that hire illegal

*This chapter was originally published in Slobodan Djajic, ed., *International Migration: Trends, Policy and Economic Impact*, London: Routledge Publishing, 2001, pp. 180–203. © 2001 Taylor & Francis; reprinted with permission.

aliens as maids or nannies" [Borjas (1999: 206)]. This is a common perception, as reflected in the following statement by Ray Borane, the major of Douglas, Arizona in a bitter *New York Times* editorial condemning the employers of undocumented workers: "Do you have any idea what havoc you cause in our area and in other border towns, all because some of you hire illegal immigrants to make your beds, mow your lawns and cook your meals?" [Borane (1999: A10)].

Since most undocumented workers remain in the U.S. economy largely undetected, existing profiles of illegal immigrants emerge mostly from the accounts of journalists or from particular case studies (with small samples) carried out by social scientists. The study by Chiswick, for example, consisted of a sample of 292 illegal immigrants, most of them from Mexico. And the studies upon which the National Academy of Sciences based its earlier statement about illegal immigrants were predominantly of Mexican migrants, such as North and Houstoun (1976), which had a sample of 793 undocumented Mexican immigrants, apprehended by the INS at the border, and Massey (1987), whose sample consisted of 232 Mexican illegal immigrants interviewed in their region of origin in Mexico. The comments by Major Borane, as most surfacing in the press, are based on immigrants close to the U.S.–Mexico border. The fact is that the views currently displayed in public discussions of illegal immigration are subject to the limited data utilized to describe this population.

This paper provides an analysis of the labor market performance of illegal immigrants in the United States through the use of a national sample of undocumented workers surveyed by the U.S. Department of Labor in 1989. The survey, released for public use in 1996, is the Legalized Population Survey (LPS), which includes a random sample of 4,012 illegal immigrants who were residing in the U.S. in 1987/88 when they sought legal permanent residence through the Immigration Reform and Control Act of 1986 (IRCA). This Act had as one of its major components an illegal immigrant amnesty program, through which illegals meeting certain requirements were able to obtain lawful permanent resident status [for more details, see Gonzalez Baker (1990, 1997) and Rivera-Batiz (1991)]. It allowed undocumented immigrants who had been continuously residing in the U.S. since January 1, 1982 to be eligible for temporary resident status. Once a person applied for temporary resident status, he or she was also eligible for permanent resident status, so long as the application was filed on or before November 6, 1990.

The sample of undocumented workers in the LPS was interviewed in 1987 and 1988, before they became legal permanent residents. Detailed information was collected from them relating to their labor market and general socioeconomic experience in the U.S. at the time that they applied for legalization. The LPS sample is therefore representative of all illegal immigrants in the U.S. who came forward with the necessary documentation to seek legalization. Although most observers agree that a large portion of the illegal alien population residing in the U.S. in 1987 and 1988 was reached by IRCA's amnesty program, it is also likely that short-term, temporary workers were not as widely reached by the program. IRCA did make a special provision for the amnesty of illegals working in agriculture (the Special Agricultural Worker or SAW program), but the LPS survey did not include this population in its sample. Because of these caveats, it may be useful to think of the LPS data (and the analysis in this paper) as representing those illegal immigrants who intended to remain permanently in the United States, and not to temporary migrants. Still, the LPS data set provides the most extensive information available yet on the experiences of illegal immigrants in the United States. For more details on the LPS data, see Smith, Kramer and Singer (1996) and Tienda *et al.* (1991).

Despite the widespread perception of illegal immigrants as predominantly unskilled persons with low levels of schooling, our analysis of the LPS data provides a sharply different picture. Because close to half of all the undocumented in the U.S. come from Mexico, one must make a differentiation in the analysis between Mexican and non-Mexican illegals. This has a major impact, as the characteristics of the Mexican immigrants, who have been frequently studied in the previous literature, are quite different from those of the rest of the illegal immigrant population. The paper shows that the central image of the illegal immigrant in the U.S., presented on television and newspapers as well as on academic journals, as an unskilled, low-income worker surreptitiously crossing the Rio Grande is misleading and ignores the great diversity present in this population.

Section 14.2 provides an overview of illegal immigration in the United States and it also presents a discussion of the characteristics of undocumented workers, as shown by the LPS, and compares them with those of the overall immigrant population, as determined from Census data. Section 14.3 proceeds to compare the socioeconomic status and labor market situation of Mexican and non-Mexican illegal immigrants. Section 14.4 focuses on the factors determining differences in earnings between Mexican and non-Mexican undocumented workers, presenting the empirical human capital model utilized to analyze the role of education, age, location, and an array of other factors in explaining wages. Section 14.5 then presents the results of the empirical earnings functions and studies the differences in the estimated labor market rates of return to various individual characteristics among Mexican and non-Mexican illegal immigrants. Section 14.6 summarizes the conclusions of the paper.

14.2 Illegal Immigration in the United States

The illegal immigrant population residing in the United States has been gradually rising over the last 15 years. Since by definition this population cannot be officially counted, one must rely on indirect methods to estimate its size. The most reliable estimates of undocumented workers in the U.S. have been obtained in recent years using the so-called residual methodology. This methodology calculates the number of illegal immigrants as the difference between the total number of immigrants who are counted in the U.S. at any given moment in time and the number of legal immigrants residing in the country. For instance, Warren and Passel (1987) found that there were 8.0 million immigrants counted in the 1980 U.S. Census of Population while there were 5.9 million legal immigrants residing in the U.S. at the time, as determined by INS data, leaving a residual of 2.1 million undocumented immigrants counted in the 1980 Census.

As Table 14.1 presents, studies using the residual methodology conclude that the number of undocumented immigrants in the U.S. rose to 4.8 million in 1987, going down to 2.2 million in 1988 after the

Table 14.1. Estimates of the Illegal Immigrant Population in the United States, 1980–1998.

Year	Number of undocumented immigrants
1980	2,100,000
1986	3,200,000
1987	4,800,000
1988	2,200,000
1990	2,600,000
1992	3,400,000
1994	3,750,000
1998	4,700,000

Sources: Warren and Passel (1987), Woodrow and Passel (1990) and Fernandez and Robinson (1994). The 1998 estimate is an extrapolation of the growth for 1994–1998 based on the 1988–1994 average annual increase.

legalization component of the 1986 Immigration Reform and Control Act went into effect. Since that time, the number of illegal immigrants has gradually climbed again. The most recent estimates of the U.S. Bureau of the Census place the number of undocumented immigrants at 3.7 million in 1994. Since the average net increase of the illegal population each year between 1988 and 1994 was 275,000, one can impute that the number of illegal immigrants in the year 1998 was about 4.7 million, about the same as it was in 1987. Note that insofar as the residual methodology estimates represent a count of illegal immigrants responding to Census surveys, they may suffer from an undercount problem. Recently, the INS has estimated the illegal immigrant population in 1996 to be 5 million [see Immigration and Naturalization Service (1999)].

Among the population of illegal immigrants, the largest share comes from Mexico. Approximately one out of every two undocumented workers residing in the United States originates in Mexico. Table 14.2 presents the composition of undocumented workers residing in the U.S., by country of origin. As Table 14.2 depicts, Mexican immigrants are followed by migrants from El Salvador, Guatemala, Canada, Haiti, the Philippines, and Honduras.

Table 14.2. Undocumented Immigrants in the U.S., by Country of Origin, 1998.

Country of origin	Total number of undocumented immigrants	Percentage of total undocumented population
Total, U.S.	4,700,000	100.0%
Mexico	2,538,000	54.0
El Salvador	315,000	6.7
Guatemala	155,000	3.3
Canada	113,000	2.4
Haiti	99,000	2.0
Philippines	89,000	1.9
Honduras	85,000	1.8
The Bahamas	66,000	1.4
Nicaragua	66,000	1.4
Poland	66,000	1.4
Colombia	61,000	1.3
Other	1,047,000	22.3

Source: The distribution of illegal immigrants is based on INS estimates for October 1996. The total number of illegals by country for 1998 is based on the 1996 distribution multiplied by the total number of illegals estimated for 1998.

What are the characteristics of undocumented workers in the U.S.? Are the stereotypes mentioned in the introduction correct? The existing literature is not much help on this issue since it uses small samples consisting mostly of illegal immigrants who entered the country through the U.S.–Mexico border. But according to INS statistics, the majority of undocumented workers has not entered the U.S. unlawfully but instead has come in by legal means, with tourist, student or work visas that are later allowed to expire. The INS has estimated that slightly over half of the illegals residing in the U.S. in 1994 had first entered the country legally. With legitimate visas in their hands, prospective illegals can simply walk through the inspection booths at U.S. ports of entry. Once they overstay their visas, they blend quietly into American society, avoiding detection and any contacts with the INS.

The characteristics of visa overstayers appear to be quite different from those of illegal border crossers. For instance, the country of origin of illegal immigrants varies significantly according to the method used by the migrants to enter the U.S. As estimated by the INS, most migrants from Mexico have entered the country by crossing the border illegally. So do many from Central America (El Salvador and Guatemala). However, most illegals from Canada, Poland, the Philippines, Haiti, the Bahamas and Italy initially entered the country lawfully. In the case of Polish citizens, the INS estimates that, in 1994, only 1 percent had initially crossed the U.S. border unlawfully.

The geographical distribution of illegal immigrants in the U.S. also diverges by the method of entry into the country. Undocumented workers crossing the U.S.–Mexico border stay mostly in the U.S. southwest. By contrast, the majority of those who initially enter the country legally end up in the Northeastern United States, mostly in New York or New Jersey. Table 14.3 displays INS estimates showing that the illegal immigrant contingent residing in New York and New Jersey is dominated by countries such as Ecuador, Ireland, Israel, Italy, Egypt, Pakistan, Philippines, Poland, Portugal and Yugoslavia, the immense majority of whom entered the country with lawful visas at the international airports at Newark in New Jersey and Kennedy in New York.

The limited existing profiles of visa overstayers suggest that the characteristics of these immigrants differ greatly from the traditional picture of the illegal immigrant. They appear to have superior educational attainment and to have achieved greater socioeconomic progress when compared to illegal border crossers. For instance, consider the case of Nuccio R., a 24 year old Italian immigrant who came to the U.S. on a tourist visa but stayed after the visa expired. Interviewed by the New York Times after four years of illegal residence in the U.S., Nuccio, a high school graduate, had "a full-time job in a relative's delicatessen, a car, a driver's license, credit cards and his own apartment" [New York Times (1995): pp. A1, B5].

This vision of visa overstayers as a population with sharply different characteristics when compared to illegal border crossers is confirmed by the Legalized Population Survey (LPS). In contrast to other surveys of undocumented workers, the LPS includes a national cross-section of those illegal immigrants in the U.S. who applied for legalization in 1987 and 1988 under the provisions of the Immigration

Table 14.3. Illegal Immigrants in New York and New Jersey, 1994.

Country of origin	Number of illegal immigrants
A. New York	
Italy	31,000
Poland	27,000
Ecuador	27,000
Dominican Republic	24,000
Trinidad & Tobago	24,000
Colombia	22,000
Jamaica	21,000
El Salvador	20,000
Ireland	20,000
Israel	15,000
Pakistan	15,000
New York total	**529,000**
B. New Jersey	
Portugal	17,000
Poland	11,000
Italy	9,000
Colombia	9,000
Ecuador	7,000
Philippines	7,000
Haiti	6,000
El Salvador	6,000
Yugoslavia	4,000
Egypt	4,000
Mexico	4,000
New Jersey total	**137,000**

Source: The data is for 1994, from the Immigration and Naturalization Service.

Reform and Control Act of 1986. Based on the public use LPS sample, Table 14.4 presents data on the characteristics of illegal border crossers and visa overstayers and compares them with those of the overall immigrant population as determined by the 1990 U.S. Census of Population and Housing.

One can notice, first of all, that illegal border crossers are on average younger than visa overstayers and have a greater concentration of men. On both of these accounts, visa overstayers have a profile that

Table 14.4. Characteristics of Illegal Border Crossers, Visa Overstayers and All Immigrants.

	Illegal border crossers	**Visa overstayers**	**All immigrants in 1990 census**
Sex (% male)	60.3%	51.9%	50.6%
Age (average, in years)	31.9	36.6	37.5
Recent Migrant (% who moved to the US in the last ten years)	84.5%	80.0%	43.2%
Educational Attainment (Average years of schooling completed by persons aged 25 or older)	7.1	11.6	10.7
College attendance (% of persons 25 years of age or older who completed at least one year of college)	6.7%	41.0%	37.5%
Professional and technical occupations (% of all persons 16 years of age or older in these occupational categories)	8.3%	28.2%	34.6%
Family income (annual, 1989)	$18,808	$21,372	$42,241
Family income per person (Family income divided by number of persons in the family)	$6,218	$9,054	$11,775
Residence in California (%)	54.5%	31.4%	12.9%

Source: Legalized Population Survey and 1990 U.S. Census of Population and Housing; authors' computations.

is closer to the average immigrant residing in the U.S. than to illegal border crossers. The same holds true of education. The average educational attainment of visa overstayers is much higher than that of illegal border crossers. According to the data in the LPS, the average years of schooling of adult visa overstayers in 1987–88 was 11.6, compared to 7.1 among illegal border crossers. In fact, the schooling of visa overstayers was closer to — and even exceeded — that of the overall immigrant population, which had an average of 10.7 years of schooling in 1990. Furthermore, 41 percent of all visa overstayers had received at least one year of college education, compared to only 6.7 percent among illegal border crossers. Again, this compares favorably with the overall immigrant population, 37.5 percent of which had completed at least one year of college.

These differences in educational attainment are reflected in the diverse occupational distributions of the visa overstayers and illegal border crossers. For instance, although only 8.3 percent of illegal border crossers 16 years of age or older were holding professional and technical occupations in 1987–88, as many as 28.2 percent of the visa overstayers were in this category. The latter is very close to the corresponding proportion among the overall immigrant population, which was 34.6 percent in 1990.

Despite the similar demographic characteristics of visa overstayers and the overall immigrant population in the U.S., there are also major differences. Both visa overstayers and illegal border crossers have been residing in the U.S. for a shorter period of time than immigrants in general. As Table 14.4 shows, close to 80 percent of both groups of illegal immigrants arrived in the U.S. in the ten years previous to the LPS survey interview, compared to 43.2 percent among the overall immigrant population. There are also significant income gaps. In 1989, the annual family income per person (measured by annual family income divided by the number of persons in the family) of the overall immigrant population in the U.S. was $11,775. The annual family income per person of visa overstayers (in 1989 dollars) was substantially lower, equal to $9,054. The latter, however, sharply exceeds the family income per worker prevailing among illegal border crossers, equal to $6,218 (in 1989 dollars).

This discussion suggests that the stereotypical perception of illegal immigrants in the U.S. as unskilled Mexican workers crossing the Rio Grande is a severely distorted one since it represents only a fraction of the overall illegal immigrant population in the country. The almost exclusive attention paid by both the press and the academic literature on Mexican illegal immigrants means that we know very little on non-Mexican illegal immigrants, who are estimated to constitute more than half of all undocumented workers residing in the

U.S. Using data available from the LPS, the following section focuses on examining the comparative economic and labor market situation of Mexican and non-Mexican illegal immigrants in the U.S., showing the substantial differences that exist between these two groups of workers.

14.3 Mexican and Non-Mexican Illegal Immigrants: A Comparative Profile

This section presents a comparative profile of the socioeconomic status of Mexican and non-Mexican illegal immigrants in the U.S. using the LPS data. Previous analysis of the LPS data set has examined the overall illegal immigrant sample or specific sub-groups, but has not compared the Mexican and non-Mexican populations [see Chiswick and Miller (1996), Cobb Clark and Kossoudji (1995, 1996), and Rivera-Batiz (1999)].

We start with a discussion of differences in basic demographic and socioeconomic variables, moving later to discuss labor market variables, including a breakdown of force participation rates, unemployment rates and wages. As noted before, the data are from the Legalized Population Survey and represent the situation of illegal immigrants when they applied for legalization in 1987 or 1988. The distribution of the countries of origin of non-Mexican immigrants is the following: Central America 48.6 percent, Asia and Pacific 15.2 percent, South America 13.5 percent, the Caribbean 9.8 percent, Europe 7.5 percent, and Africa and the Middle East 5.4 percent.

Table 14.5 shows that both Mexican and non-Mexican illegal immigrants tend to have an over representation of men in their midst. Among the Mexican contingent, 58.7 percent are men while among non-Mexicans the corresponding percentage is 56.6 percent. The Mexican illegals are somewhat younger than non-Mexicans, with the average age among Mexicans equal to 31.6 years and among non-Mexicans equal to 35 years. Both groups consist mostly of migrants who moved to the United States in the ten years prior to interview, with over 80 percent in this category for both groups. However, the method of entry into the country diverges considerably

Table 14.5. Characteristics of Mexican and Non-Mexican Illegal Immigrants.

	Mexican immigrants	**Non-Mexican immigrants**
Sex (% male)	58.7%	56.6%
Age (average, in years)	31.6	35.0
Educational Attainment (Average years of schooling completed by persons aged 25 or older)	6.3	10.4
Family income per person (Family income divided by number of persons in the family)	\$5,662	\$8,429

Source: Legalized Population Survey and 1990 U.S. Census of Population and Housing; authors' computations.

among Mexican and non-Mexican migrants. For Mexican illegals, 84.8 percent entered the country by crossing the border illegally while for non-Mexicans only 53.2 percent entered through these means, the remainder crossing the border legally and later overstaying their visas.

The educational attainment of Mexican illegals is substantially lower than that of non-Mexican migrants. As Table 14.5 shows, the average years of schooling of Mexican illegal immigrants with 25 years of age or older was 6.3 years, compared to 10.4 years among the non-Mexican group. This significant difference in schooling is also reflected in the proportion of persons 25 years of age or older who had completed more than 12 years of schooling (which, in the U.S., would correspond to having received some college education). For Mexican undocumented migrants, only 4.5 percent had completed more than 12 years of schooling, while for non-Mexican illegals, the corresponding proportion was 29.2 percent.

The divergence in educational attainment of the two groups of migrants is mirrored by the gap in family income. This is measured by annual family income in 1987 (expressed in 1989 dollars). To take into account the differences in the number of persons in a family existing in Mexican and non-Mexican groups, we compute per-capita family income, obtained by dividing family income by the number of

Table 14.6. Comparative Labor Market Indicators: Mexican and Non-Mexican Illegal Immigrants.

	Mexican immigrants		Non-Mexican immigrants	
	Male	Female	Male	Female
Labor force participation rate	96.2%	62.4%	95.8%	77.8%
Unemployment rate	3.6%	4.1%	3.2%	3.3%
Weekly wage (1989 dollars)	287.8	191.9	369.6	234.8

Data for illegal immigrants are for 1987 and 1988 (wages adjusted to 1989 dollars).
Source: Legalized Population Survey.

persons in the family. Table 14.5 shows that family income per person among non-Mexican illegals exceeds the one among Mexican illegals by close to 50 percent. The average per-capita family income among Mexicans was $5,662 while for non-Mexicans it was $8,429.

Table 14.6 presents data on the major labor market indicators for Mexican and non-Mexican illegal immigrants. By definition, labor force participation rates represent the proportion of the economically active population who is either employed or actively seeking employment. The age group considered in our analysis ranges from 18 to 64 years of age, and the data are for 1987 and 1988, as obtained by the Legalized Population Survey. As can be seen in Table 14.6, the average labor force participation rate among men diverges very little between Mexican and non-Mexican immigrants. There are, however, significant differences among women. For Mexican women, illegal immigrants had a labor force participation rate of 62.4 percent, compared to 77.7 percent for the non-Mexican immigrant population.

The unemployment rates, including both Mexican and non-Mexican illegal immigrants, range between 3.2 percent and 4.1 percent depending on gender. These figures lie substantially below the unemployment rates of the overall American labor force. The national unemployment rate in the U.S. in 1987 was 6.2 percent, and in 1988 it was 5.5 percent. Although differences in demographic and human capital characteristics may help explain the lower unemployment rates of undocumented workers, the very nature of the illegal immigration decision means that these workers are willing to take jobs at wages and working conditions below those accepted by other workers. With lower reservation wages when compared to other workers in the U.S. labor market, it is not surprising that their unemployment rate is lower.

Table 14.6 also presents the weekly wages earned by employed illegal immigrants. Gender patterns observed in the general working population are reproduced among immigrants. For example, male Mexican illegal immigrants earn close to 50 percent more than their female counterparts. And among the non-Mexican undocumented population, male workers earn 57.4 percent more than female workers. There are also substantial earnings differences between Mexican and non-Mexican illegal immigrants, with the latter receiving 37.8 percent higher wages among men and 22.4 percent higher wages among women.

What explains the differences in earnings between Mexican and non-Mexican illegal immigrants? Are the gaps in educational attainment specified earlier the major force or are other, yet unidentified factors more important? The following sections explore in detail the factors behind the differences in weekly wages among the various illegal immigrant groups just discussed.

14.4 The Earnings of Mexican and Non-Mexican Illegal Immigrants: The Empirical Model

The framework adopted here to examine the determinants of wages follows the standard empirical human capital literature in postulating that the natural logarithm of the wage rate of a worker i of sex j is given by:

$$\log \mathrm{W_{ij}} = \text{ß}'\mathrm{X_{ij}} + \mathrm{U_{ij}} \tag{1}$$

where $\mathrm{W_{ij}}$ is the hourly wage rate received by the worker, ß is a vector of coefficients to be estimated, $\mathrm{X_{ij}}$ is a vector of individual human capital, occupational and demographic characteristics affecting wages, and $\mathrm{U_{ij}}$ is a stochastic disturbance term.

The human capital variables in the vector $\mathrm{X_{ij}}$ include, first of all, years of schooling, represented by the variable EDUCAT. In addition, to reflect the skills acquired by the person through seniority and aging in the labor market, we include years of on-the-job experience, proxied by the variable EXPER (measured as age minus years of schooling completed minus six). The variable EXPERSQ, equal to the square of years of on-the-job experience, is also introduced in the equation to reflect variable returns to experience. On the assumption of positive, but diminishing, returns to on-the-job experience, it is anticipated that the variable EXPER would have a positive coefficient and EXPERSQ a negative coefficient in the earnings equation.

English language proficiency has been found to be a key human capital variable influencing the earnings of immigrants. Employment opportunities may be severely limited if the immigrant's knowledge of the English language is not sufficient. On the other hand, ethnic enclaves can allow broad leeway for immigrants to find jobs even if their English proficiency is absent. The measure of English proficiency utilized in this paper is symbolized by the variable NOENGLISH, which is equal to one if the person does not know how to speak English at all, and zero otherwise. The existing research examining the role played by English language proficiency on labor market outcomes generally finds a positive impact of English proficiency on earnings [see, for example, Chiswick and Miller (1996), and Rivera-Batiz (1990, 1996)].

The presence of disequilibria in the labor market, as well as the existence of compensating wage differentials, implies that various occupations may be endowed with different wages, holding worker characteristics constant. As a result, our wage equations introduce a set of occupational dummy variables. These are: PROFTECH, equal to one if the person was employed in managerial, professional, technical, sales and administrative occupations, and zero otherwise; FARMING, equal to one if the immigrant was employed in agricultural occupations, and zero otherwise; OPERAT, if the worker was an operator, fabricator or laborer, and zero otherwise; and PRODUCT, if the person was in precision production, craft and repair occupations, and zero otherwise. The excluded, baseline, occupations are service occupations. Since the baseline service jobs generally offer comparatively lower wages in the American economy, we expect the occupational dummy variables to be positively associated with earnings, perhaps with the exception of FARMING.

Workers supply various amounts of hours per week on their jobs. Labor supply can influence earnings, not only because more hours worked per week, at a given hourly wage rate, will increase weekly earnings, but also because the hourly rate for overtime work may be higher than for the regular workday. To incorporate variable labor supply into our earnings analysis, we include a variable denoted by HOURS, equal to the number of hours per week that the person supplies in the labor market. It can be expected that, holding other things constant, increased hours of work per week will be associated with higher weekly wages.

Migratory and work decisions are most of the time made on the basis of family considerations. A more intense level of effort, and higher earnings, may be associated with marriage, especially if the family has children. In addition, if spouses and children are residing in source countries, married immigrants will have an incentive to increase their effort levels, and therefore will receive higher weekly earnings, in order to increase the amount of remittances that they can send to their spouses abroad. A dummy variable, SINGLE, is included in the analysis to reflect possible differences in earnings between single and married persons. The variable is equal to one if the person is single and zero otherwise.

The longer immigrants reside in a country, the higher their earnings. There are two explanations for this connection. Firstly, as postulated by Chiswick (1978) and Duleep and Regets (1999), immigrants make a wide range of investments over time after they arrive in a country. These investments may be in the form of increased schooling or on-the-job training, which would be proxied by variables already included in our analysis. However, immigrants also make other types of productive investments, such as developing employment networks that can assist them in finding employment opportunities, and acquiring greater information on local, host-country labor market institutions, which can improve job search efficiency and lead to higher-paying job offers. Alternatively, Borjas (1995, 1999) has suggested that more recent immigrant cohorts in the U.S. have lower "quality" than previous ones, thus also receiving lower wages, holding everything else constant. Therefore, the longer an immigrant has been in the U.S., the older the immigrant cohort with which he or she is associated, and the lower the earnings. To incorporate the impact of recency of immigration into the analysis, we define a dummy variable RECENT to be equal to one if the immigrant moved to stay as a resident of the U.S. in the ten years previous to interview, and zero otherwise. Note that, whether because of labor market assimilation or because of "lower quality" recent cohorts, one expects the variable RECENT to have a negative impact on immigrant earnings.

Another explanatory variable utilized in the wage equations is geography, which is represented by the variable CALIF, a dummy variable equal to one if the migrant resided in California and zero otherwise. Since the largest share of both Mexican and non-Mexican immigrants locates in California, the agglomeration of these migrants can be expected to generate ethnic enclaves and networks that could exert a positive impact on earnings. In addition, the extent of the labor market for undocumented workers may also be greater in California, as illegal immigrant employers seek to locate near their employees. On this basis, it can be expected that, holding other things constant, illegal immigrants will be more likely to find higher-paying employment opportunities in California than elsewhere. This may be particularly the case for Mexican illegal immigrants since California represents the prime location of both legal and illegal Mexican immigrants. Portes and Bach (1985) have explained the superior economic performance of the Mariel Cuban immigrants relative to that of Haitian immigrants in the 1980s as deriving from the employment opportunities available to the Cuban immigrants in the Cuban-American ethnic enclave of the Miami area. A similar case can be made regarding the employment of Mexican illegal immigrants in Mexican ethnic enclaves in California.

The discussion so far suggests that the wage equation to be estimated should be given by:

$$\log W_{ij} = \beta_0 + \beta_1 \mathrm{SOMEHIGH}_{ij} + \beta_2 \mathrm{HIGHCOM}_{ij} + \beta_3 \mathrm{COLLEGE}_{ij} + \beta_4 \mathrm{EXPER}_{ij} + \beta_5 \mathrm{EXPERSQ}_{ij} + \beta_6 \mathrm{NOENGLISH}_{ij}$$

$$+ \beta_7 \text{PROFTC}_{ij} + \beta_8 \text{FARMING}_{ij} + \beta_9 \text{OPERAT}_{ij}$$
$$+ \beta_{10} \text{PRODUCT}_{ij} + \beta_{11} \text{HOURS}_{ij} + \beta_{12} \text{SINGLE}_{ij}$$
$$+ \beta_{13} \text{RECENT}_{ij} + \beta_{14} \text{CALIF}_{ij} + U_{ij} \quad (2)$$

where all the variables are as defined above.

14.5 The Earnings of Mexican and Non-Mexican Illegal Immigrants: Results

The empirical model discussed in the last section is applied here to examine the weekly wages of Mexican and non-Mexican illegal immigrants in the United States using the LPS data. Individuals with no responses on the relevant questions used to determine individual characteristics (such as earnings, educational attainment, etc.) were eliminated from the analysis. In addition, following the custom in the literature, the sample was circumscribed to persons 18 to 64 years of age, the age group most likely to be fully-involved in the labor market. Only employed workers were considered. With these restrictions, the samples utilized in the wage equations estimated in this paper include 2,171 Mexican and 2,569 non-Mexican immigrants.

The LPS sample provides information on the weekly wages of illegal immigrants in the week before they applied for legalization. Since the window for applications was from May 5, 1987 to May 4, 1988, the data available on wages for illegal immigrants corresponds to either 1987 or 1988. In order to convert them to a common denominator, both the 1987 and 1988 data were adjusted for inflation and expressed in 1989 dollars. It is these adjusted, real wages (expressed in 1989 dollars) that are discussed throughout the following analysis.

Table 14.7 presents the sample means for the variables introduced in the wage equations, by Mexican/non-Mexican origin (place of birth) and gender. The first row shows the average values for the dependent variable, the logarithm of the weekly wage. As noted earlier, the average weekly wages for men are substantially higher than for women and this is reflected in the data presented in Table 14.7, for both Mexican and non-Mexican immigrants. At the same time,

Table 14.7. Sample Means, Mexican and Non-Mexican Illegal Immigrants.

	Mexican		Non-Mexican	
Variable	**Male**	**Female**	**Male**	**Female**
Log Weekly Wage	5.569	5.138	5.730	5.323
EDUCAT (Average years of schooling completed)	6.8	6.8	10.7	10.0
EXPER (Years of Experience)	18.7	19.1	17.7	19.5
EXPERSQ (Experience Squared)	466.0	486.3	411.9	490.6
ENGLISH (Proportion does not speak English)	0.463	0.561	0.233	0.345
PROFTC (Proportion employed in professional, technical, sales and managerial occupations)	0.069	0.126	0.242	0.263
FARMING (Proportion employed in agriculture)	0.125	0.037	0.022	0.004
OPERAT (Proportion employed as operators, fabricators and laborers)	0.391	0.377	0.294	0.201
PRODUCT (Percentage employed as precision production, craft and repair workers)	0.195	0.051	0.186	0.024
SERVICE (Percentage employed in services)	0.220	0.409	0.254	0.508
HOURS (Number of hours worked per week)	42.6	39.0	42.9	39.0
SINGLE (Proportion never married)	0.313	0.318	0.355	0.320
RECENT (Proportion who migrated to the U.S. ten years or less before survey)	0.840	0.764	0.865	0.862
CALIF (Proportion residing in state of)	0.612	0.656	0.380	0.457
Number of observations	1,494	677	1,569	1,000

the wages of Mexican immigrants are significantly lower than those of non-Mexican immigrants. This gap holds for both men and women.

The lower wages of Mexican illegals compared to non-Mexican workers may be the reflection of mean differences in the characteristics of the two groups. Table 14.7 documents some of these key differences. Mexican illegal immigrants have substantially lower levels of education than non-Mexican undocumented workers. The sample means for the variable EDUCAT show that the average years of schooling of male Mexican illegal immigrant workers in the LPS sample was equal to 6.8 years, compared to 10.7 years among their non-Mexican counterparts. There is a similar educational gap among women. For female Mexican illegal immigrant workers, the mean years of schooling was 6.8 years, compared to 10.0 years among non-Mexicans.

Another major difference between Mexican and non-Mexican workers is their English language proficiency. Table 14.7 shows that the proportion of Mexicans who expressed that they could not speak English at all was 46.3 percent among men and 56.1 percent among women. By comparison, the equivalent percentages for non-Mexican workers were 23.3 percent for men and 34.5 percent for women.

The distribution of employment by sector also varies between Mexican and non-Mexican workers. The latter have a substantially greater proportion of employment in professional, technical, managerial and administrative occupations. Among men, 24.2 percent of non-Mexican illegals were employed in these occupations, compared to only 6.9 percent among Mexicans. For women, 26.3 percent of non-Mexican workers were employed in this sector, compared to 12.6 percent among Mexicans. On the other hand, Mexican undocumented workers are over-represented in agricultural occupations.

There are also some differences in the length of time that immigrants have been in the United States. Mexican illegal immigrants have resided in the U.S. for a longer period of time than non-Mexicans. Indeed, among Mexican illegal immigrants, 84 percent of all men and 76.4 percent of all women arrived in the U.S. during the decade before their interview in 1987 or 1988. But for the non-Mexican group, 86.5 percent of all men and 86.2 percent of all women declared that they had arrived in the U.S. in the decade before their interview in 1987 and 1988.

The majority of Mexican immigrants in the data, over 60 percent, resided in California. Given the geographical proximity to Mexico, and the fact that the comparatively large Mexican ethnic enclave in Los Angeles and other parts of California provides a comparative advantage for the employment of legal and illegal immigrants, it is not surprising that most Mexican immigrants locate in that state.

In terms of the remaining variables, Table 14.7 shows that there are no major differences between Mexican and non-Mexican workers in terms of marital status or years of on-the-job experience. The average value of these variables is similar among the two groups of illegal immigrants.

Tables 14.8 and 14.9 present the key results of our empirical analysis. Table 14.8 shows the coefficients of the estimated wage equations for men while Table 14.9 depicts the results for women. Note that the signs of the regression coefficients on the explanatory variables are all identical in the four equations. Furthermore, the signs are all in line with our expectations, as stated earlier. On the other hand, there are some significant differences in the magnitude of the coefficients across equations.

Tables 14.8 and 14.9 show that rates of return to education are significantly higher among non-Mexican undocumented workers. For instance, holding other things constant, an additional year of schooling provides a 1.5 percent increase in the weekly earnings of male Mexican workers, but for non-Mexican illegals the corresponding increase is more than twice, 3.2 percent. Among Mexican women, an additional year of schooling increases earnings by approximately 2 percent, but for non-Mexicans, the rate of return is much higher, equal to 3.5 percent. The higher rate of return to education among non-Mexican immigrants may be due to several factors. One possibility is that the non-Mexican immigrants moving to the U.S. may be self-selected on the basis of having a greater transferability of their schooling to the American labor market. If non-Mexican immigrants perceive their move to the U.S. as permanent, then prospective migrants with human capital skills easily-transferable to the U.S.

Table 14.8. Regression Estimates, Mexican and Non-Mexican Illegal Immigrants, Male Wage Equation.

	Mexican illegal immigrants		Non-Mexican illegal immigrants	
Independent variable	**Parameter estimate (s.e.)**	**T-statistic**	**Parameter estimate (s.e.)**	**T-statistic**
INTERCEPT	4.4495* (0.0886)	50.23	4.2961* (0.0933)	46.03
EDUCAT	0.0145* (0.0036)	4.01	0.0317* (0.0036)	8.77
EXPER	0.0205* (0.0036)	5.71	0.0220* (0.0043)	5.12
EXPERSQ	−0.0004* (0.0001)	−6.10	−0.0004* (0.0001)	−4.02
NOENGLISH	−0.0997* (0.0209)	−4.76	−0.1084* (0.0320)	−3.39
PROFTECH	0.1164* (0.0425)	2.74	0.2168* (0.0357)	6.08
FARMING	0.0097 (0.0347)	0.28	−0.0344 (0.0823)	−0.42
OPERAT	0.0994* (0.0256)	3.88	0.0551 (0.0319)	1.73
PRODUCT	0.2713* (0.0298)	9.10	0.2679* (0.0358)	7.47
HOURS	0.0161* (0.0011)	14.21	0.0167* (0.0011)	14.82
SINGLE	−0.1114* (0.0237)	−4.72	−0.0731* (0.0270)	−2.71
RECENT	−0.0517 (0.0271)	−1.91	−0.0503 (0.0353)	−1.43
CALIF	0.1009* (0.0200)	5.05	0.0243 (0.0245)	0.99
Adjusted R-SQ	0.26	—	0.28	—

* = Statistically significant at a 99 percent confidence level.
** = Statistically significant at a 95 percent confidence level.

will have a stronger incentive to migrate. Once in the U.S., they will benefit from this by obtaining higher-paying jobs. If Mexican immigrants, on the other hand, perceive their move as temporary, then the transferability of their skills to the American labor market is not as

Table 14.9. Regression Estimates, Mexican and Non-Mexican Illegal Immigrants, Female Wage Equation.

	Mexican illegal immigrants		Non-Mexican illegal immigrants	
Independent variable	**Parameter estimate (s.e.)**	**T-statistic**	**Parameter estimate (s.e.)**	**T-statistic**
INTERCEPT	3.9641* (0.1316)	30.11	3.9526* (0.0957)	41.31
EDUCAT	0.0197* (0.0067)	2.94	0.0354* (0.0418)	8.50
EXPER	0.0113 (0.0059)	1.91	0.0158* (0.0047)	3.37
EXPERSQ	−0.0002 (0.0001)	−1.87	−0.0002** (0.0001)	−2.34
NOENGLISH	−0.1868* (0.0392)	−4.77	−0.1850* (0.0319)	−5.79
PROFTECH	0.2833* (0.0574)	4.93	0.3418* (0.0347)	9.85
FARMING	0.2554* (0.0947)	2.70	0.3721 (0.2060)	1.81
OPERAT	0.2990* (0.0407)	7.35	0.1580* (0.0349)	4.53
PRODUCT	0.3679* (0.0789)	4.66	0.0726 (0.0854)	0.85
HOURS	0.0170* (0.0018)	9.49	0.0158* (0.0012)	13.36
SINGLE	−0.0855** (0.0389)	−2.20	−0.0893* (0.0291)	3.07
RECENT	−0.0936** (0.0407)	−2.30	−0.0503 (0.0385)	1.31
CALIF	0.1528* (0.0368)	4.16	0.0568** (0.0266)	2.14
Adjusted R-SQ	0.32	—	0.40	—

* = Statistically significant at a 99 percent confidence level.
** = Statistically significant at a 95 percent confidence level.

significant in their migratory decision and the immigrant contingent will not be positively self-selected on the basis of human capital characteristics (see Chiswick 1999 and Taylor 1985). The lower mean level of schooling among Mexican illegal immigrants may also explain the lower rates of return to education. With U.S. rates of return to education and employment opportunities expanding rapidly at the top of the distribution (for college graduates), non-Mexican illegals may find more profitable job opportunities than the collapsing low-wage labor markets facing Mexican undocumented workers.

The economic returns to labor market experience also vary across the various groups considered, although the major differences are on the basis of gender. As with the rate of return to education, the rate of return to experience among both men and women is somewhat higher for non-Mexican immigrants. To understand this result, note that the variable RECENT, associated with years of residence in the U.S., is being held constant while we consider changes in EXPER. Given the number of years that an immigrant has been residing in the U.S., changes in the EXPER variable are directly related to changes in the number of years of experience the worker has had abroad. One way to interpret the higher EXPER coefficient in the non-Mexican worker equation is that it shows that the returns in the U.S. labor market of an increase in years of experience abroad are proportionally higher for the non-Mexican worker than for the Mexican immigrant.

This pattern, in turn, may be determined by the relative success of non-Mexican illegal immigrants in matching their occupational experience abroad with that in the United States. The LPS data set does include information on the occupations held by undocumented workers in their countries of origin just before moving to the U.S. When one compares the occupations held by illegals in the U.S. with those they held abroad, 22.5 percent of the non-Mexican workers had jobs in the same occupational category while only 14.2 percent of Mexicans had matching jobs. For many non-Mexican undocumented workers, then, their labor market experience abroad is more valuable in the U.S. because they are more likely to find jobs in the U.S. labor market similar to those they held in their own countries. This, in turn, may be due to the greater stability provided by legal entry into the country, which, at least for a certain period of time, allows non-Mexican immigrants, who have a greater concentration of visa overstayers, to seek and obtain jobs that more closely match their experience.

Lack of ability to speak English, as reflected by the variable NOENGLISH, has a consistently negative influence on earnings, for both Mexican and non-Mexican migrants. The impact, however, appears to be much more significant for women. Among Mexican and non-Mexican men, the inability to speak English lowers earnings by approximately 10 percent, holding other things constant. But among women, the corresponding drop is approximately 19 percent, almost twice as high. This result, however, reproduces previous research on the impact of English proficiency on earnings [see Rivera-Batiz (1990, 1996)]. Women may be penalized more heavily for lower English proficiency due to the types of jobs they tend to hold (such as clerical or service sector jobs), which require more frequent usage of English.

The occupational dummies are generally positive in Tables 14.8 and 14.9 suggesting that the various categories, including professional and technical, managerial, sales and administrative support workers, operators, fabricators and laborers, all tend to have higher earnings than service sector occupations. This positive association of certain occupational categories with higher earnings is quantitatively important. For instance, non-Mexican male and female undocumented workers employed in professional, technical, managerial or administrative support occupations can earn on average of 22 and 34 percent higher earnings, respectively. The occupational wage premium received by white collar workers is lower, but still positive, for Mexican illegals.

Hours worked are significantly related to weekly earnings for all groups considered. In addition, single workers earn substantially less than married workers, and residence in California is generally linked to greater earnings, everything else held constant, especially among Mexican immigrants.

14.6 Conclusions

The results of this paper contradict many of the prevailing views held by both the public and academics alike on undocumented workers in the United States. Using the 1989 Legalized Population Survey (LPS), the research presented here provides data that are based on a national sample of illegal immigrants, instead of relying on the small samples of predominantly Mexican undocumented workers utilized in the existing literature.

The analysis first shows that the perception of illegal immigrants as unskilled workers with low levels of schooling is incorrect since it only characterizes Mexican immigrants. Among non-Mexican illegals, the paper shows that the mean years of schooling for persons aged 25 years of age or older was 10.4 years, which is about the same as the average years of schooling of the overall immigrant population counted in the 1990 U.S. Census of Population. By contrast, Mexican illegal immigrants were found to have an average of 6.3 years of schooling.

The schooling differences between Mexican and non-Mexican undocumented workers are even stronger when one looks at the proportion of the population 25 years of age or older who had completed at least one year of college (13 or more years of schooling). Among Mexican illegals, the proportion was 4.5 percent but among non-Mexican undocumented workers the proportion was equal to 29.2 percent. For comparison purposes, 37.5 percent of all adult immigrants in the 1990 Census had completed at least one year of college education.

These figures coincide with data on the proportion of the workforce employed in professional, technical, managerial and administrative occupations, which was equal to approximately 9 percent among Mexican illegals and 25 percent among non-Mexican illegals, compared to 35 percent for the overall immigrant population residing in the U.S. in 1990.

The paper shows not only that educational attainment among non-Mexican illegal immigrants was sharply higher than among Mexican undocumented workers but also that the rates of return to education were significantly greater for the former. Estimating empirical human capital earnings equations, the paper shows that the average rate of return to education among Mexican undocumented male workers was 1.5 percent per additional year of schooling while for non-Mexican male workers, the corresponding figure was 3.2 percent, more than twice. Among women, the Mexican rate of return to education was 2 percent, compared to 3.5 percent among non-Mexican female workers. Returns to experience are also greater for non-Mexican immigrants.

The higher rates of return to human capital among non-Mexican illegal immigrants are consistent with the view that non-Mexicans moving to the U.S. may be self-selected on the basis of a greater transferability of their schooling to the American labor market. If, for instance, non-Mexican immigrants perceive their move to the U.S. as permanent, then prospective migrants with human capital skills that are more productive in the U.S. will have a stronger incentive to migrate. Once in the U.S., they will benefit from their "special" skills by obtaining higher-paying jobs. If Mexican immigrants, on the other hand, perceive their migratory move as temporary, then the transferability of their skills to the American labor market is not as significant for their future economic progress and the Mexican immigrant cohort will not be positively self-selected on the basis of human capital characteristics. In any case, the lower mean level of schooling among Mexican illegal immigrants may also explain their lower rates of return to education. With U.S. rates of return to education and employment opportunities expanding rapidly at the top of the distribution (especially for college graduates), non-Mexican illegals may find more profitable job opportunities than Mexican undocumented workers facing collapsing low-wage labor markets. Finally, the fact that a large share of non-Mexican illegal immigrants are visa overstayers means that their initial entry into the country is legal and, for a certain period of time, allows the workers the stability to seek higher-paying employment opportunities. Among Mexican illegal immigrants, the great majority of whom enter the U.S. by crossing the border illegally, the situation may not be as propitious.

Despite the substantially higher earnings that non-Mexican illegal immigrants display compared to Mexican illegals, one must not forget that both groups of workers earn substantially less than the overall immigrant population. Non-Mexican male illegal workers earned 73 percent less than their counterparts in the general immigrant population; among women, the shortfall was 71 percent. For Mexican workers, male illegals earned 35 percent less than the overall immigrant population, with the gap equal to 39 percent among women (these figures are based on weekly wages earned by each group, expressed in 1989 dollars). Although a fraction of these wage gaps are due to differences in educational attainment and other demographic characteristics, a substantial share is due to the presence of discrimination and exploitation of undocumented workers in U.S. labor markets [see Rivera-Batiz (1999, 2000) for an analysis of the shortfall in the earnings of illegal Mexican workers relative to legal workers].

This paper has shown the great heterogeneity present among undocumented workers in the United States. Unfortunately, public policy discussions regarding illegal immigrants in the U.S. too often rely on stereotypical images of these workers that do not adequately represent the totality of this population. It is hoped that, by presenting a more comprehensive profile of illegal immigrants, this paper will help in generating more informed debate on undocumented workers in the future.

References

Borane, Ray (1999) 'Do You Hire Illegal Immigrants?,' *The New York Times*, August 30, p. A10.

Borjas, George J. (1990) *Friends or Strangers: The Impact of Immigrants on the U.S. Economy*, New York: Basic Books.

——— (1995) 'Assimilation and Changes in Cohort Quality Revisited: What Happened to Immigrant Earnings in the 1980s?,' *Journal of Labor Economics*, 13: 201–245.

——— (1999) 'The Economic Analysis of Immigration,' in O. Ashenfelter and R. Freeman, eds., *Handbook of Labor Economics* (Amsterdam: North Holland Publishing Company).

——— (1999), *Heaven's Door: Immigration Policy and the American Economy*, Princeton: Princeton University Press.

Borjas, George J. and Marta Tienda (1993) 'The Employment and Wages of Legalized Immigrants,' *International Migration Review*, 27: 712–747.

Chiswick, Barry R. (1978) 'The Effects of Americanization on the Earnings of the Foreign-Born,' *Journal of Political Economy*, 86: 897–922.

——— (1984) 'Illegal Aliens in the United States Labor Market: An Analysis of Occupational Attainment and Earnings,' *International Migration Review*, 18: 714–32.

——— (1988) *Illegal Aliens: Their Employment and Employers*, Kalamazoo, Michigan: W.E. Upjohn Institute for Employment Research.

——— (1999) 'Are Immigrants Favorably Selected?,' *American Economic Review*, 89: 181–185.

Chiswick, Barry and Paul Miller (1996) 'Language Skills and Earnings among Legalized Aliens,' paper presented at the 1997 American Economic Association Meetings, New Orleans, mimeo.

Cobb-Clark, Deborah A. and Sherrie A. Kossoudji (1995) 'Finding Good Opportunities within Undocumented Markets: U.S. Occupational Mobility for Latino Workers,' Center for Economic Policy, Australian National University.

Cobb-Clark, Deborah A. and Sherrie A. Kossoudji (1996) 'Coming Out of the Shadows: Learning About Legal Status and Wages from the Legalized Population,' Center for Economic Policy, Australian National University.

Duleep, Harriet and Mark Regets (1999), 'Immigrants and Human-Capital Investment,' *American Economic Review*, 89: 186–91.

Fernandez, E. and J. Gregory Robinson (1994) 'Illustrative Ranges of the Distribution of Undocumented Immigrants by State,' Technical Working Paper No. 8, U.S. Bureau of the Census.

Gonzalez Baker, Susan (1997) 'The Amnesty Aftermath: Current Policy Issues Stemming from the Legalization Programs of the 1986 Immigration Reform and Control Act,' *International Migration Review* 31: 5–27.

Gonzalez-Baker, Susan (1990) *The Cautious Welcome: The Legalization Programs of the Immigration Reform and Control Act*, University Press of America, Lanham, Maryland.

Immigration and Naturalization Service (1999) 'Illegal Alien Resident Population,' United States Department of Justice, mimeo., August 11; http://www.ins.usdoj.gov/illegalalien/index.html

Massey, Douglas S. (1987) 'Do Undocumented Immigrants Earn Lower Wages that Legal Immigrants: New Evidence from Mexico,' *Intl. Migration Review*, (21): Summer, 236–274.

Massey, Douglas S. and Audrey Singer (1995) 'New Estimates of Undocumented Mexican Migration and the Probability of Apprehension,' *Demography* 32: 203–213.

National Research Council (1997) *The New Americans: Economic, Demographic, and Fiscal Effects of Immigration*, Washington, D.C.: National Academy Press.

North, Douglas S. and Marion Houstoun (1976) 'The Characteristics and Role of Illegal Aliens in the United States Labor Market: An Exploratory Study,' mimeo., Linton and Co., Washington, D.C.

New York Times (1995) 'In the U.S. for a Visit, Many Stay Illegally,' *The New York Times*, A1, B5.

Portes, Alejandro and R. Bach (1985) *Latin Journey: Cuban and Mexican Immigrants in the United States*, University of California Press, Berkeley.

Reichert, Josh and Douglas Massey (1979) 'Patterns of US Migration from a Mexican Sending Community: A Comparison of Legal and Illegal Immigrants,' *International Migration Review*, 13: 599–623.

Rivera-Batiz, Francisco L. (1990) 'English Language Proficiency and the Economic Progress of Immigrants,' *Economics Letters*, 34: 295–300.

——— (1991) 'Introduction to U.S. Immigration Policy Reform in the 1980s,' in Francisco L. Rivera-Batiz, Selig Sechzer and Ira Gang, eds., (1991), *U.S.*

Immigration Policy Reform in the 1980s: A Preliminary Assessment, New York: Praeger Publishers, 1–22.

______ (1996) 'English Language Proficiency, Quantitative Skills and the Economic Progress of Immigrants,' in H. Orcutt Duleep and P. Wunnava, eds., *Immigrants and Immigration Policy: Individual Skills, Family Ties and Group Identities*, JAI Press, Greenwich, Connecticut, 214–235.

______ (1999), 'Undocumented Workers in the Labor Market: An Analysis of the Earnings of Legal and Illegal Mexican Immigrants in the United States,' *Journal of Population Economics*, 12: 91–116.

______ (2000), 'Underground in American Soil: Undocumented Workers and U.S. Immigration Policy,' *Journal of International Affairs*, 53: 25–37.

Smith, Shirley, Roger Kramer and Audrey Singer (1996) *Characteristics and Labor Market Behavior of the Legalized Population Five Years Following Legalization*, Immigration Policy and Research Division, Bureau of Intl. Labor Affairs, U.S. Dept. of Labor, Washington, D.C.

Taylor, J. Edward (1985) 'Selectivity of Undocumented Mexico-US Migrants and Implications for U.S. Immigration Reform,' The Urban Institute, Working Paper No. PDS-85-4.

Tienda, Marta, G.J. Borjas, H. Cordero-Guzman, K. Neuman and M. Romero (1991) 'The Demography of Legalization: Insights from Administrative Records of Legalized Aliens,' NORC, University of Chicago, Chicago.

United States Department of Commerce (1993) *1990 U.S. Census of Population and Housing 5% Public Use Microdata Sample*, Bureau of the Census, Washington, D.C.

United States Department of Labor (1996) *Legalized Population Survey Public Use File*, Bureau of International Labor Affairs, Washington, D.C.

Warren, Robert and Jeffrey Passel (1987) 'A Count of the Uncountable: Estimates of Undocumented Aliens Counted in the 1980 United States Census,' *Demography*, 24: 120–135.

Woodrow, Karen and Jeffrey Passel (1990) 'Post-IRCA Undocumented Immigration in the United States: An Assessment Based on the June 1988 CPS,' in F. Bean, B. Edmonston and J. Passel, eds., *Undocumented Migration to the United States: IRCA and the Experience of the 1980s*, Washington, D.C.: The Urban Institute.

Chapter 15

Can Border Industries Be a Substitute for Immigration?*

15.1 Introduction

The continuous flow of workers from Mexico to the United States has given rise to a wide range of proposals aimed at containing the migratory tide. At the top of the list is usually Mexican border industrialization, the incarnation of the view that immigration should be controlled at the border, through the creation of an economic fence absorbing the potential migrants. Border industrialization received a strong boost in the mid-1960's with the establishment of the Mexican Border Industrialization Program (BIP). The BIP combines trade, fiscal, and other incentives to encourage the formation of assembly plants (maquiladoras) in Mexico, particularly in the border region. Though the BIP is only part of a wider border industrialization process, it has been particularly connected to US immigration policy. Indeed, the BIP was established in the aftermath of the bracero program (that ended in 1965) and its main purpose was to absorb the former braceros into the Mexican labor force so as to prevent their illegal migration to the United States. In this paper, I examine the impact of the BIP on immigration to the United States.

*This chapter was originally published in *The American Economic Review,* Vol. 76, No. 2, May 1986, pp. 263–268.

This paper was written while I was a Visiting Associate Professor at the Regional Science Department of the University of Pennsylvania. I have benefitted from comments by Michael J. Piore.

15.2 Assembly Plants, Wages, and Employment in the Border Region

The significance of illegals in Mexican–U.S. migration suggests that the key determinant of U.S. non-refugee immigration is the socio-economic incentive to move and not immigration quotas, which are not binding. How do border industries affect the incentives to migrate to the United States? The conventional wisdom associates the assembly plants with rising employment opportunities and improved standards of living in Mexico, both of which presumably reduce migration to the United States. What are the facts in this respect?

Consider the impact on wage rates. As in most other Latin American countries, wage rates in Mexico are highly controlled by the government, and organized labor is also closely involved in wage setting, with the government often responding to pressures from the Confederation of Mexican Workers (CTM) to raise administered wages. Maquiladora workers, however, are usually unorganized, part of the package that attracts assembly plants to the area. There is a limit, though, to the downward wage flexibility accorded these firms: the Mexican Minimum Wage Commission sets minimum wages according to type of job and geographical region. Though violation of minimum wage laws is hard to detect and enforcement more difficult among domestically owned plants, foreign-owned firms are usually more closely monitored and less likely to violate the labor laws. Since the majority of the maquiladoras in the border region are U.S.-owned or controlled, one can expect them to pay close to, or above, minimum wages.

Surveys of maquiladoras in Mexico show that, under usual circumstances, they will offer wage rates in the range of 5 to 30 percent above the corresponding official minimum wages (see Michael Seligson and Edward Williams, 1981, pp. 46–49, and Joseph Grunwald and Kenneth Flamm, 1985; Monica Gambrill, 1981, partly contests these conclusions). Since minimum wages are higher in the border region relative to the rest of Mexico, these represent above-average wages in Mexican manufacturing. They do not represent, however, a significant reduction of U.S.-Mexico real wage differentials. By moving to the United States, illegal migrants could obtain as much as an 800–1300 percent increase above the Mexican minimum wages, depending on occupation, region of employment, etc. Furthermore, with minimum wages not adjusted to keep up with inflationary pressures, the differential between Mexican border real minimum wages and wages available in comparable occupations in the United States has not increased to any perceptible amount since the establishment of BIP and has declined in recent years, particularly if the occupations are unskilled, as most maquiladora employment is (real hourly wages paid to production workers in assembly plants have declined by more than 25 percent since 1979). What about employment creation? One of the standard criticisms of industrialization initiatives in Latin America has been the perception that the industries established are highly capital- and skilled-labor intensive, providing scant gains in terms of unskilled employment creation. This is clearly not true of assembly plants. Grunwald–Flamm report that in 1979, Leopoldo Solis calculated that capital per worker in a sample of assembly plants was six times lower than that in an average of all Mexican manufacturing; more recent data suggests a narrowing of this differential to three, still a remarkable difference. Indeed, the BIP has been extremely successful in terms of increasing employment in the border region. From 1969 to 1985, the employment of the assembly plants in Mexico grew from 15,000 to 240,000. It is projected that by the end of 1986 more than 800 assembly plants employing close to 300,000 workers will be in operation along the border; this makes the assembly industry one of the major employers in the area.

The fact that the BIP has provided the border region with high rates of employment growth at wages above the Mexican average has led to the conclusion that "by encouraging migration from more remote areas of Mexico to the border, these programs may actually have encouraged illegal immigration to the U.S." (Pastora San Juan Cafferty et. al., 1983, p. 192). The border region's population has indeed grown enormously over the last 40 years, at a much higher rate than other regions. And the main factor behind this growth has been interregional migration, from the south to the north. It has been reflected in high rates of urban growth. For example, the rate of growth of population from 1970 to 1980 in Tijuana was 96 percent; in Mexicali: 85 percent; Ciudad Juarez: 67 percent; Reynosa: 75 percent, and Matamoros: 87 percent, while the national average rate of urban growth was 37 percent (see Niles Hansen, 1985). It is clear that a large share of the border's population growth serves as a pool from which illegal migrants to the United States are drawn. Can we, as Cafferty et al. note above, associate a significant part of this growth with the BIP?

Some of the available evidence suggests that the BIP "contributes only marginally to internal migration to northern Mexico and international migration to the U.S." (Seligson and Williams, p. 169). The main explanation behind this conclusion is the fact that the employment practices of the assembly plants screen out as potential employees most of the labor force that migrates interregionally within Mexico and/or that is likely to migrate illegally to the United States. The maquiladoras' employees are overwhelmingly border-area born, many of them local female workers entering the labor market for the first time. Over 70 percent (and at times close to 90 percent) of the maquiladora labor force is female. As is well known, illegal migrants to the United States are predominantly male workers. Thus, the assembly plants do not offer a viable job alternative for them.

Furthermore, the maquiladoras currently offer very few forward and backward linkages to the Mexican economy. They specialize in importing most, if not all, of their raw materials and parts from the United States, exporting the finished product out of Mexico. This means that the main indirect employment creation of the maquiladoras in Mexico occurs through the services that emerge to cater to the demands of the assembly plants and their labor force. Though some job creation has occurred through these means, a large leakage occurs because of spillovers across the border. A large fraction of the income of maquiladora employees, for example, is spent across the border in U.S. goods and services (see Seligson and Williams). One can conclude that, in its present condition, the impact of the BIP appears to be minimal in terms of either attracting workers to the border, or of reducing incentives for illegal migration to the United States. The growth of the border area population cannot be attached in any significant way to the border assembly industry.

The situation, however, appears to be changing. Not only do the more recent assembly plants established in the border have higher capital–labor ratios, they also use higher male–female labor ratios. This means that the turnover rate for male workers in these firms must be low enough to make them competitive with female workers. Assembly plant managers frequently justify their hiring of females on the basis that, unlike male workers, they are less likely to quit their jobs once they have accumulated enough to pay for the costs of migrating illegally to the United States, that is, paying the smugglers (coyotes) and temporary living expenses. It is possible that the more recent assembly plants are supplying jobs with some advancement opportunities and with non-menial tasks, making them somewhat differentiated from the kind of employment provided by traditional maquiladoras. They might thus be providing attractive employment opportunities to potential migrants, discouraging those workers with relatively high aversion for illegal migration from moving further north. Whatever the reason for the employment shift, and assuming it continues, would it help in reducing migration to the United States?

15.3 Employment Creation, Expectations, and Labor Migration

The impact of the maquiladoras on migration to the United States is dependent on whether they are able to raise employment by more than they increase the labor supply in the border area through induced migration from southern regions. If an excess supply of labor is generated at the border, with surplus workers becoming either openly unemployed or underemployed, it is likely that there will be an spillover into illegal migration to the United States.

It is in the nature of the migratory process, particularly in developing countries, that it involves key speculative aspects. Though information about employment opportunities in destination areas is usually available — through networks of friends, relatives, etc. — it is impossible to know in advance exactly how many positions will develop or how many applicants will seek employment. This is particularly so when the distances involved are large, as they are in the case of interregional migration. In addition, since migration will usually be undertaken for an extended period of time (depending on the temporariness of the migration), there is an intertemporal aspect involved: expectations must be formed not only about current but also about future employment prospects, particularly if the worker is participating in unskilled labor markets with relatively low rates of tenure. Expectations formation, then, is central to determining the impact of job creation on induced labor flows and, as a consequence, unemployment and/or underemployment.

Suppose, for simplicity, that production in the border region, over any given time period t, is undertaken through the use of capital, K_t, and labor, N_t, by means of a Cobb–Douglas production function $Y_t = AK_t^a N_t^{1-a}$, where A and a are parameters representing the (fixed) technology used. In determining the demand for labor, firms set marginal productivity equal to the own-price real wage in the border, W_t^d, or in natural logarithms

$$\log W_t^d = \log A(1-a) - a \log N_t + a \log K_t. \tag{1}$$

Labor supplied to the border is assumed to take a log-linear form

$$\log L_t = b_0 \log[(W_t^d N_t/L_t)/W_t^0] + \sum_{k=1}^{T} b_k \log[(W_{t+k}^d/W_{t+k}^0) \times E[N_{t+k}|I(t)]/E[L_{t+k}\backslash I(t)]], \tag{2}$$

with L_t equal to the labor force in the border region, and W_t^0 the wage rate in the rest of Mexico. The first term in the right-hand side of equation (2) shows the influence of the differential in expected earnings in period t between the border and other regions on the labor supplied to the border. It is assumed that the probability of employment in the border is, a la Harris-Todaro, given by the employed labor force divided by the available labor supply in the region. Though this represents a situation where all jobs turn over and are randomly allocated among available workers in each time period, it greatly simplifies the exposition and could be modified without altering the results. It is also assumed that the probability of employment in the south is one, though the wage differential between border and southern regions is greater than one. The wage differential is assumed to be exogenously determined by the government and expected to change in an exogenous way according to the declared interregional equality goals of the government. The parameter b_0 represents the elasticity of the border labor force at time t with respect to the expected wage in the border relative to that in southern regions at time t.

The second term in equation (2) depicts the influence of the future interregional differentials in expected earnings (i.e., in periods $t+k$, where k goes up to T, the time horizon) on current labor supplied to the border, L_t. These expected earnings differentials are calculated in a similar fashion as that in period t, except that the future wages and probabilities of employment in the border, N_{t+k}/L_{t+k} are based on the expectations of migrants conditional on the information they have available at time t, $I(t)$. The parameters b_k depict the elasticity of labor supply to the border at time t with respect to $t+k$ expected wages.

Equation (2) is a simplified dynamic labor supply function (of the type discussed by James Heckman and Thomas Macurdy, 1980), and can be obtained from an intertemporal optimizing model of labor migration. Time preference and discounting are embodied into the b parameters, that are all assumed to be positive. The idea behind the latter is that, everything else held constant, higher relative expected earnings in the border, whether at time t or $t+k$, raise the present value of lifetime earnings in that area, inducing south to north migration and augmenting the border's labor force. The b_k's could, however, be negative if there are strong intertemporal substitution elasticities. Higher expected earnings in future time periods $t+k$ relative to the current time period t could induce some migrants to delay their decision to migrate, reducing the border labor force at time t. I assume this effect is small enough so it does not change the positive sign of the b_k's.

Subtracting (2) from (1) and simplifying yields

$$\log(N_t/L_t) = [1/(1+b_0)]Z_t - [1/(1+b_0)] \times \sum_{k=1}^{T} b_k \log[E(N_{t+k})/E(L_{t+k})], \tag{3}$$

where

$$Z_t = (1-a)\log A(1-a) + \log K_t - 1/a \log W_t^d - \sum_{k=0}^{T} b_k \log(W_{t+k}^d/W_{t+k}^0).$$

Equation (3) states that the employment rate in the border at time t is related to a group of exogenous variables at time t, denoted by Z_t and to the future expected employment rates at times $t+k$. The latter affect present (time t) employment rates, since they influence the present value of migrant earnings and therefore the current amount of interregional labor migration to the border. How do we model the formation of expectations regarding future employment rates? A first hypothesis is rational expectations — the expectations of migrants have to be consistent with the model of the border labor market described in equations (1)–(3). Using equation (3), for example, the expected employment rate for period $t+1$ is

$$\log E[N_{t+1}]/E[L_{t+1}] = [1/(1+b_1)]E[Z_{t+1}] - [1/(1+b_1)] \times \sum_{k=2}^{T} b_k \log(E[N_{t+k}]/E[L_{t+k}]).$$

Substitution into (3) and forward iteration results in

$$\log(N_t/L_t) = [1/(1+b_0)]Z_t - [1/(1+b_0)] \times \sum_{k=1}^{T} [b_k/(1+b_k)]E[Z_{t+k}] \tag{4}$$

where, for expositional simplicity, equation (4) considers only the direct effects of the expected exogenous variables at time $t+k+j$ on the employment rate at time t and ignore the, relatively minor, chain effects of $E[Z_{t+k+j}]$ on N_t/L_t by affecting $E[N_{t+k}]/E[L_{t+k}]$.

Equation (4) shows the equilibrium employment rate as a function of a vector of current exogenous variables and of a vector of expected future values of those exogenous variables. Most models of labor migration ignore the role of expectations in shaping the migration decision. This is unfortunate as the mechanics of the process of migration is intimately linked to expectations. For instance, equation (4) shows that current employment rates (and therefore unemployment rates) are affected in different ways by creation of employment opportunities in the border region depending on whether the changes are anticipated or unanticipated. An expected increase in the capital stock in the border at time $t+1$, a rise of $E[K_{t+1}]$ in our terminology, reduces the current employment rate, N_t/L_t. The reason is because, through the process of interregional migration, the relative labor force in border areas is positively affected by expectations of future employment in the region. The anticipated capital accumulation does not increase employment immediately, though, generating in the short run only a rise in the unemployment rate. In terms of equation (4), if there is anticipated capital accumulation in period $t+1$, the impact on current unemployment — as a proportion of the labor force — is, everything else constant, equal to

$$dU_t/L_t = d\log L_t = [b_1/(1+b_0)(1+b_1)]d\log E[K_{t+1}] > 0,$$

where, for benchmark purposes, it is assumed that there is full employment initially ($L_t = N_t$), and where $dN_t = 0$ since the employment disturbance occurs in period $t+1$. The effect is particularly strong if the anticipated employment creation is permanent (so that all $E[K_{t+k}]$ rise) and not transitory (as in the case of only a rise in $E[K_{t+1}]$).

Unanticipated new border programs or investments, such as an unanticipated increase in the capital stock at time t, K_t, do not tend to increase short-run unemployment rates in the border as expected disturbances do. Algebraically, the impact on unemployment is given by $dU_t/L_t = -[1/(1+b_0)]d\log K_t$, which is negative, meaning that unemployment, as a proportion of the initial labor force, declines in response to the unanticipated disturbance. This is diametrically opposite to the case of an anticipated job expansion, in which unemployment increases, and is strengthened if the unanticipated disturbance is temporary and the anticipated one permanent. The explanation is that unanticipated disturbances do not have the speculative impact that anticipated disturbances have. In the case of unanticipated capital accumulation, responses are made on the basis of created jobs not anticipated ones.

This is a key point when expectations are not realized, which is likely to arise in the presence of forecasting errors (under uncertainty), or when expectations formations are based on inaccurate information or extraneous beliefs, deviating systematically from fundamentals (for a discussion of these deviations in financial and foreign exchange markets, and their relation to speculative bubbles, rational or not, see Olivier Blanchard, 1979; Rudiger Dornbusch, 1982). Within the present context, unrealized anticipations of future employment in the border would cause migrants, many of whom have moved there on the basis of those expectations, to face unanticipatedly high probabilities of unemployment and/or underemployment in the area. Some would then be forced to migrate to the United States. This is not a trivial matter as the maquiladoras are highly mobile firms and can switch locations with relative ease. Border employment creation could therefore be highly sensitive to unanticipated events curtailing Mexico's competitiveness in attracting assembly plants, and/or to business cycles.

My discussion suggests that border industrialization, when expected to be sustained over time, and if a feasible alternative for migrant workers, is likely to generate widespread interregional migration to the border area and could potentially raise the level of unemployment and underemployment there in the short run. Similar behavior is known to occur in relation to urban job creation and rural–urban migration and, as I have described, can be explained by the speculative aspects of the process of migration.

15.4 Concluding Remarks

In sum, I hope to have thrown strong doubts on the view that the Mexican border assembly industry reduces labor inflows to the United States and, on the contrary, shown that border industries could actually encourage such migration. But even if border industrialization could reduce migration to the United States, there remains the question of whether it would be to the national advantage of the United States to encourage it by stimulating, say, direct foreign investment in the area. In other words, could not such a move be counterproductive, meaning that immigration would provide greater economic benefit (or lower net loss) to the United States? My companion paper (1985) has dealt in detail with this issue.

References

Blanchard, Olivier J., "Speculative Bubbles, Crashes and Rational Expectations," *Economics Letters*, 1979, 387–389.

Cafferty, Pastora San Juan et al., *The Dilemma of American Immigration: Beyond the Golden Door*, New Brunswick: Transaction Books, 1983.

Dornbusch, Rudiger, "Equilibrium and Disequilibrium Exchange Rates," *Zeitschrift fur Wirtschafts- und Sozialwissenshaften*, September 1982, 102, 573–599.

Gambrill, Monica C., "Employment in the Maquiladoras, the Case of Tijuana," (transl.), *Papers and Proceedings* of First Conference on Regional Impacts of U.S. -Mexico Economic Relations, July 1981, 2, 245–259.

Grunwald, Joseph and Flamm, Kenneth, *The Global Factory: Foreign Assembly in International Trade*, Washington: The Brookings Institution, 1985.

Hansen, Niles, "The Nature and Significance of Border Development," in Lay James Gibson and Alfonso Corona Renteria, eds., *The U.S. and Mexico: Borderland Development and the National Economies*, Boulder: Westview Press, 1985.

Heckman, James J. and MaCurdy, Thomas E., "A Life Cycle Model of Female Labor Supply," *Review of Economic Studies*, January 1980, 47, 47–74.

Rivera-Batiz, Francisco, "Is Direct Foreign Investment a Substitute for Labor Inflows?: A Review of the Issues and Policy Implications," paper presented at the Western Economic Association Meetings, Anaheim, July, 1985.

Seligson, Mitchell A. and Williams, Edward J., *Maquiladoras and Migration Workers in the Mexico-United States Border Industrialization Program*, Austin: University of Texas Press, 1981.

Chapter 16

A Kinder, Gentler Immigration Policy: Forget Comprehensive Reform — Let the States Compete*

16.1 Introduction

Ever since Congress passed the Immigration Reform and Control Act, in 1986, attempts at a similar comprehensive reform of U.S. immigration policies have failed. Yet today, as the Republican Party smarts from its poor performance among Hispanic voters in 2012 and such influential Republicans as former Florida Governor Jeb Bush have come out in favor of a new approach, the day for comprehensive immigration reform may seem close at hand. President Barack Obama was so confident about its prospects that he asked for it in his State of the Union address in February 2013.

Now, the U.S. Senate looks poised to offer illegal immigrants a pathway to citizenship. But a top-down legislative approach to immigration could nonetheless easily die in Congress, just as the last serious one did, in 2007. Indeed, the president's domestic problems with health care and foreign problems with Syria have already cast a shadow over the prospects for reform.

Even if a bill did manage to pass, the sad fact is that it would work no better than the 1986 law did. That act was based on the

*This chapter was co-authored with Jagdish N. Bhagwati and originally published in *Foreign Affairs*, Vol. 92, No. 6, November/December 2013, pp. 9–15. © 2013 Council of Foreign Relations.

assumption that punishments, such as sanctions on employers and heightened border security, and incentives, such as an increase in the number of legal immigrants allowed to enter the country and amnesty for illegal immigrants already there, could eliminate illegal immigration altogether. That assumption proved illusory: the offer of amnesty may have temporarily reduced the stock of illegal immigrants, but it was not enough to eliminate it. Nor did employer sanctions and border enforcement reduce the flow of new illegal immigrants.

The challenges to eliminating illegal immigration are, if anything, greater today than they were in 1986. For one thing, in order to make today's proposals politically feasible, their authors decided to offer illegal immigrants not immediate unconditional amnesty but a protracted process of legalization. Confronted with this approach, a large share of the estimated 11 million illegal immigrants now living in the United States would likely choose to remain illegal rather than gamble on the distant promise of naturalization.

Nor would reform dissuade new illegal immigrants from joining those already in the country. Extrapolating from the recent drop in apprehensions near the Rio Grande, some analysts have argued that since the flow of illegal immigrants has already slowed to a trickle, the issue has lost its urgency. This notion is misguided. One cannot focus just on the area around the Rio Grande, since only half of all illegal immigrants residing in the United States entered the country by unlawfully crossing the U.S.–Mexican border, according to a 2006 study by the Pew Research Center. Moreover, whatever drop-off has occurred is mostly the result of the recent economic slowdown in the United States and will not prove permanent. As long as wages in the United States greatly outstrip those in poor countries, the United States will remain a mecca for potential immigrants, legal and illegal.

Not only would immigration reform fail to achieve its goal of eliminating illegal immigrants; it would also lead to increasingly draconian treatment of them. In order to appease anti-immigrant groups, the Senate's immigration reform bill provides for stricter enforcement of the U.S.–Mexican border, along with $40 billion in funding. But past experience suggests that such regulations are an exercise in futility: they do little to slow the influx of illegal immigrants while greatly increasing the risk to their lives as they try to cross the border over more dangerous terrain, aided by unscrupulous smugglers who may abandon them mid-journey.

Given these realities, the United States should stop attempting to eliminate illegal immigrants — since that will never work — and focus instead on policies that treat them with humanity. Doing so would mean adopting a variety of measures to diminish the public's hostility to illegal immigrants. Principal among them would be a shift from a top-down approach to a bottom-up one: letting states compete for illegal immigrants. States with laws that were unfriendly to illegal immigrants would lose them and their badly needed labor to states that were more welcoming. The result would be a competition that would do far more to improve the treatment of illegal immigrants than anything coming from Washington.

16.2 Impossible Difficulties

Americans can be schizophrenic when it comes to illegal immigration, suffering from a sort of right-brain, left-brain problem. The right brain sympathizes with illegal immigrants, since they are immigrants, after all, and the United States was founded on immigration. But the left brain fixates on their illegality, which offends Americans' respect for the rule of law. Negotiating a viable compromise between those who wish to throw illegal immigrants out and those who wish to embrace them has always proved exceptionally difficult.

As the historian Mae Ngai has shown, U.S. immigration policy in the 1920s and 1930s was as conflicted as it is today, with proponents of deportations pitted against pro-immigrant humanitarian groups. Further complicating matters is Americans' sense of fairness. Liberals have called on Congress to offer illegal immigrants a path to citizenship, but unlike most other countries, the United States has an enormous backlog of potential immigrants who have dutifully lined up for entry — an issue that Spain, for example, did not face when it granted its illegal immigrants amnesty in 2005.

Many Americans consider it unfair to let immigrants who have broken the law join the same line that those who followed the rules are in. The proponents of amnesty have, in consequence, cluttered up their proposed policy with various restrictions and requirements that make it far less attractive than a forthright granting of full citizenship.

Like past reform proposals, the current one offers illegal immigrants a long road to legality. But the longer the process, the greater the risk that a new Congress will reverse the old. Many illegal immigrants may prefer not to accept that risk and instead stay illegal. Furthermore, as the immigration scholars Mark Rosenzweig, Guillermina Jasso, Douglas Massey, and James Smith have shown, around 30 percent of U.S. immigrants achieve legal status despite having violating immigration laws in the past. Taking these factors into account, it is reasonable to predict that of the estimated 11 million illegal immigrants, only half would take an offer of amnesty, perhaps less.

Just like the chimera of legalizing away the stock of illegal immigrants, the notion that the flow of new illegal immigrants can be shut off is also deeply impractical. For instance, attempts at expanding legal immigration in the hope that it will reduce the incentive for illegal immigration would require, at minimum, vastly expanded legal admissions. Yet even though trade unions have given up their long-standing opposition to legalizing illegal immigrants — which they figure will boost their membership — they oppose significantly expanding legal admissions. Unions have long blamed immigration for the stagnation of workers' wages, just as they have blamed outsourcing and trade liberalization. In fact, the AFL-CIO recently suggested that it should be involved in determining how many legal guest workers the United States will admit in the future. When President George W. Bush proposed a more expansive guest-worker program, unions helped kill the measure, and they would fiercely fight any efforts to liberalize legal immigration this time, too.

It is also dubious that draconian enforcement measures, at the border or internally, would actually intimidate would-be illegal immigrants, no matter what mix of punishments and inducements Congress legislates. Unlike in 1986, almost every U.S. immigrant is now more secure: their ethnic compatriots will, as they already do, go to bat for better treatment, raising their voices against such measures.

But the biggest hurdle that immigration reform faces is that as long as immigration restrictions exist, people will continue to enter the United States illegally. The government can send as many Eliot Nesses to Chicago to nab as many Al Capones as it wants, but the bootlegged liquor will keep flowing across the Canadian border as long as Prohibition remains in place.

16.3 Immigration Inhumanity

Short of dismantling all border restrictions, then, no policy could magically eliminate illegal immigration. Yet not only would a reform bill be ineffective; it could also be harmful. If a comprehensive reform bill were passed, there is a serious danger that policymakers, operating on the flawed assumption that there should then be no reason for illegal immigrants to exist, might enact even harsher measures against them.

In fact, merely attempting to secure support for a reform bill is certain to harm illegal immigrants. Their experiences under President Bill Clinton and Obama have not been reassuring. Although Democrats have generally been more sympathetic to illegal immigrants than have Republicans, both Clinton and Obama, in their attempts to secure bipartisan consensus on immigration reform, implemented ruthless measures against illegal immigrants.

In the wake of the Immigration Reform and Control Act, the U.S. government ramped up enforcement at the border, which reached new heights during the Clinton administration. Ditches were built and fences constructed. To seal off common routes of entry into the United States, the government mounted military-style actions with names that seemed straight out of a war room: Operation Blockade, in El Paso in 1993; Operation Gatekeeper, in San Diego in 1994; and many more. The border security budget skyrocketed, rising from $326 million in 1992 to $1.1 billion by the time President George W. Bush took office, in 2001. The number of U.S. Border Patrol agents stationed at the southwestern border nearly tripled. In the end, these measures did little to stem the inflow. The demographer Jeffrey Passel of the Pew Research Center has estimated that the average net annual influx of illegal immigrants crossing the Rio Grande rose from

324,000 in the first half of the 1990s to 654,800 in the second half of the decade.

What stricter enforcement did do was force illegal immigrants to bypass safer crossing points and travel through the desert instead. Desperate immigrants made no secret of their desire to keep trying to sneak across the border despite heightened enforcement, often attempting again and again until they got through. But crossing the desert meant that they had to pay smugglers, known as coyotes, who left carloads of illegal immigrants for dead when they feared apprehension by U.S. Border Patrol personnel.

At best, the Clinton administration's policies had a marginal impact on illegal border traffic and led to a major decline in the welfare of those trying to enter the country illegally. They also failed to achieve their larger objective of getting legislation through Congress; the "keep them out" and "throw them out" lobbies were too strongly opposed to any compromise.

Obama has ramped up border enforcement, too, but he has also deported record numbers of illegal immigrants already living in the United States. In 2011, he expanded the Secure Communities initiative, a joint effort between state and local governments — the federal authorities have even ordered uncooperative states, such as New York, to fall in line — that uses integrated databases to track down illegal immigrants. According to official statistics, the number of deportations (excluding apprehensions at the border itself) has risen under Obama, to 395,000 in 2009. In 2001, under George W. Bush, deportations numbered only 189,000.

The focus on border enforcement is misguided. In part, it owes to the false equation of lax border control with the influx of terrorists. There is little evidence of that link: even the 9/11 hijackers entered the United States legally. Moreover, correcting for the effect of the recession on attempted crossings, it is clear that the impact of Obama's policies has been far from dramatic in deterring illegal immigration.

But the distress caused to illegal immigrants has been great. As a 2011 report from Human Rights Watch detailed, tens of thousands of immigrants are shuffled from jail to jail awaiting deportation. Once again, the country has gained little and lost much.

16.4 Race to the Top

With top-down immigration reform unworkable and inhumane, Americans need to shift their focus to treating their inevitable neighbors with humanity. That objective cannot be pursued through Washington. It must come from elsewhere: competition among states. States that harass illegal immigrants, such as Alabama, Arizona, Georgia, Indiana, and South Carolina, will drive illegal immigrants to more welcoming states, such as Maryland, New York, Utah, and Washington. As the former lose badly needed cheap labor to the latter, the political equilibrium will shift toward those who favor policies that help retain and attract illegal immigrants.

Of course, states cannot intrude on the parts of immigration enforcement over which the federal government has exclusive authority, such as border control and civil rights. But there are a number of steps states can take to make life easier for illegal immigrants, such as issuing them driver's licenses and making accessible to them everything from health care to university scholarships.

Illegal immigrants are already voting with their feet, leaving or bypassing states that treat them harshly and flocking to those with more benign policies. In 2011, hours after a federal judge in Alabama upheld most of the state's strict immigration law, illegal immigrants began fleeing. Frightened families, *The New York Times* reported, "left behind mobile homes, sold fully furnished for a thousand dollars or even less." The article continued: "Two, 5, 10 years of living here, and then gone in a matter of days, to Tennessee, Illinois, Oregon, Florida, Arkansas, Mexico — who knows? Anywhere but Alabama."

Ample statistical evidence demonstrates this pattern. From 1990 to 2010, when tough border enforcement policies (which naturally focused on the border states) were in vogue, Arizona, California, New Mexico, and Texas saw their collective share of illegal immigrants decline by 17 percent. In California alone, the percentage of all illegal immigrants residing there fell from 43 percent to 23 percent. Similarly, the economists Sarah Bohn, Magnus Lofstrom, and Steven Raphael have calculated that Arizona's 2007 Legal Arizona Workers Act, which banned businesses from hiring illegal immigrants, led to a notable decline in the proportion of the state's foreign-born Hispanic population.

The resulting blow to economic activity has often been drastic; employers in agriculture and construction, for example, regularly complain about the absence of workers. Fortunately, however, as business interests begin to agitate in favor of easing up on illegal immigrants, state capitals will start taking note. Already, many groups in the unwelcoming states have begun to question their states' draconian immigration enforcement laws and argue for more modest measures. After Alabama passed its immigration law, for example, business leaders complained to lawmakers about the resulting labor shortages. After the Legal Arizona Workers Act went into effect, in 2008, the state's contractors' trade association even joined civil rights groups in seeking the law's repeal. That same year, the U.S. Chamber of Commerce filed a lawsuit challenging the constitutionality of an Oklahoma law that required employers to verify the work status of their employees.

As this dynamic plays out, states will begin to compete for illegal immigrants, who will then face less harassment and be able to better integrate into their communities. Democrats and Republicans who care about human rights should welcome this change. More important, so should Republicans who prize states' rights. A race to the top in the treatment of illegal immigrants is a viable path to reform that would greatly advance human rights in the United States.

There are other ways to improve the lives of illegal immigrants that also do not involve Washington. Consider the problem of Mexicans who risk their lives traveling through the desert while attempting to cross the border and who occasionally damage the property of Texan ranchers. With no method to recoup their losses, the affected ranchers found it tempting to join forces with the Minutemen vigilantes who used to patrol the border. To reduce ranchers' hostility toward illegal immigrants, the Mexican government should set up a fund that compensates ranchers who can establish credible claims of damage. Since the stories of such damages tend to outstrip the reality, the fund need not be particularly large to go a long way in defusing the hostility.

Another way to improve the plight of illegal immigrants would be for Mexico to help pay for the education and medical expenses of those illegal immigrants coming from Mexico that are otherwise borne by the U.S. government. Although a number of studies show that illegal immigrants represent a net contribution to U.S. government coffers, the common perception that American taxpayers must bear these costs and that Mexico should share some of the burden of its own citizens breeds resentment. Were the Mexican government to make such a contribution, it would serve as a gesture of goodwill that could help reduce the hostility toward illegal immigrants.

16.5 Concluding Remarks

"Give me your tired, your poor, your huddled masses," reads the poem by Emma Lazarus that adorns the Statue of Liberty, which once welcomed the millions of immigrants arriving at Ellis Island. It is well past time to revive that sense of humanity, and the diverse recommendations outlined here can help the United States do just that. Whether or not they come with Washington's permission, immigrants to the United States nonetheless deserve the compassion Lazarus promised.

Part 5

Attitudes towards International and Interregional Migrants

Chapter 17

Economic Strain, Education and Attitudes towards Foreigners in the European Union*

17.1 Introduction

The flow of foreigners to the countries of the EU has exploded in recent years. The 1990s and 2000s have seen the share of the population changes in the EU accounted for by net immigration exceed that of natural population growth (Organization for Economic Co-operation and Development (OECD), 2012). For some countries, migration has played a dominant role in population growth. In Germany, the natural increase of the population since the 1970s has been negative and net immigration fully accounts for population growth. The same phenomenon has emerged in Greece, Italy, and Portugal; natural population growth has turned negative, population rising only as a result of net immigration.

The outcome has been a substantial increase in the population proportion accounted for by foreign nationals. Table 17.1 shows that, between 1985 and 2010, the percentage of foreigners in Austria's

---

*This chapter was co-authored with Ira N. Gang and Myeong-Su Yun and originally published in *Review of International Economics*, Vol. 21, No. 2, May 2013, pp. 177–190. © 2013 Blackwell Publishing.

Table 17.1. The Fraction of Foreigners in the European Population (Percentage of the Population, by Country).

Country	Percentage of population at: 1985	1998	2010
Austria	4.0	9.1	11.1
Belgium	8.6	8.7	10.2
Denmark	2.3	4.8	6.2
Finland	0.3	1.6	3.1
France	—	6.4[a]	6.0
Germany	7.2	8.9	8.3
Ireland	2.3	3.0	9.7[b]
Italy	0.7	2.1	7.6
Luxembourg	26.7	35.6	44.1
The Netherlands	3.8	4.2	4.6
Portugal	1.0	1.8	4.2
Spain	0.6	1.8	12.4
Sweden	4.6	5.6	6.8
UK	3.1	3.8	7.4

[a]Data is 1990; [b]Data is for 2006.
Source: OECD (1998, 2001, 2012).

population rose from 4.0% to 11.1%, in Denmark from 2.3% to 6.2%, in Luxembourg from 26.7% to 44.1%, and in Germany from 7.2% to 8.3%. For some countries, these figures even underestimate the significance of immigration, as they include only foreign-born individuals who are not citizens or have not been naturalized. In Sweden, for example, foreign nationals constituted 6.8% of the population in 2010 but the total foreign-born population, including foreign nationals as well as naturalized foreign immigrants and Swedish citizens born abroad, was 14.8%. By comparison, the proportion of the foreign-born in the population of the USA, a country famed for its open immigration policy, was 12.9% in 2010.

The recent economic debacle faced by the EU has led to a slowdown of immigration. The annual inflow of permanent immigrants into the countries of the EU included in the OECD database declined from 2.5 million in 2007 to 1.9 million in 2010.[1] In Ireland, the inflows dropped from 89,600 in 2007 to 17,400 in 2010; and in Spain the reduction in the inflow of migrants during this time period was from 691,000 to 300,000. There have also been substantial departures of foreigners from some countries. Still, the foreign population in Europe continues to rise. Even in Spain, the foreign population rose from 5.3 million in 2007 to 5.7 million in 2010.

The growth of immigration in Europe has been associated with an increase of anti-foreigner attitudes in a variety of countries. From Germany to the UK, the number of racially or ethnically motivated incidents reported to the police has increased over time. The trend began in the late 1980s and continued in the 1990s. In the UK, the number of incidents grew from 4,383 in 1988 to 13,878 in 1998.[2] In Germany, in November 1991, more than 100,000 Germans demonstrated against the rising violence against foreigners (Marshall, 1991). Yet, several Turks died in 1993 as a result of fires set in their buildings by anti-foreigner extremists. In recent years, negative attitudes towards immigrants have been increasingly displayed in the growth of political movements with anti-immigrant platforms, including France, the Netherlands, Hungary, and Greece. Individual acts of violence have also been widely noted in the press, from Germany (Moore, 2009) to Greece (Alderman, 2012). In July 2012, Human Rights Watch argues that in Greece "migrants and asylum seekers face a hostile environment, where they may be subject to detention in inhuman and degrading conditions, risk destitution, and xenophobic violence" (Human Rights Watch, 2012).

What explains the rise in negative sentiments towards foreigners among some segments of the European population? Is economic strain in host countries, in the form of stagnant earnings and rising unemployment, the key to understanding anti-immigrant activities or are non-economic factors, such as prejudice and racism, more influential in determining such behavior? This paper explores the determinants of the attitudes of European citizens towards foreigners using Eurobarometer Surveys. In 1988, 2003, and 2008, the surveys included specific questions measuring attitudes towards immigrants and immigration. The answers to these questions are used in this paper to carry out a statistical analysis of key factors influencing the attitudes of EU citizens towards foreigners and their changes over time.

17.2 The Determinants of Anti-Immigrant Attitudes

There is now extensive research studying the determinants of natives' attitudes towards foreigners in host countries. Some studies examine the theory of how different individuals or interest groups may be affected by immigrants and how these may influence their attitudes (Benhabib, 1996; Ortega, 2005). Others focus on analysis of survey and other data to study how attitudes towards foreigners are formed (Bauer *et al.*, 2000; Card *et al.*, 2012; Dustmann and Preston, 2001; Facchini and Mayda, 2012, Facchini *et al.*, 2011, Gang and Rivera-Batiz, 1994a,b; Gang *et al.*, 2010; Mayda, 2006; Scheve and Slaughter, 2001).

A common explanation for anti-immigrant attitudes is based on immigrants' economic impacts. It is hypothesized that in countries facing economic strain, with stagnant or collapsing income and/or employment opportunities, immigrants will be partly blamed for the economic stress thus generating the resentment of the native-born population. Whether immigration does lower wages or reduce employment opportunities is a matter of debate. Evidence on the impact of immigrants on European labor markets is inconclusive, often finding small effects of immigration on employment.[3] Studies on the USA also find small wage and unemployment effects of immigration.[4] Indeed, economic theory warns us against hastily assuming that a flow of immigrants into an economy will raise the unemployment of natives or reduce their wages. If immigrants are complements to the native-born, the foreign labor inflow increases the demand for natives, thus raising rather than lowering their employment.[5]

This debate on the economic effects of immigration may not be directly relevant to the formation of attitudes of natives towards immigrants, which are based on *perceptions* about how immigrants affect the economy, perceptions that are not necessarily based on reality. Even if the measured employment or wage effects of immigrants are very small, people may be influenced by rumors and stories reported in the media or heard in the streets about the "immigrant invasion" taking jobs away from them. Those who are directly competing with immigrants for jobs and who may be seeking a factor to blame for job losses, may be more responsive to these rumors and biased stories, developing strong negative attitudes towards foreigners — particularly if the press and politicians make the topic a big issue.

This leads to another major explanation for the emergence of negative sentiments towards immigrants: ethnic or racial prejudice, whose strength is often related to the presence and concentration of immigrants within particular communities. In the USA, historically, there is substantial evidence that racial prejudice was a major factor behind restrictionist movements that reduced immigration flows from particular countries or regions, such as China and Mexico. Racial prejudice has also been found in many of the anti-immigrant activities documented in the last few years in European countries. The xenophobia is reflected in isolated incidents, such as the hundreds of African migrants who had to be evacuated from the town of Rosarno in Italy after they clashed with town locals (Castelfranco, 2010). It is also reflected in the rise of anti-foreigner extremist groups and anti-immigrant political parties. Card *et al.* (2012) have found that attitudes towards race and ethnicity reflected in compositional amenities of a locality are more important than economic factors in determining attitudes toward immigration policy.

17.3 The Eurobarometer Survey and the Empirical Model

The analysis in this paper uses data on attitudes obtained from Eurobarometer Surveys in order to study the relative role played by economic strain and racial prejudice in forming attitudes towards immigrants. The surveys give rise to unique data sets on public opinion consisting of cross-sections of a geographically distributed random sample of households across Europe (see Reif and Melich (1991) and Melich (1999) for detailed descriptions of the procedures followed in each country). In addition to information on household economic and demographic behavior, the 1988, 2003, and 2008 Eurobarometer surveys contained questions on attitudes towards immigrants and foreigners. This paper measures attitudes towards foreigners on the basis of the responses of residents of EU countries to two questions. In 1988, they were asked: "Is the presence of (non-European Community) foreigners good or bad for the future of our country?" The variable ANTI-FOREIGNERS is constructed to equal one if the respondent declares that foreigners are "bad" or "a little bad" for the future of their country, and zero otherwise. This qualitative variable will be the dependent variable in a probit analysis studying the impact of various explanatory variables on the probability of a person displaying negative attitudes towards foreigners in 1988. For 2003 and 2008, the question used to determine anti-immigrant sentiments is: "Do immigrants contribute a lot to your country?", with the ANTI-FOREIGNERS variable equal to one if persons answered "tend to disagree" or "totally disagree." in response to the question, as opposed to totally agree or tend to agree, which is assigned a zero.

Table 17.2 presents the attitudes of European residents towards foreigners, on the basis of the ANTI-FOREIGNERS variable just defined. The first row shows overall opinions of the Eurobarometer survey sample, with the first column showing the results for the Eurobarometer sample in 1988, the second one for 2003 and the third

Table 17.2. Attitudes of European Residents towards Foreigners.

	Percentage anti-foreigner as of:		
Labor force status	**1988**	**2003**	**2008**
Overall sample	31.43	50.95	44.99
Employed/Salaried	31.84	50.00	43.04
Unemployed	31.42	58.23	54.33
Student	26.23	41.96	36.60
Housework	28.95	51.72	46.86
Retired	38.05	56.15	51.16

Note: ANTI-FOREIGNERS has a value of one when the respondent says that foreigners or immigrants do not contribute a lot to their country.

Source: Eurobarometer surveys 30.0 (October/November 1988), 60.1 (October–November 2003) and 69.2 (March–May 2008), authors' calculations.

one for 2008. As can be seen, in 1988, 31.43% of all respondents answered that foreigners were "bad" or "a little bad" for the future of their country. By 2003, the percentage of people who believed that immigrants contributed negatively to their country had gone up to 50.95%. However, by 2008, the anti-immigrant responses had declined to 44.99%.

What explains negative attitudes towards foreigners? Why was there such a marked increase in anti-foreigner sentiment among native European residents from 1988 to 2003 and then a decline from 2003 to 2008? The previous section points out that one answer may lie in the economic strain encountered by the population. In a large part of Europe, a slowdown in growth and rising unemployment characterized the 1980s and 1990s while the mid-2000s saw a generalized booming economy. In Germany, for instance, unemployment rose from 6.3% in 1988 to 9.3% in 2003, but then declined to 7.6% by 2008. In France, the unemployment rate rose from 8.3% in 1989 to over 10% in the 1990s and to 8.6% in 2003, but dropped to 7.5% in 2008. In Italy, unemployment rose from 7.9% in 1988 to 8.5% in 2003, declining to 7.9% in 2008. In Spain, unemployment rates that rose to over 19% in the 1990s dropped sharply in the 2000s and by early 2008 the unemployment rate was 8.6%. Rising unemployment in the 1990s could have sparked anti-foreigner attitudes: those who are fired and laid-off seek a target to blame their ills on. The significant drop in unemployment — and rising real wages — in the mid-2000s could explain the significant fall in negative attitudes towards immigrants between 2003 and 2008.

Table 17.2 decomposes the 1988, 2003, and 2008 Eurobarometer samples into various labor force categories, which includes those who are employed (with a salaried job), the unemployed, self-employed, and those out of the labor force, which include students, house workers and retired people. To a greater or lesser extent, the pattern of rising and then declining anti-foreigner sentiment is reflected for all labor force categories. In addition, the unemployed display sharply rising negative attitudes, increasing from 31.42% in 1988 to 58.23% in 2003 and remaining relatively high at 54.33% in 2008. A similar pattern holds for retired people.

Although interesting, the simple correlations obtained from Table 17.2 can only be suggestive. In order to systematically identify the effects of various economic and ethnic/racial factors on the formation of anti-foreigner attitudes, a probit analysis of the ANTI-FOREIGNERS variable defined earlier is carried out. In the probit analysis, the probability of observing negative attitudes towards foreigners is defined as Prob(ANTI-FOREIGNERS = 1) = $\Phi(X\beta)$, where Φ is a standard normal cumulative distribution function, β is a set of estimated coefficients and X includes various explanatory variables.

In addition to explanatory variables capturing labor force status, the analysis includes a number of background and demographic variables. First, the age of the person is used to incorporate a generational impact on earnings. Two variables: AGE (number of years) and AGESQUARE (number of years of age squared divided by 100) are introduced to reflect decreasing or increasing effects of age on attitudes. In addition, the variable EDUCATION (years of schooling) is introduced. It is expected that education is inversely associated with negative attitudes towards immigrants, partly because most educational systems willfully act to reduce prejudice and bias, and partly because more educated European residents are less likely to be negatively affected by the less-skilled foreigners whose visibility is noted in the press or by extremist political movements; in fact, they may have benefitted from low-wage foreigners if the skilled and unskilled are complementary inputs.

The analysis also considers differences in attitudes based on gender, including a dummy variable MALE, which is equal to one if the person was male and zero otherwise. Another dummy variable, MARRIED, is equal to one if the person is married and zero otherwise. One expects this variable to be associated with more negative attitudes towards foreigners because any perceived negative economic effects of the immigrants will be magnified for married persons, who have to manage the economic affairs of a multi-person household that is likely to include children or other dependents. Finally, a set of country fixed effects is introduced to control for differences in attitudes resulting from country-specific forces, such as may be caused by differences in average income per-capita and ethnic composition of the population.

17.4 Results

This study focuses on the attitudes of the citizens of EU countries aged 16–70 years, not of foreign origin and not in the military. Respondents who did not answer questions as to their nationality, education, age or gender were removed from the sample. The remaining sample of citizens of the EU was equal to 9,775 in 1988, 11,461 in 2003 and 10,076 in 2008.[6]

Table 17.3 shows the mean characteristics of the samples. The average age rises from 40 years in 1988 to almost 42 years in 2003 and to 44.3 years in 2008. The educational attainment of the sample also rises, from 11.2 years of schooling in 1988 to 12.0 in 2008. About half of the samples (49%) consist of men, and over half are married. In 1988, 39% of the sample was employed in wage/salary jobs, but this rises to 45.7% by 2008. Those who are unemployed are 6.2% in 1988, rising to 7.1% in 2003, remaining about the same in 2008. Those retired rise from 12.3% in 1988 to 15.6% in 2008.

The estimated probit coefficients are reported in Table 17.4. The result that stands out is the coefficient on education, which is strongly negative, suggesting that persons with more years of schooling have significantly less negative attitudes towards foreigners. In addition, the estimated coefficient rises sharply through time, especially from 2003 to 2008 — the impact of schooling in suppressing or discouraging negative attitudes towards foreigners is getting stronger over time. Whether because more skilled workers feel less threatened by immigrants or because the reduced ignorance associated with rising schooling has a stronger impact on racism and xenophobia, the suggestion is that educated Europeans have sharply lower negative attitudes towards immigrants since the late 1980s, and particularly in the 2000s.

The probit results in Table 17.4 show the partial correlation between attitudes towards foreigners and various, disaggregated labor market groups, including the employed, unemployed, retired, self-employed, and non-retirees out of the labor force (note that

Table 17.3. Sample Means.

Variable	1988	2003	2008
Negative attitudes towards foreigners[a]	31.43	50.95	44.99
Age	40.0 (15.7)	41.7 (15.1)	44.3 (15.1)
Education	11.2 (3.0)	11.9 (2.9)	12.0 (2.9)
Male	0.489 (0.499)	0.484 (0.499)	0.488 (0.499)
Labor force status			
Employed	0.388 (0.487)	0.459 (0.498)	0.457 (0.498)
Unemployed	0.062 (0.2421)	0.071 (0.256)	0.072 (0.258)
Student	0.113 (0.316)	0.108 (0.310)	0.099 (0.298)
Household work	0.202 (0.402)	0.124 (0.329)	0.119 (0.324)
Retired	0.123 (0.328)	0.147 (0.354)	0.156 (0.360)
Married	0.595 (0.491)	0.509 (0.499)	0.518 (0.499)
France	0.053 (0.225)	0.078 (0.268)	0.083 (0.276)
Belgium	0.096 (0.294)	0.078 (0.268)	0.082 (0.274)
The Netherlands	0.068 (0.253)	0.079 (0.269)	0.083 (0.276)
Germany	0.087 (0.282)	0.076 (0.265)	0.123 (0.328)
Italy	0.101 (0.301)	0.076 (0.265)	0.087 (0.282)
Luxembourg	0.029 (0.169)	0.044 (0.206)	0.039 (0.193)
Denmark	0.093 (0.290)	0.075 (0.264)	0.079 (0.271)
Ireland	0.090 (0.286)	0.081 (0.272)	0.090 (0.286)
UK	0.106 (0.308)	0.105 (0.306)	0.096 (0.294)
Greece	0.092 (0.290)	0.076 (0.265)	0.823 (0.275)
Spain	0.092 (0.289)	0.077 (0.267)	0.078 (0.268)
Number of Observations	9,775	11,461	10,070

[a] Includes both "the presence of foreigners is bad for the country" and "foreigners do not contribute a lot to the country"

Note: Standard deviation in parenthesis.

Source: Eurobarometer surveys 30.0 (October/November 1988), 60.1 (October–November 2003) and 69.2 (March–May 2008), authors' calculations.

students are the reference group). The statistical significance of the coefficients on the dummy variables varies substantially across these groups and across years. However, it does appear that being unemployed is generally associated with more strongly negative attitudes towards immigrants, particularly in 2003 and 2008. To determine whether the labor force status variables influence, as a group,

Table 17.4. Probit Analysis of Anti-Foreign Attitudes.

Variable	1988	2003	2008
Intercept	−0.698 (0.132)*	−0.321 (0.116)*	0.050 (0.137)
Age	−0.000 (0.007)	0.003 (0.006)	0.005 (0.007)
Agesq	0.001 (0.008)	−0.005 (0.007)	−0.008 (0.008)
Education	−0.037 (0.006)*	−0.051 (0.005)*	−0.084 (0.005)*
Male	0.047 (0.032)	−0.002 (0.025)	0.151 (0.029)*
Married	0.046 (0.034)	0.038 (0.027)	−0.021 (0.029)
Labor force status			
Employed	0.050 (0.059)	0.103 (0.053)**	0.087 (0.067)
Unemployed	0.069 (0.076)	0.215 (0.001)*	0.241 (0.083)*
Student	0.141 (0.072)**	0.113 (0.065)	0.017 (0.079)
Household work	0.075 (0.072)	0.090 (0.065)	0.113 (0.079)
Retired	0.140 (0.078)**	0.172 (0.066)*	0.153 (0.078)
France	0.917 (0.075)*	0.751 (0.064)*	0.659 (0.068)*
Belgium	1.085 (0.066)*	1.196 (0.065)*	1.153 (0.069)*
The Netherlands	0.392 (0.073)*	0.868 (0.065)*	0.617 (0.070)*
Germany	0.756 (0.066)*	1.028 (0.056)*	1.017 (0.063)*
Italy	0.415 (0.065)*	0.692 (0.065)*	0.870 (0.068)*
Luxembourg	0.037 (0.101)	0.586 (0.075)*	0.482 (0.084)*
Denmark	0.941 (0.069)*	0.933 (0.067)*	0.755 (0.073)*
Ireland	0.209 (0.074)*	0.684 (0.063)*	0.259 (0.067)*
UK	0.453 (0.064)*	0.906 (0.059)	0.704 (0.065)*
Greece	0.301 (0.067)*	0.920 (0.064)*	0.893 (0.068)*
Spain	0.078 (0.070)	0.572 (0.064)*	−0.074 (0.071)
Number of Observations	9,775	11,461	10,070

Note: Standard deviations in parenthesis. *, ** Represents statistical significance at a 99% and 95% level of confidence, respectively.

Source: Eurobarometer surveys 30.0 (October/November 1988), 60.1 (October–November 2003) and 69.2 (March–May 2008), authors' calculations.

attitudes towards foreigners, the null hypothesis that all the labor force status coefficients are equal to zero was tested. Although the chi-square statistic for this joint hypothesis test is not statistically significant in 1988, it is significant at the 95% confidence level in 2003 and at the 99% confidence level in 2008.

Finally, the country coefficients reported in Table 17.4 show some variation in the extent of anti-foreigner sentiment in various countries relative to Portugal, which is the excluded country in the equation. Belgium, Germany, and Denmark consistently show higher negative attitudes towards immigrants, although Greece and Italy display rapidly rising negative sentiments between 1988 and 2008.

17.5 Changes in Attitudes: A Decomposition Analysis

This section provides an analysis of which factors — employment status, education, country-specific fixed effects, etc. — are most significant in understanding the rising negative attitudes towards immigrants in Europe between 1988 and 2003, and their decline from 2003 to 2008. There are two broad approaches to explaining changes in attitudes over time. One relies on the possibility that the characteristics of individuals giving rise to negative attitudes towards immigrants have changed over time, increasing or decreasing the dislike of foreigners. For instance, those who feel that they are being hurt by immigrants via current competition in the labor market (such as the employed, whose wages may decline as a result of immigration, or the unemployed, whose employment opportunities may shrink), as well as those who feel they were hurt by the labor market competition suffered from immigrants in the past (the retired population), can have strong negative feelings towards foreigners. If the number of these labor market competitors of immigrants rises in the population, one expects that the society will suffer from more negative attitudes towards foreigners. Indeed, in the Eurobarometer surveys, the proportion of the population that was unemployed rose between 1988 and 2003, and 2008, and the probit analysis shows this indeed partly explains rising negative sentiments towards foreigners. More generally, one can define this type of explanation as a *characteristics effect*, because it reflects how changes in the average characteristics of individuals over time affect the likelihood of negative attitudes towards foreigners.

Suppose instead that average individual characteristics in the sample were not different in 1988, 2003, and 2008. A second approach to explaining the rising negative attitudes towards foreigners relies on the possibility that the effects of the given individual characteristics on attitudes have changed over time. For example, suppose that those individuals who are unemployed become more frustrated over time as a result of the economic strain they suffer. This may spillover into stronger negative attitudes towards foreigners. This increased bias against foreigners may not necessarily be connected to rising unemployment or a more sluggish economy, but rather to the fact that unemployment and recession generates more strongly negative effects on the attitudes of certain groups of people towards immigrants. Consider, for example, the coefficients of the variables UNEMPLOYED in the probit equations explaining negative attitudes towards foreigners. The coefficients reported in Table 17.5 rise from 0.069 in 1988 to 0.215 in 2003 and 0.241 in 2008, suggesting that the unemployed had more strongly negative attitudes towards foreigners in 2008 than in 1988. At an aggregate level, this may explain rising incidents of violence or bias against immigrants. Since this type of effect is associated with changes in the coefficients of the probit equations between 1988, 2003, and 2008, whether connected to unemployment or other variables, it is referred to as a *coefficients effect*.

Studying characteristics and coefficients effects was first carried out by Oaxaca (1973) and Blinder (1973). Their work has led to an extensive literature decomposing differences in dependent variables over time (or between groups). The implementation and extensions of their analyses have generally been in the context of wage differentials (in general, any continuous variable), although recent extensions allow for discrete dependent variables (Yun, 2004). The decomposition method proposed by Yun (2004) is used in this paper.[7]

The likelihood of having anti-foreigner attitudes for individual i is estimated by $\Phi(X_i\beta)$, where X_i is $1 \times K$ vector of independent variables, β is a $1 \times K$ vector of coefficients and Φ is the standard normal cumulative distribution function. The observed rate to have anti-foreigner attitudes is asymptotically equal to the sample average of individual likelihood to have anti-foreigner attitudes, or $\overline{P} = \overline{\Phi(X\beta)} = \frac{1}{N}\sum_{i=1}^{N}\Phi(X_i\beta)$. Algebraically, changes between years A and B in the average probability of having anti-foreigner attitudes $(\overline{P}_A - \overline{P}_B)$, where $A = 2003$ and $B = 1988$

Table 17.5. Decomposition Analysis of Changes in Anti-Foreigner Attitudes.

(a) Change in anti-foreigner attitudes between 1988 and 2003

	Characteristics effect		Coefficients effect	
	Estimate	**Share (%)**	**Estimate**	**Share (%)**
Aggregate Effect	0.0007	−0.34	0.1959*	100.34
Sub-Aggregate Effect				
Age and its square	0.0003	0.16	0.0013	0.67
Years of education	−0.0067	−3.41	−0.0612**	−31.32
Gender	0.0000	0.00	0.0002	0.11
Marriage	−0.0008	−0.41	−0.0001	−0.03
Countries	0.0064	3.29	−0.0022	−1.12
Labor market status	0.0001	0.03	0.0009	0.48
Intercept	0	0	0.2569*	131.54

Note: Percentage share of differences in predicted probabilities of anti-foreigner attitudes between 2003 and 1988 (0.1953 = 0.5095 − 0.3143) are reported.

*, ** Denote significance at the 99% and 95% level of confidence, respectively.

Source: Eurobarometer Survey, 1988, 2003; authors' calculations.

(b) Change in anti-foreigner attitudes between 2003 and 2008

	Characteristics effect		Coefficients effect	
	Estimate	**Share (%)**	**Estimate**	**Share (%)**
Aggregate Effect	−0.0047**	7.93	−0.0549*	92.07
Sub-Aggregate Effect				
Age and its square	−0.0011	1.77	0.0114	−19.08
Years of education	−0.0017*	2.81	−0.1479*	247.95
Gender	0.0002	−0.32	−0.0128*	21.43
Marriage	0.0002	−0.41	−0.0008	1.30
Countries	−0.0031*	5.22	0.0015	−2.49
Labor market status	0.0007	−1.13	−0.0012	1.93
Intercept	0	0	0.0948	−158.97

Note: Percentage share of differences in predicted probabilities of anti-foreigner attitudes between 2008 and 2003 (−0.0597 = 0.4499 − 0.5095) are reported.

*, ** Denote significance at the 99% and 95% level of confidence, respectively.

Source: Eurobarometer Survey, 2003, 2008; authors' calculations.

(or 2008 and 2003), may be decomposed into two components, i.e., $\overline{P}_A - \overline{P}_B = [\overline{\Phi(X_A\beta_B)} - \overline{\Phi(X_B\beta_B)}] + [\overline{\Phi(X_A\beta_A)} - \overline{\Phi(X_A\beta_B)}]$, where the first and the second components in the right-hand side represent the characteristic effect and coefficient effect; and an "over bar" represents the value of the sample's average.

This decomposition provides us with the overall coefficient and characteristic effects. In order to find the relative contribution of each variable to changes in negative attitudes towards foreigners between say 2008 and 2003, in terms of characteristic and coefficient effects, we employ a decomposition equation for the probit model (as proposed by Yun, 2004);[8]

$$\overline{P}_A - \overline{P}_B = \sum_{k=1}^{K} W_{\Delta X}^{k}[\overline{\Phi(X_A\beta_B)} - \overline{\Phi(X_B\beta_B)}]$$
$$+\sum_{k=1}^{K} W_{\Delta\beta}^{k}[\overline{\Phi(X_A\beta_A)} - \overline{\Phi(X_A\beta_B)}],$$

where $W_{\Delta X}^{k} = \frac{(\overline{X}_A^k - \overline{X}_B^k)\beta_B^k}{(\overline{X}_A - \overline{X}_B)\beta_B}$, $W_{\Delta\beta}^{k} = \frac{\overline{X}_A^k(\beta_A^k - \beta_B^k)}{\overline{X}_A(\beta_A - \beta_B)}$, and $\sum_{k=1}^{K} W_{\Delta X}^{k} = \sum_{k=1}^{K} W_{\Delta\beta}^{k} = 1$, where $\overline{X}_A^k$ and $\overline{X}_B^k$ are average values of explanatory variables k for groups A and B , respectively.[9]

Table 17.5 reports the results of this decomposition analysis. The probit equations upon which the decompositions are based upon were presented in Table 17.4 and represent the results of the analysis for 1988, 2003, and 2008. First, in Table 17.5(a), the change in the probability of having negative attitudes towards foreigners between 1988 and 2003 is decomposed into its components in terms of changes in characteristics or coefficients. This probability, which is the percentage of the sample who believed foreigners "do not contribute a lot" to their country, rises sharply by 19.53 percentage points (from 31.43% to 50.95%) between 1988 and 2003. The top row in Table 16.5(a) presents the overall effects of characteristics vs coefficients in explaining the increased negative attitudes towards foreigners, while the sub-aggregate effects depict the role of various groups of variables.

As Table 17.5(a) shows, the rising anti-foreigner attitudes in Europe between 1988 and 2003 are completely explained by changes in coefficients, not characteristics. In fact, changes in the characteristics of persons appear to be linked to a reduction in anti-foreigner attitudes. Specifically, the increased schooling between 1988 and 2003 is associated with a decline in anti-foreigner attitudes of 3.4%. In terms of the coefficients, the rising impact of years of schooling in reducing negative sentiments towards foreigners was significant and acted to reduce anti-foreigner attitudes by 31.3%. These would explain a reduction in negative sentiments towards immigrants. So, what explains the rise of anti-foreigner opinions?

Table 17.5(a) indicates that a rising intercept in the probit equation lies behind the increased negative attitudes. One interpretation of this result can be based on the studies seeking to measure the impact of discrimination in determining wages in the labor market. These studies suggest that since the intercept refers to the impact of variables not included in the analysis (meaning variables other than age, education, etc.), it may reflect the importance of discrimination and prejudice in reducing wages, as opposed to individual characteristics, such as education and experience. In the present context, since changes in the characteristics included in the analysis cannot explain the increasingly negative attitudes between 1988 and 2003, the rising intercept is consistent with rising xenophobia and prejudice against foreigners in the period between 1988 and 2003. From this point of view, despite the ameliorating effect of education in reducing negative attitudes towards foreigners, the overall increase of prejudice and bias appears to explain the rising negative attitudes towards immigrants.[10]

Table 17.5(b) shows the analysis of the changes in anti-foreigner sentiments between 2003 and 2008. In contrast to the earlier period, during these years there was a drop in negative attitudes towards foreigners. As before, the effects of characteristics are relatively minor, with increased years of schooling being associated with a 2.8% reduction in negative attitudes towards foreigners. The changes in coefficients again lie behind the decline in negative attitudes towards immigrants, but in contrast to the 1988–2003 period, during 2003–2008 it is the rising coefficient on education that explains the significant drop in negative sentiments. This means that the strength of the ameliorating impact of education on anti-foreigner attitudes rose sharply. The impact of a given level of schooling on attitudes towards immigrants increases substantially between 2003 and 2008, and this is associated with a reduction in the negative sentiments towards foreigners that more than compensates for the continuing overall rising trend in prejudice and bias (reflected by the increased intercept coefficient) that continues in the mid-2000s.

17.6 Summary and Conclusions

This paper has examined the relative significance of some of the key forces that influence the attitudes of EU citizens towards foreigners. Using attitudinal survey data from the 1988, 2003, and 2008 Eurobarometer surveys, variables that potentially determine attitudes towards immigrants have been analyzed, including the role of labor market status, educational attainment, and racial/ethnic bias. Estimating probit equations of the likelihood that people in the sample had negative attitudes towards foreigners, the paper provides an analysis of the connections between an array of explanatory variables and these attitudes.

We find a sharp increase in anti-foreigner attitudes in Europe between 1988 and 2003 and a decline between 2003 and 2008. In 1988, 31.43% of the sample felt that foreigners did not contribute a lot to the future of their country, but by 2003 as much as 50.95% felt that immigrants did not contribute to their countries, and by 2008 this had dropped to 44.99%.

What are the factors that explain these shifting attitudes towards foreigners? People who directly compete (or have competed) in the labor market with immigrants have stronger negative attitudes towards foreigners, *ceteris paribus*. This includes the unemployed but also other, employed workers who may perceive that their wages are negatively affected by immigrants.

Educational attainment is found to be a strong antidote to anti-foreigner sentiments. Both rising educational attainment and increasing effectiveness of education in reducing anti-foreigner sentiments lie behind the turnaround in negative attitudes towards immigrants from 2003 to 2008. At the same time, the decomposition results suggest there may be a long-term, rising trend in racial bias and xenophobia sustaining anti-foreigner sentiment. While this trend is more than compensated by the effects of education between 2003 and 2008, in the earlier period, from 1988 to 2003, it was strong enough to give rise to increasingly negative attitudes towards foreigners.

The data available for this study ends in 2008 and is preceded by a period of declining unemployment and economic boom in some European countries, such as Portugal, Ireland, and Spain. This situation, however, has sharply turned around since that time. Europe currently faces an extended recession, rising unemployment and an uncertain economic future. Insofar as economic strain is associated with negative attitudes towards immigrants, the current economic situation is likely to reverse the reductions in anti-foreigner sentiments between 2003 and 2008.

Notes:

[1]The countries included in the OECD database are: Austria, Belgium, Denmark, Finland, France, Germany, Ireland, Italy, Netherlands, Norway, Spain, Switzerland, and Sweden. The definitions of "foreigners" or the "foreign-born" in a population may differ depending on the country (OECD, 2012, 335), as international migration data have not been standardized.

[2]The number of incidents reported to the police greatly underestimates the actual number of such incidents since most remain unreported. In 1996, the British Crime Survey estimated that 143,000 offences against ethnic minorities (transgressions considered by the victim to be racially-motivated) had been committed the year before [Channel 4 (2000)].

[3]See the extensive literature surveyed in Bodvarsson and Van den Berg (2009) and Giordani and Ruta (2011).

[4]See Card (1990) for empirical evidence on this issue relating to the Mariel immigrant flow. See also Ottaviano and Peri (2012).

[5]For a discussion of the issue of complementarity between immigrant and native-born workers, see Rivera-Batiz and Sechzer (1991) and Gang and Rivera-Batiz (1994a).

[6]The sample is restricted to respondents in countries that were members of the EU in 1988: Belgium, Denmark, France, Germany, Greece, Ireland, Italy, Luxembourg, the Netherlands, Portugal, Spain, and the UK.

[7]What Yun (2004) proposed is a general method to decompose differences in the first moment for nonlinear models (see also Powers and Yun, 2009).

[8]In order to obtain a proper weight, the following approximations are used; first, an approximation of the value of the average of the function, $\overline{\Phi(X\beta)}$, with that

of the function evaluated at the average value of exogenous variables, $\Phi(\overline{X\beta})$; second, a first order Taylor expansion to linearize the characteristics and coefficients effects around $\overline{X}_B\beta_B$ and $\overline{X}_A\beta_A$.

[9]For computing asymptotic standard errors of the characteristics and coefficients effects, see Yun (2005a). Robustness issues, known as the index or parameterization problem and the identification problem, have been dealt with in more detailed decompositions. A decomposition equation with a different parameterization $[\overline{\Phi(X_A\beta_A)} - \overline{\Phi(X_B\beta_A)} + [\overline{\Phi(X_B\beta_A)} - \overline{\Phi(X_B\beta_B)}]]$, was computed; the results are not substantially different from those presented and are available from the authors. Another issue when interpreting the decomposition results is that the coefficients effect in the detailed decomposition is not invariant to the choice of omitted groups when dummy variables are used (Oaxaca and Ransom, 1999). The solution suggested by Yun (2005b, 2008) is used here, which shows that, if alternative reference groups yield different estimates of the coefficients effects for each individual variable, it is natural to obtain estimates of the coefficients effects for every possible specification of the reference groups and take the average of the estimates of the coefficients effects with various reference groups as the "true" contributions of individual variables to differentials. While appearing cumbersome, this can be accomplished with a single estimation. One can transform the probit estimates into a normalized equation and use the normalized equation for the decomposition.

[10]It is possible that there is an unobservable variable — other than prejudice or bias — which could explain the rising intercept coefficient. Yet probably no missing variable is as important as prejudice and xenophobia in explaining negative attitudes towards foreigners.

References

Alderman, Liz, "Greek Far Right Hangs a Target on Immigrants," *The New York Times*, July 11, 2012, p. A1.

Bauer, Thomas K., Magnus Lofstrom, and Klaus F. Zimmermann, "Immigration Policy, Assimilation of Immigrants and Natives' Sentiments toward Immigrants: Evidence from 12 OECD Countries," *Swedish Economic Policy Review* 7 (2000): 11–53.

Benhabib, Jesse, "On the Political Economy of Immigration," *Economic European Review* 40 (1996): 1737–43.

Blinder, Alan S., "Wage Discrimination: Reduced Form and Structural Estimates," *Journal of Human Resources*, 8 (1973): 436–55.

Bodvarsson, Orn B. and Hendrik Van den Berg, *The Economics of Immigration: Theory and Policy*, Berlin: Springer-Verlag (2009).

Card, David, "The Impact of the Mariel Boatlift on the Miami Labor Market," *Industrial and Labor Relations Review* 43 (1990): 245–57.

Card, David, Christian Dustmann, and Ian P. Preston, "Immigration, Wages and Compositional Amenities," *Journal of the European Economic Association* 10 (2012): 78–119.

Castelfranco, Sabina, "Violence Forces Evacuation of African Immigrants from Southern Italian Town," *Voice of America News*, January 10, 2010.

Channel 4 Hate Commission, *Hate Crime Report*, London (2000).

Dustmann, Christian and Ian P. Preston, "Attitudes to Ethnic Minorities, Ethnic Context and Location Decisions," *Economic Journal* 111 (2001): 353–73.

Facchini, Giovanni and Anna Maria Mayda, "Individual Attitudes towards Skilled Migration: An Empirical Analysis across Countries," *The World Economy* 35 (2012): 183–96.

Facchini, Giovanni, Anna Maria Mayda, and Prachi Mishra, "Do Interest Groups Affect U.S. Immigration Policy?" *Journal of International Economics* 85 (2011): 114–28.

Gang, Ira N. and Francisco L. Rivera-Batiz, "Labor Market Effects of Immigration in the United States and Europe: Substitution vs. Complementarity," *Journal of Population Economics* 7 (1994a): 157–75.

———, "Unemployment and Attitudes Toward Foreigners in Germany," in Gunter Steinmann and Ralph Urich (eds), *Economic Consequences of Immigration in Germany*, Heidelberg: Physica-Verlag (1994b): 121–54.

Gang, Ira N., Francisco L. Rivera-Batiz, and Myeong-Su Yun, "Changes in Attitudes toward Immigrants in Europe: Before and After the Fall of the Berlin Wall," in Gil S. Epstein and Ira N. Gang (eds), *Migration and Culture*, Bingley, UK: Emerald Group (2010): 649–76.

Giordani, Paolo E. and Michele Ruta, "The Immigration Policy Puzzle," *Review of International Economics* 19 (2011): 922–35.

Human Rights Watch, *Hate on the Streets: Xenophobic Violence in Greece*. Washington, DC: Human Rights Watch (2012).

Marshall, Tyler, "100,000 Germans Decry Attacks on Foreigners," *Los Angeles Times*, November 10, 1991.

Mayda, Anna Maria, "Who is Against Immigration? Cross-country Investigation of Individual Attitudes toward Immigrants," *Review of Economics and Statistics* 88 (2006): 510–30.

Melich, Anna, *Eurobarometer 48: Holiday Travel, October–November 1997*. Ann Arbor, MI: Inter-university Consortium for Political and Social Research Producers and Distributors (1999).

Moore, Tristana, "In Germany, a Disturbing Rise in Right-Wing Violence," *Time Magazine*, December 23, 2009.

Oaxaca, Ronald, "Male–Female Wage Differentials in Urban Labor Markets," *International Economic Review* 14 (1973): 693–709.

Oaxaca, Ronald and Michael R. Ransom, "Identification in Detailed Wage Decompositions," *Review of Economics and Statistics* 81 (1999): 154–57.

OECD, *Trends in International Migration (SOPEMI)*, Paris: OECD (1998, 2001).

OECD, *International Migration Outlook*, Paris: OECD (2012).

Ortega, Francesco, "Immigration Quotas and Skill Upgrading," *Journal of Public Economics* 89 (2005): 1841–63.

Ottaviano, Gianmarco I. P. and Giovanni Peri, "Rethinking the Effects of Immigration on Wages," *Journal of the European Economic Association* 10 (2012): 152–97.

Powers, Daniel A. and Myeong-Su Yun, "Multivariate Decomposition for Hazard Rate Models," *Sociological Methodology* 39 (2009): 233–63.

Reif, Karlheinz and Anna Melich, *Euro-Barometer 30: Immigrants and Out-Groups in Western Europe, October–November 1988*, Ann Arbor MI: Inter-University Consortium for Political and Social Research Producers and Distributors (1991).

Rivera-Batiz, Francisco L. and Selig L. Sechzer, "Substitution and Complementarity between Immigrant and Native Labor in the United States," in F. Rivera-Batiz, S. Sechzer and I. Gang (eds), *U.S. Immigration Policy Reform in the 1980s: A Preliminary Assessment*, New York: Praeger (1991): 89–116.

Scheve, Kenneth F. and Matthew J. Slaughter, "Labor Market Competition and Individual Preferences over Immigration Policy," *Review of Economics and Statistics* 83 (2001): 133–45.

Yun, Myeong-Su, "Decomposition Differences in the First Moment," *Economics Letters* 82 (2004): 273–78.

Yun, Myeong-Su, "Hypothesis Tests when Decomposing Differences in the First Moment," *Journal of Economic and Social Measurement* 30 (2005a): 295–304.

Yun, Myeong-Su, "A Simple Solution to the Identification Problem in Detailed Wage Decomposition," *Economic Inquiry* 43 (2005b): 766–72.

Yun, Myeong-Su, "Identification Problem and Detailed Oaxaca Decomposition: A General Solution and Inference," *Journal of Economic and Social Measurement* 33 (2008): 27–38.

Chapter 18

Education and Attitudes towards Internal Migrants in China*

18.1 Introduction

The number of internal migrants in China accelerated after the early 1980s. Before that time, the so-called hukou household registration system restricted severely rural to urban movements. Imposed in the 1950s, the hukou system requires that every person register their permanent residence and type of work (agricultural or non-agricultural) with local government authorities. In order to migrate, the person either requests an official change of hukou location — which was originally very difficult but has progressively become easier since the 1980s — or migrates without such change of residence, either by using temporary migration permits or other means (non-hukou migrants). The official estimates based on the 2010 Census are that the number of non-hukou migrants in China was about 260 million, up from about 30 million in the late 1980s (Chen and Feng, 2012, p. 3).

*This chapter was co-authored with Na Feng and a lengthier version was originally published in Na Feng, ed., *Essays on Education, Political Movements and Income Growth in China*, Ann Arbor, Michigan: Proquest Publishing LLC, 2016, pp. 122–187. © 2016 Na Feng.

The authors are grateful to Mun C. Tsang, Andrew J. Nathan, Ronald E. Findlay and Henan Chen for their valuable comments and suggestions. The chapter was presented at the Center for Chinese Education at Teachers College, Columbia University and the comments of participants at the seminar are gratefully acknowledged.

These migrants are often referred to as the country's floating population or *liu dong ren kou* (Goodkind and West, 2002, and Li, 2006). Given that they have not changed hukou location, most of these migrants do not have access to local social safety nets as well as to public education and health benefits.

Internal migrants in China tend to be relatively young, male and with low educational attainment (Chen, 2011). Data from the 2004 Rural Migration Survey of the National Bureau of Statistics (RMS) show that as much as 45 percent of the migrants were 25 years of age or younger. They are relatively unskilled, with estimates from the 2004 RMS showing that 83 per cent of migrant workers had completed no more than nine years of schooling. Most migrants are men, with data from the 2004 RMS indicating that two-thirds were male. The lower likelihood of women to migrate is connected to the greater involvement of women in taking care of children and older family members, which forces them to remain in rural areas.

The next section provides a discussion of the literature on attitudes towards internal migrants in China and a review of the international literature on opinions towards migrants. Later sections describe the data utilized in this essay, the research methodology, results, and conclusions.

18.2 Attitudes towards Migrants in China

There is now a substantial literature examining the socioeconomic status of migrants in China, including their wages (Wang, Oropesa and Firebaugh, 2013; Leng, 2012; Gagnon *et al.* (2009); and Demurger *et al.*, 2009), employment (Roberts, 2001, and Quheng and Gustaffson, 2006), occupations (Kondo and Ou, 2010), job search processes (see Giuletti *et al.* (2012) and Long, Appleton and Song, 2013), labor market discrimination (Meng and Zhang, 2001; Demurger *et al.*, 2009, and Gagnon *et al.*, 2009), education of their children (Lai *et al.*, 2014; Chen and Feng, 2012, and Tan, 2010), and other aspects of their socioeconomic status (Peilin and Feng, 2011, and Tan, 2010).

There is, however, not much formal, statistical research examining the opinions and attitudes of the general population towards migrants. Evidence of negative attitudes confronting migrants has surfaced from psychological and sociological studies (see Wong, Chang and He, 2007; Wong and Song, 2008, and Roberts, 2002). And a number of studies have suggested that the lack of protections and public benefits faced by many non-hukou migrants, combined with their lower average levels of schooling and low socioeconomic status, appear to have generated a group of the population which is considered as inferior by their fellow Chinese. The potential for discrimination and abuse has been noted by organizations such as Amnesty International (see Amnesty International, 2007) and supported by case studies, qualitative analysis and journalistic reports and documentaries on the troubles of the migrants themselves. As Guan (2010, p. 22) observes:

"Although migrants play an indispensable role in economic growth in China, they are frequently portrayed negatively. Rural-to-urban migrants... are perceived as a threat to social stability, and are often linked to the increase in crime rates in cities. They are also perceived as competing with unemployed urban residents who have been laid off from the state-owned enterprises... Indeed, the hostility displayed by urban citizens has hurt migrants' self-image and self-esteem, and has widened the social gap between migrants and citizens."

There is some research examining attitudes towards migrants in urban China, but the studies have been small in scale and focused on specific cities or urban areas in the country. In the mid-1990s, Solinger (1999) conducted a survey of urban residents, asking their general opinions towards migrants. He found that 74 per cent of Shanghainese blamed migrant workers for at least three of the following four urban problems: crime, transport problems, unemployment and environmental degradation. A similar result is obtained by Nielsen, Nyland, Smyth, Zhang and Zhu (2006), who carried out a comprehensive survey of the attitudes towards migrants of 885 local urban residents working in 23 enterprises in 6 cities in Jiangsu Province, which is one the coastal provinces attracting large numbers of migrant workers. They found that 62.0 per cent of urban locals felt migrant workers responsible for up to three out of four problems: unemployment, overcrowding, security and hygiene in the city.

The perceptions of urban residents towards internal migrants in China are reminiscent of the attitudes displayed towards immigrants in recipient countries. In fact, some of the sociological literature on attitudes towards internal migrants argues that one can conceptualize the negative views towards these migrants by urban residents as being similar to those attached to ethnic or even racial bias. Following the sociological literature, Zhou *et al.* (2011) note that there are "similarities between racism in western countries and discrimination against migrant workers by urban residents in China... the term 'race' here seen broadly and defined as a concept that signifies and symbolizes social conflicts... The segregation of hukou has resulted in the formation of two distinct ethnic groups, the urban and the rural (cheng hanzu and xiang hanzu), and the gap between the two is deep-rooted and difficult to cross."

Given the similarities in the experiences faced by rural migrants in Chinese urban cities and those of immigrants in recipient countries — and given the shortage of research by economists or other social scientists on the determinants of attitudes towards internal migrants — the next section provides a brief review of the literature on the determinants of attitudes towards immigrants in the United States and European countries.

18.3 Education and the Determinants of Attitudes towards Migrants

The literature studying the determinants of the attitudes of natives towards foreigners in recipient countries is extensive. Some of these studies are concerned with the theory of how different individuals or interest groups may be affected by immigrants and how these may influence their attitudes (Benhabib, 1996, and Ortega, 2005). Others focus on empirical analysis of survey and other data to study how attitudes towards foreigners are formed (Gang, Rivera-Batiz and Yun, 2013; Facchini and Mayda, 2012; Card, Dustmann and Preston, 2012; Gang, Rivera-Batiz and Yun, 2010; Mayda, 2006; Bauer, Lofstrom, and Zimmermann, 2000); Krueger and Pischke, 1997; and Gang and Rivera-Batiz, 1994).

One of the most common explanations for anti-immigrant attitudes is based on the economic impact of the migrants. It is hypothesized that in countries where economic strain is present, with stagnant or collapsing income and/or employment opportunities, immigrants will be partly blamed for the economic stress thus generating the resentment of the native-born population. Whether immigration does in fact act to lower wages or reduce unemployment opportunities is a matter of debate: the statistical connection between economic variables and attitudes towards migrants found in previous research is based on *perceptions* about how migrants affect the economy, perceptions that are not necessarily based on reality. For example, there is now ample research showing that the economic impact of immigration on the wages and employment opportunities of natives varies and, overall, the impact is small (see Ottaviano and Peri, 2012; Gang and Rivera-Batiz, 1994; Rivera-Batiz and Sechzer, 1991, and Card, 1990). But people may be influenced by rumors and stories reported in the media or heard in the streets about the immigrant invasion which is taking jobs away from them. Those who are directly competing with immigrants for jobs and who may be seeking a factor to blame for job losses, may be more responsive to these rumors and biased stories, developing strong negative attitudes towards foreigners particularly if the press and politicians make the topic a big issue.

Indeed, another major explanation for the emergence of negative sentiments towards immigrants is ethnic or racial prejudice, whose strength is often related to the presence and concentration of immigrants within particular communities. In the United States, historically, there is substantial evidence that racial prejudice was a major factor behind restrictionist movements that reduced immigration flows from particular countries or regions, such as China and Mexico. Racial prejudice has also been found in many of the anti-immigrant activities documented in the last few years in European countries.

Educational attainment is a variable that has been found in the previous literature to constrain negative attitudes towards immigrants. For instance, Gang, Rivera-Batiz and Yun (2013) examine the determinants of attitudes towards immigrants among European Union citizens, and the changes in these attitudes between 1988, 2003 and 2008. Using a multivariate statistical analysis of the determinants of attitudes towards immigrants, they find that educational attainment is a strong antidote to anti-migrant attitudes. They conclude that rising average schooling in Europe as well as more positive attitudes towards immigrants by the highly educated has ameliorated anti-immigrant attitudes (see also Facchini and Mayda, 2012; Krueger and Pischke, 1997; Mayda, 2006).

The negative connection between increased schooling and anti-migrant sentiments found in the literature may be due to the fact that in most countries and regions of the world, migrants tend to have significantly lower education than natives in the recipient countries or areas. As a result, more educated residents in recipient areas may not feel that they are directly competing with migrants in the labor market and therefore that their jobs or wages are under threat because of increased migration. In fact, they may see the migrants as complements, benefiting them instead of potentially hurting their economic status. Less educated natives, on the other hand, may perceive they are directly competing with the migrants, fueling anti-migrant sentiments.

Alternatively, education may reduce negative attitudes towards migrants because in many countries school and university curricula emphasize civility and tolerance towards persons of different backgrounds and seek to reduce the ignorance often linked to prejudice. As persons go through school systems that favor diversity and promote the integration of migrants, anti-migrant attitudes may diminish.

But some studies have not found that increased education reduces in significant way negative attitudes towards migrants. Indeed, this is the result of several studies in China. Sociologists Y. Zhou, Y. Wang and W. Chen (2011, p. 2), for example, find that: "there is... a negative relationship... between education and attitude toward equality for migrant workers." Increased educational attainment may generate anti-migrant attitudes for a number of reasons. For one, if the migrants are highly-educated, then natives with more schooling may fear for their jobs. But in China, for example, rural to urban migrants tend to be less educated than urbanites, so other explanations are necessary. One hypothesis is that urban anti-immigrant attitudes may be connected to fears that increased migration will deteriorate the quality of life in recipient regions, due to congestion, increased crime, etc. These perceptions may not be based on reality, but fueled by prejudice and bias. They may therefore affect more intensely the more-educated population that is isolated from where the migrants live and may react more intensely to any instances where migrants have been involved in crimes.

In addition, the school systems in recipient areas may not be contributing towards reducing anti-migrant attitudes. In China, as noted earlier, the hukou system has acted effectively to make migrants a separate group in society, segregating migrant children from the children of urban residents, and generating a population with limited legal rights, stimulating the perception that they are inferior to urban residents. Indeed, some sociologists have argued that urban populations with higher socioeconomic status in China may have developed a sub-culture of privilege that distances them from migrants, who are considered as belonging to a different sub-culture towards which they do not have any positive attitudes (see Irwin, 1999).

So, what is the impact of education on attitudes towards migrants in China? The following sections examine the data and empirical strategies adopted in this paper.

18.4 The Determinants of Attitudes towards Migrants in China: Empirical Methodology

This paper utilizes the 2005 wave of the Chinese General Social Survey (CGSS), which includes a series of detailed questions asking respondents to identify their opinions towards migrants. The CGSS is an annual survey carried out since 2003 by Renmin University, the Hong Kong Sciences and Technology University, and other universities and organizations in China. The surveys draw random cross-sectional samples of the population in China each year and interview a set of individuals 18 years of age or older, asking them a core set of detailed background questions on their socioeconomic status as well as that of the households where they reside.

These are four questions relating to attitudes towards migrants in the CGSS used in this paper: (1) Are you willing to work with them? (2) Can you tolerate them living in your neighborhood? (3) Can you tolerate them living next to you? (4) Are you willing to invite them as guests in your home? (5) Do you consent that your sons, daughters and other relatives court them?

The dependent variable used in the estimation for each question is a categorical variable equal to one or zero based on the responses to the attitude questions. For instance, the responses to the question: "Can you tolerate [migrants] living in your neighborhood?" are coded into a variable PRO-MIGRANT, which is equal to one if the person answered yes and zero if the person answered no. Each question is analyzed separately, as a different dependent variable examined independently of the others. Only individuals residing in urban areas are included. For each question, the analysis will be carried out first including both males and females but later the analysis is separated for males and females.

In order to identify statistically the relative influence of the variables just listed on attitudes towards migrants, a separate probit analysis of each of the five PRO-MIGRANT variables defined earlier is carried out. In the probit analysis, the probability of observing positive attitudes towards migrants on the part of person i of gender m (where m=1 for male and m=2 for female) is defined as being equal to:

$$\mathrm{P_{im}} = \mathrm{Prob_{im}}(\text{PRO-MIGRANT} = 1) = \Phi(\beta\text{'}\mathrm{X_{im}}),$$

where Φ is a standard normal cumulative distribution function, β is a set of estimated coefficients and X includes various explanatory variables to be specified below.

More specifically:

$$\begin{aligned}\beta\text{'}\mathrm{X_{im}} &= \text{ß}_{0\mathrm{M}} + \text{ß}_{1\mathrm{m}}\mathrm{EDUC_{im}} + \text{ß}_{2\mathrm{m}}\mathrm{MALE_{im}} + \text{ß}_{3\mathrm{m}}\mathrm{AGE_{ij}} \\ &\quad + \text{ß}_{4\mathrm{m}}\mathrm{UHUKOU_{im}} + \text{ß}_{5\mathrm{m}}\mathrm{ETHNIC_{im}} + \text{ß}_{6\mathrm{m}}\mathrm{SOCIALC_{im}}\end{aligned}$$

$$+ ß_{7m}\text{INTENSITY}_{im} + ß_{8m}\text{MARITAL}_{im}$$
$$+ ß_{9m}\text{COASTAL}_{im} + ß_{10m}\text{CENTRALR}_{im}$$
$$+ ß_{11m}\text{FINCOME}_{im} + ß_{12m}\text{FULLYEMP}_{im}$$
$$+ ß_{13m}\text{UNEMP}_{im} + U_{ij} \quad (1)$$

where U_{ij} is a stochastic disturbance term and the explanatory variables represent the different forces that may lead individuals to have negative or positive opinions towards migrants, as defined next.

1. EDUC, representing educational attainment or years of schooling. It is expected that education is inversely associated with negative attitudes towards migrants, partly because educational systems usually act to reduce prejudice and bias, and partly because more educated residents are less likely to be negatively affected by the less-skilled migrants who have flowed into China's cities. However, as discussed in the last section, some of the existing literature on China's migrants has found increased education is not associated with more positive attitudes towards migrants.
2. MALE is a dummy variable equal to one if the person is male and zero if female. This variable could be positive or negative as there may be different forces affecting how male and female urban residents see migrants. The economic approach would suggest that since most migrants are male, it would be male urban residents who — holding other things constant — would feel more threated by the increased labor market presence of the migrants. On the other hand, sociologists have argued that social conventions may not favor urban women having friendships with migrant men, which could generate more negative attitudes of urban women towards migrants. There may be other social forces that could make females have more negative attitudes towards migrants. Wang and Schwartz (2015) find that rural [migrant] women are much more likely to marry urban men than rural men are to marry urban women. The increased competition in the marriage market may therefore make women in urban areas have more negative attitudes towards migrants, holding everything else the

same, while the increased supply of potential marriage partners for urban men would make them more positive towards migrants.

3. AGE, to incorporate a generational impact on attitudes. One could expect that, since younger persons may have been exposed to more diverse urban environments and, therefore, may be less ignorant about migrants, they would have more positive attitudes towards them. On the other hand, migrants tend to be young workers and young urbanites may be more fearful of competition with them in urban labor markets, which would generate negative attitudes towards the migrants.
4. UHUKOU is equal to one if the person had an urban hukou and zero otherwise. Since only urban residents are included in the analysis, persons with a non-urban hukou (UHUKOU=0) would have been officially registered in rural households and would generally be migrants, while those with an urban hukou (UHUKOU=1) would be urban natives or urbanites. Although one would expect migrants to have more positive attitudes towards other migrants, so that the variable would have a negative coefficient, some of the immigration literature suggests that because of potential competition with other migrants it is possible that the variable could have a positive coefficient.
5. ETHNIC is equal to one if the person declares he or she is a member of the Mongolian, Manchu, Hui, Tibetan, Zhuang, Uygur or other ethnic or national minority group, and zero otherwise. Although most of the population in China is part of the Han ethnicity, there are a variety of ethnic minority groups in the country. Because these groups may be in greater competition with the migrants, it could be expected that they would have more negative attitudes towards them.
6. SOCIALC is a variable that ranges from 1 to 5 and is based on the question: are you familiar with your neighbors? With answers ranging from not familiar at all (SOCIALC=1) to very familiar (SOCIALC=5). It is expected that persons who are more familiar with their neighbors are more likely to be less ignorant and stereotypical of migrants and would, therefore, have more positive attitudes towards them.

7. INTENSITY, an index that intends to measure whether the person has had more contacts with migrants. It is derived from the following questions asked by the 2005 CGSS: Have you had a migrant person as your co-worker? Are there any of them living in your neighborhood? Are there any of them living next to you? On the basis of these three questions, the index, INTENSITY, was developed to measure the intensity of the contact between the interviewee and migrants. If the answer to all the questions is yes, the value of the index is 3 and if the answer is no to all questions, then the index is 0, and so on. The index will rise according to the extent to which the person has had more contacts with migrants. Note that a greater presence of migrants in the neighborhood or workplace where the person resides (which would be reflected in higher values of the INTENSITY index) might lead to stronger negative attitudes towards them. As noted earlier, the literature on attitudes towards immigrants finds that increased intensity of contact with immigrants is often associated with negative attitudes towards the immigrants, but the fears and racial and ethnic prejudice associated with immigrants may not be translated to internal migrants in China, whose contribution to Chinese economic growth is widely recognized, and are generally part of the Han Chinese majority. Instead, increased intensity of contact between migrants and urbanites may lead to a reduction of ignorance about them, greater understanding of the plight of these hard working individuals, and to a more positive attitudes towards them and their contribution to Chinese society.
8. MARITAL, reflecting the role of marital status. It is introduced as a dummy variable, equal to one if the person is married and zero otherwise. One expects this variable to be associated with more negative attitudes towards migrants because any perceived negative economic effects of the migrants will be magnified for married persons, who have to manage the economic affairs of a multi-person household that is likely to include children and/or other dependents.
9. COASTAL, which is a dummy variable equal to one if the person resides in a coastal province, which includes: Shanghai, Beijing,

Tianjin, Zhejiang, Guangdong, Liaoning, Shandong, Fujian and Jiangsu, and zero otherwise. CENTRAL is a dummy variable equal to one if the person resides in a central province of China, including Hebei, Shanxi, Jilin, Heilongjiang, Anhui, Jiangxi, Henan, Hubei, Hunan, Guangxi, and Hainan, and zero otherwise. These variables are introduced as fixed effects to control for differences in attitudes due to region-specific forces. It is expected that urban residents in the coastal and central provinces may have more negative attitudes towards migrants because of the greater labor market competition these residents face from the migrants, who have migrated in more numbers to these coastal areas.

10. FINCOME is a variable equal to the family income reported by the respondent. Previous studies examining attitudes towards immigrants tend to find that higher socioeconomic status is associated with more positive attitudes towards migrants, whether because of lower fears about possible negative impacts of migrants on jobs and wages, or because those with higher socioeconomic status may have business interests that benefit from migrants. But the existing, sociological literature on attitudes towards internal migrants in China (Irwin, 1999; Zhou, Wang and Chen, 2011) does not find that more persons living in households with greater income have more positive attitudes towards migrants. Note, however, that the previous literature on Chinese attitudes towards migrants have used very limited datasets and these hypotheses need a closer examination using the more comprehensive set of questions available in the 2005 CGSS, as examined in the present paper.
11. A set of explanatory variables denoting employment status are included, which includes fully-employed (FULLYEMP), and partly employed/unemployed (PART/UNEMP), as opposed to the remaining categories, which represent persons out of the labor force. As was noted above, the existing literature on attitudes towards immigrants suggests employment status is a major factor influencing attitudes. It is expected that persons who are unemployed will have stronger negative attitudes towards

migrants, relative to other categories, because of the fears that migrants may be taking their jobs. On the other hand, those who are fully-employed would have more positive attitudes since they do not have to be afraid of the competition faced by the migrants and, instead, may see migrants as being complementary inputs.

18.5 Results

The results presented in this section pull together the male and female samples of the 2005 CGSS. The next section reports the results disaggregated by sex. The probit coefficients are reported first and marginal probabilities are discussed later.

Sample Means

Table 18.1 shows the distribution of answers that were given by sample participants to the five questions they were asked to respond in the 2005 CGSS regarding their attitudes towards migrants. The table shows that a substantial portion of the Chinese urban population had negative attitudes towards the migrants. With respect to question 1, asking whether the person was willing to work with migrants, 73.2% said yes and 26.8% said no. But as additional questions were asked, the percentage with pro-migrant attitudes declines. For question 2, asking whether they would tolerate the migrants living in their neighborhood, the percentage saying yes was 67.2 percent. For question 3, asking whether they would tolerate migrants living next

Table 18.1. Attitudes of Urban Residents in China towards Migrants.

Attitudes question	% Yes	% No
1. Are you willing to work with them?	73.2%	26.8%
2. Can you tolerate them living in your neighborhood?	67.2%	32.8%
3. Can you tolerate them living next to you?	58.0%	42.0%
4. Are you willing to invite them as guests to your home?	52.0%	48.0%
5. Do you consent to your sons, daughters and relatives courting them?	42.3%	57.7%

Source: CGSS, 2015.

to them, the percentage of urbanites saying yes drops to 58 percent. For question 4, asking if they would be willing to invite the migrants as guests to their home, the percentage saying yes drops further to 52 percent, and for question 5, asking if they would consent to having their sons, daughters and relatives courting a migrant, only 42.3 percent answered yes.

The purpose of this paper is to study what factors can explain the negative attitudes towards migrants displayed in Table 18.1. The focus of the following discussion is on the results of the probit analysis for question 1. Note, however, that the signs and statistical significance of the coefficients on the various explanatory variables for each question do not tend to differ significantly by question; only their absolute value tends to vary. In any case, the results for questions 2 through 5 are presented in Feng (2016).

Table 18.2 displays the sample means for the probit equation that uses a pooled male and female sample of persons in the 2005 CGSS. The sample consists of 46.7 percent males and 53.3 percent

Table 18.2. Sample Means for Probit Equation, Pooled Male and Female Sample.

Variable	Sample mean
EDUC (Years of schooling)	9.7 years
MALE (% Male)	46.7%
AGE	44.7 years
UHUKOU (1=urban hukou, 0=rural hukou)	91.0%
ETHNIC (1=minority, 0=majority Han Chinese)	4.9%
SOCIALC (1=not close to neighbors, 5=very close)	3.4
INTENSITY (0=no contact with migrants, 3=substantial)	1.7
COASTAL (1=residence in coastal provinces, 0 otherwise)	45.6%
CENTRAL (1=residence in central provinces, 0 otherwise)	35.6%
MARITAL (1=married, 0=not married)	80.5%
FINCOME (Family income in previous year)	27,818 Yuan
FULLYEMP (1=Fully employed, 0=otherwise)	39.2%
PART/UNEMP (1=Unemployed or Part-time Employed)	22.9%
OUTLF (1=out of labor force, 0 otherwise)	37.9%
Number of observations	6,074

Source: 2005 CGSS.

females. Persons who did not answer one or more of the questions used to determine educational attainment, age, etc. were eliminated from the analysis. The number of missing observations was equal to 7.5 percent of the total sample used in this essay and so it does not constitute a serious problem. The rate of excluded observations was 7.1 percent for men and 7.8 percent for women.

As Table 18.2 shows, the average years of schooling in the sample was 9.7 years, their mean age was 44.7 years, 91 percent of them had a permanent household urban hukou (were not migrants or urbanites), 4.9 percent were in a minority ethnic or national group, 45.6% lived in the coastal provinces, and 80.5 percent were married. In terms of the index of social closeness, SOCIALC, defined with a range of values from 1 to 5, with 1 implying the person was not familiar with his or her neighbors and 5 very familiar, the average value for the sample was 3.4. For the index of INTENSITY — with extreme values equal to 0 if the person had no migrant co-workers or neighbors, and three if they had migrant co-workers, migrants living in the neighborhood and migrants living next to them — the average value was 1.7. In terms of the economic variables included in the analysis, the sample mean for annual family income was 27,818 yuan, 39.2 percent of the sample was fully-employed, 22.9 percent were either unemployed or employed part-time, and 37.9 percent were out of the labor force.

Results, Pooled Male and Female Sample

What explains positive versus negative attitudes towards migrants? Table 18.3 displays the estimated coefficients for the probit equations that include the explanatory variables identified earlier. The first column presents the results including only social, demographic and personal characteristics of the individuals while the second column adds the economic variables (family income and employment status). The dependent variable is based on the answers to question 1, equal to one if the person was willing to work with migrants and zero if he or she was not willing to work with migrants.

The first result seen in Table 18.3 is that the coefficient on education, though positive in value, is statistically insignificant at any conventional level of confidence. This contradicts the existing

Table 18.3. Probit Analysis of Pro-Migrant Attitudes with Pooled Male and Female Sample.

Explanatory variable	**Social variables coefficient, t value**	**Social + eco variables coefficient, t value**
CONSTANT	0.6915* (5.3)	0.5809* (4.0)
EDUC	0.0026 (0.5)	−0.0010 (−0.2)
MALE	0.1596* (4.3)	0.1431* (3.6)
AGE	−0.0109* (−7.9)	−0.0097* (−5.9)
UHUKOU	−0.2721* (−3.7)	−0.2664* (−3.4)
ETHNIC	0.0235 (0.3)	−0.0065 (−0.1)
SOCIALC	0.0354** (1.9)	0.0414** (2.1)
INTENSITY	0.3807* (21.9)	0.3805* (20.9)
MARITAL	0.0636 (1.3)	0.0588 (1.1)
COASTAL	−0.2521* (−4.8)	−0.2877* (−5.2)
CENTRAL	−0.1505* (−2.8)	−0.1525* (−2.7)
FINCOME	—	0.00015* (2.6)
FULLY EMPLOYED	—	0.1097** (2.1)
PART/UNEMPLOYED	—	0.0541 (1.0)
No. of Observations	6,074	5,642
Chi-Square Statistic	715 (99% confidence level)	690 (99% confidence level)

Note: t statistic in parenthesis. One star represents statistical significance at a 99% level of confidence and two stars at a 95% level.

international literature, which finds that increased educational attainment is usually associated with positive attitudes towards migrants. However, it is consistent with the limited literature that has examined opinions about migrants in China (Irwin, 1999; Zhou, Wang and Chen, 2011).

What could explain this result? One hypothesis, mentioned earlier, is based on the power of education to reduce ignorance and prejudice against migrants. In countries subject to immigration, governments in the recipient nations often emphasize the importance of assimilating the migrant population, a task that is spearheaded by the school system. So, the curricula of schools include cross-cultural, inclusive modules, and the teachers are trained in culturally sensitive methods, which are then communicated to children of all races and ethnicities in schools. But because migrants are not from any particular ethnic or national minority group in China, the education system in urban China has not incorporated into its curriculum or in its teacher training any components that deal with the treatment of migrants. In fact, since for decades the government's official policies have effectively discriminated against the urban migrant population, including the provision of schooling for the children of migrant workers, one could argue that this segregation may have contributed to the absence of more positive attitudes towards migrants among the urban Chinese.

Is gender a significant factor in attitudes towards migrants? Table 18.3 shows that men tend to have much more positive attitudes towards migrants, with the coefficient on the MALE variable in the first column of Table 18.3 being statistically significant at the 99 percent level of confidence. This again does not support the economic approach, which would argue that since most migrants are male, they would be most likely to compete with male urbanites — holding other things constant, including education — and urban males would therefore have more negative attitudes towards them. Instead, the results in Table 18.3 support arguments that have been made by sociologists in relation to the gender and migration phenomenon in China. First, social conventions that frown against urban women having friendships with migrant men would imply that urban women would be more segregated from most migrants and this could generate more negative attitudes towards them. Second, sociologists argue that the marriage market in urban China favors urban men marrying rural women, which might make urban men have more positive attitudes towards the migrants while urban women, who would not consider migrant men as an attractive marriage possibility, would have more negative attitudes towards them. These hypotheses seem to be supported by the results of the research in this dissertation.

Table 18.3 reports that older urban residents have more strongly negative attitudes towards migrants. This tends to contradict the simple economic approach, which argues that since migrants tend to be young workers, the urban young population would be more fearful of competition with them in urban labor markets, which would generate negative attitudes towards the migrants, holding other things constant. The alternative, more sociological, hypothesis is that younger urbanites may have been exposed to more diverse urban environments and, therefore, would be less ignorant about migrants, and have more positive attitudes towards them, everything else the same.

Do migrants have more positive attitudes towards other migrants? One would expect that social and family links as well as solidarity sentiments would make migrants have more positive attitudes towards other migrants, but some of the immigration literature suggests that because of potential labor market competition, migrants could have more negative attitudes towards other migrants. In Table 18.3, the variable UHUKOU is equal to one if the person had an urban hukou and zero if he or she had a rural hukou. As shown, the coefficient on this variable is negative and statistically significant at the 99 percent confidence level, suggesting that rural migrants do have more positive attitudes towards fellow migrants than urban residents.

Table 18.3 also examines how being part of an ethnic and national minority might affect attitudes towards migrants. The variable ETHNIC is equal to one if the person is a member of a minority and its coefficient, although positive in column 1, is not statistically significant at conventional levels of confidence, suggesting minority groups do not appear to have more positive or negative views towards migrants, holding other things constant.

People who are more familiar with their neighborhood are bound to be more informed about the actual behavior and situation of migrants and less likely to follow more ignorant, stereotypical views of this population. That is why the coefficient on the variable SOCIALC is expected to be positive, being associated with more positive attitudes towards migrants. The values of this variable ranges from 1 to 5, with a one associated with a person who is not "familiar with their neighbors" and 5 is "very familiar" with their neighbors. As reported in Table 18.3, the probit coefficient is positive and statistically significant at the 99 percent level of confidence, confirming the expectation that people who are more familiar with their neighborhoods have more positive attitudes towards migrants.

Table 18.3 reports the effects of the variable INTENSITY, an index that varies from 1 to 3, with a value of 3 meaning that the person has migrants as coworkers, in the neighborhood and living next to him or her, while a zero means that the person has no migrants present at work or in the neighborhood or vicinity. Based on the literature on attitudes towards immigrants, one would expect to find that an increased presence of migrants would have a negative impact on attitudes because (1) it may generate greater fears that the migrants will take jobs away and reduce wages, (2) it may trigger prejudicial fears that the urban environment (cleanliness, safety, etc.) will deteriorate because of the visibility of the migrants. But, as was explained in a previous section, the existing international literature is based on attitudes towards immigrants, where racial and ethnic prejudices play a major role. These phenomena may not therefore apply to internal migrants in China, whose contribution to Chinese economic growth is widely recognized, and are generally part of the Han Chinese majority. By contrast, an increased presence of migrants may be associated with prosperity by urbanites, triggering more positive attitudes towards them. Also, an increased migrant presence may lead to greater face-to-face contact with them and may reduce misconceptions and stereotypes about them. Indeed, the coefficient on the INTENSITY variable is both positive and statistically significant at the 99 percent level of confidence, confirming these hypotheses for the case of internal migrants in China.

The variable MARITAL is a dummy variable equal to one if the person is married and zero otherwise. Based on the previous literature, the hypothesis is that this variable is associated with more negative attitudes towards migrants because married persons tend to have greater demands on their economic situation, especially if they have children or relatives living with them, and this can trigger fears that the migrants will take jobs from them. This does not appear to be supported by the data: the coefficient on MARITAL is not statistically significant at conventional levels of confidence and, in any case, is positive.

In contrast to some of the results obtained so far, the conventional wisdom based on the previous literature seems to prevail in the results for the explanatory variables, COASTAL and CENTRAL, which are equal to one if a person resides in provinces in these geographical areas. The hypothesis, based on the previous literature, is that both of these variables should have negative signs because these provinces have been inundated with migrants and urban residents in them may fear that the migrants will take jobs from them or lower wages. The coefficients on both, COASTAL and CENTRAL, are negative and statistically significant at the 99 percent confidence level.

The second column of Table 18.3 presents the results of adding a set of crucial economic variables that are hypothesized to have an impact on attitudes towards migrants. These are: annual family income (FINCOME), a dummy variable equal to one if the person was fully-employed and zero otherwise (FULLYEMP), and another dummy variable equal to one if the person was partly employed/unemployed and zero otherwise (PART/UNEMP), as opposed to the remaining categories, which represent persons out of the labor force. Note that, as one compares columns 1 and 2, the signs of the coefficients on the statistically significant variables discussed earlier do not change, and the value of the coefficients remains of the same order. So, the following discussion focuses on the results obtained on the economic variables added to the equation.

The first of these variables is annual family income (FINCOME). The existing international literature tends to find that higher socioeconomic status is associated with more positive attitudes towards migrants because (1) it reduces fears about possible negative impacts of migrants on jobs and wages, and/or (2) those with higher socioeconomic status may have business interests that benefit from migrants. But the sociological literature on attitudes towards internal migrants in China (Irwin, 1999; Zhou, Wang and Chen, 2011) does not find that persons living in households with greater income have more positive attitudes towards migrants. They explain this result by arguing that urban populations with higher socioeconomic status may have developed a sub-culture of privilege that distances them from migrants. But the previous literature have had very limited datasets available. What does an analysis of the 2005 CGSS find?

The results in the second column of Table 18.3 support the hypothesis that greater family income is associated with positive attitudes towards migrants, with the coefficient on FINCOME positive and statistically significant at the 99 percent level of confidence.

The coefficient on the fully-employed variable is positive and statistically significant at the 95 percent level of confidence. This is consistent with the hypothesis that the fully-employed should have more positive attitudes towards migrants since they do not have to be afraid of the competition faced by the migrants and, instead, may see migrants as being complementary inputs. The coefficient on the unemployed/partially employed variable, is positive, but it is not statistically significant at conventional confidence levels.

The coefficients in Table 18.3 do not provide a measure of how each explanatory variable affects the likelihood of pro-migrant attitudes towards migrants, as they need to be combined with the values of the explanatory variables in order to calculate marginal effects. Table 18.4 presents the marginal effects calculated at the sample means, as provided by the MARGINS command in STATA. These show how the probability of having more positive attitudes towards migrants is altered when the explanatory variable changes, holding other variables constant. The variables MALE, UHUKOU, INTENSITY, COASTAL, CENTER AND FULLYEMP appear to provide the stronger effects on the probability of employment, per unit changed in the explanatory variable. For instance, the second column of Table 18.4 shows that being female tends to reduce the probability of having positive attitudes towards immigrants by 0.0418.

The result that gender has a significant effect on attitudes towards migrants leads to the question as to what factors may explain these differences. Do education, age or other variables operate differently in affecting the opinions of men and women towards migrants? The next section examines this issue.

Results, Male and Female Samples Disaggregated

Table 18.5 displays the differences in attitudes towards migrants on the basis of gender, as represented by the responses on the five questions present in the 2005 CGSS. In all cases, women tend to have

Table 18.4. Marginal Probabilities of Pro-Migrant Attitudes with Pooled Male and Female Sample.

Explanatory variable	Equation: Social variables marginal effect (dy/dx)	Equation: Social + eco variables marginal effect (dy/dx)
EDUC	0.0008 (0.5)	−0.0003 (−0.2)
MALE	0.0469* (4.3)	0.0418* (−3.7)
AGE	−0.0032* (−8.0)	−0.0028* (−5.9)
UHUKOU	−0.0799* (−3.7)	−0.0778* (−3.4)
ETHNIC	0.0069 (0.3)	−0.0019 (−0.1)
SOCIALC	0.0104** (1.9)	0.0121** (2.1)
INTENSITY	0.1119* (24.6)	0.1111* (23.5)
MARITAL	0.0187 (1.3)	0.0172 (1.2)
COASTAL	−0.0741* (−4.8)	−0.0841* (−5.2)
CENTRAL	−0.0442* (−2.8)	−0.0445* (−2.7)
FINCOME	—	0.00005* (2.6)
FULLY EMPLOYED	—	0.0320** (2.1)
PART/UNEMPLOYED	—	0.0158 (1.0)
No. of Observations	6,074	5,642

Note: t statistic in parenthesis. One star represents statistical significance at a 99% level of confidence and two stars at a 95% level.

Source: 2005 CGSS.

Table 18.5. Attitudes of Urban Residents in China towards Migrants: By Gender.

Attitudes question	Male %Yes	Male %No	Female %Yes	Female %No
1. Are you willing to work with them?	76.2%	23.6%	70.4%	29.6%
2. Can you tolerate them living in your neighborhood?	69.5%	30.5%	65.3%	34.7%
3. Can you tolerate them living next to you?	59.8%	40.2%	56.5%	43.5%
4. Are you willing to invite them as guests to your home?	54.1%	45.9%	49.6%	50.4%
5. Do you consent to your sons, daughters and relatives courting them?	44.8%	55.2%	40.2%	59.8%

Source: CGSS, 2005.

Table 18.6. Sample Means for Probit Equation, Separate Male and Female Samples.

Variable	Sample mean	
	Male	Female
EDUC (Years of schooling)	10.3 years	9.1 years
AGE	45.0 years	44.4 years
UHUKOU (1=urban hukou, 0=rural hukou)	92.0%	90.2%
SOCIALC (1=not close to neighbors, 5=very close)	3.4	3.5
INTENSITY (0=no contact with migrants, 3=substantial)	1.7	1.6
COASTAL (1=in coastal provinces, 0 otherwise)	45.7%	45.6%
CENTRAL (1=residence in central province, 0 otherwise)	35.4%	35.8%
MARITAL (1=married, 0=not married)	79.7%	81.3%
FINCOME (Family income in previous year)	29,450 yuan	26,388 yuan
FULLYEMP (1=Fully employed, 0=otherwise)	47.7%	31.8%
PART/UNEMP (1=Unemployed or Part-time Employed)	21.0%	24.5%
OUTLF (1=out of labor force, 0 otherwise)	31.3%	43.7%
Number of observations	2,634	3,008

Source: 2005 CGSS.

less positive attitudes towards migrants. For example, in response to question 1, "are you willing to work with them (migrants)," 76.2 percent of men answered yes while 70.4 percent of women did. Similar outcomes are obtained for the other questions.

As before, the focus in this paper will be on explaining the answers to question 1. However, note that the sign of the coefficients obtained do not vary significantly depending on the question analyzed, although the marginal effects may change (see Feng, 2016).

The sample means for the variables used in the probit equations disaggregated by gender are presented in Table 18.6. These sample means do not diverge much between the two groups, although men do have 1.2 more years of schooling, women have about 90 percent of the average family income men have, and there is an almost 16 percentage point difference in the percentage of fully-employed in the male and female sample, with men having the substantially higher proportion,

Table 18.7. Probit Analysis of Pro-Migrant Attitudes: Separate Male and Female Samples.

Explanatory variable	Equation for males coefficient, t value	Equation for females coefficient, t value
CONSTANT	0.9285* (4.0)	0.4792* (2.6)
EDUC	0.0024 (0.3)	−0.0060 (−0.8)
AGE	−0.0103* (−4.0)	−0.0098* (−4.3)
UHUKOU	−0.2711** (−2.2)	−0.2660* (−2.7)
SOCIALC	0.0111 (0.4)	0.0668* (2.5)
INTENSITY	0.3927* (14.4)	0.3713* (15.2)
MARITAL	0.0340 (0.4)	0.0830 (1.2)
COASTAL	−0.3166* (−3.9)	−0.2732* (−3.7)
CENTER	−0.1756** (−2.1)	−0.1403 (−1.9)
FINCOME	0.00003* (2.5)	0.000007 (1.0)
FULLY EMPLOYED	−0.0336 (−0.4)	0.2203* (3.1)
PART/UNEMPLOYED	−0.1535 (−1.7)	0.1928* (2.7)
No. of Observations	2,634	3,008
Chi-Square Statistic	311 (99% confidence level)	378 (99% confidence level)

Note: t statistic in parenthesis. One star represents statistical significance at a 99% level of confidence and two stars at a 95% level.

Source: 2005 CGSS.

which is also reflected in much higher rates of women out of the labor force when compared to men. Despite these differences, the values of the sample means for most of the other determinants of attitudes are similar for men and women, so one would expect that the less positive attitudes towards migrants by women may be due to the impact these variables have on attitudes (differences in the coefficients and marginal effects of the explanatory variables).

Table 18.7 shows the coefficients of the estimated probit equations disaggregated by gender and Table 18.8 presents marginal effects. Several variables have different signs in the male and female equations. Education is one of them, although the coefficients are not statistically significant at conventional levels of confidence. In the male equation, the coefficient is positive while in the female equation it is negative, suggesting that, for women, higher education tends to be associated with more negative attitudes towards migrants. For men,

Table 18.8. Marginal Probabilities of Pro-Migrant Attitudes with Separate Male and Female Samples.

Explanatory variable	**Equation for males marginal effect (dy/dx)**	**Equation for females marginal effect (dy/dx)**
EDUC	0.0007 (0.3)	−0.0018 (−0.8)
AGE	−0.0028* (−4.1)	−0.0030* (−4.4)
UHUKOU	−0.0741** (−2.1)	−0.0816* (−2.7)
SOCIALC	0.0030 (0.4)	0.0205* (2.5)
INTENSITY	0.1073* (16.1)	0.1138* (17.0)
MARITAL	0.0093 (0.4)	0.0254 (1.2)
COASTAL	−0.0865* (−3.9)	−0.0838* (−3.8)
CENTER	−0.0480* (−2.1)	−0.0430 (−1.9)
FINCOME	0.000007* (2.5)	0.000002 (1.1)
FULLY EMPLOYED	−0.009 (−0.4)	0.0676* (3.1)
PART/UNEMPLOYED	−0.0420 (−1.7)	0.0591* (2.7)
No. of Observations	2,634	3,008

Note: t statistic in parenthesis. One star represents statistical significance at a 99% level of confidence and two stars at a 95% level.

Source: 2005 CGSS.

the opposite holds, but the impact is not statistically significant. These results continue to support the conclusion arrived earlier that increased schooling is not reducing negative attitudes towards internal migrants in urban China.

The labor force status variables also appear to have different effects for men and women. For men, being fully employed — and to some extent unemployed/partly employed — have negative effects on attitudes towards migrants, although the coefficients are not statistically significant. For women, the coefficients on both of these variables are positive and statistically significant at the 99 percent level of confidence. The implication is that, for men, persons who participate in the labor force tend to have a more negative view of migrants while, for women, being in the labor force is linked to more positive attitudes towards migrants. This result is consistent with men having a more competitive labor market position relative to migrants (as if they were substitutes in production) while women do not see themselves as competing with migrants in the labor force (as if they were complements in production).

18.6 Conclusions

This paper has examined the relative significance of some of the key factors that influence the attitudes of urban Chinese citizens towards migrants. Using survey data from the 2005 CGSS, the role of educational attainment, age, family income, labor market status, and a set of other variables that potentially influence attitudes towards migrants was analyzed. Estimating probit equations of the likelihood that the respondents in the sample had positive attitudes towards migrants, the research shows the connections between a range of explanatory variables and these attitudes.

The research carried out in this paper indicates that educational attainment does not dampen negative attitudes towards migrants in China. This is different from the results obtained by previous international research on attitudes toward immigrants, in which education has been found to have a negative influence on anti-migrant sentiments. Even when the analysis is disaggregated on the basis of gender there is no statistically significant connection between increased schooling and positive attitudes towards migrants.

The conclusion that increased schooling is not associated with more positive attitudes towards migrants in China has serious implications about educational institutions in the country. At an international level, in many countries and cities that receive substantial numbers of immigrants, governments emphasize the importance of assimilating migrants, who are often of diverse ethnic and racial groups. This task is spearheaded by the school system, through cross-cultural curricula and teacher training. Those with more education thus receive information that combats stereotypes and prejudice. But in China, because migrants are not from any particular ethnic or national minority group in China, the education system does not appear to have incorporated into its curriculum or in its teacher training any components that deal with the treatment of migrants. And government policies — such as the hukou system — that have effectively discriminated against the urban migrant population, even making difficult the schooling of the children of migrant workers, may have contributed to the absence of more positive attitudes towards migrants among more educated urban populations.

The development of a plan to incorporate migrant-sensitive curricula and teacher training into schools and college may be essential to diminish negative attitudes towards the migrant population. Unfortunately, some aspects of the existing curriculum in China's schools clash with such reforms and would need to be drastically altered. More specifically, the suzhi 素质 (personal quality) discourse which was gradually adopted by the school system, presumably to make the population "better-behaved," "more refined," or "higher-quality" (see Murphy, 2004), has used migrants as a negative stereotype, portraying them as uncultured, ignorant and unrefined people whose behavioral characteristics should be avoided at all costs. As Anagnost (2004) reports: "The discourse of population quality (renkou suzhi) may have first appeared in the 1980s, in state documents...that attributed China's failure to modernize to the "low quality" (suzhi di) of its population, especially in rural areas...By the early 1990s it became a key term in the party-state's policy statements...The discourse of suzhi appears most elaborated in relation to...the rural migrant, which exemplifies suzhi in its apparent absence." Any educational policy changes intended to reduce negative attitudes towards migrants should eliminate the targeting of migrants as representing an uneducated, uncultured population, showing them instead as being an essential building block of China's economy.

The analysis in this paper also suggests that the hukou system that has governed migration policy in China for decades needs to be reformed in order to end the institutional marginalization of migrants in urban areas. As noted before, a person's hukou (registration) is determined by his/her place of birth and it is difficult to have an official change of hukou from rural to urban areas. Since social benefits, including public education and health benefits, are attached to the person's hukou, the system has excluded migrants from having the same rights as urban residents. Experiments to modify the hukou system have emerged in some areas, such as Guangdong. And in

2014, China's State Council announced a set of hukou policy reforms intended to allow migrants greater access to public services in cities, such as in education, health care and social security. But the reform is gradual and favors towns and small cities while in larger cities (above 3 to 5 million in population), changes in registration will remain difficult for migrants. A deeper reform needs to be implemented.

On a more positive note, the research in this paper finds that as migrant presence grows in their workplaces and neighborhoods, as detected by respondents in the 2005 CGSS survey, urban residents actually become more positive in their attitudes towards migrants. This contradicts some of the previous literature, which finds that an increased presence of migrants worsens attitudes towards them because it engenders fears that they will take jobs away from natives or that the urban environment (cleanliness, safety, etc.) will deteriorate. But the multivariate analysis carried out in this paper does not find these fears in China. Instead, possibly because migrants are seen as providing a valuable contribution to Chinese economic growth, and perhaps because they are generally part of the Han Chinese majority, an increased concentration of migrants does not worsen attitudes towards them.

Gender is found to have a significant connection to attitudes towards migrants. Men tend to have much more positive attitudes. This is again different from the existing literature, which finds that since most migrants are male, they compete with male urbanites and generate more negative attitudes towards them. Instead, in urban China, perhaps because social conventions frown against urban women having friendships with migrant men, or because the marriage market in urban China favors urban men marrying rural women, men tend to have more positive attitudes towards the migrants than urban women.

References

Amemiya, Takeshi (1995). *Advanced Econometrics*, Cambridge: Harvard University Press.

Amnesty International (2007). *The People's Republic of China Internal Migrants: Discrimination and Abuse.*

Anagnost, Ann (2004). "The Corporeal Politics of Quality (Suzhi)," *Public Culture*, 16 (2): 157–177.

Bauer, Tomas K., Magnus Lofstrom, and Klaus F. Zimmermann (2000). "Immigration Policy, Assimilation of Immigrants and Natives' Sentiments toward Immigrants: Evidence from 12 OECD-Countries," *Swedish Economic Policy Review* 7: 11–53.

Benhabib, Jesse (1996). "On the Political Economy of Immigration." *Economic European Review* 40: 1737–1743

Bodvarsson, Orn B. and Hendrik Van den Berg (2009). *The Economics of Immigration: Theory and Policy*, Berlin: Springer-Verlag.

Card, David (1990). "The Impact of the Mariel Boatlift on the Miami Labor Market," *Industrial and Labor Relations Review* 43: 245–257.

Card, David, Christian Dustmann and Ian P. Preston (2012). "Immigration, Wages and Compositional Amenities," *NORFACE Migration Discussion Paper No. 2012-13.*

Chen, Yuanyuan and Shuaizhang Feng (2012). "Access to Public Schools and the Education of Migrant Children in China," *IZA Discussion Paper No. 6853, Institute for the Study of Labor, Berlin, September.*

Chen, Yu (2011). "Rural Migrants in Urban China: Characteristics and Challenges to Public Policy," *Local Economy*, 26: 325–336.

Clemens, Michael (2013). "What do we Know about Skilled Migration and Development?," *Migration Policy Institute Policy Brief, September.*

Demurger, Sylvie, Marc Gurgand, Li Shi and Yue Ximing (2009). "Migrants as Second-Class Workers in Urban China? A Decomposition Analysis." *Journal of Comparative Economics*, 37 (4): 610–28.

Dustmann, Christian and Ian P. Preston (2001). "Attitudes to Ethnic Minorities, Ethnic Context and Location Decisions," *Economic Journal* 111: 353–373.

Facchini, Giovanni and Anna Maria Mayda (2012). "Individual Attitudes towards Skilled Migration: An Empirical Analysis across Countries," *The World Economy* 35: 183–196.

Facchini, Giovanni, Anna Maria Mayda and Prachi Mishra (2011). "Do Interest Groups Affect U.S. Immigration Policy?," *Journal of International Economics* 85: 114–128.

Fend, Hu (2014). "Risk Attitudes and Self-Employment in China," *China and the World Economy*, 22 (3): 101–120, May–June.

Feng, Na (2016). *Essays on Education, Political Movements and Income Growth in China.* Ann Arbor, Michigan: UMI Publishing.

Gagnon, Jason, Theodora Xenogiani and Chunbing Xing (2009). "Are all Migrants Really Worse off in Urban Labor Markets: New Empirical Evidence from China?" *OECD Development Centre Working Paper No. 278.*

Gang, Ira N. and Francisco L. Rivera-Batiz (1994). "Labor Market Effects of Immigration in the United States and Europe: Substitution vs. Complementarity," *Journal of Population Economics* 7: 157–75. (a)

Gang, Ira N. and Francisco L. Rivera-Batiz (1994) "Unemployment and Attitudes towards Foreigners in Germany," in Gunter Steinmann and Ralph Urich (eds.) *Economic Consequences of Immigration in Germany*, Germany: Physica-Verlag, 121–154. (b)

Gang, Ira N., Francisco L. Rivera-Batiz and Myeong-Su Yun (2010). "Changes in Attitudes toward Immigrants in Europe: Before and After the Fall of the Berlin Wall," in Gil S. Epstein and Ira N. Gang (eds.) *Migration and Culture*, Bingley: Emerald Group Publishing, 649–676.

Gang, Ira N., Francisco L. Rivera-Batiz and Myeong-Su Yun (2013). "Economic Strain, Education and Attitudes towards Foreigners in the European Union," *Review of International Economics*, 21 (2): 177–190.

Giuletti, C., M. Guzi, Z. Zha and K. Zimmermann (2012). "Social Networks and the Labor Market Outcomes of Rural to Urban Migrants in China," *paper presented at the Conference of the European Association of Labor Economists.*

Goodkind, D. and L. West (2002). "China's Floating Population: Definitions, Data and Recent Findings," *Urban Studies*, 39 (2): 237–250.

Guan, Jian (2010). "Stigma toward the Rural-to-Urban Migrant in China: A Qualitative Study," *Interpersona*, 4 (1): 21–34.

Hairong, Yan (2008). *New Masters, New Servants: Migration, Development and Women Workers in China*, Durham: Duke University Press, 2008.

Huhe, Narisong (2014). "Understanding the Multilevel Foundation of Social Trust in Rural China: Evidence from the China General Social Survey," *Social Science Quarterly*, 95 (2): 581–597.

Huafeng, Zhang (2010). "The Hukou System's Constraints on Migrant Workers' Job Mobility in Chinese Cities," *China Economic Review*, 21 (1): 51–64.

Irwin, J. (1999). "Shanghai's Migrant Millions," *UNESCO Courier*, June, 32–35.

Kondo, Ayako and Dongshu Ou (2010). "In Search of a Better Life: The Occupational Attainment of Rural and Urban Migrants in China," *Working Paper No. 793, Institute of Social and Economic Research, Osaka, Japan, September.*

Kessler, Alan E. and Gary P. Freeman (2005). "Public Opinion in the EU on Immigration from Outside the Community," *Journal of Common Market Studies* 43: 825–850.

Krueger, Alan B. and Jorn-Steffen Pischke (1997). "A Statistical Analysis of Crime Against Foreigners in Unified Germany," *Journal of Human Resources* 32: 182–209.

Lai, Fang, Chengfang Liu, Renfu Luo, Linxiu Zhang, Xiaochen Ma, Yujie Bai, Brian Sharbono and Scot Rozelle (2014). "The Education of China's Migrant Children: The Missing Link in China's Education System," *International Journal of Educational Development*, 37 (1): 68–77. July.

Leng, Lee (2012). "Decomposing Wage Differentials between Migrant Workers and Urban Workers in Urban China's Labor Markets," *Journal of Comparative Economics*, 23: 337–340.

Li, B.Q. (2006). "Floating Population or Urban Citizens? Status, Social Provision and Circumstances of Rural-Urban Migrants in China," *Social Policy and Administration*, 2: 174–195.

Long, Wenjin, Simon Appleton and Lina Song (2013). "Job Contact Networks and Wages of Rural-Urban Migrants in China," *IZA Discussion Paper No. 7577, Institute for the Study of Labor, Berlin, August.*

Mayda, Anna Maria (2006). "Who is Against Immigration?: A Cross-Country Investigation of Individual Attitudes toward Immigrants," *Review of Economics and Statistics*, 88: 510–530.

Meng, Xin and Junsen Zhang (2001). "The Two-Tier Labor Market in Urban China: Occupational Segregation and Wage Differentials between Urban Residents and Rural Migrants in Shanghai," *Journal of Comparative Economics*, 29 (3): 485–504.

Murphy, R. (2004). "Turning Peasants into Modern Chinese," *The China Quarterly*, 177 (1): 1– 20.

Nielsen, Ingrid, Chris Nyland, Russell Smyth, Mingqiong Zhang and Cherrie Jiuhua Zhu (2006). "Effects of Intergroup Contact on Attitudes of Chinese Urban Residents to Migrant Workers," *Urban Studies*, 43 (3): 475–490.

Ortega, Francesc (2005). "Immigration Quotas and Skill Upgrading," *Journal of Public Economics*, 89: 1841–1863.

Ottaviano, Gianmarco I. P. and Giovanni Peri (2012). "Rethinking the Effects of Immigration on Wages," *Journal of the European Economic Association* 10: 152–197.

Peilin, Li and Tian Feng (2011). "The New Generation of Migrant Workers: Social Attitudes and Behavioral Choices," *Chinese Journal of Sociology*, 31 (3): 1–23.

Qin, He and Al Xiaoquing (2012). "A Study of the Wage Gap Faced by Migrant Workers from the Perspective of Industry Segmentation," *Working Paper*, Beijing Union University.

Quheng, Deng and Bjorn Gustafsson (2006). "China's Lesser Known Migrants." IZA *Discussion Paper No.2152, Institute for the Study of Labor, Berlin.*

Rivera-Batiz, Francisco L. and Selig L. Sechzer (1991), "Substitution and Complementarity between Immigrant and Native Labor in the United States," in F. Rivera-Batiz, S. Sechzer and I. Gang, (eds.) *U.S. Immigration Policy Reform in the 1980s: A Preliminary Assessment.* New York Praeger Publishers: 89–116.

Roberts, K. (2001). "The Determinants of Job Choice by Rural Labor Migrants in Shanghai," *China Economic Review*, 12 (1): 15–39.

Roberts, K. (2002). "Rural Migrants in Urban China: Willing Workers, Invisible Residents," *Asia Pacific Business Review*, 8: 141–158.

Scheve, Kenneth F. and Matthew J. Slaughter (2001). "Labor Market Competition and Individual Preferences over Immigration Policy", *Review of Economics and Statistics* 83: 133–145.

Shi, Li (2008). "Rural Migrant Workers in China: Scenario, Challenges and Public Policy," *Working Paper No. 89, International Labour Organization, Geneva.*

Solinger, D. (1999) *Contesting Citizenship in Urban China: Peasant Migrants, the State and the Logic of the Market.* Berkeley, CA: University of California Press.

Tan, Guangyu (2010). "Under the Same Blue Sky? Inequity in Migrant Children's Education in China," *Current Issues in Comparative Education*, 12 (2): 31–40. Spring.

Wang, Xiaozhou, R. Oropesa and G. Firebaugh (2013). "Permanent Migrants to Cities in China: Hukou Origin and Earnings among Men in an Era of Transformation," *Migration and Development*, 2 (1): 37–56.

Wang, Haining, Zhiming Cheng and Russel Smyth (2013). "Compensating Wage and Income Differentials for Occupational Risk: Migrant Workers in China's Pearl River Delta," *Working Paper, Department of Economics, Monash University.*

Wang, F. and X. Zuo (1999). "Inside China's Institutional Barriers and Opportunities for Urban Migrants," *American Economic Review*, 89: 276–280.

Wang, Yu and Christine Schwartz (2015). "Intermarriage and Social Exclusion in China," *Working Paper No. 2015-01, Center for Demography and Ecology, University of Wisconsin at Madison.*

Wong, D.F.K. and H.X. Song (2008). "The Resilience of Migrant Workers in Shanghai, China: The Roles of Migration Stress and Meaning of Migration," *International Journal of Social Psychiatry*, 54 (1): 1–31.

Wong, D.F.K., Y.L. Chang and X.S. He (2007). "Rural Migrant Workers in Urban China: Living a Marginalized Life," *International Journal of Social Welfare*, 16 (1): 32–40.

Xu, Qingwen and Neal Palmer (2011). "Migrant Workers' Communities in China: Relationships among Social Networks, Life Satisfaction and Political Participation," *Psychosocial Intervention*, 20 (3): 281–294.

Yiu, L. (2010). "Education, Social Stratification and Social Attitudes in Urban China," *paper presented at the Comparative and International Education Society Annual Conference, Chicago, Illinois.*

Yu, Xueying (2014). "Is Environment a 'City Thing' in China? Rural-Urban Differences in Environmental Attitudes," *Journal of Environmental Psychology*, 38 (1): 39–48, June.

Zhao, Yue (2005). "Objective and Subjective Social Distance to Migrants in Urban China," *paper presented at the Population Association of America, Washington, D.C.*

Zhao, Y. (1997). "Labor Migration and Returns to Rural Education in China," *American Journal of Agricultural Economics*, *79*, 1278–1287.

Zhou, Y., Y. Wang and W. Chen (2011). "Unfinished Promise: Socioeconomic Status and Attitudes towards Equality for Migrant Workers in Urban China," *Working Paper, Prairie Metropolis Centre, University of Alberta.*

Zhou, Dong (2014). "The Long Term Impacts of the Cultural Revolution on Economic Performance of Urban Migrants in China," *Working Paper, Department of Economics, University of California at Riverside.*

Part 6

Interregional Migration and Geography

Chapter 19

Modeling Urban Agglomeration: Producer Services, Linkage Externalities and Specialization Economies*

19.1 Introduction

The determinants of agglomeration in space have been a central topic in urban and regional economic theory for centuries, from the early work of Adam Smith [1776, Book I, Chapters I–III] associating city size with increased trade and economic growth, to the recent literature connecting urban growth with consumer heterogeneity [see Fujita and Rivera-Batiz (1988)]. One factor that the empirical evidence suggests is important but has not received much attention in the theoretical literature is the role played by business services in generating external economies of scale in urban industrial production. As Henderson [1986, p. 271] states: "in a larger city a manufacturing firm may be able to contract out various service and specialized production activities to firms specialized in those activities," an advantage that is not available to firms located in small

*This chapter was originally published in William G. Vogt and Marvin H. Mickle, eds., *Modeling and Simulation, Vol. 19*, North Carolina: Instrument Society of America, 1988, pp. 113–119.

This chapter was written while I was a Visiting Associate Professor at the Regional Science Department of the University of Pennsylvania.

towns. The increased productivity that this allows induces firms to agglomerate. Evidence from the United States and Brazil suggests that this kind of external economy — referred to as 'linkage externality' by Krugman (1987) — substantially explains agglomeration economies [see Henderson (1983, 1986), Segel (1976) and Moomaw (1985)]. It is purpose of this paper to provide a simple urban-theoretical model illustrating the role played by specialized business services in generating linkage externalities and agglomeration in space.

We conceptualize the business services sector as supplying an array of specialized, differentiated intermediate inputs within a market structure of Chamberlinian monopolistic competition. We thus follow recent literature formalizing the role played by differentiated intermediate products in production [see Ethier (1982), Helpman and Krugman (1986, chapter 11), Romer (1986, 1987), and Rivera-Batiz (1988b)]. In particular, the present paper constitutes a simplified version of Rivera-Batiz (1988c), where the present paper emphasizes exclusively the production aspects of agglomeration while ignoring the consumption agglomeration effects discussed in Rivera-Batiz (1988c).

19.2 Producer Services and Urban Linkage Externalities

We begin by describing an urban area with an exogenously-given labor force, L. Geographically, the city consists of a center (export node) around which lies a circular central business district (CBD) enclosing the city's industrial sector. The CBD is assumed to have a radius equal to $\hat{u}$, so that the amount of space available for industrial use is equal to $\pi\hat{u}^2$. Outside the CBD lies a circular area where households reside. The total amount of space for residential use is equal to $\pi(u^2 - \hat{u}^2)$, where u denotes the city's outside boundary.

Urban industrial output, X_m, is assumed to result from the use of labor, L_m, capital and/or space, K_m, and a set n of producer services. The latter are differentiated and sold under monopolistic competition. Product differentiation among service sector firms arises from the fact that the industrial sector demands a wide array of different types of services requiring highly specialized tasks. Thus any modern industrial complex needs maintenance services that include tasks relating to electricity, water and heating, office equipment, including computer and Xerox machine servicing, industrial machinery service and maintenance, transport services, banking and insurance, legal services, and so on. Indeed, the degree of specialization of the tasks demanded by the industrial sector is so large and diverse that the number of services actually supplied by the market is always much smaller than the potential one. There is, as a consequence, always scope for further specialization.

The production function for the city's industrial good is assumed to be given by:

$$X_m = L_m^a K_m^b V_m^c, \quad a + b + c = 1 \tag{1}$$

where X_m is industrial production, K_m we will assume — for convenience — to consist of industrial space, the parameters a, b and c are positive fractions, and V_m is a sub-production function of the array of business services used by industry.

For simplicity, the sub-production function V_m is assumed to be of the CES type:

$$V_m = \sum_{i=1}^{n} S_i^{\sigma}, \quad 0 < \sigma < 1 \tag{2}$$

with S_i equal to the amount of each service demanded by industry and σ a parameter to be interpreted shortly.

Given the symmetric way in which services enter the production function, V_m, and the similarity of their cost, and therefore supply, functions — to be established below — the amount of each service that industry will purchase is identical. As a result, the aggregate quantity demanded of business services is equal to $S_m = nS_i$. Equation (2) can therefore be transformed into:

$$V_m = S_m n^{(1-\sigma)/\sigma}. \tag{3}$$

Inserting this expression into equation (1), and some manipulation, yields:

$$X_m = n^{c(1-\sigma)/\sigma} L_m^a K_m^b S_m^c. \tag{4}$$

Equation (4) states that urban industrial production is related to the quantities of labor, capital and producer services demanded and to the number of producer services used.

That the number of services used by industry has an effect an output independent of that of their quantity demanded is an outcome of the form of the sub-production function for services, V_m, and reflects the presence of specialization economies in the use of producer services. A rise in the number of producer services available increases the output of industrial goods, even if the industry keeps their total quantity demanded the same (S_m constant), because the services used become more specialized and, consequently, more effective, resulting in smoother production and increased output.

Note that the form of (4) is such that it can be interpreted as representing a standard Cobb-Douglas production function with inputs given by labor, space and services, and a shift parameter equal to $n^{c(1-\sigma)/\sigma}$. This shift parameter depicts linkage externalities to the extent that an increase in urban industrial production leads to an increased extent of the market for services, inducing greater specialization in the service industry and, therefore, enhanced industrial productivity.

The parameter σ is positive, indicating that the sub-production function V_m is concave and that increased variety of services results in specialization economies. As the value of σ goes to 1, however, the exponent of the number of services, n, in equation (4) approaches zero and the influence of n on X_m disappears. The reason is that, as σ goes to 1, the sub-production function, V_m, becomes the simple sum of the quantities of services used by the industrial sector. That is, in this case, each service is a perfect substitute for another. With services homogenous, there is then no influence of the number of services on industrial production; only total quantity demanded, S_m, has an impact. On the other hand, as the value of σ declines towards zero, the exponent of n in equation (4) increases, and the importance of diversity in services on industrial productivity becomes more important.

Industrial profits, R, are given by:

$$R = P_m L_m^a K_m^b V_m^c - WL_m - r_m K_m - \sum_{i=1}^{n} P_i S_i$$

where W is the wage rate in the city, r_m is the rental rate on industrial space, P_i is the price charged for the services supplied by a business service firm i, and P_m is the price of the industrial output of the city in world markets. It is assumed that the latter is exogenously-given.

From the first order conditions for profit maximization, the following expression can be derived for the urban wage:

$$W = aP_m L_m^{a-1} (\pi \hat{u}^2)^b S_m^c n^{c(1-\sigma)/\sigma}. \quad (5)$$

This shows that the urban wage rate is influenced by employment, the price of the industrial good produced in the city, by the parameter a associated with the marginal product of labor, the amount of space used by the sector, the total quantity demanded of business services and the number of services available. We now proceed to specify the determinants of the latter two variables, which are endogenously-determined.

19.3 The Producer Services Market: Diversity, Pricing and Output Decisions

Ample evidence tends to indicate that services are relatively labor intensive. We thus assume that each firm supplying producer services uses only labor as an input, whose requirements are given by:

$$L_i = c_o + c_1 S_i \quad (6)$$

where c_o represents a fixed labor input requirement and c_1 is a variable labor input requirement. The technology used by all service firms is considered to be identical, implying that c_o and c_1 are the same for all firms i.

Given the labor requirements depicted by (6), each firm's total costs are equal to WL_i. Average costs are then given by: $AC_i = Wc_1 + Wc_o/S_i$, reflecting the presence of internal economies of scale in the production of services. Marginal costs, finally, are equal to Wc_1, a constant for each single firm in the market. The equality of marginal cost to marginal revenue suggested by profit maximization indicates that:

$$Wc_1 = P_i(\varepsilon - 1)/\varepsilon. \tag{7}$$

Since marginal revenue is related to the elasticity of demand facing each firm, ε, we must specify this variable in order to determine the profit-maximizing price and output of each service.

Calculating the elasticity of demand facing one firm in a market composed of a large number of other firms selling related, differentiated services can be quite complicated. The discussion can be greatly simplified, however, if the market structure within which services operate is assumed to be one of Chamberlinian monopolistic competition [see Chamberlin (1931) and Dixit-Stiglitz (1977)]. Within this framework, each producer is assumed to act in a Cournot-Nash fashion in conjecturing that other firms in the sector will not change their output in response to changes in the firm's own price. In addition, Chamberlinian monopolistic competition assumes that there is a large enough number of firms in the market such that the influence of each firm on the total output of the sector is insignificant.

Under the Chamberlinian assumptions, it is easy to show [see Rivera-Batiz (1988c)] that the price elasticity facing a single service is:

$$\varepsilon = 1/(1 - \sigma). \tag{8}$$

Observe that since σ is a fixed parameter, the demand curve facing a service firm exhibits constant elasticity. However, as σ is exogenously increased toward 1, this elasticity tends to rise to infinity. The explanation is that, as σ approaches 1, the services demanded by industry become closer substitutes, increasing the competition among them and raising the responsiveness of quantity demanded to any particular firm's change in price.

Substitution of the expression for the elasticity of demand shown by equation (8) into equation (7), and some simplification, yields:

$$P_i = c_1W/\sigma. \tag{9}$$

Equation (9) can be interpreted as stating that each service sector firm sets its price at a mark-up above its variable and marginal costs, c_1W. The markup is inversely related to the parameter σ, reflecting the role played by product differentiation in allowing firms to increase price above marginal cost. As σ decreases toward 0, the services required by the industrial sector become more strongly differentiated from each other, allowing any given number of firms operating in the market to increase their price markets. Since all firms face identical cost and demand parameters — c_o, c_1 and σ are the same for all i — the profit-maximization prices they charge will be the same.

Entry of firms into the service sector guarantees that the industry's equilibrium is one with no unexploited profit opportunities. Zero profits exist when total revenue, P_iS_i, equal total cost, WL_i. Using equations (6) and (9), the zero profits equilibrium occurs at a level of output equal to:

$$S_i = \sigma c_o/(1-\sigma)c_1. \tag{10}$$

Since each firm has the same σ, c_o and c_1 parameters, equation (10) indicates that each service sector firm will produce the same equilibrium level of output.

The equilibrium number of firms in the producer services sector is also derived from the zero profits condition and is given by:

$$n = c_1(1-\sigma)S_m/\sigma c_o. \tag{11}$$

This states that, given the aggregate demand for services, $S_m = nS_i$, the equilibrium number of firms in the sector is inversely related to the output supplied by each firm. An increase in the aggregate demand for services, on the other hand, raises the equilibrium number of firms.

Since services and labor are the main variable inputs of the industrial sector, one can specify how the demand for one is related to the demand for the other. The results are:

$$S_m = c\sigma L_m/ac_1 \tag{12}$$

and

$$n = (1-\sigma)cL_m/c_oa. \tag{13}$$

Equations (12) and (13) show that business services and industrial labor are complements in production. An increase in the use of industrial labor raises the demand for producer services, increasing the equilibrium number of service firms and the aggregate quantity of services supplied by that sector.

Given a fixed number of households in the city, L, each supplying a fixed amount of labor, $H = 1$, the assumption of perfect competition in the labor market implies the following full employment condition: $L_m + L_s = L$, where L_s represents the total amount of labor employed in the business services sector. But $L_s = (\frac{c}{a})L_m$. Therefore: $L_m = [a/(a+c)]L$. Substitution into (12) and (13) above, and further use of equation (5) results in:

$$W = \gamma L^{(\frac{c}{\sigma})+a-1} \tag{14}$$

where:

$$\gamma = a^a P_m \left(\frac{1-\sigma c}{c_o a}\right)^{c/\sigma} \left(\frac{\sigma c_o}{1-\sigma c_1}\right)^c \pi^b \hat{u}^{2b}[1/(a+c)]^{(\frac{c}{\sigma})+a-1}. \tag{15}$$

This shows how the urban wage rate is related to the urban labor force and to an array of exogenous variables that include the price of the industrial good produced in the city, P_m, the space available to the urban industrial base, and technology parameters.

Note that the impact of changes in the labor force of the city, L, on the wage rate is of ambiguous sign. On the one hand, the conventional effect of an increase in the labor force is to reduce the city's wage rate due to diminishing returns. However, in the present context, an increase in the size of the urban population increases the size of the industrial sector and, therefore, it shifts upwards the demand for producer services. The latter leads to an expansion in the variety of such services. With a wider diversity of service firms available, the industrial sector can obtain more specialized services and its productivity is therefore enhanced. This productivity increase is then embodied into higher wage rates. The net impact of increased population on the equilibrium wage rate in the city is related to the relative importance of the 'diminishing returns' and the 'increased productivity or linkage externality' effects.

19.4 Household Utility, Linkage Externalities and Urban Equilibrium

Each household j consumes housing or space, K_{jh}, and an array of internationally-traded industrial sector goods that we aggregate into a composite, C_{jT}. The household utility function is, for simplicity, assumed to be log-linear:

$$U_j = \theta \log C_{jT} + (1-\theta)\log K_{jH} \tag{16}$$

where θ is a positive fraction.

Utility is maximized subject to the following budget constraint:

$$P_T C_{jT} + r_h K_{jH} = W \tag{17}$$

where P_T is an index of the prices of goods purchased by consumers (assumed to be exogenously-given), and r_h is the rental rate on housing paid by households, observe that individual labor supply, H, is normalized to equal 1, implying that household labor income is equal to the market wage rate, W. In addition, it is assumed that spending is made out of wages, meaning that rental income is either saved or accrues to non-city dwellers.

With equations (16) and (17), we can set-up the constrained optimization problem facing the individual household j in the city. The resulting first-order conditions can then be aggregated among individuals (assuming identical tastes) to yield the city's demand for goods and housing. Equating the demand for and supply of residential housing implies:

$$\frac{W}{r_h} = \pi(u^2 - \hat{u}^2)/[(1-\theta)L]. \tag{18}$$

Equation (18) shows the inverse relationship between the city's labor force and its real wage deflated by the rental cost of housing: an increase in the number of households in the city raises the demand for space, resulting in an equilibrium increase in rental rates which reduces real wages.

The indirect utility function for a household in the city is:

$$U_j = \theta \log\left(\frac{\theta W}{P_T}\right) + (1-\theta)\log(1-\theta)W/r_h.$$

Substituting equations (14) and (18) results in:

$$U_j = \log(\theta\gamma/P_T)^{\theta}[\pi(u^2 - \hat{u}^2)]^{1-\theta} + \left[\left(\frac{\theta c}{\sigma}\right) + a\theta - 1\right]\log L \quad (19)$$

where $\gamma > 0$ is as defined by equation (15).

The second term of equation (19) clearly depicts the possible positive and negative effects of increased urban population, L, on household utility, as specified by:

$$\mathrm{d}U_j = \left\{\theta\left[\left(\frac{c}{\sigma}\right) + a\right] - 1\right\} dL/L.$$

This derivative can be positive or negative, depending on the relative strength of the following forces:

1. The degree of differentiation among business services, σ. An increase in urban population raises the level of urban industrial production, widening the extent of the market for business services and, therefore, their level of specialization. This increases industrial productivity and tends to raise urban wages, a gain to households in the city. The stronger the differentiation among services, the larger the impact on industrial productivity and urban wages.
2. The share of business services on total revenues in the industrial sector, c. The linkage externalities mentioned in (1) have a stronger impact on industrial productivity when business services become relatively more important in industry.
3. The share of housing on the total spending of consumers $(1-\theta)$. An increase in urban population raises rental rates on housing and, consequently, lowers real wages. The larger the share of housing on total household spending, the stronger the negative impact of the higher rental rates on household utility.
4. The physical productivity of labor parameter a. An increase in urban industrial employment tends to lower urban wages due to the presence of diminishing returns. As the parameter a rises,

however, diminishing returns lose importance and the negative Impact on household utility shrinks.

Up to this point, we have considered the impact of an exogenous increase in the urban labor force. Let us suppose, however, that households are free to migrate in and out of the city under consideration to other given cities or rural areas. What will determine the equilibrium population level to the city under consideration?

The equilibrium distribution of households to the city occurs at that point at which there are no incentives to migrate among locations. On the simplifying assumption that all households have identical preferences, equilibrium is reached when

$$U_j = U_o \tag{20}$$

where U_o represents the maximum alternative level of utility that any household can achieve in the rest of the economy. We assume that the latter is exogenously-given. Substitution of the expression for U_j in equation (19) into (20) then yields the equilibrium population in the city.

Observe that, if $\mathrm{d}U_j/\mathrm{d}L > 0$, the equilibrium labor force suggested by (20) will not be stable. In this case, an increase in population above the equilibrium level specified by (20) will raise household utility in the city above that in the rest of the economy, inducing further migration. Urban growth becomes explosive unless external diseconomies (environmental externalities or congestion) are introduced. It is necessary for a stable equilibrium, then, for $\mathrm{d}U_j/\mathrm{d}L$ to be negative. In this case, note that, the stronger the specialization economies associated with the service sector — that is, the larger the θ and c parameters — the bigger the equilibrium labor force of the city.

19.5 Concluding Remarks

Our analysis in this paper has been simplified. Our goal has been to show the basic building blocks of a model that describes urban agglomeration economies endogenously, with the economic processes generating the external effects explicitly specified. The model can be extended to incorporate commuting costs and land use heterogeneity within the city. The service sector could also be modeled more extensively by introducing inputs other than labor and by considering alternative market structures, such as oligopolistic competition. Questions regarding the sub-optimality of the equilibrium and the existence of tax-subsidy schemes intended to achieve a pareto optimum could be answered. Alternative sources of agglomeration economies could be introduced, such as from the labor market side [see, for example, Kim (1987)], or through alternative production externalities, as for instance, when one considers the effects of urban growth on technical change [see Rivera-Batiz (1988a)]. This should be a matter for further research.

References

Chamberlin, E.H., *The Theory of Monopolistic Competition*, Harvard University Press, Cambridge, 1931.

Dixit, A.K. and J. Stiglitz, "Monopolistic Competition and Optimum Product Diversity," *American Economic Review* 67, 1977, 297–308.

Ethier, W., "National and International Returns to Scale in the Modern Theory of International Trade," *American Economic Review* 72, 1982, 389–405.

Fujita, M. and F. Rivera-Batiz, "Agglomeration and Heterogeneity in Space: An Introduction", *Regional Science and Urban Economics* 18, 1988, 1–5.

Helpman, E. and P. Krugman, *Market Structure and Foreign Trade: Increasing Returns, Imperfect Competition and the International Economy.* The MIT Press, Cambridge, 1986.

Henderson, J.V., *Economic Theory and the Cities.* Academic Press, New York, 1977.

______, "Industrial Bases and City Sizes," *American Economic Review* 73, 1983, 164–168.

______, "Efficiency of Resource Usage and City Size," *Journal of Urban Economics*, 19, 1986, 47–70.

Kim, S., "Diversity in Urban Labor Markets and Agglomeration Economies," Papers of The Regional Science Association, 62, 1987, 57–70.

Krugman, P., "Strategic Sectors and International Competition," in R.M. Stern, ed., *U.S. Trade Policies in a Changing World Economy*, MIT Press, Cambridge, 1987, 207–232.

Moomaw, R.L., "Firm Location and City Size: Reduced Productivity Advantages as a factor in the Decline of Manufacturing in Urban Areas," *Journal of Urban Economics*, 17, 1985, 73–89.

Rivera-Batiz, F.L., "Technical Change, Market Structure and Agglomeration Economies," Paper presented at the Location Theory Workshop, University of Pennsylvania, Philadelphia, April 1988. (a)

———, and L. Rivera-Batiz, "The Effects of Direct Foreign Investment in the Presence of Increasing Returns Due to Specialization," Paper Presented at the Midwest International Economics Meeting, University of Minnesota, Minneapolis, April 22–24, 1988. (b)

———, "Increasing Returns, Monopolistic Competition and Agglomeration, Economies in Consumption and Production," *Regional Science and Urban Economics* 17, February 1988, 125–153. (c)

Romer, P.M., "Growth Based on Increasing Returns Due to Specialization," *American Economic Review* 77, 1987, 56–62.

———, "Increasing Returns, Specialization and External Economies: Growth as Described by Allwyn Young," Rochester Center for Economic Research, Working Paper No. 64, 1986.

Segel, D., "Are There Returns to Scale in City Size?," *Review of Economics and Statistics* 58, 1976, 339–350.

Smith, A., *The Wealth of Nations.* Penguin Books Ltd., Middlesex, 1776.